Parental Alienation

How to Understand and Address Parental Alienation Resulting from Acrimonious Divorce or Separation

L.F. Lowenstein

RHP

Russell House Publishing

Published in 2007 by
Russell House Publishing Limited
4 St George's House
Uplyme Road
Lyme Regis
Dorset
DT7 3LS

Tel: 01297 443948
Fax: 01297 442722
e-mail: help@russellhouse.co.uk

British Library Cataloguing-in-Publication Data:

A catalogue record of this book is available from the British Library

ISBN: 978-1-905541-10-2

Typeset by: TW Typesetting, Plymouth, Devon
Printed by: Biddles Ltd, King's Lynn

Russell House Publishing
Russell House Publishing aims to publish innovative and valuable materials to
help managers, practitioners, trainers, educators and students.
Our full catalogue covers: social policy, working with young people, helping
children and families, care of older people, social care, combating social
exclusion, revitalising communities and working with offenders.
Full details can be found at www.russellhouse.co.uk and we are pleased to send
out information to you by post. Our contact details are on this page.
We are always keen to receive feedback on publications and new ideas for
future projects.

Contents

Part Three: Treating PAS

Dedication

This book is dedicated to a child, one of so many that I have tried to help, to see how important it is to have the love and care of both parents. To the child who said "I don't need my mother (father); I only need my father (mother)" I would like to reiterate the importance of having the love and care of both parents. Where I have succeeded via mediation for you (the child) to see sense I know it will be appreciated for a lifetime.

If I have failed it was not for want of trying. I only hope that you as a child, adolescent, or adult will yet realise the importance of not just one, but both, loving parents before it is too late. Do not blame yourself for what has happened in the past. The fault was not with you, but rested elsewhere as is so clearly explained in the book. Make amends now by seeking that loving contact you denied yourself, when you truly needed this. The parent you have so unfairly rejected because of their love for you will welcome you back with open arms and a loving heart.

Acknowledgements

Many thanks are due to the mothers and fathers who contributed to this book by explaining how they have suffered as victims of parental alienation. I have personally represented some of them in court and, hopefully, helped with their problems. In some cases I have succeeded: in others, unfortunately, I have failed. This has been the main reason for writing this book.

I would like to thank most wholeheartedly one parent in particular, Dennis von Bergh, who championed my work and made it accessible worldwide by setting up a website. His help and friendship have been invaluable. I would also like to thank those who have printed my articles and helped to further the cause for change in the courts regarding the treatment of the alienated parent and the injustices they have suffered.

I would also like to acknowledge and thank those who have contributed to this book in any way including Shaun O'Connell (Fathers for Justice). Many others have contributed but have wished to remain anonymous.

I would like to acknowledge the help provided by Gail McFarlane of the University of Southampton Library in providing information on research about parental alienation: I owe her a tremendous debt of gratitude.

I would also like to thank most especially my good wife Kathleen who typed up the chapters and the original articles on which this book is based. Without her I do not believe it would have seen the light of day.

Finally, I would like to thank Geoffrey Mann of Russell House Publishing for his confidence in accepting this book for publication and Martin Jones for his editorial and production work. Otherwise it might just be gathering dust on my office shelves along with many others.

About the Author

Dr LF Lowenstein gained his BA at the University of Western Australia in 1958 before going on to study at the University of London for his MA in 1960, his Diploma in Clinical and Educational Psychology in 1962 and his Ph.D in 1966.

After a period as Chief Educational Psychologist for Hampshire he has worked over the past 20 years as a forensic psychologist in the area of clinical psychology, educational psychology and general problems related to psychological changes within individuals. He also undertakes Legal Aid work.

He belongs to the Association of Educational Psychologists, the International Council of Psychologists, the Society of Clinical Psychiatrists, the UK Register of Expert Witnesses, the Academy of Experts, the British Academy of Forensic Sciences, the American Psychological Association, APIL Expert Witness Database, the AVMA Database, the Expert Witness Directory and Expert Witness.

Dr Lowenstein is also an Associate Fellow of the British Psychological Society, Vice Chairman of Children of High Intelligence and a Fellow of the College of Teachers.

He has acted in a large number of cases and written over 390 articles involving forensic cases, personal injury, Parental Alienation Syndrome and family and children issues.

Dr Lowenstein's expertise covers child abuse problems, minimum and maximum brain damage, psychological aspects of delinquent or criminal activities, failure to receive education according to their special needs, Parental Alienation Syndrome and child custody disputes.

He also deals with adults, emotional and behavioural problems, serious crimes where there is a psychological factor explaining the behaviour, crimes committed as a result of subnormality or moral imbecility, Munchausen Syndrome, and clients accused of sex offences, rape, fetishes, homicide, substance abuse, alcoholism, kleptomania, arson, road rage (aggression in driving), fitness to plead, educational problems such as dyslexia, dyspraxia, dysorthographia, brain injury, and special needs, problems facing children such as child sex abuse; Parental Alienation Syndrome (PAS), child custody disputes, personal injury, post-traumatic stress disorder and other stress-related illness, minimal brain dysfunction.

Dr Lowenstein also undertakes personality testing, aptitude testing and interest testing and has worked on mediation and conciliation work with couples. Within business and industry, there have been requests for help in resolving personality clashes and improving communication, participation and morale within small and large organisations and the assessment of employees for promotion etc.

Foreword

Parental Alienation and Parental Alienation Syndrome (PAS) are recent concepts that have emerged as the divorce and separation rates have soared to new heights. Incidents of parents using their children to 'get back' at a former partner or as leverage within a failed relationship is occurring at an increasing rate and the alienation of one parent by the other as new relationships are formed or old relationships terminated is on the rise. Dr Lowenstein has clearly spent a great deal of time and energy working in the field and it is readily apparent throughout his book. From the first chapter in which he poses the question, 'Do children need fathers?', he dissects the problems inherent with the syndrome and goes on to offer clear, straight forward strategies for treating PAS.

The book is divided into three sections. The first clearly delineates the difficulties and problem areas associated with PAS. His discussion of the causes and effects of divorce leads intuitively to his discussion of the development of PAS in child custody disputes and the effects it has on both the former partners as well as the children involved in those disputes. He presents an extensive list of indicators by which professionals and others can recognise PAS at an early stage, going on to give an equally extensive list of interventions directly targeted at those identified concerns.

The second part focuses on the role of the Judiciary in PAS and the effects of divorce. He demonstrates an almost surgical ability to isolate and identify the problems. His chapter on what the legal profession should know is again clearly based on his extensive experience within the field and is approached in his typically direct and forthright manner.

Treatment of those involved in PAS forms the third and final thrust of the book. His familial approach combined with his obvious concern for all parties forms the basis of his therapeutic style in which mediation replaces provocation and the adversarial stance is supplanted by cooperation. Throughout, his concern for the children caught up in PAS remains a core focus. His discussion of the broader issues of PAS raises numerous areas for future investigation and study.

Throughout the book, Dr Lowenstein's expertise in the area and his concern for those involved are woven into a discussion that is both sensitive and objective. He draws on both research and personal experience to raise the reader's awareness of both the process and the effects of PAS. His clear and direct writing style is easily read and understood. This is a book that will take a pivotal position in anyone's research into the area of PAS. Likewise it is a 'must read' for those working in the area of separation, divorce, mediation and child risk.

Dennis R Trent, PhD.
President of the International Council of Psychologists

Grief

Barbara F. Steinberg, PhD

A parent who has been alienated from their child's life experiences extreme loss. Often we are asked by a targeted parent, 'How do I deal with this on-going pain?'

First, know that you are not alone. There are others, both mothers and fathers, who have similar experiences, and who are in deep agony over the loss of contact and meaningful relationship with their children.

Second, know that you are not crazy. In our culture we are not encouraged to experience our grief. We are taught to be strong, to rise above it, to tough it out, to get over it and get on with life. Sometimes that is wise counsel if we linger in our pain, and our outrage becomes the complete focus of our life affecting our work, our social life and our spirit. However, the loss of a child whether by death or by exclusion from that child's life is beyond the realm of most parents' ability to cope. In the beginning of an alienation process, we believe, as parents, this is not really happening. We deny that the other parent of our child is capable of these vengeful acts, and we choose not to believe our child, whom we love deeply, would ever treat us in such hurtful ways. Denial is the strongest emotional defense mechanism we have at our disposal, and it is the one on which we rely the most. For most parents, because they truly want contact and relationship with their child, their denial does not hold up under time or with the reality of the disconnection they experience.

Third, many parents feel confusion, which suggests they are not able to identify and process the bunch of emotions they are experiencing in their gut. Usually, these can be separated into feelings of deep sadness, intense anger, extreme outrage, and desperate blame. To keep from being overwhelmed by this internal 'bucket of worms', many parents detach from the situation, which they believe is an act of self-preservation. Some bargain with themselves using the following logic, 'My child will forget what's happened when they turn eighteen so I'll just wait'. Both strategies are akin to whistling in the dark.

Fourth, targeted parents want to know how to deal with these strong emotions in healthy ways, because if allowed to remain unreleased, they often gain a life of their own and emerge in inappropriate ways and at inopportune times toward others who do not understand or deserve the depth and intensity of the feeling. Sometimes, these emotions are held internally. In an attempt to self-medicate the resulting pain, the targeted parent turns to addictive behaviors or substances. Eventually, if strong emotions are held internally for a long period of time, they can convert into physical problems, which plague the individual for the remainder of their life. So the dilemma remains, what do I do with my pain? Keeping a journal or diary is helpful, but strong emotions require active self-interventions. Many parents report feeling relief from their deep sadness by allowing themselves to cry and scream. If you believe this might assist you in your process, to avoid embarrassment, it is wise to isolate yourself perhaps in a quiet, natural place so you can grieve in an unrestrained and unobserved way. It is also helpful to take a sequence of your child's pictures so you can activate your feelings of loss. Intense anger is a physical activator so you will need to participate in a focused activity such as bowling, driving golf balls at a range or hitting balls in a batting cage. A less expensive approach is throwing ice cubes at a sturdy wall, an activity, that parents report, gives a sense of relief and release from ever tightening bands of anger. Outrage describes a parent who feels misunderstood so there needs to be some attention paid to 'telling your story'. The problem is finding a receptive listener who has the patience and energy to hear the saga of hurt, frustration and humiliation more than once. Targeted parents can tell their story into a small tape recorder; they can write their story by hand into a journal, a loose-leaf notebook or a diary. They can use a word processor and store it on computer disc, or if they are creatively inclined, they can write poems to their children. Some parents have already published their story in books and poetry. Of importance here is the intention to alleviate the outrage of misunderstanding that proclaims, as a parent, you are unimportant, even nonessential in your child's life. Also, it is important that you be heard, and that you remind yourself you are still a parent by keeping your child's pictures around you. Another approach is to involve yourself in the parenting role with other children as a Godparent, as an involved uncle or aunt, as a big brother or big sister. Validating yourself as a parent can go a long way to heal feelings of outrage.

Finally, desperate blame is probably the most difficult bereavement issue to process. Some blame is justifiable: the other parent, the other parent's family, the legal and social services system, your child, yourself. However, the only one under your jurisdiction of control is yourself so this is the part that you work with in three separate ways.

First, it is critical, regardless of the attitude and reception from the other parent, from the other parent's family and from your child that you stay in positive contact with them. Civility and cordiality in face-to-face contact is essential regardless of what is said in your presence or behind your back. In addition, sending your child cards, letters and little packages on unimportant days is appropriate. Also, communicating with your child by telephone, by e-mail and by facsimile can be effective. If you have completely lost contact with your child, then set your priority to find them and restore contact at least from a distance. If this is impossible, then collect items and memorabilia in a special box or trunk reserved for your child and the possibility of future contact.

Second, become active as a citizen for positive change, and learn about the strengths and weaknesses of the system you blame for preventing you from having parenting opportunities with your child. This action may not change the disposition of your situation, but you may make the system a better place for other targeted parents and their children.

Third, for your sake and for the sake of your relationship with your child, it is imperative that you forgive the other parent. Notice there was no mention of forgetting what has happened, or how you have been treated, but again, for restoring your emotional balance and your ability to cope with life challenges in healthy ways, you will need to forgive the alienator. For some, this is a spiritual journey, and for others the path is a secular one. What is important is that you go about this process in a unique way that you believe will work for you so the specter of losing your child is diminished, and your health and well being are in restoration.

The Parental Alienation Awareness Organization

. . . lauds the publication of Dr Lowenstein's book, *Parental Alienation: How to Understand and Address Parental Alienation Resulting From Acrimonious Divorce or Separation*. Sadly, Parental Alienation (PA) is a global phenomenon that has ramifications for the structure and well-being of children and families world-wide. We welcome the information this book provides on the complex, many-faceted issue of PA.

The Parental Alienation Awareness Organization is a web-based, international organization dedicated to helping the public and the professionals who work with children and families, become aware of behaviors that have painful and damaging effects on children. We are guided by the research of prominent experts in the field, as well as the experiences of families affected by PA. Such activities as 25 April, Parental Alienation Awareness Day, have helped focus attention on this world-wide problem.

These behaviors, under the comprehensive term of Parental Alienation, have the lasting effect of damaging the bond between a child and a loving parent. They frequently result in devastating emotional problems for the child. These maladaptive consequences can range from confusion, divided loyalties, depression and anxiety, to difficulties with their own relationships.

However, it is not important what the terminology is: what is important is the recognition of a set of behaviors, which, in their execution, do a great deal of psychological harm to a child. Such damaging behaviors are most often observed during divorce and custody situations. They may be subtly conveyed via non verbal expressions of negative feelings about the other parent, or blatantly demonstrated via negative or untrue statements and interference with communication and visitation of that parent.

Most states in the United States, require divorcing parents to take a mandatory course which addresses these behaviors. Laws dealing with custody criteria recognise the importance of the child residing with the parent who is more likely to encourage a positive relationship with the other parent. Parental Alienation Awareness Organization recognizes the importance of courts to consistently follow custody guidelines, issue sanctions for those who would violate these laws and provide for interventions and reintegration programs for those families affected by alienating behaviors. We believe the best interest of the child is met when they have the love, guidance, and support of both parents in their lives, regardless of the marital relationship.

Regardless of terminology, a thorn by any other name hurts just as much.

Sarvy Emo President/Co-Founder
Robin Denison Vice President/Co-Founder
http://www.parental-alienation-awareness.com

Introduction

It is my view that an introduction should do much more than just summarise the book that follows: it should also look into the future and provide remedies in the form of suggestions as to how things can be improved for the current and future generations. This will also be the task of the conclusion at the end of the book.

The breakdown of relationships between parents

One has to admit that families today are not as stable and secure as was the case a century ago. Without some form of direction things are likely to continue to get worse rather than better in this regard. Almost 50 per cent of relationships, whether married or not, break up leaving children frequently to suffer the consequences of losing one of their parents, sometimes permanently. This is more often than not the father.

Parenting children of broken relationships

Marriages or other unions rarely end on a note of harmony. One or both parents are unhappy with the way the relationship has turned from love to disharmony, and what one can only term 'implacable hostility'. This is a term often preferred by the judiciary rather than the term 'parental alienation' (PA) or 'parental alienation syndrome (PAS). Whether we like it or not parental alienation is often the consequence of hatred of one or both parents toward the other. As an alleged expert in the area of implacable hostility between parents or parental alienation I have had contact with hundreds of mothers and fathers who have been separated and who have contacted me for the purpose of providing help and advice as to what they can and should do to continue to have contact with their children.

My advice has always been to continue, whenever possible, to act as loving and responsible parents. This means putting the needs of the children always first. Children are likely to have the best chance of growing up and becoming happy adolescents and adults, when their parents put aside their grievances and work together to rear their children using the most positive ways available. The children do best when they have been provided with information by both parents that the other parent loves and cares for them as much as ever. This means doing everything possible to portray the other parent in a favourable rather than hostile light. This unfortunately does not occur in the case of PA or PAS.

Parents must encourage children to have good and regular contact with the other parent, ideally on a 50 per cent basis for each. This is not always possible and this is obviously recognised. It is however something to be aimed for. The result of this approach leads children to feel that while their parents cannot agree to live with one another, this does not detract from both still feeling the love and care for their children as they did in the past. This can only occur when both parents speak well of the other and 'sincerely' encourage the children to have good contact with the other parent. When this occurs it is infertile ground for either parental alienation or parental alienation syndrome. Unfortunately, as a clinical forensic psychologist and expert witness to the courts, I have often found disharmony between parents in cases of divorce or separation. The first casualties are the children who have been moving consciously or unconsciously into the web of hostility which exists between the parents. Such children suffer both in the short and long-term and frequently help to foster another generation of unhappy children when they are themselves adults. This occurs when such children as adults often perpetuate the parental alienation with their own children which they suffered in the past.

It is important to state that there should never be contact between a parent and a child who has practiced abuse with that child, whether this be in the form of emotional, physical or sexual abuse. This point is made clear in many areas of the book. Here supervised contact is still possible. With the successful treatment of the abusing parent, direct contact with the abusing parent can occur. Direct contact can only ultimately be possible after careful assessment by an experienced psychologist or psychiatrist. It is always vital to keep in the forefront of one's mind that a child's physical and psychological state is of primary concern.

Children also need to be protected from damaging influences derived from a hostile parent towards a former partner being communicated directly, or subtly, to the child. This should also be considered a form of child abuse. PAS or PA needs to be dealt with firmly by recommendations made by the expert following an intensive examination.

Working with children of broken relationships

The victimised child and the alienated parent require rescue from the embittered brainwashing which is possible by one parent in order to 'pay back' the non custodial parent for real or imagined past grievances. The role of the expert, and conclusions reached by the expert, are of little value if not supported by the judiciary. Proof of the process of PAS occurring should lead to a number of actions. This includes financial penalties being paid by the alienator. In the final instance it may mean the removal of the child to the alienated parent and this may be necessary in order to protect the child from further 'brainwashing'. Sometimes the child may be removed to a more neutral environment such as placing a child into care.

Judicial decisions about children of broken relationships

Judges are criticised in the book which follows by being often superficially 'child-centred'. If the child indicates that they want nothing to do with the absent parent with whom there was previously a happy relationship, judges will often wrongly deduce that the child's feelings and views are 'valid' and must be respected and acted upon. There is rarely any mention as to why the child fails to wish contact with a former loving parent. The answer, although in the murky depths of confusion and wrong interpretations, is due to the brainwashing that the child has received from one parent, usually the custodial parent.

The way forward is discussed in many chapters of Part Three of the book. The conclusion also stresses the importance of necessary changes to the social system which need to be made in law to alter parental attitudes and behaviour.

The purpose of this book

This book has been written for two major reasons:

1. To protect and support children and adults who have been made the victims of tragic and corrupting processes of parental alienation. The victims are both fathers and mothers, as well as the grandparents, important influentials of the children, who are often forgotten.
2. To create awareness in the judiciary and society as a whole of certain injustices currently being practised against absent parents. It is to acknowledge the fact that PA destroys families who could be supporting children as they go through life. This is often done with the judiciary failing to support experts who find where the problem is. It is my view that good parents should be able to continue to act with care, love and responsibility towards the next generation, despite the break up of the parental relationship.

Parental Alienation Syndrome?

Whether we use the term 'parental alienation' or 'parental alienation syndrome' matters not at all. The term syndrome refers to a number of co-existing symptoms that make up the condition of PA. The term PAS has not as yet been officially recognised by the American Psychological Association (APA) or the British Psychological Association as existing, albeit there is considerable evidence that PA as well as PAS is present when there is an acrimonious relationship between the parents. In what follows, ignoring the current non acceptance by the APA of PAS, the two terms will be used as having equivalent meaning which most individuals can recognise. The book will make clear which are the group symptoms (syndrome) of PAS explained in Chapters 2, 8 and 12.

The structure of this book

The book has been divided into three major sections but there is often a considerable overlap or interaction between the sections. Part One essentially deals with the problems encountered by parents and their children when parental alienations occurs. The section begins with an introduction to PAS and attempts to understand post-divorce or post-separation conflicts (Chapter 4) and how to deal with this tragic phenomenon.

How both children and parents suffer as a result of the implacable hostility between the parents are discussed in a variety of chapters including Chapters 2, 3, 6 and 7. Since the larger proportion of alienated parents are fathers, Chapter 1 poses a pertinent question: 'Do children need fathers?' Naturally the question is answered in the affirmative since children need *both* parents to do best.

It is important to recognise the signs of PAS and these are delineated and discussed fully throughout the book and most especially in Chapters 8, 9 and 10. This first section as well as Sections Two and Three draws frequently from the international research concerning parental alienation, its signs, causes and consequences. Chapter 7 presents evidence of how children have both short and long-term problems as a result of the alienation process.

Part Two is concerned with the role of the judiciary. Judges have to make decisions for the benefit of children. Judges are not psychologists. They are influenced by so-called experts but more so by the law or legal process. Many experts tend to rely on what children say and how they behave in connection with contact disputes. Judges need to be made aware how easily children are manipulated by disaffected parents and the insidious effects of this disaffection.

It is vital for judges and others to look beneath the superficial statements of a child regarding an absent parent who in the past played some, or even an important, role in their lives. Judges need to make decisions that are based on the real facts as to why a child wishes none, or little, contact with an absent parent. This could lead to real justice for non custodial parents and will benefit the child tremendously (Chapter 11).

Part Three is concerned with the important task of seeking to remedy the situation of parental alienation or parental alienation syndrome. It is my basic principle that both parents **have the right and the responsibility to guide their children appropriately**. How this is worked out firstly depends on the parents themselves. If they fail to agree, then the psychologist and others can help to remedy conflicts. If this fails then the legal system also plays an important role. Both the expert and the courts need to form an alliance to help parents to resolve their differences in regard to the welfare of their children. Often very hard decisions have to be made and stuck to.

Sometimes there is a need for mediation to take place and this is discussed more fully in Chapters 18–20. Both parents and their children, frequently need some form of treatment for the harm already done as parents dispute how, if and when contact is to be arranged between the children and the absent parent. Chapters 22–28 deal with this in some depth. The difficulties involved in dealing with this task is discussed in Chapter 21 especially.

Who this book is for

To the benefit of the child

The expert and the courts of law need to be focused on finding a solution which is to the benefit of the child in the short as well as long-term. There is now considerable research that indicates the harm that can be done to children in the short and long-term as a result of parental alienation conflicts. Parents in conflict with implacable hostility towards one another frequently make untrue or exaggerated accusations against another parent. This includes allegations of physical or sexual abuse and other accusations. These allegations must be rigorously investigated and either substantiated by the facts or not substantiated. It is unfortunate that children are involved in the acrimony between their parents. The expert with the help of the judicial system, working together, can achieve much in the way of justice for all concerned. In this way a new generation of adults can result that are well adjusted rather than the opposite.

Alienated Parents' Stories

Story 1

Dr Lowenstein is a very brave man to write about a matter which governments in the western world are ignoring. Parental Alienation Syndrome (PAS) is hotly debated in many countries as being an excuse to hide the abuse or violence of demonised men and fathers. Gender wars serve no-one in the long-term especially not the children.

I was a male victim of domestic violence and suffered it for over two and a half years before leaving the family home. I didn't take the children as I had been threatened with death if I did so. Social services stated that the violence did not matter as we no longer live together so there was less risk of the children witnessing it. The mother had a long history of emotional and psychological problems and borderline personality disorder.

My son was locked in the bedroom regularly from the age of two and a half to five. My daughter believes this never happened, my son was told by the stepfather he knew what he was doing was wrong but that he was beating children up. He also had memories from when he was two and a half.

I was stopped from seeing my children on October 28th 1999 when my daughter told social services she wanted to live with her father. This was after I had raised issues relating to the care of the children by the mother. Social services had carried out an assessment of risk without meeting me and only interviewed the judge and court welfare officer.

They ignored serious symptoms such as daytime wetting and related urinary tract infections in my daughter and behavioural problems in my son. She stated under oath: 'I have worked with thousands of families and I can tell you I can sense without even knowing when a mother's emotionally unstable. I don't even have to look at them, I can sense it a mile off'.

My son still has behavioural problems at school, has been referred to child and family guidance since 1997, was referred to a psychiatrist in 2005 and had counselling for low self esteem and lack of confidence, yet the CAFCASS Guardian states that he is fine.

My children's surnames were changed at their schools and GP in 2003 yet I only found out by chance when I obtained an original school report with different surnames on it. The school had sent me a forged school report with cut and paste surname change on it.

I cannot describe what feelings you go through when you meet the closed world of the Family Division. I went through shell shock, numbness, disbelief and sheer and utter anger. How naïve I was then. I used to believe the mantra that we have the best legal system in the world. Now I use all that I have learnt to assist others in the UK version of Auschwitz.

In April 2001 I received a four page letter from my daughter stating how much she loved me and missed me. The court ignored the letter. In 2002 I appealed to the Court of Appeal and in the words of Mr. Justice Sumner lost my case, when he said in his judgement: 'If he is unable to separate his own intense feelings about the injustice to him and the poor care that this mother gives, the children will not have a proper relationship with their mother if there is the risk that her standing with them will be undermined'.

I went to the European Court of Human Rights who refused the case as not all domestic remedies had been used. Eventually in 2005 I managed to remove the circuit judge from my case and in December 2005 met my children again along with a Guardian and a high court judge. They were no longer my children. They hated the whole of my family including their aunts, uncles, grandparents and even six year old cousin.

They alleged that I had manipulated them by 'making things look so good'. Words they had been told by a social worker. What was I supposed to do – abuse them? Is that reason for social services to end all contact in their blind support of the mother and to cover up their failings?

I cannot describe the pain of seeing your own children hate you on banalities. The degree of brainwashing was so complete that they didn't even recognise the absurdities of what they were saying. After that meeting with my children I gave up teaching after being signed off for stress by my GP.

The children had false memories, some memories had been erased, and they mimicked the mother and stepfather. They said that they had been told everything by the mother and stepfather. When I tried to disabuse the children by telling them the truth the judge intervened and stopped me.

The children enjoyed the meeting as a game. The Guardian for CAFCASS just repeated their words in her report and then stated under oath that she believed the children believed their words to be true. The High Court Judge then stated 'it only matters if it comes from their hearts'. I was aghast. The CAFCASS Guardian stated that Dr Lowenstein would be seen to be biased as he mentions PAS.

PAS dictates the children's words. The children's wishes and feelings are now being taken verbatim in many cases in the family courts and without addressing PAS the children's best interests is denied.

Parental Alienation Syndrome is a very real and serious form of child abuse and although I had some reservations about the criteria used by Dr Richard Gardner, having met them face to face I have no doubt whatsoever that PAS is very real.

I was a teacher with training in science, anger management and special needs yet have been denied contact with my own children for almost seven years. A living bereavement when I can teach any child in the country except my own. All that I say here has already been said in open court.

Without training in PAS for all child welfare workers more such miscarriages will occur. The blind and zealous pursuit of women's interests and not the children's cannot be in the best interests of the future well being of our society and social cohesion although men can also alienate there is an imbalance overall.

I applaud the stance of Dr Lowenstein in raising this issue and bringing it to the public's attention. At the time of going to press my latest appeal is before LJ Wall on the issue of PAS. On 7th July LJ Wall stated that re L, V, M and H was not a report on PAS as often quoted by CAFCASS. He may be brave enough to admit that PAS exists, then again he may not.

I hope my own children will read this book. They then might understand that their father loves them and has done all in his power to seek remedy and there has not been a single day when he does not think of them.

Alienated father

Story 2

It is a sad and unwelcome realisation having to face the fact that your marriage or relationship that you had fully committed to for all the right reasons is no more. You also have to deal with the harsh truth of somehow having contributed to the failure of one of the most important human relationships we all aspire to making successful. To also have to cope with your children being emotionally 'forced' to choose between being with their mother or father and feeling powerless to stop this process is even more heartbreaking.

Witnessing your children being systematically turned against you over a period of time is probably the most painful experience a parent can go through. It is like a living bereavement. The original loving relationship you treasured with your children and they took for granted and valued with you has been fundamentally destroyed. Instead this relationship is now manifested by your children's verbalised hatred, physical attacks and complete vilification of you. They tell you that they do not love you, have never loved you, they no longer want you in their life and denounce you as their mother or father. You ask yourself how can this be? What have you done to have caused this? Are you truly the monster your children suggest you are?

This problem is not a gender issue, mothers and fathers alike have suffered, however the biggest sufferers of all are the children who have been denied a relationship with a loving, caring and devoted parent, for completely fabricated and unacceptable reasons. This problem is not a country-related, social, cultural or religious issue either. It can affect any parent living anywhere in the world from any walk of life.

There are no winners in a situation like this – only losers, with the biggest losers being our children. All parents must be made aware of the very real consequences of such actions – for their children's sake.

How can such alienation happen? Unhappily, quite easily and is continuing to happen at an increasingly alarming rate as marriages and relationships continue to fail in the fragile family environment of the early 21st century.

What is this problem and can it be diagnosed and prevented? There has been increasing awareness in Family Courts particularly in the UK, US and Australia over the last few years about a problem referred to as Parental Alienation. The late Dr Richard Gardner, an eminent US Child Psychiatrist through his work during the 1970s and 1980s began seeing a distinct pattern of child behaviour he had not encountered before. He described this in his key note presentation at the International Conference on the Parental Alienation Syndrome (PAS) held in Frankfurt/Main, Germany, October 18–19, 2002[1] as follows:

> *In this new disorder, I not only saw programming ('brainwashing') of the child by one parent to denigrate the other, but also self-created contributions by the child in support of the alienating parent's campaign of denigration against the alienated parent. Because of the child's contribution I did not consider the terms **brainwashing**, **programming**, or other equivalent words to be sufficient. Furthermore, I observed a cluster of symptoms that typically appear together, a cluster that warranted the designation **syndrome**. Accordingly, I introduced the term **Parental Alienation Syndrome** to encompass the **combination** of these two factors that contributed to the development of the syndrome.[2] In accordance with this use of the term I have suggested this definition of the parental alienation syndrome:*
>
> > *The Parental Alienation Syndrome (PAS) is a childhood disorder that arises almost exclusively in the context of child-custody disputes. Its primary manifestation is the child's campaign of denigration against a good, loving parent – a campaign that has no justification. It results from the combination of a programming (brainwashing) parent's indoctrinations and the child's own contributions to the vilification of the target parent. When true parental abuse and/or neglect is present, the child's animosity may be justified and so the parental alienation syndrome explanation for the child's hostility is not applicable.*

The term 'syndrome' to describe this behaviour has been a central element in the PAS controversy. At present PAS is not recognised as such by the US based Diagnostic and Statistical Manual of Mental Disorders (DSM) classification, published by the American Psychiatric Association (APA). This is the standard classification of mental disorders used by mental health professionals in the United States and across the world. It is intended to be applicable in a wide array of contexts and used by clinicians and researchers of many different orientations (e.g. biological, psychodynamic, cognitive, behavioural, interpersonal, family/systems).[3] The next edition of the DSM, DSM-V, is not scheduled for publication until 2011 at the earliest.[4]

We should **not** have to wait until 2011 to do something about this growing problem, whether or not it is called a syndrome. In addition, it should not be a critical issue whether this parental conduct is referred to as parental alienation, hostile-aggressive parenting or implacable hostility, which are terms used by the courts and psychiatrists and psychologists to describe such behaviour.

Consider the following true statements which give an indication of the very powerful and destructive elements of parental alienation:

I did not know I could still love both Mummy and Daddy.

Alienated child aged 5 years old

It does a child no good to have a denigrated view of a parent even if merited but it is very troubling when it was not merited. There could be serious effects as the child gets older.

I remain painfully aware what a sad and difficult case this is and of the risk of getting it wrong. At the same time I must point out that the risks associated with doing nothing are also very significant indeed.

Alienated mother

If the situation continues as it has done, certainly from my experiences over the last six years within the UK Family Court proceedings arena, more and more children will become alienated from loving, caring, committed and perfectly safe parents as a result of the failure of the courts to stem the tide from acrimonious divorces. The problem is compounded by the unacceptable delays in hearing such cases in court, seeking expert clinical input to adequately and appropriately advise the courts of such problems and imposing effective sanctions on parents who are insidiously or overtly 'preventing' their children from having a normal and fulfilling relationship with their other parent.

What of those children already alienated? Recognising and preventing the problem manifesting itself at the outset is by far the easier solution. Normalising severely alienated children is almost impossible. In extreme cases this may require taking the critical steps of removing the children from the controlling parent that they appear to absolutely adore,[5] or even possible removal to care through the initiation of Care Proceedings.[6] This is because the controlling parent is deemed by the children to be 'all good'. Slowly, and with appropriate expert support, the children need to be re-introduced to the alienated parent who they have been influenced to believe is 'all bad'.

Educating everyone who is involved in child residency cases about parental alienation is therefore vitally important. Having highly respected and credible experts such as Dr Ludwig Lowenstein publish key findings about parental alienation based on clinical experience is also critical as part of the continuing education process.

As a decent, loving, heartbroken mother who has witnessed her two children systematically alienated from her over the last six years I am indebted to Dr Lowenstein for asking me to provide a parent's view of parental alienation. My world has been shattered, my value system destroyed, I have to live on a daily basis knowing that I have not been able to cuddle, kiss or be an intrinsic part of my two children's lives for four years now. They will not even speak to me on the phone any more yet live only 10 miles away. They are 10 and almost 8 years old. I fear for their continuing emotional development having been forced to exclude me from their lives. I hope and pray that in time they are able to find their way back to me. I have had to come to terms that this is unlikely to happen for many years until, perhaps, they are old enough and independent of mind enough to understand the truth. However there is no guarantee of this.

For Adam and Eli – I will always be here for you.
Lisa Cohen
Alienated Mother

References

1. Gardner, R.A. (2002) The Parental Alienation Syndrome: Past, Present, and Future. Keynote address presented to the International Conference on the Parental Alienation Syndrome (PAS), Frankfurt/Main, Germany, October 18-19, 2002. http://www.rgardner.com/refs/ar22.htm
2. Gardner, R.A. Counselling Children in Stepfamilies. Elementary School Guidance and Counselling, 19: 1, 40-9.
3. Diagnostic and Statistical Manual of Mental Disorders (DSM). 4th edn. http://dsmivtr.org/
4. DSM-V Prelude Project: Research and Outreach. http://www.dsm5.org/
5. V v V [2004] EWHC 1215 (Fam) http://www.familylawweek.co.uk/library.asp?i=237
6. C v C Neutral Citation Number: [2005] EWHC 2935 (Fam) http://www.familylawweek.co.uk/library.asp?i=1482

Story 3

This is a special book about parental alienation, an only too common result of inter human relationships where the incompetence of one, or both, of the parents of a child, to deal with the emotions involved around a divorce, leads to a hate campaign against the other parent. The result displays in the child; (verbal) abuse against, and ultimately rejection of, the targeted parent as well as a surviving mechanism where the child displays perfectly normal behaviour to absolutely abnormal situations.

It was Dr Richard Gardner MD who first described the Parental Alienation Syndrome (PAS) back in 1985. His entrepreneurial approach led to further research and fierce discussions. These discussions about PAS became a war zone where the ultimate aim of the discussions moved from the best way to solve abnormal situations for children to debating the existence of PAS, leading to personal vendettas against believers. The first psychologist in the United Kingdom to step into this minefield was Dr Ludwig Lowenstein.

When I got divorced in 1996 and was facing a major personal crisis, I had never heard of PAS, Dr Gardner or even Dr Lowenstein. I was facing trouble enough trying to secure the loving bond I had developed with my, then, two year old daughter Byron (meaning source, spring or well).

It proved to be impossible to agree with Byron's mother in order to reach an agreement about a contact arrangement. It took many interventions by the court to achieve this. These interventions included a 'Penal Notice', forcing Byron's mother to obey the court's directions or face being sent to prison due to being guilty of contempt of court, and later a 'Munby J's approach', when the judge ordered a contact visit to take place, and at the same time ordered the mother to report in writing and in person to the same judge, at a specific date and time with specific reasons as to why this contact visit did not take place, should this be the case. Of course under these conditions Byron's mother gave way and reluctantly allowed the visits.

Following each court order Byron's mother increased the pressure on Byron. Handovers became more and more difficult and strenuous. It took Byron increasingly longer to adjust upon arrival in my home, enduring stalking phone calls by her mother. Byron became more and more unapproachable, unresponsive and unmanageable. I noticed a loyalty conflict with Byron but fortunately we were able to address this sensibly and she still enjoyed her time spent with her paternal family. Later on Byron welcomed my new partner and especially her three children who were of the same age group. When these relationships developed positively, Byron's mother increased her hate campaign. The situation became impossible to bear for any girl of ten years old. My weekly phone calls to Byron, as ordered by the court, were not answered, messages left were not replied to, her mother subsequently cancelled contact visits without notice and the matter was before the court again.

As a result the court appointed Dr Lowenstein as the forensic child psychologist and asked him to perform a psycho-diagnostic assessment of the three parties involved, examine their interfamilial relationships and make recommendations with the purpose of re-establishing contact between father and daughter. Dr Lowenstein concluded that Byron had identified with her mother totally and regarded her father as an outsider who could be marginalised. Byron obviously felt that she had a much greater control of her own life and had greater freedom if she allied herself to her mother at the cost of her father. Dr Lowenstein advised the court to intervene with mediation to all three parties with the purpose of helping Byron to understand why her parents behaved differently towards her, and how she could fit in with both parents. At the same time Dr Lowenstein sought some form of compromise between the parents that would give them both the opportunity of playing an appropriate role with Byron so that she could benefit from this.

The court then ordered the three of us to attend Dr Lowenstein's mediation sessions to reach a solution. After nearly nine years since our divorce (by now Byron was eleven years of age) these mediation sessions proved to be the ultimate divorce challenge so far. I found the mediation process a difficult period. However, it was an experience I would not have wanted to miss. Never did I anticipate the aggression and hostility that I encountered during these sessions. Byron and her mother made unreasonable demands, used aggressive wording expressing false accusations, even up to the point of physical abuse of Byron by myself and touching her in inappropriate places. The hostility had further increased but Dr Lowenstein intervened and explicitly assessed that the alleged abuse had not taken place. A short while later this was spontaneously confirmed by Byron in the presence of her mother!

Our case, and particularly the interaction with Byron and her mother inspired Dr Lowenstein to write his article 'How does one identify and treat false accusations of sexual abuse in parental alienation situations?' the subject of Chapter 25.

When it appeared that Byron and her mother were not willing to make any progress on the road to re-establishing contact between Byron and myself, Dr Lowenstein then intervened through therapy focussing on Byron. I was present when he performed the therapy and witnessed her positive change of posture during the therapy session. Dr Lowenstein started by addressing the therapy process sensitively and confronted Byron with the way she behaved towards me. He continued by asking what she felt like with me, to which she answered that she felt uncomfortable, but could not explain why. When there still was no progress in her attitude, which was even on the brink of becoming impertinent, Dr Lowenstein made a strong appeal to her conscience and responsibility. She then was confronted with her own statements made in the previous sessions. To emphasise the seriousness of this situation Dr Lowenstein continued by speaking slowly, in a lowered voice, confronting Byron with her own words. She felt trapped by her own words and reacted with shouting, crying and sobbing. I was perplexed by the way she misbehaved and felt ashamed.

As her father I decided to step in, asking Byron to look me right in the eyes and repeat her allegations, but this time directly to me. She found this very confrontational and admitted that these had never happened. Dr Lowenstein then addressed Byron as to what she was rejecting and how her father tried to be a positive influence in her life. During this part I continued showing Byron pictures of people she loved and memories of fun times she shared with our family. When Dr Lowenstein addressed Byron and explained she was 'doing wrong towards her father', she finally changed her attitude. The situation was tense, but never went out of control. Dr Lowenstein succeeded fully in making Byron aware of her irresponsible and outrageous behaviour, what she had rejected and how much she had appreciated this earlier in her life. It was as if she had awakened from a trance. At the end of this particular therapy session, Byron became co-operative and behaved like any child would do towards her father. We spoke together about nice things and happy memories and I was very pleased and grateful to observe that she was feeling relieved, fully at ease and had totally changed her behaviour. When we were on our own, (when the therapist had left the room for a moment) Byron and I could especially share moments of intimacy and joy for the first time in ages. She was her own self again and displayed a heartbreaking amount of affection and warmth. Again our case inspired Dr Lowenstein to write another article 'How can one overturn the programming of a child against a parent?' which is also included in this book as Chapter 15. The dialogue reflects our therapy session.

At the end of this crucial session when her mother joined in, Byron was liberated to know that she could show me some affection again and that she had the backing of Dr Lowenstein to demonstrate this warmth in the presence of her mother. In the months following this precious moment however, Byron's mother continued the alienation and managed to reverse any progress that had been made by Dr Lowenstein, myself and Byron.

In his final report to the court, Dr Lowenstein set out how the mediation sessions had taken place and gave his conclusion that the mother had conducted 'parental alienation' towards the child, against the father. He substantiated his findings with many examples and suggested a continuation of mediation for all three parties and therapy for Byron and her mother.

The court, however, was slow to intervene with adequate measures that could have secured the successful repair in the relationship between Byron and myself. Instead of a quick return to the original contact arrangements and the start up of further professional therapy and mediation for the three of us, as recommended by the court appointed forensic child psychologist, I had to participate two months later, in supervised contact visits, with a representative of the alienator present.

It was obvious that Byron's mother had continued and increased her hate campaign and of course the court's approach did not have any chance to lead to regular unsupervised visits. At the start of the court proceedings the judge had stated that if contact would not be back to normal within half a year, he would reinstate this contact with the force of the court. When push came to shove however the judge appeared to be a sheep in wolf's clothing and he declined taking the announced appropriate action. I have not seen, nor have I had, any contact with Byron since the last successful mediation session with Dr Lowenstein in August 2005. The court system was slow to take proper measures and by doing so rewarded the aggressive alienating parent. The court system failed, and the child is the victim. The child became a child of war.

This is where my side of the story on parental alienation ends, for the moment.

Dr Lowenstein's story in this case however continued. Despite his sensitive approach, Byron's mother filed a complaint with the British Psychological Society against Dr Lowenstein's professional conduct during the mediation sessions. After detailed investigations by the British Psychological Society, all of her complaints turned out to be unjustified.

So my case may have been a disappointment for me and my daughter, yet it had the two important outcomes mentioned above. **Byron is a recognised victim of parental alienation**. This may not have been in time to help Byron and me in safeguarding our relationship through the court, but I hope it will be in time for other parents in their quest for contact whilst suffering from parental alienation.

It will take time before the legal system acknowledges the findings of parental alienation, which seems to be the crux of the case. It will take even more time before this system will deal with this kind of misbehaviour in a more effective way. Dr Lowenstein may not have achieved this so far but as a champion for the acceptance and existence of parental alienation in the UK he has made that 'small step for man but giant leap for mankind'. This book makes an important contribution towards the expansion of knowledge of parental alienation and its consequences for the children, who are the ultimate victims of this villainous process.

I am deeply indebted to Dr Lowenstein for his involvement in Byron's situation. I am privileged to have worked with him in the mediation sessions and feel honoured by his request to write this preface.

I look forward to the day that I can inform him about Byron and I picking up the threads of our lives together again, because I am sure this day will come.

Gottfried Vendig Brensohn

'*Lieve Byron,*
   Whenever, wherever, you will always be welcome with us.
Liefs,
Pappa'

Except for Dr Lowenstein's, all the names have been altered. The daughter's name has been changed to Byron in respect of Byron Katie; author of the self help book *Loving What Is*. (Katie, B. (2002) *Loving What Is: How Four Questions can Change Your Life*. New York: Harmony Books (http://www.thework.com))

Part One

The Problems Associated With Parental Alienation and Parental Alienation Syndrome

Chapter One

Introduction: do children need fathers?

David Blunkett was in the news for wishing to have contact with his unborn child. Hopefully, he will not face the problem of having little or no contact with his child that many fathers have previously had. I will not give a direct answer to the question posed in my title but the answer will become clear as I go along.

As an expert witness for many years I have acted as an independent psychological consultant to the courts, requesting mostly that fathers, but also mothers, are given opportunities for contact with their children. Very often the parties are in dispute over contact, especially fathers. In most cases those seeking contact and wishing to play a vital role in the life of a child have been fathers. Some fathers have sought such contact over many months and even many years. In some cases after a great number of attempts of seeking to play a role in their children's lives they have given up. This is unfortunate and damaging to the child, especially in the long term.

In most cases the separation between the partners has been hostile and this hostility has been maintained long after separation and divorce and passed on to the children, usually by the mother. The custodial parent, usually the mother, has tended to make it difficult, sometimes impossible for the father to maintain and build upon a relationship with a child or children due to the implacable opposition which many mothers have for such contact.

There has often been a process of 'alienation' or 'poisoning the mind' of the child against the father by denigrating him in the eyes of the child. This tends to be denied by the mother. She claims to have made every effort to encourage a child to be receptive to being with the father. But suddenly or gradually the child who was previously so close to the father is now disinclined to meet with him!

If contact is provided, it tends to be minimal or very restricted. Sometimes a mother will insist, with no valid reason, that a former partner should only have contact by post, supervised contact or unsupervised contact but fairly restricted contact. In the extreme, mothers have changed the name of the child without the

father's knowledge or permission when the mother has formed a new relationship.

The judicial system has gone along with the unfair and unjust procedures over many years. It is for this reason that there now exist such organisations as 'Fathers 4 Justice' and also 'Shared Parenting' etc. Some of the measures employed have not been to everyone's satisfaction when they have reached the headlines in recent times. However, I and many others, whilst not always condoning the methods, have understood and sympathised with the frustrations endured by many fathers. It is because fathers have been unable to achieve justice by legal or legitimate means that this behaviour has developed into more extreme forms of rebelliousness.

My own position as an expert witness has equally been frustrated by the implacable and outmoded legal system in place today which does not adequately deal with these matters. It is my view that the child needs to maintain positive contact with both loving parents. The exceptions are when one or both parents are violent or abusive, either sexually, physically or emotionally, towards the child. The fact that one parent may have to resort to being the litigant does not give that parent a positive persona to the child or to others. It is unfortunate that the custodial parent will sometimes use the power of control as an argument when accusing the father of assertions of abuse, these being false.

I favour both natural parents providing time, guidance, and love towards a mutually conceived child or children. Ideally this should be on a 50/50 basis. One cannot, however, hold to this precise sharing of time in every case. One should however, use this as a starting point. (It must be said that there are few judges who agree with me at this time: it is encouraging, however, that a few do agree.) This view however, is not normally accepted by the judiciary. They still cling to the opinion that mothers should be the most prominent, or even the only, care providers. Fathers are considered to be at the periphery, virtually rejected from family life. At present there are numerous single parents, both male and female, who are care givers. At least one third of these care providers who have custody of a child are now men. These men are as capable as mothers of caring for their children.

After many years of seeking appropriate or even any contact with a child some fathers unfortunately give up the struggle, despite the sadness they feel in having to do so. When some contact exists, this contact is not only restricted and therefore unnatural, such as no overnight stays with the father being allowed, but often unsatisfactory in many other ways. It is also tragic that the father sometimes has to overcome the reluctance of the child to be with him because of the 'brainwashing' against himself which has been perpetrated by the mother and often her family. It is also very difficult for fathers to develop a long-term relationship when they have not seen their child for a considerable period of time, or the interval between seeing their child is too long.

Not only are fathers excluded or limited in contact with their children but also the child is prevented from having contact with father's extended family. Judges, it appears, are loathe to treat mothers in any punitive manner. This is even when mothers actively prevent contact for non valid reasons. Such obstinate behaviour by mothers occurs even when courts state that mothers must co-operate.

One judge, who will be nameless, stated 'What would you have me do if a mother refuses to obey the ruling of the Court. Imprison her?'

To this I replied with a similar question: 'What would you do if the father had custody and the mother wished for equitable contact. Would you not then consider some punitive action?'

The same judge then considered the matter: 'Would penalising or imprisoning the mother in the final analysis not be harmful to the child who we must most importantly protect?'

To which I replied: 'Of course the child must be protected, but does it not also harm the child in the short and long-term to be deprived of a loving and caring father?'

The judge had no answer to this.

Therefore, based on my experience, woe betide any expert witness who supports a father in seeking contact, especially on a 50/50 basis, that is shared residence, when a mother is implacably imposed to such an arrangement. I have sought fair and equal contact for fathers with their children in cases in which I have been involved

but my experience with some judges has been disappointing.

I deem it most important for a child now and in the future to be cared for by two loving parents. The ideal is for both parents playing an equal part in the child's upbringing. Much of the troubles of society today are due to the fact that many children do not have the benefit of two loving parents being involved in their lives. This results in educational problems, truancy, delinquency and future problems in their own relationships. Father's role with their sons is of particular importance in preventing delinquency as much research has indicated. Daughters also who have a positive relationship with their fathers are more likely to be able to establish a good relationship with males as adults.

In some cases I have been viewed as being a biased psychological expert when I have recommended joint residency. I could not understand, and neither could the fathers, why I was not seen as being 'independent' in my conclusions and recommendations because of this opinion that fathers and mothers have both rights of an equal nature for the care and love of their children.

In at least one case, irrelevant allegations have been made of my own derelictions by a biased mother and her solicitor with the objective of discrediting me, my judgement, my recommendations and my good name. Some judges fortunately have the good sense to note these irrelevant ploys as they were merely for the purpose of denigrating me so that my views would be discounted. It was especially unfortunate that one well-prepared report which I considered to be independent was considered to be biased and was not even considered by the court. I personally could not see where one recommended equal partnerships in rearing a child could be considered as 'biased'. In one recent case, a whole report was discredited, as I suspect was because of my recommendation to equal contact. I was not even allowed to be present at the hearing. My message therefore to expert witnesses involved in family matters, and parental alienation especially, is to beware!

There is no room in our current judicial system for new and better ideas regarding justice and fairness for fathers with some judges. Indeed why does the case of access or contact have to be a judicial issue? Might this matter be better served outside of such a forbidding, worrying and costly scenario? Despite this, I will continue to represent fathers seeking contact with their children and hoping that with time and good arguments, views will change and fathers and indeed mothers will be justly treated by the courts on a 50/50 basis or as close as possible.

In this way, children will in future benefit in the short and long term. Children need both parents to have the best possible chance of growing into emotionally healthy and adjusted adolescents and adults. This is also a vital way of improving society on the whole in the future.

Chapter Two

Parental Alienation Syndrome (PAS)

PAS has been practised for as long as marital or relationship conflicts have occurred. It is the conscious action of one parent turning against another to oust the other parent from the affection, love and respect or regard of their children. It works more effectively when used against younger, passive children and less so with older, more assertive children. It is unlikely to occur in a stable, harmonious relationship between parents who encourage the children to regard the other parent similarly, and work together to bring up their children appropriately with socialised standards of behaviour. Where marital disharmony does occur PAS is not necessarily a consequence, as many parents consider their parental role as of the greatest importance. They will encourage the former partner to participate in guiding and caring for their children, and afford them equal importance in the upbringing. Such parents engender the important principle that whilst parents may not be able to love one another it does not mean that their love for their children is any the less. Sometimes the parted couples can even establish a friendly relationship towards one another which is desirable for their children. To achieve this some parents need guidance from an outside professional. In this way, despite the marital split, parenting patterns persist.

Why does PAS occur?

PAS occurs as a result of a relationship in conflict, to which must be added the pathological condition of the alienator. They suffer from the need to control totally the process of rearing the children after an acrimonious separation. It is known to be most common in females. Sometimes this results from the need to retaliate against the former partner who may have been the rejector of the relationship. Depths of early childhood experiences and alienation from their own parents also play a part.

Depriving a former partner of positive contact with his children is a powerful weapon. Some alienators go so far as to accuse the former partner, often unjustly, of physically, emotionally and even sexually abusing the child or children merely to get their own way. This results in the involvement of social workers, the police and leads to the humiliation of the alienated parent, often unjustly. Under these circumstances, most alienated partners often give up the fight to seek contact with their child. The alienating parent will often use this against him by informing the child: 'You see how little he cares for you'; 'Wasn't I right about him?' The child will more often than not fail to understand the lack of logic of what takes place and support the mother's position since she is present most of the time and has usually been the main carer. Sometimes a new partnership has emerged. It is then the object of the alienator to promote the affection and closeness of the children with the new partner and to forget the role of the alienated parent, usually the father.

In the very rare instances there occurs poor parenting by one partner or even criminal activities such as paedophilia. Such parents should be removed from the parenting role at least until they have been treated for their problems.

Who is most likely to practise PAS?

More than 75 per cent of mothers practise PAS, as against 25 per cent of men who alienate. Partly this is due to the view, despite the changes in social and cultural norms, that the mother is the centre of family life. Hence an alienating mother feels she has the greater input and responsibility in caring for the child than the father. Mothers who are on their own feel it is only right that they should have the main or only right to make decisions concerning their children. They will, therefore, use any weapon, fair or foul, to make certain that they have the ultimate power over their children. Among the weapons used are accusations by the mother that the father is unfit to care for or even spend any time with the child. This may be due to allegations of sexual misconduct, alcohol or drug misuse, immorality or poor mental state or lifestyle or possibly criminal involvement. Due to the closeness of the mothers and children, the children will often believe the worse of the other parent.

Such mothers alienate themselves from the real needs of the child in order to maintain their total contact and to eliminate the contact and relationship with the other parent. When litigation is threatened, the alienating parent becomes even keener in her determination to have complete control. She will say to the child: 'See what your father is doing now? He is trying to have me imprisoned'. This turns the child against the father even more as they see the mother as the 'victim'. Hence, she has involved and continues to involve the child in her battle with the father and the process of programming and brainwashing the child until the child sees matters as the programmer sees them and turns against the father. The child's behaviour, therefore, becomes increasingly more difficult when the father is present and the child may even refuse to go with him. Sometimes in-laws, allied to one or the other, may influence matters further. Hence the child uses the same hostility and acts accordingly. The mother in turn is deeply gratified to have achieved her objective and may even disclaim that she is doing anything to influence the child and may state that she is actively encouraging the child to cooperate. The result is that the child will behave in an inimical, unfriendly and hostile way towards the alienated person, usually the father. In this situation, the mother may well believe her own lies. Some mothers overindulge their children in order to provide their children with the view that 'mother offers them most'. This is combined with persistent denigration of the other parent.

It is of interest to note that many parents who seek to programme their children in the above way have often been subjected to the same treatment themselves. They are, therefore, very familiar with the techniques that can be used effectively. They are perpetuating a vicious and destructive pattern to the next generation.

The likely consequences to the alienated person and the children

Children hate to see their parents in acrimony because it reduces their sense of security and they feel in jeopardy. The successful indoctrination, programming and brainwashing of a child leads to bitterness, sadness and anger in the unjustly accused parent and prevention of the parent in exercising their rights, obligations and love for the child. They will either give up the right, or there will be an acrimonious conflict wherein the child suffers confusion and ultimately alienation towards one of the parents. This may go on for many years.

Fear is sometimes induced in the child towards the alienated parent. This is ultimately often translated into attacking and humiliating them. Fear induction is especially likely to be successful with younger children. Eventually such children consider the alienated parent to be 'bad', 'inadequate' and of little value to them. Such parents eventually are forced to play a peripheral role or no role at all, except as financial providers. When the mother's economic position is greater than father's, for instance, there is a desire to eliminate father even from the role of provider. Some fathers become so desperate as to contemplate suicide or use alcohol or drugs as a means of escape. This merely verifies the picture which mothers frequently inculcate in their children – that their father is an alcoholic or drug addict. Some children, seeing the once stable parents embroiled in this kind of warfare, turn against both parents and become depressed, underachieve at school or turn to delinquency.

Only later in life do children sometimes become aware of the wrong which has been done and the way they have been used as 'pawns' and programmed against all the opposing 'reality'. Then the antagonism of the maturing adult turns against the alienating parent, as they grow up and become aware through maturity and learning to think for themselves that the alienated parent has suffered a great injustice at the hands of the alienator and themselves. As a consequence they feel a sense of desperate guilt, which can become a helpless kind of regret and has no way of being assuaged if the parent has died or has vanished.

How is PAS carried out?

Parents who use PAS often see themselves as 'victims' and like to think their children see them as 'victims'. They tend to seek revenge and will encourage the children to believe that the other parent is at fault, by claiming that 'she', the victim and programmer, has been cruelly and unjustly treated. They will also assuage and engender the view that their former partner suffers from a number of moral and personal problems. Slanderous or exaggerated statements are made constantly to the child about the alienated parent. Alienating parents will over-state or even create vices such as: 'He's an alcoholic, drug taker, womaniser, has no sense of responsibility, drives dangerously, etc.' All such statements and many more, are repeated to the child continually.

Of all such statements the most damaging to the alienated parent is that of sexual or physical abuse, when there are no justifiable reasons for such allegations being made. The repercussions can be that the alienated parent can be judged guilty by allegations alone, and often has to undergo a painful investigation and suspicion to disprove such allegations. However, where this is substantiated by a court there should be no question of continued access to the child in question until treatment has been undergone and it is felt safe by all involved for contact to resume.

Intervention in the form of therapy is usually necessary in order to counteract false allegations. Such help will be met with a mixture of hope by the alienated parent and often resentment, and lack of co-operation by the alienator and often by the alienated child. The alienator will use or promote anything which will achieve their objective of hurting, denigrating and if possible eliminating the alienated parent's control or contact with the child.

Other ways of carrying out the process of alienation via programming and thereby brainwashing children can be seen by:

1. Observing the behaviour and listening to the statements of children towards the alienated party.
2. By noting the control the alienating parent seeks and obtains in order to eliminate the alienated parent.
3. By noting the marital disharmony as well as the acrimony when the parents separated subsequently.
4. By noting the contradictory statements and behaviour demonstrated by the programmed child when interviewed.
5. By taking note of the character assaults which the alienating parent makes which are often not verifiable: e.g. that the former partner is immoral, lacks parenting skills, drinks heavily, uses drugs, is emotionally unstable or unreliable or is dishonest, etc.
6. By noting the unchildlike statements made which have been programmed by the alienating parent.

Another manifestation of PAS is the child being totally under the influence of the alienating parent, by believing and repeating what the alienating parent says, in attacking and humiliating the other party, and refusing to have contact or very limited contact with the alienated person.

There are many other direct as well as subtle ways in which the process of programming and brainwashing is carried out. Here are some of them:

1. Encouraging the child to disobey and show a lack of respect for the alienated parent.
2. By promoting an alliance between the child and alienator against the other parent.
3. Showing opposition to the other parent's child-rearing methods and communicating this to the child.
4. Bribing and overindulging the child to create comparative poverty of enjoyment with the other parent, when they are with that parent.
5. Suggesting and actually changing the surname of the child to reduce the influence and memory of the other birth parent.
6. The programmer playing the part of a 'martyr' claiming how badly they were treated by the alienated parent.
7. Making the child afraid of the alienated parent.
8. Encouraging the child to hate being with the other parent.
9. Showing the other parent to be bad.
10. Instilling in the child the view that the other parent wants to take the child away from the programmer and even to kidnap the child.
11. Making the child feel anxious, rejected and insecure if the child does not comply with the programmer.
12. The programmer encourages the child to keep secrets while spying and reporting on the alienated parent.
13. Moving away or living some distance from the alienated parent.
14. Sowing the seeds of not obeying the alienated parent.
15. Showing negative non-verbal communication such as turning the body away when speaking of the alienated parent or making derogatory faces about the alienated parent, when speaking on the telephone.

Treating the effects of PAS

It is vital that a professional such as a clinical psychologist or psychiatrist be involved as soon as possible to deal with PAS. This is to prevent the damage caused by PAS from becoming impervious to improvement. The professional must be aware of PAS, and also its origin.

Both parents and the child must be evaluated individually with the professional being aware of the presence and effect of PAS on all concerned. Sometimes unannounced home visits are indicated. Having established that none of the parents are a danger to the child, efforts must be made to develop a voluntary 'modus vivendi' on who should have the children and when, thus avoiding PAS by either parent. One must term this a 'two-step plan'. If the initial process of voluntary help being provided with both parents and the child is ineffective, a more firm approach must be adopted, including the involvement of the legal system.

Interviews with all members of the warring factions should be insisted upon by the court. Frequently there is much opposition to this by one party or the other. Only the court can insist on all being done as the professional (expert witness) requests. Failure to co-operate with the expert witness indicates to the court what the next step needs to be. It is preferable for one expert witness to deal with both parties, rather than each to have their own who will side with their particular position rather than considering the overall complexity of the problems and the concern over the child's needs. This is not always possible however in an 'adversarial' atmosphere.

Interviews and tests used must be carried out sensitively and impartially. Videotaping may be used when allowed by the participants. When this is not allowed, who objects and why should be noted! The videotapes can be studied by all involved in seeking to make the best possible decisions.

Where PAS continues by one or both parties, legal sanctions need finally to be found with the alienating parent being given psychological treatment and, failing this, being forced to discontinue such behaviour. When this fails in the extreme, such parents should lose custody of the child, and the child placed with co-operating in-laws who permit full contact of the child with the previous alienated parent. It is also possible that the alienating parent could be fined or imprisoned with the alienated parent being given regular contact and even custody of the child.

This would need to be done with the greatest of care since the children have often been programmed so fully against the alienated parent. What is required is a period of deprogramming, with the help of a clinical psychologist. In this way the child may be allowed to understand the following:

- Why the programming occurred.
- What can be done to gradually improve and cement the child's relationship with the alienated parent.

Therapists involved in helping such children should seek to develop a greater insight into such children concerning PAS.

What is the judicial recourse?

There is an increase in the alienated parent turning to the legal profession and the courts if all other methods have failed. They feel justice must surely prevail when an independent judge is made aware of PAS. This is now common in the United States, but less so in the UK. Judges are naturally influenced by a number of traditions and are unaware in many cases, of the effects of PAS. These traditions are:

1. Mothers, on the whole, are thought more suitable than fathers to have custody of the children.
2. The older children should have the final say about whom to be with. This does not, however, consider the programming which the alienated parent has carried out beforehand.
3. In the case of a younger child, many judges again favour the mother as main custodian or sole custodian, all things being equal. If they favour the other parent they may well be viewed as unfair.
4. Sometimes judges will recommend family therapy or some involvement of psychiatrists, paediatricians or clinical psychologists to assess and treat the conflict between opposing parents. These professionals also often fail to respond to the PAS which has eliminated or reduced the role being played by the alienated parent. They, too, may put too much emphasis on what children say they want, being unaware of PAS.

It is vital that decisions are made which are fair and just for all concerned. PAS cannot be allowed to prevent one capable but hostile parent from depriving another stable and capable parent of their parenting role. Any parent who practises PAS must ultimately be dealt with severely by the court. PAS is a kind of brainwashing which leads to suffering for all concerned, either in the short or long-term. Both parents must be viewed as having the right and the obligation to play a vital role on the care, guidance and love provided for their children.

The judiciary must realise that many potential litigious parents who have been the victims of adverse brainwashing of their children give up the fight. They do this for a variety of practical reasons including:

- The feeling that they are doing more harm to their children than good by fighting over them.
- Lack of financial resources.
- The view that they simply do not think they can win against a determined, alienating former parent.
- It takes much determination and is extremely time consuming, when one is already fully stretched in earning a living in order to provide for the children.

It is unfortunate that many children view the fact that a parent does not fight for them in the courts, as a rejection of them by that parent. It is time to redress the balance.

Justice of the Peace, Jan. 1999, 163: 3, 16: 47–50

Chapter Three

Causes and consequences of divorce

Most research concerning divorce and separation comes from the United States. Between the mid 1980s and 2002, 46 research articles appeared, mostly dealing with the causes of separation and divorce and only very few with the repercussions and treatment approaches. Other countries providing research include the UK (6), Holland (3), China (2), Australia (2). The remainder present one piece of research from Saudi Arabia, Finland, Sweden, Israel, Japan, Ireland, and Switzerland. One piece of research concerned itself with international comparisons of separation and divorce.

Goldstein (1999) noted that divorce rates show a levelling off mainly due to the fact that there is now considerable cohabitation, that is, living together without marriage. One piece of research made an effort to examine the power of an oral history interview in predicting stable marital relationships versus divorce. Carrers et al. (2000) was able to predict with 84.4 per cent accuracy, those marriages that were likely to remain intact rather than those that did not. The oral history date predicted 81 per cent and 87.4 per cent accuracy of these couples separating or remaining together. The 87.4 per cent prediction was whether divorce occurred within the first five years while the 81 per cent predicted accuracy over a longer period.

Daly and Wilson (2000) considered why some marriages appeared to last. He drew information from the Darwinian theory which argued that the human mammal selected the marital alliance as the best adaptation for ensuring its survival through sexual reproduction. With the decline in religious influences considerable family changes have occurred in the United States during the past four decades (Brooks, 2002). This had led to an increasing proportion of single parent families. Public concern with family decline increased steadily after 1980. A study by Pinsof (2002) noted that during the last half of the twentieth century, for the first time in history, divorce replaced death as the end point of the majority of marriages.

Most research, as indicated, is based on the causes of divorce. Relatively little is concerned

with the consequences of divorce and even less in seeking to find remedies or prevention for separation and divorce. These three areas of researched causes will now be explored intensively.

Causes of divorce

It should be remembered that divorce does not occur for a single reason and that frequently there are a number of factors involved as to why divorce and separations occur. A summary of these now follows:

1. Women's independence.
2. Too early marriage and arranged marriages.
3. Economic and financial factors.
4. Poor intellectual, educational and social skills.
5. Liberal divorce laws.
6. Sexual factors leading to incompatibility.
7. Role conflicts.
8. Alcoholism and substance abuse or risk taking behaviour.
9. Differences between the partners leading to acrimony.
10. Religious factors.
11. Attitudes to divorce.
12. Various other factors.

Women's independence

Over the years women have gained in independence due to their often developing a career in the work setting. Ermisch (1986) felt that marital disillusion often occurred when women had the experience of working and following their own career. This influenced women's earning capacity and gave considerable risk to marital disillusion especially when there were other problems present as well. A Japanese study by Ogawa and Ermisch (1994) found that in Japan the divorce rate had more than doubled since the mid 1960s. This was attributed to female paid employment which had increased rapidly in the past few decades. This was especially the case for women who took up full time employment. Hence it was found by Heath and Ciscel (1996) that many women remained in marriage merely because they had no alternative but to do so, having no earning power, and opportunities to be economically independent from their spouses.

Ruggles (1997) found the rise of female employment in non-farm-type occupations was closely associated with growth of divorce and separation. Moreover, higher female labour-force participation among black women and lower economic opportunities for black men accounted for race differences and marital instability before 1940, and for more of such differences in subsequent years.

Many women who took up careers frequently lacked the career support from their spouses. This was noted by Dolan and Hoffman (1998).

Divorce or separation between partners frequently affected their total earnings which is one of the reasons why many partners remained together, to prevent this from occurring (Ressler and Waters, 2000). It was also noted, however, that increases in female earnings significantly increased divorce rates, undoubtedly due to the fact that the woman in an unhappy marriage now found herself capable of sustaining herself and possibly her family on her own wages.

An interesting phenomenon over recent years is that women file for divorce more often now than men, despite deep attachments to their children who they know are being harmed by such divorces. Many women in retrospect report the fact that they are happier being single than when they were married (Brinig and Allen, 2000). Many women also file for divorce for the purpose of having sole custody of the children.

Sayer and Bianchi (2000) explored whether a wife's economic independence destabilised marriage and heightened the risk of divorce. There was an initial positive association between a wife's percentage contribution to the family income and divorce, but the relation was reduced to non-significance as soon as variables measuring gender ideology were introduced into the model. The analysis indicated that measures of marital commitment and satisfaction were better predictors of marital disillusion than measures of economic independence. The studies of the influence of women's work on the risk of divorce were carried out by Poortman and Kalmijn (2002) in a Dutch study. Of particular importance were the factors that led to divorce due to the intensity of the wife's work, the status of the wife's work and the potential success she achieved on the labour market in comparison with her husband. The result showed that working women had a 22 per cent higher risk of divorce than women who did not work.

Too early marriage and arranged marriages

Only one study concerned itself with too early marriage. This was a Chinese study by Zeng et al. (1992). This study demonstrated that the level of divorce in China was extremely low, in comparison with other developed and developing countries. Similar findings from other studies indicated that the risk of divorce for women who married before the age of 18 was higher than those married after 20. Arranged marriages had a risk of divorce which was about 2.5 times as high as the non-arranged marriage. It was also noted that divorces were higher in urban than rural areas. Other things being equal, women with more children had a lower risk of divorce. Son-preference exerted an effect on marriage dissolution. Women with no son had significantly higher risk of divorce than those with at least one son.

Economic and financial factors

A study by Whittington and Alm (1997) showed that women and men respond to tax incentives in their divorce decisions. It must be said that the couples involved in this rather mercenary approach to divorce were a small proportion of those seeking divorce. Most couples tended to find themselves in financial difficulties from one side or the other, or in some cases, both sides as a result of separation and divorce. Frequently it results in unemployment and the reliance on state benefits in Great Britain. In most cases there is an association between emotional factors and subsequent partnership break ups (Kiernan and Mueller, 1998). The authors summarised that people who embarked on partnerships at an early age, cohabitants, those who had experienced parental divorce, and those who were economically, somatically and emotionally vulnerable had higher risks of divorce.

An international study of regional differences in divorce rates was carried out by Lester (1999). The author explored social correlates of regional divorce rates for seven nations: Finland, France, Hungary, Japan, Switzerland, Taiwan, and the USA, finding little consistency. The most consistent social correlates were found to be unemployment and, to a lesser extent, population size, homicide rates, percentage of elderly people, birth rates, death rates, and crime rates.

A study of young Americans who wished to divorce showed that economic factors played an important role in many who sought separations and divorces (Burgess et al., 1997). Similar results were obtained by Waters and Ressler (1999). A final study by Finnas (2000) showed that in Finland an increasing level of income of the husband also decreased the divorce risk, whereas the trend was the opposite one in respect to the wife's income. It was also found that tenants in this study ran a 50 per cent higher risk of divorce than home owners.

Poor intellectual, educational and social skills

Many investigators found that divorce risks decreased as you moved from groups with little education or social capital to groups with more (Hoem, 1997). This negative educational gradient fits with the notion that people with more education are better at selecting spouses and better at making a marriage work. Similarly, Dronkers (2002) in a Dutch study found a relationship between intelligence and divorce risk during the early 1990s for two different Dutch longitudinal cohorts, for which intelligence measures during their childhood were available. A positive relation between intelligence and divorce risk was found for 50 year olds born around 1940: divorced respondents had a lower average intelligence than respondents who stayed together. A negative relation between intelligence and divorce risk was found also for 30 year olds born around 1958: divorced respondents had a lower average intelligence than respondents who stayed together.

Liberal divorce laws or the ease of obtaining divorces

Several studies have shown that the ease of gaining a divorce through liberal laws has undoubtedly increased the likelihood of divorce. This has been shown to be the case in post-war growth of divorces in Great Britain (Smith, 1997). The rising incidence of divorce was explained chiefly also by the growth in the real earnings of women, which had increased post-divorce welfare by providing a measure of financial independence. This coincides with the factor identified above, the greater power of women in their role in society.

Similar results were obtained in the United States as noted by Friedberg (1998). Most states in America switched from requiring mutual consent to allowing unilateral or no-fault divorce between 1970 and 1985. Since then the national divorce rate more than doubled after 1965. A later study by Smith (1998) noted that while in England and Wales the emphasis was initially on fault divorce decrees, no-fault divorce decrees dominated in Scotland. The paper proposed an explanation for this remarkable contrast based on cost incentives generated by procedural and legal interventions with the respective legal systems. The introduction of the Simplified Procedure in Scotland and the reduction in the time bar to divorce in England and Wales were seen as causal factors for a greater number of divorces occurring. The introduction of liberal no-fault divorce laws, therefore, had a significant effect on the divorce rate in England and Wales (Binner and Dnes, 2001).

Sexual factors leading to incompatibility

Despite the great emphasis on sexual problems between a couple, only two studies dealt directly with this. Mazur and Booth (1998) noted that in men high levels of endogenous testosterone seemed to encourage sexual behaviour and tended to come into conflict with a harmonious marriage. There appeared therefore to be a relationship between testosterone secretion in men and this leading to divorce. Allen and Brinig (1998) examined differences in sex drive between husbands and wives and how this affected bargaining strengths during marriage, particularly at times when divorce occurred. The basic argument followed from the fact that sex drives varied over an individual's life cycle and were frequently different for men and women. The spouse having the lower sex drive at any time in the marriage had the controlling right over whether or not sexual intercourse occurred, with a consequent increase in bargaining power.

Such powers influenced the marriages and the likelihood of adultery and divorce.

Role conflicts

Despite the fact that role conflicts predominating frequently led to marital disharmony only two studies were published in this area. Abdel Hameed Al Khateeb (1998) in a study of Saudi Arabian families, including 95 Saudi working women, suggested that Saudi families had changed to some degree. Marital aspects such as housing and bride-price had changed faster than cultural ones. One important change, however, that had taken place in a Saudi family, was the dynamic of marital relationships. Whereas originally this relationship was characterised by the exaggerated respect wives were expected to show their husbands in their daily interactions, now mutual respect and understanding were increasingly evident in the marital relationship. Women's attitudes to equality between the sexes tended to be more progressive than those of men and different expectations had caused role conflict in the family and an increase in the divorce rate. Although men had lost some of their social and religious authority in the family, their economic and general authority remained intact. The Saudi family was a male dominated institution with important decisions being made by men. Cultural norms, civil roles, and judicial legislations supported men's authority in the family and society. An American study also found that incongruence between spouses and gender beliefs, expectations, and behaviours affected marital stability through negative marital interactions, causing identity disruption, and resulted in distancing, marital instability, and in some cases divorce (Pasley et al., 2001).

Alcoholism and substance abuse

Only two recent studies concerned themselves with the role of alcohol in producing problems in marriage. Alcohol consumption and divorce rates in the United States were studied by Caces et al. (1999). The results provided support for both the effects of heavy drinking on divorce rates and the effects of divorce on expenditures for alcoholic beverages. The association between health related behaviours and the risk of divorce in the United States was noted by Fu and Goldman (2000). The

findings indicated that physical characteristics associated with poor health, namely obesity and short stature, were not significantly related to risks of marital dissolution for either men or women. On the other hand, risk taking behaviour such as smoking and drug use was strongly related to higher risks of divorce for both sexes. Overall, results emphasised the need to accommodate health related variables in the dominant economic and social psychological theories of marital dissolution.

Various differences between partners in the relationship

Janssen et al. (2000) asked the question: 'Do marriages in which partners do not resemble each other with respect to age, educational level, occupational status, religion, ethnic background, and social origin have larger probabilities of divorce than marriage in which partners have similar characteristics?' Event history models showed that all forms of heterogamy (being different) led to higher divorce rates and that heterogamy with regard to age, educational attainment, and religion had the largest impact. Both the lack of similarity in taste and preference, and lack of social support affected the risk of divorce, with the effect of the former twice as strong as the effect of the latter. The interpretation of the effects of heterogamy, i.e., being different, on divorce was partial; the effects of educational and religious heterogamy were explained to a larger extent. Other factors important in relationships and frequently neglected were positive time spent by the spouses with one another. This was a significant predictor for women, but less so for men, as to whether the marriage actually worked. For men, unsociable marriages were significant as leading to problems between the parties. This was not, however, found to be the case for women (Terling-Watt, 2001).

Religious factors

A Swiss study by Charton and Wanner (2001) indicated that Switzerland had more than 25 per cent of marital unions end in divorce. This high prevalence of divorce was thought to be linked to the fact that marriage was a forced ritual for many Swiss partners. Factors modifying the probability of divorce were discussed in the paper on the basis of the 1994/95 Family and Fertility Survey data. Survival models allowed for measuring factors influencing the risk of divorce. Among individual factors, the absence of the practice of religion and a former divorce of parents seemed to have a positive effect on the risk of divorce. Other factors included age of the spouses and having had a premarital union. The presence of children in the union also had an impact in preventing separation and divorce. It seemed that the meaning of divorce was increasingly linked to the significance and positive attitudes attributed to marriage.

An interesting study by Broyles (2002) examined the religiosity and attitudes towards divorce. Researchers had shown that religion played a role in predicting whether there was a greater likelihood of obtaining a divorce when marital problems arose. Although the research in this area was quite intensive, little research existed about how religiosity affected one's attitudes towards divorce. The results indicated that there was in fact a significant negative correlation between religiosity and attitudes towards divorce, which suggested that religion does play a role in one's consideration as to whether or not to seek to obtain a divorce.

Attitudes to divorce

A study by Kim and Kim (2002) found that a once-divorced person may hesitate to divorce again as is the case in Asian countries, due to the fear of being labelled as pathological or abnormal. This contradicted the view that multiple divorces were likely to occur in certain individuals.

In Ireland divorce was banned under the Irish Constitution. Despite there being thousands of separated people in Ireland in the early 1980s, the proposal to introduce divorce was vociferously opposed in referenda in 1986 and 1995. The campaign also claimed that divorce would open the floodgates to marriage breakdown. The availability of divorce in Ireland since 1997 had not, however, borne out these dire predictions (Burley and Regan, 2002).

Other factors

One study concerned itself with the death of a child leading to divorce (Schwab, 1998). The death of a child put a tremendous strain on the marital relationship and was fairly common among bereaved parents. It appeared, however, that the majority of marital relationships survived the strain brought about by a child's death and were often even strengthened in the long run. The quality of the marital relationship prior to the child's death, cause of death, and circumstances surrounding the death produced differential outcomes for the marital relationship.

Attitudes to marriage and divorce are vital in determining whether a divorce or separation is likely to occur as noted by Amato and Rogers (1999). When the marital quality deteriorates, those with attitudes favouring divorce are more likely to take that step, as opposed to those who hold fast to their marriage vows.

A British study by Kiernan and Cherlin (1999) indicated that a longitudinal survey of a British cohort born in 1958 found that by the age of 33 offspring of parents who were divorced were more likely to have dissolved their own first partnerships. This finding persisted after taking into account age at first partnership, and type of first partnership (marital, premarital, cohabitation union, and cohabiting union). Also important were indicators of class background, childhood and adolescent school achievement and early behaviour problems. Some of these factors were associated with partnership dissolution in their own right, but the association between parental divorce and second generation partnership dissolution was largely independent of them.

The costs of divorce were also considered a factor as to whether this occurred (Bougheas and Georgellis, 1999). The effect of war on divorce has also been noted by Anderson and Little (1999). Empirical tests showed that World War II significantly increased divorce rates, but rates did not significantly increase because of the Korean War and the Vietnam War.

Barlow (1999) noted that the divorce rate among Christians was higher than that of the average population. This statistic was cause for concern and changes in church preparation for marriage occurred. Although instructions for pastoral premarital counselling existed, most churches did not follow the minimum guidelines. Churches needed a new proactive model for building good marriages rather than mending broken ones. The question is frequently asked whether marital instability occurred as a result of the individual's parents having sought divorce in the past. Wolfinger (2000) tested the hypothesis that individuals and households in the USA who experienced many parental relationship transitions were more likely to reproduce these behaviours as adults by dissolving multiple marriages. The hypothesis was confirmed, and the findings were essentially unchanged when controlling for socioeconomic characteristics of both respondents and their families of origin.

The effect of children being born has also been considered as possible grounds for divorce as noted by Hoge (2002). The author showed how the transition to parenthood became a personal crisis for some fathers and mothers. It prompted them to run away to search for extramarital affairs, or lapse into addictions. This may well lead to preparation for parenthood education. Those who initiated divorces frequently married again. Sweeney (2002) examined the ways in which the decision to begin and to end relationships were interrelated. Results suggested that initiators tended to enter subsequent unions more quickly, although this differential diminished considerably three years after separation. There is also evidence that initiators of divorce or separation were in a stronger position for remarriage and the possibility of forming another relationship was good. Whether this relationship lasted, however, depended on what positive lesson had been learned from previous relationships.

Consequences of divorce

The consequences of divorce can be summed up into four main areas:

1. The diminishing of the father's role in the family.
2. Poor impact on the children.
3. Emotional problems for a number of persons involved.
4. Reduced living standards.

The diminishing of the father's role in the family

A number of studies have indicated the father's role is diminished considerably as a result of divorce. This was due to mothers usually receiving custody of children. This could lead to a parental alienation situation termed Parental Alienation Syndrome (PAS) (Lowenstein, 1998a,

1998b, 1999a, 1999b, 1999d, 2001a, 2001b; Gardner, 1992, 1998, 2001). Within two generations, the primary reason that American children were deprived of a father shifted from a father's death to a woman's choice of a separation or divorce (Coney and Mackey, 1998). Prior to the 1960s, the major cause of becoming deprived of a father was death of a father through illness or accident. After the 1960s the children became deprived of a father primarily because of the mother's decision to petition for a divorce or to become a single parent mother. This situation has been termed by many the 'crisis in America: Father's absence' (Ancona, 1998). Much blame of violence, gangs, rape, crime, and substance abuse has been attributed to the dissolution of the family which caused primarily the loss of paternal functions. In short, society was seen to be becoming imbued with being able to cope without fathers. Some women and others frequently ask: Why do we need fathers'? Certainly the consequences of fatherless families were seen to be the cause of a number of problems in many cases.

Poor impact on children

There have been a number of studies to indicate the harm that can be done to children and parents by divorces or separations which lead to dissolution of the family. Booth (1999) reviewed changes in divorce rates over the last century. Explanations for the changes were evaluated and future trends were projected. The implications of future trends, especially as they related to children, were examined. The author contended that the negative relationship between parental divorce and children's wellbeing appeared long before the divorce took place. Also, children whose parents exhibited low conflict levels before divorce suffered more than those whose parents exhibited moderate to high conflict. These and other findings were explored so that those divorces that entailed high long and short-term risks for children could be identified, and dealt with.

Children's adjustment in conflicted marriage and divorce was studied by Kelly (2000). Children of divorced parents as a group had more adjustment problems than did children of never-divorced parents. The view that divorce per se was the major cause of these symptoms had to be considered in the light of newer research documenting the negative effect of troubled marriages on children. Divorcing parents tended to describe their children as presenting more problems than parents who were not divorced, as noted by Burns and Dunlop (2000) in an Australian study. Data from a longitudinal sample of Australian men and women who were adolescents at the time of their parental divorce again presented considerable problems in such youngsters. Analysis of parent/child data described children of divorced parents as presenting more problems than children whose parents had not been divorced. Such children as adults were more wary about committing to relationships. These children whose parents described them (13–16 year olds) were less socialised and more problematic and had more relationships as adults. Those who as teenagers described themselves less positively also reported themselves as having poorer relationships as adults.

Emotional problems for a number of persons involved

A study of marrying a man with 'baggage,' in the case of second wives, was examined by Knox and Zusman (2001). Results showed that subjects who perceived that their stepchildren had caused problems in their marriage reported less happiness with their marriage, and more thoughts about divorce. There were also more regrets about remarrying their husbands. Sixty-six percent of these individuals reported feeling that their family continued to be affected by the first family of their husband and they felt resentful over the financial obligations of their husband due to the first family. Thirty-four percent of the subjects felt jealous of their husband's first wife.

A study of the non-custodial parent and infants was carried out by Ram et al. (2002). Infants perceived divorce as a violation of the routine of everyday life. They were forced to cope with the collapse of their most familiar unit of care giving frame. This double parenting had been vital for proper growth and development and often caused developmental arrest or regression in the infant. Despite the dearth in empirical research data, there has been a growing recognition among professionals of the vital role played by the non-custodial parent in the post-divorce adjustment of the infant. Parental conflict and

other parental factors, which influenced the non-custodial parent/infant relationship, were potentially hazardous to a smooth and proper development of the child. This was due to one parent, usually the custodial parent, trying to turn children against the other parent (usually the father). This then led to parental alienation (PA) or a Parental Alienation Syndrome (PAS) as already mentioned.

Educational problems were also more likely to occur in children according to Evans et al. (2001) and they were more likely to have suffered from the emotional problems resulting from divorce. Results from an Australian study showed that divorce in Australia costs seven-tenths of a year of education, mainly reducing secondary school completion. Furthermore, it was found that parental remarriage did not ameliorate the educational damage caused by parental separation or divorce.

Reduced living standards

As a result of divorce a number of investigators have found reduced living standards in the participants of the initial marriage (Wells, 2001). This appeared to affect both parties in the former marital relationship. Contrary to conventional thinking, the majority of partnered men in the USA lost economic status when their union dissolved (McManus and DiPrete, 2001). Although most men experienced a decline in living standards following union dissolution, men's outcome was heterogeneous, and the minority of men who relied on their partners for less than 20 per cent of pre-dissolution income, typically gained from separation and divorce. The data of the study showed clearly the great economic interdependence in partnerships. This trend appeared to increase the proportion of men who suffered a reduced standard of living following a separation.

Remedy and treatment for individuals likely to suffer from separation or divorce

There are relatively few studies compared with the aetiology of separation and divorce in the area of remedies and treatment. McIsaac and Finn (1999) described their parental education programme for high conflict families. Participants were 26 parents (couples) referred by the family court. The method emphasised an educational approach teaching conflict resolution skills. This course was rooted in the tenets of cognitive restructuring: if parents think differently about the other parent and their shared task of raising their children they will feel and act differently. The authors believed many of the difficulties between parents were caused by the negative perception of the other parent created during the spousal relationship.

They also believed the key to successful co-parenting was to reframe these perceptions emphasising cooperation and joint problem solving. Furthermore, they believed as the cooperation and joint problem solving improved, this improvement was likely to be positive and have a reinforcing effect. Finally, the authors believed parents needed to learn to separate conflict in the spousal role from conflict in the parenting role. A follow-up review of these parents found that 13 of these highly conflicted parents used the concepts constructively. The other 13 parents appeared to need more help, indicated by their return to mediation. Mediation was also considered the way forward by Lowenstein (2000).

Davila and Bradbury (2001) hypothesised that attachment insecurity would be associated with remaining in an unhappy marriage. One hundred and seventy-two newly married couples participated in a four year longitudinal study with multiple assessment points. Hierarchical linear models revealed that compared with spouses in happy marriages and divorced spouses, spouses who were in stable but unhappy marriages showed the highest level of insecurity initially and over time. Spouses in stable, unhappy marriages also had lower levels of marital satisfaction than divorced spouses and showed relatively high levels of depressive symptoms initially and over time.

Results suggested that spouses at risk of having unhappy marriages could be identified early and would benefit from interventions that increase the security of spouses' attachment to each other. Finally, Walker and McCarthy (2001) emphasised the role of marriage counselling in England and Wales as a way of preventing divorce and separation. In recent times Lowenstein (2000, 2002) found mediation processes of great value in preventing divorce, or in dealing with parents after divorce to accept the importance of their continuing positive parenting role. It was vital to involve both parties in the relationship to promote the capacity for sharing parenting despite marital break up.

Journal of Divorce and Remarriage, 2005, 42: 3–4: 153–71

Chapter Four

Post divorce conflict: understanding and resolution

Introduction

What follows will consider a number of important issues relating to divorce. It must be said that not all divorces are likely to lead to problems or conflicts but unfortunately many do. This is especially the case when there are children on the scene. This often results in custody wars and lack of co-operation between the legal and mental health professions (Gunsberg and Hymowitz, 2005). In what follows we will consider the adjustment of parents to the best interest of the child; the causes of conflict between former close partners; prevention of these conflicts; the reaction of parents to divorce and the conflicts which sometimes result in relation to children. Finally we will consider the use of mediation in resolving post separation conflict.

The best interest of the child and adjustment of parents to this

Whenever there are children on the scene it is vital to argue what is 'in the best interest' of the children and how these can be met by the parents who formally loved one another, or at least wished to be together. No longer loving one another should not in any way intrude on the love of both parents for their child and the love of the child for each of these parents. Anything less is not in the child's best interest. Determinations about what is in the best interest of the child are often difficult when trying to decide between the wishes of the mother and father.

When a parent enters into a new romantic relationship, including remarriage, decisions regarding the best interests of the child must take into account three or possibly four care-givers. In some instances, the issue becomes one of father versus step-father and mother versus step-mother, regarding who will be the primary care-givers and what role each plays in guiding the development of the child. It is here that the distinction between parental rights and obligations becomes more crucial for the forensic evaluator or expert witness. The manner in which

step parents have dealt with obligations to their own children can provide important indicators about the way that they will interact and influence the environment of the children in a blended family. The willingness, as well as the ability of the step-parents to assist in meeting parental obligations, is one that should be given great weight in making custodial recommendations (Klein, 2005).

There are relatively few objective measures available for assessing the adjustment of parents and how best to deal with conflicts between them. Zimmerman et al. (2004) have used the Divorce Adjustment Inventory to assess the adjustment of custodial mothers or fathers. The authors assess healthy or unhealthy levels of psychological functioning. The Symptom Checklist 90-Revised (SCL-90-R) has also been used. These tests provide a baseline for reported negative symptomatology among divorced women, and confirm the efficacy of a divorce education. The objective of the programme is in reducing psychological symptoms, and support the use of the Divorce Adjustment Inventory Revised in assessing post-divorce family functioning.

Kapinus (2004) asks three questions regarding divorce and individuals concerned:

1. What influence do parents' attitudes towards divorce have on offspring's attitudes?
2. How are offspring's attitudes towards divorce influenced by parental divorce, and do the effects vary depending on the gender of the child?
3. How do the conditions surrounding parental divorce influence young adults' attitudes?

Results indicate that parents have the greatest influence on offspring during their late teen years. Fathers have more influence on some attitudes than mothers. The gender of parents has no effect on the influence of parents' attitudes on daughters. In contrast to prior research, this study finds that parental divorce continues to influence offspring's views of divorce after controlling parents' attitudes only for daughters, not for sons. The relationship between family structure, cohesion and adaptability as well as parental anger is associated with children's behaviour problems. According to Dremen (2003) high levels of family cohesion and adaptability are predicted to be related to fewer behaviour problems. Post-divorce conflicts and diminished closeness to father following the divorce have different effects on sons and daughters attitudes. Girls seem to have more problems at high levels of maternal anger. The main impact on daughters concerns their view of the male figure. This could mean that daughters may well have difficulties in establishing a positive relationship with the opposite sex and view males in a negative manner. Sons will have difficulties with not having identified with a significant male such as their father, they have problems of self-esteem and feelings of abandonment. They will often have behaviour problems due to a lack of clear hierarchies and parental assertiveness. Boys in general take more notice of the male figure than they do of the female figure. All these aspects are damaging for the child when they reach their teens and also in the long-term when they wish to establish a relationship with members of the opposite sex and establish a family of their own. Difficulties with their own attitudes and behaviour may have a significant impact on their relationship problems and their responsibility within a relationship.

A number of examiners have assessed the negative and positive adjustment of divorced custodial parents across several areas of functioning, including depression, hostility, alcohol use, and well-being (Hilton and Kopera-Frye, 2004). Differences among custodial mothers and fathers were evaluated, followed by a series of hierarchical regressions that were used to evaluate factors contributing to negative and positive outcomes for the two groups. Compared to custodial fathers, custodial mothers were significantly younger, less likely to co-habit, and they had less income and more economic strain. In terms of their functioning, mothers experienced greater depression and hostility than fathers, but they were less likely to drink excessively. There were no differences in the family functioning, life satisfaction, personal mastery, or well-being of custodial mothers and fathers. It was concluded that custodial parents differed in their negative adjustment, but not their positive adjustment, and that custodial

fathers had fewer problems with adjustment than custodial mothers.

Several types of post-divorce parental relationships were discovered by Baum (2004). Similar to previous typology three types of co-parental relationships were identified: co-operative, parallel, and conflictual.

Causes of conflict between parents after divorce

Divorces do not occur 'out of the blue' or without cause. Divorces are usually made up of strong emotions, mis-perceptions, or stereotypes, and very often poor communications and repetitive negative behaviour (Taylor, 2003). How adults behave following divorce and seeking to avoid conflict depends on their level of narcissism and self-differentiation and also their modes of conflict management as well as the levels of these traits in their former spouses. Higher self-differentiation was associated with a lower propensity to use the attack mode among both fathers and mothers. It was associated with a higher use of the compromise mode among the mothers but not among the fathers. Higher narcissism, according to Baum and Shnit (2003) is associated with a higher level of the 'attack mode' among the fathers but not among the mothers. The differentiation and narcissism of each ex-spouse contributed to the other's modes of conflict management style beyond the contribution made by their own personality traits. High anger levels in mothers according to Dremen (2003) are associated with more behaviour problems in children, particularly adolescents. Girls have more behaviour problems at higher levels of maternal state-anger. In contrast, boys are found to have few behaviour problems at high levels of maternal anger. It was concluded that an adolescent child's needs are for clear role hierarchies, stability, and parental assertiveness to promote optimal adjustment.

Inter-parental aggression was found to have a significant and direct negative impact on closeness. It also had a strong impact on children and most especially adolescents. Winstock and Eisikovits (2003) hypothesises that adolescents' exposure to inter-parental violence reduces affinity, a notion that may explain one link between exposure to inter-parental violence and adolescent development.

Prevention of problems relating to conflicts in divorce

One of the main difficulties with divorced parents is the raising of children in two separate households although frequently only one of the parents has custody. Preventing problems of conflicts, according to Most (2005) is to encourage parents to observe how their children are doing and seek professional guidance for them if they see struggles with education, emotions or behaviours. Parents are also encouraged to reflect upon their new roles.

Knight (2005) recommends the use of parent co-ordinators which includes education, assessment, intervention and monitoring post-divorce parents. Ideally parents who use a parent co-ordinator are likely to successfully identify difficulties in their post-divorce relationships that have an impact on their children and will make changes that improve their children's adjustment.

Above all it is vital, when conflicts loom, for early intervention. With such early intervention it is also important to include the children and their experiences of the conflict between their parents (McIntosh and Long, 2005). Anthony (2005) notes that anger management for mothers and fathers are of particular importance since this affects their children considerably. To understand anger within the family one must understand the aetiology of anger. Concerns for parents who are considering divorce, while at the same time considering the prevention of conflicts, are about custody, visitation, alimony and financial factors (Yilmaz and Fisiloglu, 2005).

A number of researchers, including Pruett et al. (2005) have noted the importance of involving both parents in the care of young children even before they begin their separation and preparing the children for this process. These families had lower conflict, greater father involvement and better outcomes for children than the control group which did not have some form of intervention such as the Collaborative Divorce Project (CDP). This project was designed to assist parents of children six years old and younger as they began the separation/divorce process. Court records indicated that these interventions led to families who were more co-operative and were less likely to need custody evaluations and other costly services. The CDP approach illustrated how prevention programmes were located by the courts. The CDP approach systematically evaluated, and aided by helping the legal system function optimally for families with young children.

It is important in post-divorce families to promote resilience and family well-being (Greeff et al., 2004). Family coherence was used as an indication of the level of the recovery after the crisis of divorce. Hence, family crises were prevented through relatives and friends and a general support system. The result of their studies showed that intra-family support, support from the extended family and others, as well as religion and open communication, and financial security were factors promoting resilience in families of divorce.

Reaction of parents to divorce

An interesting study entitled *What Grown Children Have to Say About Their Parent's Divorce* by Constance Ahrons (2004) was considered by Nock (2005). It was felt most important for children to consider that they were still a part of a family. The author believed 'good divorces' allowed adults and children to continue to live more or less harmoniously as a family. This view was based on a sample of 98 divorced couples and their children. The author considered that divorce led to a reorganised family but did not destroy it. He also reported that the majority of these adults believed that their parents' decision to get a divorce was the right one and that most did not wish their parents to remain married due to the acrimony and problems that existed at the time.

It is unfortunate that not all divorces end in such a positive way. Frequently children suffer adjustment problems at home and in school, most especially when parents are hostile towards one another. A study by Wood et al. (2004) examined linkages between divorce, depressive or withdrawn parenting and child adjustment problems at home and school. Middle class divorced single mother families (n = 35) and two-parent families (n = 174) with a child in the fourth grade participated. Mothers and teachers completed yearly questionnaires and children were interviewed when they were in their fourth, fifth and sixth grades. It suggested that the association between divorce and child externalising and internalising behaviour was partly mediated by depressive/withdrawn parenting when their children were in their fourth and fifth grades.

Parental conflict and its effect on children

The effect of divorce on children varies undoubtedly as a result of the relationship which existed and continues to exist between the parents. Bowling (2005) considers that there is no one truth about how divorce affects children. The author concludes with a call to allow children of divorce to have a voice and the opportunity to tell their stories. There is therefore a relationship between marital distress by either party and the adjustment of children (Papp et al., 2004). Such distress has a linkage with depression, withdrawn parenting, and child adjustment problems at home and at school (Repetti et al., 2004).

Frequently following divorce there is an ongoing hostility between the parents and this has adverse outcomes and reactions in children in seeking to deal with parental hostility towards one another (Taylor, 2004). A British sample of families studied by Wild and Richards (2003) aimed to compare child and parent reports of inter-parental conflict. They also studied children's emotional reactions to this conflict. Children tended to have neutral responses to inter-personal conflict if they expected that the arguments would be quickly resolved and had no negative long-term consequences. On the other hand, greater perceived frequency and intensity of inter-parental conflict, poor resolution and more child involvement were associated with negative emotion reactions in children. Such children often felt extreme sadness and self-blame. On the other hand high levels of family cohesion and adaptability were predicted to be related to fewer behaviour problems in children (Dreman, 2003).

When there are severe problems and hostility between parents, the results often indicate that such children of divorced homes have higher rates of delinquency (status offences, crimes against persons, felony, theft, general delinquency, and tobacco and drug use) when compared to children from intact homes (Price and Kunz, 2003). Other findings revealed that black and younger children were more delinquent than white and older children. Samples included both male and female children and upper class children who were more likely to be involved in delinquency than samples with only male and female children or children from other social classes. Hence high levels of parental conflict in separated families had a devastating impact on children and their development (Read, 2003).

Long-term problems for children of divorce

While divorces are never to be favoured there are 'better' divorces and 'worse' divorces. The repercussions for the parents as well as the children therefore also varies depending on the hostility or lack of hostility which continues between the parents. There is some research that indicates that people exposed to parental divorce experience a number of attitudinal effects. One such effect, is the inter-generational transmission of divorce. This involves a greater risk of divorce among those adult children whose parents were divorced (Segrin et al., 2005). The results replicated the inter-generational transmission of divorce as well as higher family conflict, more negative attitudes towards marriage, greater likelihood of marriage to a previously divorced person, and a decreased likelihood of currently being in a close relationship. Either family-of-origin conflict or negative marital attitudes mediated many of these effects. In other words, it is not parental divorce that is entirely responsible for certain relational and attitudinal effects.

It has been well established that boys frequently lose their father as a result of divorce. Divorce therefore is often a traumatic life-changing event for children, especially for boys who often lose not only a parent but also a crucial role model (Allen, 2005). Amato and Cheadle (2005), used data from the study of marital instability over the life course to examine links between divorce in the grandparent generation (first generation) and outcome in their grandchild generation (third generation). Divorce in the first generation was associated with lower education, more marital discord, weaker ties with mothers, and weaker ties with fathers in the third generation. These associations were mediated by family characteristics in the middle generation, including low education, more marital discord, and greater tension in early parent/child relationships. The results suggested that divorce had consequences for subsequent generations, including individuals who were not yet born at the time of the original divorce.

Vandervalk et al. (2004) examined the relationship between adolescent emotional adjustment and the family environment, that is the family status, the family process, and parental resources. 2,636 parent-child couples were studied. They were both intact and divorced families. The results indicated that adolescent emotional adjustment was clearly based on the family as well as on the individual. Support for the hypothesis was that growing up both in post-divorce families and in intact families with a low marital quality related negatively to adolescent emotional adjustment.

Mention has already been made of the likelihood of maladjustment among male youth as a result of an absent father. Harper and McLanahan (2004) measured the likelihood of youth incarceration among adolescent males from father-absent households, using data from the National Longitudinal Survey of Youth (N = 34,031 person-years). At baseline, the adolescents ranged from 14–17 years, and the incarceration outcome measure spanned ages 15–30 years. This study tested whether risk factors concentrated in father-absent households explained the apparent effects of father absence. The results from longitudinal event-history analysis showed that although a sizeable portion of risk that appeared to be due to father absence could actually be attributed to other factors, such as teen motherhood, low parent education, racial inequalities, and poverty, adolescents in father-absent households still faced elevated incarceration risks. The adolescents who faced the highest incarceration risks, however, were those in step-parent families, including father-stepmother families.

It must be said that due to inter-parental conflict, impaired parenting and the considerable pressures from mothers for the child to side against the father, children and adolescents frequently feel they are being caught in the middle and of having to take sides (Walper et al., 2004). This affects adolescents later in their daily relationships and suggests considerable continuity in relation to problems over time including their own marriage when they are adults (Doucet and Aseltine, 2003). Hence it must be stressed that the empirical literature on the long-term adjustment of children of divorce emphasises that there are stresses resulting from divorce and elevated risks that divorce presents for children. This should assist parents of divorce to institute more protective behaviours that may

enhance children's long-term adjustment (Kelly and Emery, 2003).

Using mediation to resolve conflict

First I will consider how to prevent conflicts between previously close adults followed by positive aspects of mediation as well as at times some of the negative repercussions of mediation. What will be further discussed will be mediation as an alternative to litigation and also the use of education and counselling to deal with post-divorce problems.

Each year, 50 per cent of all marriages now end in divorce and one million children are exposed to a divorced family in the United States alone (Taylor, 2005). Among the methods of resolving some of the issues that develop as a result of such separation and divorce, we will consider mediation between the parents. Unfortunately many adults do not believe in, nor do they trust, the process of mediation when it is ordered. Children and adolescents coming from families with high levels of marital conflicts display a variety of difficulties. Much depends on the intensity of the problems between the adults. Such problems certainly affect the self-esteem of both children and adolescents. In many cases in later life both children and adolescents develop more fearful attachment styles in comparison to those coming from families of low marital conflict (Sirvanli-Ozen, 2004). It is frequently necessary to involve psychological treatment in high conflict divorce (Boyan and Termini, 2005).

Preventing conflicts if possible

There has been relatively little research in how to prevent problems between warring adults which in turn is a way of preventing children from suffering from this conflict. Children are totally involved when marriage breaks up and conflicts arise. It has been felt by numerous investigators that children should be included in the mediation process (Moloney and McIntosh, 2004; Mackinnon et al., 2004; Louw and Scherrer, 2004). Such preventive approaches do much to reduce the negative outcomes experienced by children of divorce (Haine et al., 2003). If at all possible, a different kind of family life in which quality of relationship is the key factor needs to be established (Walker, 2003). In this way parents can institute more protective behaviour that may enhance children's short and long-term adjustment (Kelly and Emery, 2003). Rye et al. (2004) emphasise the importance of promoting forgiveness of an ex-spouse in post-divorce adjustment. This is likely to reduce the level of depression, anger and other negative emotions that frequently result from relationships breaking up.

Positive aspects of mediation

We will now consider some of the positive as well as negative aspects of mediation. Therapeutic divorce mediation is one of several interventions that hold promise for assisting highly conflicted parents to resolve disputes about their children (Smyth and Moloney, 2003). During the mediation process it is vital to introduce an intense child focus in order to reduce the conflicts between parents by asking them to consider what is most important i.e. the child and their future (Kelly, 2003a). It is always important to emphasise that it should not be a question of who wins and loses the arguments but what is the common purpose of both parents (McKnight and Erickson, 2004).

It has been well known that divorce puts the emotional, economic and educational well-being of thousands of children in danger every year. The levels of conflict between parents is a key factor in how well the children overcome the challenges that divorce creates (Schepard, 2004). Courts today seek to involve both parents in a child's life rather than having to choose between them. Mediation and education have replaced to some degree the courtroom as the primary forum for resolving parental disputes. Unfortunately, mediators and Courts of Justice, as will be seen later, do not always work together effectively.

Since April 2001 the Children and Family Court Advisory Support Service (CAFCASS) in the UK became responsible for family court work including the provision of mediation services. Family court mediation offers a gateway for social work with children and families whose needs are largely left untouched by current services. Such an organisation could thereby play an important role within the broader extension of prevention by a process of early intervention. Parenting and support services have for some time been recommended by the government of the United Kingdom. Over the past decades, mediation has

become a popular approach to reducing conflict and resolving disputes (Mantle and Critchley, 2004) but not when the hostility between the parents is pathological.

Following such mediation after divorce there are many legal consequences. Among them is the regulation of the relationship between parents and children in as far as how it relates to contact with children (Kraljic, 2005). Contact with children is often the central problem of divorcing parents. Instead of maintaining genuine relations with their children, they may abuse them for their own purposes, including practising parental alienation. Mediation should help parents and children realise that parenting does not end with divorce.

It is also very important to involve the children at some point in time in the process of mediation (Schoffer, 2005). One must listen to the child but one must also listen to the 'secret voice' that does not always speak within the child due to the fact that what the child states may not be in their best interest and is often based on prejudice, bias and a process of alienation (Lowenstein, 2005a–j; McIntosh et al., 2004; McIntosh and Moloney, 2004). McIntosh and Moloney draw a distinction between child-focused and child-inclusive practice. Child-inclusive practice, on the other hand, more formally fulfils the aspirations of the United Nations Convention on the Rights of the Child that children should be consulted when decisions about their welfare are being made. Further, child-inclusive practice as defined by McIntosh and Moloney allows for consultation without placing the burden of decision-making on the child. An article by Schoffer (2005) discusses the cost and benefits of the child's involvement and comes to the conclusion that the integration of children in mediation ought to be considered on a case to case basis. The alienation process occurs over time between divorced parents who experienced severe or pathological parental conflicts. Psychologists, psychiatrists, and psychotherapists working as parent co-ordinators have found the work extremely challenging since parents take stands that go counter to one another, especially in high conflict divorce (Boyan and Termini, 2005).

Problems of mediation

It has already been suggested that mediation is not a perfect way of dealing with the problem of conflict between parents involving children. As pointed out by Lowenstein (2005a-j) without the support of the court, when there is implacable, irrational hostility between the parents, the mediation process often is a meaningless activity. This is because children are almost always caught in the triangle of their parent's fights. This 'war' may either be open or made insidious such as when parental alienation or parental alienation syndrome is present (Goncalves and de Vincenzi, 2003). Other family members and even strangers become embroiled in the conflict. A study by Sbarra and Emery (2005) re-evaluated the long-term effects of divorce mediation on adults' psychological adjustment and investigated the relations among co-parenting custody conflicts. This revealed that fathers and parents who mediated their custody disputes reported significantly more non acceptance based on a 12 year follow-up assessment. Unfortunately this is one of the few longer term researches available.

Mediation as an alternative to litigation

There has been in practice the view based on the importance of mediation rather than litigation. This however, is not always feasible since parents, through the mediation process, hope to gain what they believe to be their own right. Mediators can only do so much to seek the co-operation of parents who may be extremely distant or opposite in their viewpoints. In the end they will require the court to support their efforts (Lowenstein, 2005a-j). There is a growing need to examine the consistency and effectiveness of child custody mediation endeavours in the USA as noted by Ortega et al. (2004). Some districts favour judge-imposed orders and other districts favour mediated settlements. As an alternative to litigation, mediation has been used to resolve conflicts in a co-operative manner to reflect the best interests of all the parties. This is easier said than done as already mentioned (Bartholomae et al., 2003; Bailey and Robbins, 2005). Parents will always seek to get the mediator to take sides. When the mediator resists this, one or both parents will turn against the mediator.

Another reason for relying heavily on mediation processes is that family disputes are the bane of overburdened court systems, especially in child access issues, and consume a disproportionate share of court resources.

Consequently, family mediation has become a viable method of helping to resolve disputes and mental health professionals are increasingly called upon to mediate child access and support disagreements (Ortega et al., 2004).

As already mentioned children have a need to be involved in this process but in the most sensitive way possible. This is because mediation, at least in a large part, must be child focused. Hence, while children should be consulted when decisions about their welfare are being made it is vital to look deeper into the decisions and feelings of children before including what they say or feel as being as meaningful as it appears to be. This is due to the fact that many children are seeking security with, usually, the custodial parent and are in many cases willing to reject the non-resident parent for no good reason (McIntosh et al., 2004). The child thus taking the side of one parent at the expense of the other is wrong. The excluded or 'side-lined' parent feels they are being treated unjustly. The child cannot in the short or long-term benefit from this state of affairs.

Education and counselling

Another approach has been used often combined with the mediation process. This is the education and counselling of parents who have found it difficult to avoid their conflict continuing, especially in relation to their children. Attendance at divorce education classes were found to be associated with whether a subject will return to court or not. Those who attended were less likely to return to court and litigation (Criddle et al., 2003).

There have been substantial changes in scientific and public perspectives regarding children's adjustment to divorce in the United States. Decades of divorce research have created a more complex and nuanced understanding of how divorce impacts on children and adolescents. The stressors and risks which divorce presents for children, the resiliency demonstrated by the majority of children, and protective factors which are associated with better judgement following divorce are described by Kelly (2003b). A distinction is drawn between painful memories and psychopathology. It is therefore felt that educating divorced parents about known risk factors for their children acts as a protective measure to enhance their children's long-term adjustment.

Family advocates and family counsellors represent the best interests of children in divorce actions (Scherrer and Louw, 2004). Regardless of how the divorce occurs, it is important to note that there are hurt parties in need of healing. Mediation and divorce education lend themselves to reduce the pain and anguish being experienced in some cases. It is only when the parents are free from the trauma associated with divorce that they may serve as a positive influence on their children (Taylor, 2004). Only by helping parents to move from entrenched disputes towards a more constructive co-parenting relationship will the best interest of the children be served (McIntosh and Deacon-Wood, 2003).

Conclusion

There are several ways to prevent and deal with conflicts between parents for the benefit of the children. These ways aim to improve situations including the treatment of individual parents using psychological techniques, using mediation and education procedures. One must be aware of the fact that these are not always effective on their own. It has been established that without the support of the court or the judiciary many procedures of mediation are unsuccessful. Hence, there are both positive and negative outcomes of mediation. Some of the less severe conflicts are resolved by mediation alone. The more severe cases require a combination of court involvement and the mediation process working co-operatively.

As a consequence of acrimonious divorce or separation there are considerable conflicts between parents that have drastic repercussions in their children in the present as well as in the short and long term. The cause of these conflicts between parents is their emotional incapacity to view the future of their own children as their primary concern despite declaring that they do so. Their mutual hostility affects the lives of their children especially when there is domestic violence.

There is a need for early intervention to prevent the problem of conflict continuing after divorce and to successfully identify and improve aspects of post-divorce relationships.

More research is needed to map the long-term effects on children of divorce and to identify how the children's lives may be influenced by the poor relationships of their parents. There is therefore an inter-generational effect of hostile divorces on future generations.

In the case of boys the loss of a father could have drastic effects on their capacity to socialise effectively. Behaviour problems may result. Fathers on the whole have more influence on son's attitudes than do mothers. In the case of girls the loss of a father may affect how they view and interact with a male figure which in turn will affect their future relationships and loyalty to a male partner . . . Pain and grieving and family resiliency are identified as the major aspects of divorce that permeate children's lives.

The loss of a mother produces insecurity for the child, depression, lack of self worth and self-blame associated with abandonment, and acting out behaviour. The cohesion and adaptability of the family contribute to the amount of behaviour problems encountered with the highest level of cohesion and adaptability being related to the fewest behaviour problems.

Chapter Five

Attempting to resolve child contact disputes

Introduction

We will discuss contact disputes as well as the still uncertain concept of parental alienation (PA) versus parental alienation syndrome (PAS). The final part will discuss the role and plight of the non custodial parent.

The author has carried out considerable work in the area of children who have been alienated by a parent and thereby prevented from effective contact with their other parent. As an expert witness the author has been involved in dealing with courtroom cases, but more often than not attempting to find some way of reconciling differences between the warring factions through the process of mediation. This has sometimes been successful but at other times has failed dismally due to the fact that the judiciary did not, on the whole, work together with the mediator (Lowenstein, 1998a, 1998b, 1999). Often it is necessary to carry out an initial investigation into the role of the parents and the attitude of the child in the dispute (Lowenstein 1999, and 2001).

It has not as yet been well understood how children suffer in the short and long term from the effects of parental alienation or parental alienation syndrome (Lowenstein, 2002) and how best to deal with the problem (Lowenstein, 2003, 2005).

Research into contact disputes

There is a considerable difference of opinion in how to involve children in decision making. The primary concern is always the child. This however, is not far behind the two adults responsible for the child's welfare since the child's welfare coincides with both parents, whenever possible, playing an important role or having responsibility for the rearing of the child/children. Children however, should have a meaningful voice in decision making (Warshak, 2003) but one must be absolutely certain from where the child's decision comes. More will be said concerning this when alienation takes place against a non resident parent. Whatever happens the child should not be placed in the position of taking sides whether this is involved in joint custody, overnight stays, relocation or any other way of both parents playing a meaningful role.

In recent times there has been a tendency for fathers to have more contact and sometimes even custody of a child due to feelings of sexual equality which is currently the view. Mothers therefore have substantial fears that they may lose custody as a result of such equality (Heiliger, 2003). Mothers realise, since they are not the main bread winner, that divorce puts the emotional, economic, and educational well-being of many children in danger. Therefore, courts today seek to involve both parents in the child's life rather than having to choose between them. Mediation and education have sometimes replaced the courtroom as the primary forum for resolving parental disputes (Schepard, 2004).

Parents are often encouraged to formulate a visitation plan that is 'reasonable'. What is reasonable in a court must also have an air of reasonableness to the parents. Unfortunately one or both parents are often unreasonable in the manner in which they make decisions on visitation and contact (Hauser, 2005).

A major issue in divorces that involve children is the allocation of parental time. In many divorces, parents work out, with greater or lesser difficulty, time sharing arrangements that satisfy both them and the court. In many other situations, parents cannot agree on how to allot time, and the court must decide on temporary or long-term plans. While sensible people have always recognised that no single time sharing arrangement is optimal for all children, often the court has to order who has custody. This can lead to one parent without access. The involvement of an expert witness who helps the court to make decisions can result in good solutions from time to time but equally can lead to parents, one or the other, turning against the solution by the expert who they feel is 'against' them (Dember and Fliman, 2005). Many parents consider an expert to be biased against them.

Contact has been high on the agenda since the UK government report, *Making Contact Work* (2002) which examined various means for facilitating contact between non resident parents and their children. More recently the issue has featured prominently in the headlines since in England and Wales a 'father's rights group' has complained about the injustice and have made demands to change the law so that fathers could have contact, or increased contact, with their children. Thus far little has been achieved in relation to better contact through these methods (Kaganas and Sclater, 2004).

Perhaps too little attention has been paid to the tremendous harm that has been done to children when parents are in conflict over their care. Parental conflict is a more total predictor of child adjustment than is divorce and conflict resolution is important to children's coping with divorce (McIntosh, 2003; Lowenstein, 2005).

Parental alienation syndrome versus parental alienation: is that the question?

The term parental alienation has been accepted as it is an undeniable fact that it frequently occurs as a result of conflicts in separation or divorce. The term parental alienation syndrome (PAS) has not as yet been recognised by the American Psychological and Psychiatric Associations or the British Psychological and Psychiatric Associations, despite there being peer reviewed discussions on Parental Alienation and Parental Alienation Syndrome.

A study from the Netherlands by Spruijt et al. (2005) reported that about 20 per cent of children did not have any contact with their non resident parent after parental divorce. There were many reasons for broken contact, one of which was the process of parental alienation, when the child denigrated and excluded the non resident parent. Parental alienation was responsible for 42 per cent of reasons for broken contact. The extent of parental alienation was classified as mild in 33 per cent of cases, and moderate in 9 per cent of cases. There were no severe cases. The authors used the term parental alienation syndrome and indicated that it occurred significantly more often when decisions with relation to children were not taken together by the parents but were determined in court. The authors considered that compulsory mediation was the better way forward in many cases of PAS. (The author of this current article indicates that this is a useless exercise unless the court works directly with the

mediator and supports their views. Only the courts have the power to impose sanctions and serve a penal notice on a parent who has been recognised to have practised parental alienation against the non custodial parent. A parent can take part in mediation to appease the court but at the same time carry on the practise of parental alienation with the child. Mediation in this case is a waste of time especially if the court does not take on board that parental alienation has taken place and action against the alienating parent needs to be taken to stop this process. Mediation alone will not do this especially if the custodial parent and alienator are entrenched in a programme of implacable hostility and still carrying on a programme of alienation in a subtle way with the child.)

Caplan (2004) considered that PAS is a group of symptoms occurring together and constituted a recognisable condition. Emery (2005) considered PAS still of minimal scientific standard and preferred the use of the term parental alienation (PA). The signs were also stressed by Shopper (2005). He felt that alienation by definition involved the estrangement or transfer of feelings away from one person and onto another. Within a family, the attempts at alienation may take the form of undeserved criticism and bad-mouthing of a parent or an emphasis on the mistakes or inadequacy of the parent. For a younger child, the distinction between dis-identifying with a character trait versus dis-identifying with a parent as a whole may be beyond the child's developmental abilities. In most cases the older child perceives that there is no denunciation of the parent as a whole but only of a circumscribed aspect of that parental behaviour.

In place of the term parental alienation syndrome, the term 'medea syndrome', or 'implacable hostility', or the 'malicious mother syndrome' can be used. These terms are used to describe a conscious or concerted effort to disrupt the child's affectionate relationship with the other parent and co-opt all of the child's affection on to oneself. In the course of the alienation, the non resident parent is portrayed as such a demonised and dehumanised individual as to render that person unfit for either affection from, or a positive relationship with, the child. Alienation in any setting or cause can best be viewed theoretically and clinically as a subtype of what the author terms 'disorder of created reality'. 'Disorders of created reality' refer to a situation in which a person's own autonomous sense of reality testing and reality appreciation are devalued, and overwhelmed and replaced by a different irrational reality concerning the rejected non custodial parent.

There are considerable problems in relation to PAS and the judiciary, who realise the non acceptance of the term by the APA or BPS and use this to avoid making decisions based upon its diagnosis. Hence PAS has been unfairly criticised by both judicial and mental health communities despite the fact that there is considerable evidence that it exists. Critics sometimes go so far as to deny it exists and then equal the term with parental alienation (PA). It has of course been well recognised that PA does exist but even then some courts have barred testimony on this, even from professionals who have dealt with the truly rejecting behaviour of an alienated child (Andre, 2004). The child as a result is often forced to reject one or other of their parents in the short term due to the false belief that the non custodial parent is a bad, horrible person, who causes problems and unhappiness for the family and the custodial parent. In the long term the child loses the parental input and contribution of the rejected parent to their upbringing. The child also faces many psychological problems in the future due to the process of alienation which will reflect on their future behaviour and happiness. This resulting damage is not in the best interests of the child. Furthermore, the child loses contact with a parent with whom they once had a close and loving relationship. The result is the sorrow and confusion of a rejected parent, and the pathology of a hateful alienating parent. Given the large number of children of divorce who are likely to be vulnerable to this condition there is potential for far-reaching and tragic circumstances for individuals, families and society. Those who reject the term PAS or the rejecting behaviour of one parent towards another consider it simplistic and not supported by findings from recent empirical research (Johnston and Kelly, 2004).

A number of attempts have been made to define both PA and PAS. All consider that it is the persistence of conflict between the two parents in regard to their children based on extreme hatred towards the non resident parent (Batchy and Kinoo, 2004). Some investigators have considered that PAS or PA are similar to the false memory syndrome (FMS) (Gardner, 2004a, 2004b). Both share in common a campaign of acrimony against a parent. Both also persist in strong negative attitudes and rejecting behaviour towards that parent with corresponding emotional enmeshment with the other parent (Johnston, 2003; Johnston et al., 2005). What is perhaps most hard to bear for the rejected parent is that they rejected where previously they were loved. All this is due to ex spouses still being in conflict with their former partner (Gagne et al., 2005). Child custody evaluators commonly find themselves confronted with resistance when they attempt to use the term parental alienation syndrome or even parental alienation during their time in courts of law. Although convinced that the individual being evaluated suffers from the disorder, they often find that the solicitors, attorneys or barristers who represent alienated parents, although they agree with the diagnosis, discourage use of the term in the evaluators reports and testimony. Even those who are biased against the whole concept of alienation consider the view that fathers, who are often the rejected parent, are actually inadequate individuals. Such injustice fortunately is not general (Van Gijseghem, 2005).

Gardner (2002 and 2003) has for a long time been a great advocate of PAS rather than PA before the judiciary. This is despite the fact that up to now DSM-IV diagnosis has not recognised the term PAS. This should not be confused however, with the fact that such a syndrome of combination of aspects are related to parental alienation as to virtually term it a syndrome. It was the hope of Gardner (2003) that PAS would be recognised in due course by the judiciary in order to make prudent decisions in child custody disputes. Some courts indeed do recognise it. Proponents of its use applaud it as a distinctly diagnosable phenomenon and appreciate the clarity it brings to diagnosis and treatment of intra and inter-family dynamics. Some critics sometimes go so far as to deny it exists. Some courts who have recognised it have made good progress while other courts bar testimony on it (Andre, 2004). Despite this there are those who still oppose its use and the concept of PAS (Emery, 2005). It is the view of the current author that it makes little difference whether the term PAS or PA is accepted as it is self evident that this situation exists and that the alienating process does much harm to children as well as their parents.

At present the extent of the problem of parental alienation is unknown and there are often multiple factors that may contribute to the refusal of children to have contact with the parent. It is however, always recommended that there be therapeutic intervention when this occurs albeit the custodial parent will often refuse or be opposed to such a procedure (Falco, 2003).

It is unfortunate that the legal systems in many areas of the world find it difficult to reverse the refusal of a child to see a parent. Courts tend to give in to the views of the child irrespective of what has caused these views to be developed (Gardner, 2003).

Are non residential parents of value?

Although the rejected parent is predominantly the father, it does also occur that mothers are the rejected party. There is now some evidence that concrete aspects are related to fathers being left out or rejected in the child's life. Snow (2003) found that divorce affected more than one million children each year in the United States. Within two years of their parents divorce, roughly 50 per cent of the children will have contact with their father less than twice per year. Conflicts tend to arise when a parent has disparate definitions and expectations of the other parent's role performance. Obstructions or threats to the enactment of good relations create conflicts between the parents. This conflict often escalates when parents see themselves as a victim of the other parent.

One study (Jones, 2004) found that when there was a good relationship between the father and his children despite divorce, academic performance in school rose. This study found that boys living without their fathers were under-functioning when compared with boys living in father-resident homes. This indicated the importance of fathers in promoting academic school performance for boys.

Hence numerous studies have found the importance of involving fathers after divorce or separation and how paternal involvement improved the adjustment of young children from zero to six years of age and older (Insabella et al., 2003).

It is unfortunate that at present non resident parents such as fathers have little input with their children aside from providing financial support. Results suggest that efforts should be made to continue to examine non resident father's involvement. Fathers should do more than provide leisure and recreational activities, which is currently the case in non resident father-child contact.

Novick (2003) pointed out the importance of Gardner's book on Parental Alienation Syndrome and how it emphasised how quickly the process of alienation should be checked and reversed to prevent it becoming an ongoing way of life. Rand et al. (2005) went so far as to insist that children be forced to visit the target parent even if they did not wish to do so. The authors felt that absence from a non custodial parent was likely to make matters worse. There should be immediate contact and this was important for maintaining a relationship with both parents in the future. Children who had enforced visitation with the target parent or were in the target parent's custody, maintained relationships with both parents unless the alienator was too disturbed pathologically and continued the alienation process. Unfortunately many alienators violated court orders with impunity.

A Dutch study by Spruijt et al. (2004) emphasised the value of the non resident parent and father having close and regular contact with adolescent young adults. Increasing frequency of contact with the non resident father over time seemed to correlate with diminishing internalising problems.

Conclusions

Parental Alienation and the Parental Alienation Syndrome is very much alive. Children are being deprived all over the world of an essential part of their childhood, their loving parents and connected loving family members. In essence they are being deprived of half of their own personality since both parents are the founders of the child. Both parents are therefore needed for a healthy development of the child. The long term effects – albeit that long term research needs to increase – are devastating for the child. The APA and BPS can no longer deny the existence of PA and PAS and should start an open dialogue on these subjects. If they do not then the APA and BPS are not meeting their responsibilities towards the healthcare of children and adolescences.

Chapter Six

Child custody disputes: ideals and realities

There has been an increase in child custody disputes over the years at least to a large extent due to the increase in marital problems, divorce and separation. Many couples now with marital or relationship disputes are not even married, but the results of breaking up the family where children are involved are the same as if the couple were actually married in the first place. What follows will be general comments, not applicable in all cases as there are many other factors that come in to play, on points which are involved in making decisions on marital custody-type cases where children are involved.

Prior to the 1900s children were considered the property of the father and automatically reverted to him. After the industrial revolution the mother's role was seen as being the most important in caring for the children, especially young children. In the late 1960s to early 1970s decisions made depended on what were 'the best interest standard'.

Psychologists became increasingly involved in helping to make decisions which took into account the interests of the child and the care they would receive from one or both parents. Certain guidelines were considered as essential although they did not apply in all cases, and in fact other aspects need to be considered from time to time.

Factors important in guiding towards appropriate custody resolutions:

- Of most prominent concern are the rights and welfare of the child. There are however, problems here from time to time since children may wish to be with one parent, for various reasons including being the subject of parental alienation syndrome (PAS).
- The wishes of the parents are also considered but they may diverge, and one parent will attempt to have greater interest, or wish for control, over the custody of a child or children. It is for the psychologist and others to assess which is best for the child primarily, but also for the parents whenever possible.
- Of primary importance in making decisions are the mental and physical health of the parents

and in the way they live and conduct themselves vis a vis the child.
- Other factors are also important including whether either party is an extreme substance abuser, or practices sexual or emotional or physical abuse.

Appropriate guidelines for psychologists and psychiatrists

There are still many problems associated with helping to make a decision in relation to parental disputes over children. Many psychologists make decisions without having seen or evaluated all the people involved in the dispute i.e. psychologists will often miss either mother or father or children. To make a most appropriate solution all of them must be assessed and decisions made on the basis of this assessment.

The adversarial system has frequently prevented an assessor, psychologist, psychiatrist, to see all parties involved in order to make such a decision. With a change in the ruling due to the Woolf Report (1999) there is now a greater likelihood that the expert witness is able to see all parties involved before a decision is made. This may mean that those parties not willing to co-operate with this assessment could cause severe difficulties in making really honest and worthwhile child custody dispute resolutions.

Those making decisions in this very important area must be experienced, qualified and have true justice in mind for the children involved as well as the parents. This means the following:

- They must be impartial in the decision they make in relation to both parents.
- In undertaking such a resolution a considerable amount of time is involved. In one study it was found that the average child custody evaluation with report writing took 26.4 hours. In addition to this psychologists and others spend an additional 3–4 hours consulting with solicitors and testifying in court.
- Also in the evaluation when appropriate are the need to test the intelligence, personality of children and sometimes parents.

- When making sole custody recommendations, this must be based on one parent being shown to be either an active substance abuser, or practising parental alienation, a parent lacking parental skills or psychological stability, or a parent lacking in emotional bonding. In the case of physical, emotional or sexual abuse these must also be borne in mind when making such decisions.
- Joint custody cases on the whole are preferred where both parents can play the maximum role in the rearing and care of their children. This might be said to be, all things being equal, the 'ideal solution'. To rear their children in a joint manner is a great advantage.
- In order for joint custody to succeed however, it is vital for the parents to separate their personal difficulties from the important parenting roles they will play in a unified manner. This can often be assisted by specialists, psychologists and psychiatrists or expert witnesses who may practice some form of mediation when there are difficulties between the parents.
- There is a time however when children are no longer in the position of having to be passive in respect to their preference. Sometime around the 15th year children should be able to make a choice as to who they wish to live with and whom they wish to see but not in a custodial situation.
- The evaluation of who should have the child or children must be based on the combination of interviews of both parents, psychological testing of both parents, and the same for the child or children in question. This should be followed by report writing and the dissemination of information.

The assessment or evaluation

The parental interview

The parental interview must be open-ended in the first instance but certain areas should be covered if one feels they are likely to be relevant in making a decision. They include the following:

- Assessment of the place of residence of both parents and most particularly the one who may have immediate custody of the child.
- The place of employment of both parents where appropriate, also the duration of the employment or security of the employment.
- The history of the individuals concerned who are employed.
- The educational history of both parents.
- Names and ages of children who may be present where the child is to reside.
- Previous psychological/psychiatric treatment that either parents may have received in the past.
- Alcohol and other substance abuse history of both parents.
- Any difficulties in relation to the law that either parent may have encountered.
- Any history of sexual abuse or assault or emotional or physical abuse.
- Current medical history of both parents.
- Any major stresses in both parent's lives.
- Previous marital history.

The interview of the child

Interviewing a child can be a difficult matter and much depends on the age of the child, intelligence and whether the child has been programmed by one parent or the other to avoid contact with the other parent. Equally children can give such answers as 'I don't know', and this usually means they do not want to answer that particular question. It is probably best to give the child some opportunity to make a choice from several suggestions such as: 'Would you like to see your mother or father more of the time, less of the time, or about the same amount of time?'

The child should also be asked how they are disciplined or punished by either parent and about the relationship between the parents. Children have often been programmed by one parent in order for that parent to have some advantage over the other parent. A long, well rehearsed litany of statements usually means that someone has programmed the child, especially if the language used is not that of a child.

The question should also be asked in connection with one or both parent's substance abusing behaviour i.e. alcohol etc. The questions that might be asked are:

- What do you do when you are with your father or mother?
- Who takes you to school?
- Who wants you to do your homework?
- Who makes certain you help in the house?

Obtaining other relevant information

Other information may be obtained from grandparents or other relatives or by visiting the home of each of the parents. School records may also be consulted.

Sometimes cognitive or intelligence tests may be administered to the child or the parents, in order to obtain information about their capacity for reasoning, memory, concentration and judgement.

Personality testing as already mentioned can be of great value. In the United States the Minnesota Multiphasic Personality Inventory I and 2 are frequently administered. There are equivalent tests in Great Britain such as the Eysenck Tests which measure psychoticism, neuroticism, introversion, extroversion, impulsiveness, empathy, and venturesomeness, and also have a lie scale, indicating the truthfulness of the individual, and can indicate by the responses made the desire of the person to be seen in a more socially acceptable light, i.e. how they feel they should be seen rather than how they actually are. They are unaware of the responses they make not being valid. It is probably best to warn anyone taking such tests that there is a measure of lies which can be avoided by being very honest in responding. On the whole this results in individuals responding with a relatively low lie score. The test has norms for males and females and by ages and is an objective measure of personality.

Chapter Seven

Problems suffered by children due to the effects of PAS

Introduction

I have been involved with, and heard a great deal about, the effects of parental alienation on the adult partners in a damaged relationship. What follows will be the impact that relationship break ups and adverse alienation procedures have on the child or children.

General aspects of children suffering from the effects of PAS

The effect of PAS has been investigated by relatively few individuals so far but I should like to acknowledge my own gratitude to one researcher, Professor Richard A. Gardner for the work he has done in this area (Gardner, 1992; 1998; 2001). In what follows we will be concentrating on the effects, both short term and long term, of parental alienation on children. Whatever one may think, children associated with parental alienation are victims, but not of their own making. Parents are responsible for the child becoming a victim and most especially the parent who is carrying out the alienation process. However we will not consider the role of the parent extensively although it must be remembered that they have an important role to play producing the product of alienation.

We will instead concentrate on the child and what their victimisation produces. Increasingly we hear a great deal about child abuse, especially sexual abuse. We hear somewhat less about emotional abuse. Parental alienation is a form of child abuse since children are being used for the purpose of parents showing their animosity towards the other half of a relationship. The animosity displayed towards the other parent who is being alienated can have a terrible affect on the child in question. Later my own research in this area will be presented indicating the effect upon the child of the alienation process. I will further consider how I feel the problem could best be remedied.

Children who are suffering within the alienation process are often unaware of its impact. They merely feel the consequences such

as developing views propagated by the alienating parent that the other parent is 'evil', 'wicked', 'stupid' or 'dangerous' or all of these. Children therefore are frequently used by the alienating parent against the other parent to act as spies or saboteurs, or generally being used for unethical purposes in relation to the alienated parent.

Additionally they are often encouraged to treat the alienated parent with a lack of respect with the purpose of humiliating that parent. The children are even encouraged to behave in a deceitful manner with that parent, as already mentioned, spying on them and any relationship they may have developed with another person, stealing from that person or lying to them. This of course will be denied by the alienating parent.

Encouraging a child to betray one of the most important members of their family, be it the father or the mother, produces within the child a tendency towards psychopathic behaviour. Once the alienating parent has denigrated the other parent to the child, the child, due to the pressure upon them and the 'power' wielded by the alienator, needs to carry on the process of denigration.

Children who suffer from the parental alienation syndrome develop a concept that one parent is the loving parent, and hence to be loved back, while the other is the hated parent who has done evil or wickedness, etc., not only towards the alienating parent but towards the child. This has consciously as well as unconsciously indoctrinated the child. This has also resulted in fear as well as hatred for the alienated parent. Virtually all indoctrination of a negative type is carried out by the mother who usually retains the child in residence. Occasionally it is the father or one of the relations to the child who may have taken over the role of parenting.

Gardner (1998) considers that there are eight cardinal symptoms of PAS in its effect on the child:

1. The campaign of denigration.
2. Weak, frivolous and absurd rationalisations for the denigration.

3. Lack of ambivalence.
4. The 'independent thinker phenomenon'.
5. Reflexive support of the alienating parent in the parental conflict.
6. Actions of guilt over cruelty to or exploitation of the alienated parent.
7. The presence of borrowed scenarios.
8. The spread of animosity to the extended family and alienated parent.

The result of alienation as I have found it is that the child develops a hatred for the other person, that is the non-resident other parent, and seeks to denigrate and vilify that parent much as has been done by the alienating parent. The destruction of one parent can have serious consequences not only immediately but in the long term. One might say the child has been robbed of the possibility of having a supportive and caring parent. Very often that parent is a father who has become a poisonous object. All memories of a good relationship have been destroyed.

Additionally, there has been brainwashing in order to make the child fearful of the alienated parent, very often the father. The animosity created through being programmed or brain washed frequently leads not merely to antagonism towards the alienated parent but also towards their whole family. This means the child will not merely lose one of its parents for support but also the grandparents of that alienated parent.

Another common reaction of children who have been programmed is to pretend to the programming parent that they have strong hatred or dislike for the alienated parent when in fact they do not at all feel this way and do not demonstrate this in the presence of the alienated parent. Hence they have practised deception and a form of lying in order to placate the programming parent while at the same time seeking to form some kind of warm relationship with the absent parent. Such deception is unlikely to lead to an individual who will be truthful and honest in other dealings now and in the future.

Sometimes the alienating parent seeks to exploit the parent who has been defiled. This is done in various ways including seeking to get money or clothes or other material objects for the children who are then used in this scheme or manipulation. The manipulator will often clothe the children in the filthiest clothes hoping the alienated parent will be forced to buy new clothes for the child. This teaches children a strategy

which is unlikely to endear them to others in the future. Such practices of deception and exploitation then may well become a repertoire of the way the children will behave in later life. Other forms of deception are when the child is called by the alienated parent on the telephone and that parent is told in front of the child that the child is not in or the child refuses to speak to them when in fact this is not the case at all. Again children are taught that lying is acceptable. This runs counter to what many parents do to instil truthfulness in their children for the purposes of being accepted by others now and in the future.

In order to endear themselves to the strong programming parent who is dominant over all the children's behaviour, the children will tell that parent that they have been starved or deprived or punished at the alienated parent's home merely to endear themselves to that parent. Here again lying and deception becomes the way which can have detrimental effects in later life. In non-PAS homes the parent who has been separated does not maintain control over the children but the custodial parent will do all that they can to promote a healthy feeling towards the other parent and to be truthful and to encourage the child or children to enjoy the company of the other parent. This does not occur but rather the reverse in the alienation type environment. Needless to say children benefit from such an attitude by non-PAS type behaviour. It is also of great importance that parents who have been divorced or separated do all they can to enhance the feelings of the child for the parent with whom they are not in residence, and vice-versa.

As children grow older they realise they are in a position of strength wherein they may be able to decide to which parent to go by manipulating situations in order to get their way. This in turn reduces the capacity of the alienating parent to utilise discipline to create the right type of ethical behaviour. This is because the alienating parent is dependent on the child to do that which antagonises or damages the targeted parent. Such children frequently become undisciplined knowing they have the power to manipulate the programming parent through fulfilling or not fulfilling the wishes of that parent towards the alienated parent.

In severe cases of PAS, children are placed in seriously unhappy situations and will frequently develop panic reactions when they are asked to visit the alienated parent. This in turn can lead to repercussions in their attitude to school and their capacity to concentrate on their education. In some cases there can be psychotic delusions in the child due to the pressure on that child to passively submit to the alienating parent. In order to overcome such serious disturbances intensive psychological treatment is required and this will be covered in another article entitled: *Dealing with Children who have been involved in Parental Alienation through Therapy*. In some cases children have been indoctrinated with the view that the alienated parent will seriously damage them in some way. Such delusions need urgently to be dealt with through therapy. Following such therapy such unfortunate children may learn to be able to be more rational and realistic in the way they view the alienated parent despite the efforts of the programming parent. This of course is a different matter to resolve in the case of very young children. In the case of older children the habit of hatred towards the target parent may make it extremely difficult but not impossible to alter the attitude of such older children towards the alienated parent.

Perhaps the most interesting scenario that occurs is when the child realises what the alienating or programming parent has been doing and eventually turns against that parent. They often seek the target parent feeling a great sense of guilt in having been a party, albeit an unwilling party, to the humiliation and harm done to the target parent who has done nothing wrong to them to deserve such treatment.

Symptoms of children suffering from the effects of PAS

Now follows a series of symptoms found in children, when they are presented over a period of time, with brainwashing or programming against another parent. The effects are both short and long term. It must be stated from the beginning that not all the symptoms about to be mentioned occur in all children who are involved in the parental alienation syndrome scenario. There will also be some difference between the very young child and the older child who has more experience of the PAS process. Again, not all the symptoms mentioned occur in all children. However, some symptoms undoubtedly will occur and affect the child unless some form of treatment is carried out which eliminates the impact of the alienating process:

1. **Anger** is a common reaction of many children to the process of alienation. The anger however will be expressed towards the target parent as the child sides with one of the parents in the relationship against the other. The fact the children are forced into this kind of situation causes considerable distress and frustration and the response often is to show aggressive behaviour towards the targeted parent in order to accommodate the programmer.

2. **Loss or a lack of impulse control in conduct.** Children who suffer from PAS are not merely suffering from aggression but also often turn to delinquent behaviour. There is considerable evidence that fathers and their presence and influence can do much to prevent and alleviate the possibility of delinquency most especially in boys.

3. **Loss of self-confidence and self-esteem.** Losing one of the parents through the programming procedure can produce a lack of self-confidence and self-esteem. In the case of boys, identification with a male figure has been curtailed, especially if the alienated parent is the father.

4. **Clinging and separation anxiety.** Children, especially very young children, who have been programmed to hate or disdain one of the parents will tend to cling to the parent who has carried out the programming. There is considerable anxiety induced by the programming parent against the target parent including threats that such a parent would carry out a great number of different negative actions against the child as well as the programming parent.

5. **Developing fears and phobias.** Many children fear being abandoned or rejected now that they have been induced to feel that one of the partners in a relationship, usually the father, is less than desirable. Sometimes this results in school phobia, that is, fear of attending school, mainly due to fear of leaving the parent who claims to be the sole beneficial partner in the formal relationship. Some children suffer from hyperchondriacal disorders and tend to develop psychological symptoms and physical illnesses. Such children also fear what will happen in the future and most especially there is a fear that the programming parent or only parent, who is allegedly the 'good parent', may die and leave the child bereft of any support.

6. **Depression and suicidal ideation.** Some children who are so unhappy at the tragic break up of the relationship are further faced with animosity between the programming parent and the targeted parent. This leads to ambivalence and uncertainty and sometimes suicidal attempts occur due to the unhappiness which the child feels brought about by the two main adults in their life.

7. **Sleep disorder** is another symptom which follows the parental alienation situation. Children frequently dream and often find it difficult to sleep due to their worries about the danger of the alienated parent and the guilt they may feel as a result of participating in the process of alienation.

8. **Eating disorders.** A variety of eating disorders have been noted in children who are surrounded by parental alienation. This includes anorexia nervosa, obesity and bulimia.

9. **Educational problems.** Children who are surrounded by the pressure of having to reject one parent frequently suffer from school dysfunctions. They may become disruptive as well as aggressive within that system.

10. **Enuresis and encopresis.** A number of very young children due to the pressure and frustrations around them suffer from bed wetting and soiling. This is a response to the psychological disturbance of losing one parent and finding one parent inimical to the rejected parent.

11. **Drug abuse and self destructive behaviour** frequently are present in children who have suffered from parental alienation. This tendency is due to a need to escape one's feelings of the abuse they have suffered through the experience and the desire to escape from it. In the extreme such self destructive behaviour can lead to suicidal tendencies.

12. **Obsessive compulsive behaviour.** This psychological reaction is frequently present in PAS children. Such children will seek to find security in their environment by adopting a variety of obsessive compulsive behaviour patterns.

13. **Anxiety and panic attacks** are also frequently present in children who have been involved in PAS processes. This may be reflected through psycho-somatic disorders such as nightmares.

14. **Damaged sexual identity problems.** As a result of the PAS syndrome children often develop identity problems, especially as they may have failed to identify with one member of the originally secure relationship.

15. **Poor peer relationships** may follow the PAS situation due to the fact that such children often are either very withdrawn in their behaviour or are aggressive.

16. **Excessive feelings of guilt.** This may be due to the knowledge deep down that the ostracised parent who has been vilified has done nothing wrong to deserve the kind of treatment perceived by the child or children. When this view occurs the child, especially when older, begins to suffer from guilt feelings.

Children who are exposed to PAS suffer in a variety of general as well as specific ways from this experience. It will often have both temporary and lasting effects on their lives. This is obviously not the intention of the alienator but it is the result of such alienation procedures and programming which causes the child to show a negative attitude and behaviour towards one of the parents. To deal with this problem a variety of therapeutic techniques are required and these will be covered in Part Three.

Long-term effect on children of PAS

There have been relatively few studies, considering the importance of the subject, on the long-term effects of parental alienation on adults. One study by Baker (2005a), indicates that there are at least seven areas where there are likely to be deficits as a result of parental alienation. This information results from a qualitative retrospective study of 38 adults who had experienced such alienation. The individuals participated in one hour semi-structured interviews during which auditory tapes transcribed verbatim. The results were then analysed for primary themes and patterns. Findings pertaining to the long term effects of parental alienation were analysed with results revealing the following:

- low self-esteem
- depression
- drug or alcohol abuse
- lack of trust

- alienation from own children
- divorce
- other specific responses of a negative nature

These seven were discussed at length with adult victims and provide a first glimpse into the lives of adult children of parental alienation.

The same author, Baker (2005b), also studied the cult of parenthood using a qualitative study of parental alienation. 40 adults who were alienated from a parent as a child participated in the study about their experiences. A content analysis was again used in the transcript and a comparison was undertaken to identify similarities between the alienating parents and cult leaders. Results revealed that adults whose parent alienated them from the other parent described the alienating parent in much the same way as former cult members described cult leaders. The alienating parents were described as narcissistic and requiring excessive loyalty and devotion, especially at the expense of the targeted parent. The alienating parents were also found to utilise much of the same emotional manipulation and persuasion that cult leaders used to heighten the dependency on them. Finally, the alienating parents seemed to benefit from the alienation in much the same way cult leaders benefited from the cult: they had excessive control, power, and adulation from their victims. Likewise the participants reported many of the same negative outcomes that former cult members experienced such as low self-esteem, guilt, depression and lack of trust in themselves and others. These findings provided a useful framework for conceptualising the experience of parental alienation and were also useful for therapists who provided counselling and treatment to adults who experienced alienation as a child.

The same result was obtained by Gardner (2004). Although the parental alienation syndrome was considered by him to be primarily a disorder of childhood, the false memory syndrome was a disorder of young adults, primarily women. They shared in common a campaign of acrimony against the parent. It was the purpose of Gardner's article to describe both the similarities and differences between these two disorders in the child and in the adult. Laughrea

(2002) attempted to develop an objective self report instrument called the 'Alienated Family Relationship Scale' (AFRS) in order to identify the alienated dynamic within the family from a young adult's perspective.

The AFRS comprised of three sections: Inter-parental conflict, alienating attitude of the father towards the mother and the mother towards the father, and the alienated attitude of the young adult towards both parents. The sample consisted of 493 undergraduate students of which 417 were from intact families and 76 were from divorced or separated families. The results suggested good reliability as well as convergent and constructive validity. The AFRS also discriminated between intact families and divorced and separated families.

It could be of some value to develop a similar test related to children who are undergoing the alienating process. At present the reliance is almost totally on interviews of the various individuals associated with the alienation process.

An earlier study concerned with the personality characteristic of children from intact and divorced and intact families studied retrospectively was that of Fox (2001). 105 college student aged students aged 18–34 years in either intact or single parented households completed questionnaires concerning feelings of well-being, social potency, achievement, social closeness, stress reaction, alienation, aggression, control, harm avoidance, and traditionalism. Results showed no significant differences between subjects in terms of personality characteristics. Female participants scored higher than males concerning social closeness, control, traditionalism, and harm avoidance.

The results of these few studies indicate that much more work needs to be done to assess post-alienation sufferers in adulthood. Only after this will it be possible to strengthen the case for treatment of individuals as children who have been programmed in this manner. It can be seen that not only does a child suffer from and is a victim of the alienation process at the time of the alienation but that this continues into later life and very often perpetuates itself.

Justice of the Peace, 2002, 166: 24: 464–6

Chapter Eight

Signs of PAS and how to counteract it

Introduction

What follows will be in two parts. The first part will deal with the signs of parental alienation or what one should look out for when dealing with children, alienators, and the victims of alienation. The second part will concern itself with remedies in dealing with the alienation process.

It must be understood that what the child wants is important but one must be absolutely certain that what the child wants is truly being reflected by what the child says. It must be understood that children who state that they do not want to see a parent, unless there has been proven sexual, physical or emotional abuse, should still strongly be encouraged to have contact with the other parent.

Children may state they do not wish to see a parent and those who deal with children in the legal profession and as psychologists and psychiatrists often feel they must listen to the child and concede that what the child wants is right for that child. This is a very wrong way of looking at things. Children often want things for themselves that are not good in the short term as well as the long term. While a major consideration when dealing with the alienation process is to do what is best for the child, we must be careful to understand that children will react in a certain way after a period of alienation by one parent. This then leads to information solely on the basis of what the child feels and thinks should happen. Children who have been alienated or programmed against a parent will often state things that are untrue, exaggerated or frivolous, despite having had a good earlier relationship with that parent.

The approach of the therapist in dealing with alienation cases is very different from the psychologist or psychiatrist dealing with a variety of neuroses or psychoses. What is required is to understand that the alienating parent can be, but not necessarily, mentally ill, or evil, or both, in the manner in which they deal with the child in order to wreak vengeance on a parent who had been close at some point in time. What such parents fail to realise is that they are harming the child both in the short

and the long term by depriving that child of a good parent merely because they are angry and wish to get back in a vengeful way against their ex partner. The child is used as a tool in this process. The alienator is not concerned for the welfare of the child but is concerned with their own desire for vengeance against the alienated individual.

Signs of Parental Alienation (PA)

A number of signs or indicators of alienation can be identified. It should be recognised that not all these signs appear in all cases, since they are numerous, but many will in fact apply to those who alienate children against the non-custodial parent. This unfortunately tends to be the father rather than the mother, although increasingly fathers are employing such techniques against mothers also. Whoever uses alienation procedures or brainwashing to get the child to hate the other parent is clearly in the wrong and is guilty of causing harm to the child both in the present and the future. There is considerable research indicating the harm that is done to children who are alienated against a parent when they are young. Increasing research has also shown that when they become adults such individuals suffer retrospectively from the damage done by an alienating parent.

What follows will be a number of signs, some of which interact with other items, and should be viewed not in isolation but in combination in this complex problem of the alienation process:

1. Lack of independent thinking from the child who is imitating the alienator's thoughts and feelings.
2. Destroying mail or even presents from the alienated parent.
3. The alienating parent tends to seek to curtail all communication between the child and the alienated parent.
4. The alienated parent is seen as the scapegoat. They are blamed for everything that has gone wrong with the child. There is no sense of ambivalence.

5. The child calls the alienated parent a liar and other abusive names similar to the alienating parent.
6. The child insults, shows disrespect, and humiliates the alienated parent often in front of the alienator.
7. Alienated parents are viewed as being despicable, faulty and deserving of being rejected permanently.
8. Parents who alienate children are seducing the child emotionally and will continue to do this while in control of the child, yet they deny that they are doing anything but encouraging the child to make contact with the alienated parent.
9. The child is made to feel guilty for any love shown towards the alienated parent. The child will deny any involvement with the alienated parent, fearful of what the alienator would do to them.
10. The child fears rejection by the programmer in case they wish to say good things about the alienated parent or wish to be with them.
11. The child is owned, controlled, and indoctrinated by the alienating parent. That parent is viewed as all good, all wise, and all powerful by the child who becomes dependent and manipulated by them. There is never any questioning that what the parent says or does is always right.
12. The child tends to paraphrase statements used by the alienating parent. The words used are often untypical of words likely to be used by a child. It is very similar to a cult type of indoctrination.
13. The child suffers from paranoia (hatred) inculcated by the alienating parent who promotes attitudes, intentions, and behaviours of a negative nature to the alienated parent.
14. The child will speak about exaggerated or contrived abuse that has been experienced from the alienated parent.
15. The child or alienating parent makes statements insinuating quasi or actual sexual, emotional, and physical abuse suffered by the child.
16. The language comes indirectly from the alienator such as, 'he touches me inappropriately,' or 'he has penetrated me,' These are all borrowed scenarios from the alienating parent.
17. Children who are alienated no longer know truth from lies.
18. The child who is alienated against the parent will often be alienated against the parent's family also.
19. The alienator will also poison the child against the therapist unless the therapist supports the alienator. Hence the therapist is seen as an enemy in the same light as the alienated parent.
20. It is not what the alienator says but how it is said. For example when telling a child 'father would like to take you out,' it can be said with joy and enthusiasm indicating positive expectations or it can be said with venom indicating negative feelings. This is what is predominantly communicated to the child rather than the verbal message.
21. The alienated child tends to see themselves in a very powerful position, especially in the severity of their antagonism shown to the alienated parent. This is all done following the programming by the alienator.
22. Female alienators will often choose female solicitors as they assume they will be able to identify with them better.
23. Female alienators are often angry due to the fact that the alienated individual has a new relationship, while she has not.
24. Some alienators move away from where their ex partner resides in order to make visits difficult or impossible.
25. Sometimes the name of the child is changed to that of the alienator or the next partner to which the alienator has attached themselves.
26. Frivolous reasons are often given for not wanting to be with the alienated parent. Even when told that if these frivolous reasons were removed the child will often claim they do not wish to be with that parent under any circumstances.
27. The child is encouraged to be with friends or play on video games in preference to being with the alienated parent.
28. A child who had a history of a good, happy and warm relationship with the now alienated parent before separation or divorce will fail to remember events in the past that made them happy. They may be suffering from amnesia of any good events due to the alienation process.

Ways to combat parental alienation during mediation and treatment

There is no easy way to combat alienation especially if it has taken place for a long period of time and the alienated parent has had little contact with the child. One might say the alienator has won and has the complete control of the child in this scenario. The two (the alienator and the child) then are a 'team' who work totally against the alienated parent for the purpose of humiliating and rejecting that parent from having contact with the victimised child.

Some of the methods that are recommended for dealing with the process of alienation may seem extreme but it is an extreme situation that one is facing when dealing with the overwhelming power of the alienator. Typical therapeutic methods are ineffective when dealing with such problems. Very firm approaches are required and these must be backed unequivocally by the court in order for them to have an effect in debriefing the victim of the alienation (the child). This sometimes places the therapist in a dangerous situation for they may be accused of being too firm in seeking to reverse the alienation effects. A combination of both reason and emotion but most of all firmness must be shown to the child to make them aware of the damage that has and is being done by continuing to live with such a negative attitude towards one parent. This is, of course, assuming that the alienated parent is innocent of all physical, sexual or emotional abuse.

Again there will be overlap in the suggestions made to reduce the effects of alienation:

1. Destroy the effects of denigration by one parent towards the other by making the child aware of the happy history before the acrimony and separation between the parents occurred.
2. Get the child to see the good points about the denigrated parent.
3. Be firm and proactive in changing attitudes and behaviour that have caused the parental alienation.
4. Try to get the alienating parent to cooperate in stopping the alienation. This is easier said than done, and many alienators will refuse to cooperate in this, although claiming otherwise. This is even the case when it is highlighted that such actions are actually harmful to the child's development.
5. Appeal to the child's conscience that they are rejecting, hurting, and humiliating an innocent party who cares for them.
6. Have the child together with the alienated parent in due course while seeking to change both attitudes and behaviour via rational emotive therapy. There is a need in this process for very firm communications.
7. Make the child aware of what a blood relative might sacrifice for that child which is not the case for strangers.
8. Warn the parent who alienates the child of the harm that they are doing to the child not just in the present time but in the future also.
9. Appeal to the child's critical thinking (intelligence and emotions) and make the child aware of the unfairness and cruelty in rejecting a loving parent.
10. Make the child aware that they need both parents without endangering the relationship with the alienating parent.
11. Make the child aware that they may lose a good parent if the process of alienation continues.
12. The child should be made aware that the extended family of the alienated parent is also being unfairly rejected.
13. Encourage the child not only to engage with the alienated parent but with the alienated parent's extended family, i.e. grandmother, grandfather, aunts, uncles, etc. This will serve to reverse the alienation process.
14. Curtail or eliminate telephone calls and other communications from the programming parent while the child is with the non-custodial parent.
15. It is important for children who have been alienated to spend as much time as is possible with the alienated parent alone so that a relationship can re-develop between them. The longer this individual contact occurs, the greater the likelihood that the alienation process will be depleted.
16. Curtail the child being used as a spy against the alienated parent.
17. In an extreme case the child should be removed from the influences of the alienating parent and be given in custody to the alienated parent or another body which may include a family member. This is to protect the child from further alienation.
18. Passivity and tolerance are ineffective when dealing with parental alienation. What is required is confrontation of a very powerful

type in order to both counteract the effects of the alienation and to reverse it.

19. The power of the court must back the mediator who is seeking to remove the alienation effects.

20. The child may need to be removed to a neutral setting such as a hospital to prevent further alienation. This is only in very extreme cases where severe psychological damage has been done to such a degree that the child suffers from delusions about the alienated parent.

21. In the case of severe alienation it is best for the alienated parent never to approach the home of the alienator but rather to use an intermediary for the transfer of contact with the child.

22. It should be remembered that the child who has been the victim of brainwashing needs to know that it is safe to be with the alienated parent without this reducing their loyalty and commitment to the other parent. Hence the alienated parent should do as much as possible to reassure the child that there is no desire to separate the child from their other parent.

23. Once they have contacted their children alienated parents should concentrate on talking about the past and the happy times together, supplemented with pictures or videos. Initially a child might be very offhand and even fail to make eye contact but this can be improved through reminders of happier times in the past and how this can continue in the future.

24. Alienated parents should not give up easily but should persevere in their efforts to make and maintain contact with their child. Constant rejection from the child is likely to be humiliating and demoralising, but persistence sometimes leads to success with the help of an expert and the support of the courts.

All these aspects involved in dealing with parental alienation are important but the details here are certainly incomplete, as there are many other ways of dealing with alienated children as well as their parents. It is important to realise that there is a great difference between therapeutic approaches in the normal sense and those that are required with parents who are alienating a child against another parent. It cannot be emphasised too strongly that without the backing of the courts the efforts of the expert involved are unlikely to be effective.

Chapter Nine

PAS as a shared psychotic disorder: 'folie à deux'

It is almost too simplistic to state that children fare best when there are two loving and caring parents who can guide these children to live in accordance with what is best in society. When parents separate or divorce, it is still possible to provide such care and guidance despite certain difficulties. Here again the love and care for children should be of primary importance for both parents. It must be based on the acceptance that both parents have an important role to play and that both parents welcome this dual relationship vis-à-vis their children even though their own relationship has been severed.

It is unfortunate, however, that often, due to the hostility between the parents or just one of the parents, the positive goal of dual parenting is often disrupted if not destroyed. This is almost always due to one parent, usually the custodial parent, seeking to sideline and even totally reject the non custodial parent being involved with the child. This is undoubtedly due to the implacable hostility which has developed leading to the break-up of the relationship.

The reason for such hostility varies. Often it is a need for revenge, influence and power, especially when the rejected parent finds a new partner. When this occurs, the alienator feels all the more the need for power and control, and to dominate by keeping the child exclusively to themselves by a relentless process of programming (Clawar and Rivlin, 1991).

Intractable hostility

Intractable hostility between the former partners in a relationship is a result which often leads to a close relationship developing between a child and one, rather than both, parents. The child has come to share the emotions of hatred for the non custodial parent. This is known as 'folie à deux'. This is due to the fear or phobia (Lowenstein, 2006b) and programming by an alienating parent, and the child has a fear of losing the security of the one remaining parent.

The inducer of the implacable hatred holds the key to the child's delusional beliefs of the absent parent. If this parent (with or without

counselling) learns to self-reflect and stimulate the child in their relationship with the other parent, then the child's delusional beliefs of the absent parent and their 'evil and wicked ways' can be eliminated. Often this is not the case and the custodial parent persists in promoting rejection of the absent parent in the child. Only by breaking the relationship between the inducer of such implacable hatred towards the absent parent can the child's delusional beliefs be eliminated. The difficulties involved in breaking this exclusive pathological bond are only too apparent. As an expert witness, my work in the courtroom is to seek a solution for a programmed child which is not to be undermined by the custodial parent while the process of mediation occurs. This will be discussed later when it is considered when a severe pathological alienation process has occurred and how best to deal with it.

The Honourable Judge Gomery of Canada put it wisely:

Hatred is not an emotion that comes naturally to a child. It has to be taught. A parent who would teach a child to hate the other parent, represents a grave and persistent danger to the mental and emotional health of that child.

Would it were that more judges would share such a view in the UK. It would prevent many injustices to children and alienated parents who are sidelined (usually but not always fathers). Such parents have limited contact with their children, if any contact at all. Some have no direct contact. These parents suffer both humiliation and sadness and more importantly the children also suffer both in the short and long term (Lowenstein, 2006a). One does not always know from the child's behaviour that there is anything amiss. Their behaviour is anything but hostile towards the absent father initially, but only later, after a period of considerable brainwashing or programming does the hostility occur, and it eventually becomes an implacable hostility, difficult to reverse.

Behaviour of children who have been alienated may display some, or all of the following:

1. They express the same hostility as does the custodial parent, hence the 'folie à deux' analogy.
2. They identify with and imitate the alienator.
3. They do not wish to visit or spend time with the absent and alienated parent.
4. The child's views of rejecting the absent parent is virtually identical with the programming of the custodial parent.
5. The children suffer from the same delusions and the irrational beliefs as the alienator in regard to the non resident parent (this occurs because the children have totally identified with the custodial parent).
6. The children feel themselves to be powerful due to their alliance with the controlling and powerful alienator.
7. They are not frightened (albeit they claim not to be) by the absent parent or the court.
8. The children have no valid reasons for rejecting the alienated parent, but will often manufacture these reasons, or exaggerate events for the purpose of rejecting alienated parents.
9. They can see nothing positive or good about the absent parent and even the absent parent's family, indeed they claim not to be able to remember anything of a positive nature in the form of memories about the absent parent.
10. They have difficulties in being able to distinguish between what they are told about the absent parent and their own recollections of that parent.
11. They appear not to feel any sense of guilt about the way they treat the absent parent if and when there is contact.
12. They appear to be 'normal', yet appear also no longer to have a mind of their own, being totally obsessed with the custodial parent and their implacable hostility towards the absent parent and frequently their extended family.

These reactions are both pathological and unfair towards the targeted parent and harmful to the perpetrator of such behaviour, that is, the child. The result is a refusal of contact with the formerly close and even loved parent (Rand, 1997). Now they feel dread, anxiety and a virtual phobia when being requested to visit that parent (Lund, 1995, Lowenstein, 2006b). If forced to do so they will physically resist, threaten to run away and actually do run away from the alienated parent back to the alienator. The child totally shares the animosity and paranoia with the programming parent. That parent will insist that they have done nothing to cause the child to behave this way. They will claim that they have encouraged contact, but it is the child who rebels so vehemently against visiting the absent parent.

Sometimes this is influenced by different rearing approaches between the two parents. The indulgent parent is usually the programmer, and this is usually the mother. The programmed parent often seeks to guide the child in a certain way and may appear to the child to be more authoritarian and demanding. This is usually the absent father. The child is being used to do what the programmer wants and will resent the parent who directs and guides (this is usually as already stated the father) (Lund 1995).

Sometimes it is the father who is over-indulgent while the child is in his custody. The absent mother fares similarly if she attempts to discipline or direct the child. The warring parents create a climate where the child feels insecure. Instead of unity there is the opposite. The child feels it has to make a choice and chooses usually that parent who has custody to whom to give their loyalty. In so doing the child feels inclined to reject the absent parent because that parent has so little power compared with the parent with whom the child resides more or less full time.

Therapists or mediators who seek to resolve parental alienation or parental alienation syndrome may antagonise the child as well as the custodial parent when efforts are made for encouraging the child to have contact with the absent parent. If the therapist goes along with the child's wishes of rejecting the non custodial parent, and many do, then the parental alienation becomes all the stronger and more difficult to reverse. This means the therapist has fallen into the trap of the alienator who will claim that it is the child's wishes not to have contact, or only minimal contact with the alienated parent (folie à trois). The courts follow suit by backing the therapist who considers the status quo best for the child. This demonstrates quite clearly how the system of parental alienation works.

Here it becomes imperative that the therapist has the basic principle of **the child needs both parents** firmly in mind. It is important that the therapist is not manipulated either by the alienator, the child, or the current unequal and pathological situation. The therapist must work in order to prevail in getting the child and the alienator to see the value of contact with both parents. As I have so often said, failure to do this increases the likelihood of little or no subsequent contact with the absent and alienated parent. 'Absence does not make the heart grow fonder'. Absence in fact creates a greater likelihood that the absence will be permanent. Little contact results eventually in no contact.

This allows the alienator to continue their work of indoctrination, virtually unchallenged, having received the backing of the court. It takes both a wise and courageous judge to seek to see beneath those 'shenanigans'. There are still too few psychologists whose principle is 'the child needs both parents' when such obdurate opposition from the alienator and the child exists.

Cartwright (1993) indicates that 'time is on the side of the alienator'. The alienator practices various ploys to prevent good contact between the child and the absent parent. Such delaying tactics are unscrupulous and unfair, but they are effective. In time, and after numerous efforts to gain good contact through the courts, the alienated parent sometimes gives up. The odds are stacked against them ever having real positive contact with their child and this gives the alienator the pathological chance to continue the alienation process. One may well ask: 'Is this real justice?' It is not only 'folie à deux' or the 'folie à trois' that has won the day but 'folie carré', to coin a new phrase with the third person in this case being the encased therapist and the fourth party being the court of law. Eventually all favourable recollections the child has had about the relationship with the absent parent disappear. This is again a reflection of how the alienator feels about the former partner as they both enact their 'folie à deux' pathological delusions.

One is often asked what effect this has on the child now and in later life. This has been discussed more fully by Lowenstein (2006a). To summarise, the child grows up relentlessly re-enacting what it has experienced in its own life. Not only does the hostility perpetuate itself towards the targeted parent but it perpetuates itself in the life of the child as they become an adult. The child as an adult has difficulties very often in relationships with a partner and re-enacts what has been learned by perpetuating the cycle of the paranoid delusions and hostility resulting in PAS.

Sometimes a child as an adult or mature adolescent will consider what has occurred and how they have been used by the alienator. This

may result in a change of thinking, due to therapy or in conversation with intimate friends. Then follows an active seeking for the lost parent. Unfortunately there is no research as to the frequency of this happening. The conjecture is that it is relatively rare. As Cartwright (1993) states:

> The child's good memories of the alienated parent are systematically destroyed and the child misses out on the day to day interaction, learning, support and love, which, in an intact family, usually flows between the child and both parents as well as grandparents and other relatives on both sides.

In many cases what occurs is that the now lost parent may no longer be available and the grandparents have undoubtedly died. Additionally, the more mature child sometimes turns against the alienator in the realisation of what has been done. Mothers are twice as likely to be responsible for parental alienation than fathers, as they tend to be on the whole, the custodial parent.

Any expert assessing or treating such problems must be scrupulously fair and independent. The overwhelmingly important principle, as already stated, must be that all things being equal, both parents whenever possible should have an equal access to care and influence on a child. The exception is when it can be shown that either parent is an abuser (sexually, physically, and emotionally) or in other ways is a danger to the child. Mothers appear to make the greatest number of complaints of sexual abuse (67 per cent) (Gardner, 1987). These allegations, more often than not, are invalid about 50 per cent of the time. Fathers are accusers of sexual abuse also in 22 per cent of cases.

The pattern of gaining control over children varies by gender. Men tend to abduct physically 60–70 per cent of the time when 'abductions' occur, whilst women use a kind of social psychological abduction (Clawar and Rivlin, 1991). Whoever has control (custody) of the child can use the child against a former partner since they see the child as an extension of themselves. In these cases they do not view the child either as independent of themselves or as belonging to the alienated parent. They hence view the alienated parent as being of no value, or having any rights over the child, despite still being the natural parent (Wallerstein and Blakeslee, 1994). There is, in addition, a denial of rights for the absent parent. There is nevertheless the desire to make the absent parent responsible towards the maintenance of the child in financial terms. This causes much acrimony, as the non custodial parent (usually the father) will complain as to why he must contribute financially without having a role to play in the child's upbringing or even regular good contact with that child. These issues, however, are strictly separated by law. Rightly so, the courts are strict on parents who do not take up their responsibility to pay for the rearing of the child. The courts should be equally as strict to parents who do not take up their responsibility to make this rearing of the child a matter in which both parents partake.

Turkat (1995) calls this disorder 'malicious parent syndrome' as the parent, usually but not always the mother, engages with the 'folie à deux' child in a relentless and multi-faceted campaign of aggression and deception against the ex-spouse. Sometimes other people are involved in this 'folie à deux' scenario and it may well be called 'folie à plus de trois'. This includes family members and friends, or even neighbours who will back the alienator. Each will support the alienator, without a qualm. They fall into the trap of attacking the absent parent and thereby prevent that parent playing any role in a child's life. Sometimes they will go so far, without first hand evidence, to claim that the absent parent is a sexual or physical abuser. Both mothers and fathers have been responsible for such totally false allegations being made. Children will be encouraged or even pressurised to lie about sex abuse or physical contact of some kind in order for the innocent parent to be eliminated totally from having any contact with the child. Hence the alienator's delusions are imposed not only on an innocent child, but many others, in a form of 'folie à plusieurs' or madness or delusion of many.

These alienating and falsely accusing parents may be diagnosed as suffering from 'a personality disorder'. This includes 'mixed, unspecified, histrionic, borderline, passive-aggressive or paranoid behaviour' (Wakefield and Underwager, 1990). Such views in these parents lead to a typical totally controlling and maintaining of a symbiotic bond with the child, and elimination of the other parent (Ross and Blush, 1990).

Such alienators impose fear of the absent parent on the child as already mentioned. This is sometimes termed 'folie imposée'. When many people or one side is involved it is termed 'folie à plusieurs' (Enoch and Ball, 2001).

What is the solution to the 'folie à deux' phenomenon?

In seeking to deal with the problem it must be emphasised strongly that what follows is only to be considered if and when the alienation is so pathological that no other course of action is available. What will have preceded such apparently drastic responses is for mediation and the edicts of the court to have had no effect in changing the alienators dangerous and damaging acts in the short but even more in the long term (Lowenstein, 2006a). This damaging action has come in the form of preventing a child having good, or any contact, by making that contact very difficult with the absent and non custodial parent.

The process of assessing whether or not parental alienation has taken place is required to be carried out by an experienced psychologist or psychiatrist. Such a person needs to look not only for the signs of PAS (Lowenstein, 2006c) but also the manner in which the dissimulation occurs. This results in the form of the child refusing any contact or having only very limited contact with a previously loved but now alienated parent. The alienation has taken place through the efforts of the custodial parent and their implacable hostility, as previously stated, towards the non custodial parent.

Once the assessment of the problem has been presented to the court, it is often recommended that efforts are made to gain the co-operation of the custodial parent and the child so that the alienated parent and the child are able to establish or re-establish some kind of positive relationship. If this succeeds and the absent parent has regular and good contact, that is the end of the matter and one can describe this to be a success in promoting good parenting on both sides.

Unfortunately this course of action, from its very inception, fails as a result of the continuing implacable hostility of the custodial parent and the process of alienation not having been reversed. Hence, while the alienator often plays 'lip-service' to the process of mediation, this is not supported by the efforts to reverse the 'folie à deux' phenomenon. The child therefore still resents, if not loathes, the alienated parent whilst giving the impression that this is in no way due to having been programmed to share the alienators implacable hostility.

This scenario is frequently missed or purposely ignored by psychologists. Instead the child's opinion is taken for granted, rather than investigating the true reasons for the child's attitude towards the alienated parent. Judges also make decisions of no or little contact with the absent parent based on 'the child's apparent wishes'. This is an act of betrayal, in fact to the child (!), lacking in sophistication and an injustice. The judicial decision is made on the basis of the brainwashed view of the child. Judges will often hide behind:

1. The expert witness' superficial opinion that a child's view cannot be ignored.
2. The expert who notes the alienation which has occurred, yet feels that it is now too late to do anything to reverse the situation, considering it now a 'damage limitation exercise'.

Expert witnesses who do not fall into these two categories are either ignored or seen as extreme in the view they express when they seek to reverse the successful alienation process by more drastic means. Such experts are viewed as being harsh, heartless and 'unrealistic'. What follows is nevertheless a solution, not often employed, which could well reverse the betrayal both of a child and an innocent and rejected parent who have been wronged. Such a parent and child have often also been betrayed by an unjust judicial system. What now follows is a more extreme approach in cases of severe pathological indoctrination or programming by the custodial parent.

Silveira and Seeman (1995) consider the only solution possible to the 'folie à deux' pathological phenomenon to be a separation of the individuals involved until the alienated parent has been able to have good contact with the child. This may appear to be a drastic solution, one which is likely to be frowned upon by those who consider themselves to be 'child centred', and this viewpoint is understandable. Let us, however,

look at the situation from the point of view of the long-term consequences to allowing 'folie à deux' to continue its unjust and damaging course of action. The child loses a good parent and the parent loses the opportunity of rearing the child they have created. Let us remember our basic principle, that the input of two parents is on the whole better than one parent, all things being equal. The long-term deprivation of a parent for a child has been delineated as leading to a perpetuation of the same situation occurring ad infinitum. Following the separation from the alienator the child should be provided with intensive therapy by a skilled therapist who understands the pathology of PAS. In addition to these points it is not justice but an injustice that has triumphed (Lowenstein, 2006d; 2006e; 2006f; 2006g).

Summary

We have considered the shared psychotic disorder 'folie à deux' which is often an integral part of the parental alienation process. The way it functions insidiously leads to the alienation of a good parent. The basis is the intractable hostility of the alienating parent against the now non resident parent. The alienator systematically destroys the child's attitude, affection and love which the child previously felt for the now absent parent. The child forms a pathological bond ('folie à deux') with the alienator.

Eventually, contact between the child and the alienated parent becomes negligible or non existent. After both mediation and a lack of response to the courts decisions, the author recommends splitting the child totally for a time from the programmer. The purpose of this is for the child to receive treatment to deal with the alienation without being under the influence of the alienator, and at the same time to have contact with the alienated parent. This should continue until good contact is possible once again with both parents.

Chapter Ten

The psychological effect of modelling (imitation) in PAS

I am often asked how children become estranged from a parent after an acrimonious divorce or separation. What follows indicates the process by which alienation occurs and examples are cited on how non alienation can also occur, as well as the negative aspects of the destruction of a relationship between one of the parents (alienation). While most alienated parents are fathers, mothers also face this alienation process and hence the sex of the partners, in what follows as illustrations, are kept ambiguous. Hence (A) will equal one parent who responds well to counselling by a psychologist and therefore avoids the process of alienation, while the other (R) has not as yet been able to avoid the process of alienation. As each speaks, including the psychologist (P), the interaction of the two indicates the process by which alienation can also be avoided.

The illustrations also demonstrate, as they are recorded by tape recorder, both positive and negative verbal and non verbal communications which equally result in positive and negative relationships respectively. These recordings have been made with the consent of all the parties involved. It is important to begin with how the custodial parent prevents a process of negative behaviour (parental alienation) from developing with the help of the psychologist. This does much to prevent harm to the child in the short and long term (Clawar and Rivlin, 1991; Blush and Ross, 1987; Gardner, 2000, 2001; Lowenstein, 2005a–k). Before illustrating this with two actual cases as seen by this author, it is vital to look briefly at the theoretical work on modelling leading to parental alienation. By modelling is meant the child identifying closely with the custodial parent and responding accordingly to the wishes of that parent, whether these are subtle or direct.

There is considerable evidence that parental alienation results from a custodial parent acting with hostility or fear towards a former spouse. This then results in a child developing similar if not identical reactions towards the non custodial parent with whom the child had had a good relationship earlier. (Clawar and Rivlin, 1991; Blush and Ross, 1987; Gardner, 2000, 2001; Lowenstein, 2005a–k).

Bandura and Rosenthal (1966) were some earlier investigators who noted that fear or alienation could be acquired through modelling, that is, through observation and imitation. Hence a child may observe or hear a parent act or speak with fear or antagonism towards an absent parent and thereby equally develop the same fear and hostility towards that absent parent through imitation. The absent parent, by their absence, are unable to defend themselves. The child also becomes totally identified with the custodial parent and that parent's position of fear and hostility towards the non custodial parent (Fredrikson, Annas and Wik, 1997).

Fear, anxiety and hostility are inculcated in the child by a hostile parent, often towards the absent parent, either the father or the mother. This frequently leads to avoidance behaviour by the child in the short and long term through operant conditioning. Hence antagonism could develop eventually for the whole gender of the alienating parent (male or female). This can lead to the avoidance of the whole gender group due to generalisation effects. This again is due to the preservation of the emotions and attitudes over the long term (Kim and Hoover, 1996; Wells et al., 1995). This could also result in a generalised anxiety disorder via a stimulus generalisation.

Now follow excerpts from two, consent given, tape recorded interviews. The first (A) was a parent who was amenable to a change of attitude and hence to the avoidance of alienating, through the guidance of the psychologist. The second (R) was more resistant to avoiding alienating a child against the former partner.

Illustration 1: How PA can be prevented or curtailed

The custodial parent A could be either the father or the mother, P is the psychologist.)

A: Doctor, I don't know how to deal with my daughter. We have both been let down by my partner who left me for someone else:

P: In the first instance you should be accurate in what you say to your child. You should tell her that her parent has not left her (the daughter) but has left you (the wife or husband). You should make it absolutely clear to the child that the absent parent loves her as much as when they resided with her.

A: How then do I explain my being alone and them leaving me?

P: You should make it clear that there have been differences between yourselves (the parents) which made it difficult to live together but that this does not in any way change your child's feelings towards your former partner. You should make it absolutely clear that you are both the child's parents and that you both love the child.

A: I feel so bereft and alone with the burden of looking after and bringing up a family on my own.

P: I understand how you feel. Your former partner probably does also and possibly feels some guilt. You were undoubtedly close at one time.

A: Yes we were, but no longer. I must look ahead but how to do this is not easy.

P: There are many couples who after a time become friends once the grieving and animosity has ended.

A: I don't see how I can ever forgive them.

P: You may never forgive or forget but now it is time to think of your daughter first and foremost and how best to provide for your daughter's emotional security. That means continuing to involve your ex-partner in the life of that child. You are one of the most important members of your daughter's life. She has already seen one parent leave and may have witnessed acrimony and unhappiness of the two persons which mean most to her in her life. Your daughter must continue to depend on you and your former partner for her future emotional development, security and capacity for living a reasonable happy life. Please make certain that your daughter and the other parent is aware of that.

A: It makes sense when you say what you say and I will try to make my ex-partner play an important part in our child's life.

P: How are you going to make sure this is communicated to the child? You will have to speak well of your ex-partner regardless of how you may feel about their treatment of yourself. You will have to speak well and mean it and sincerely encourage your child to have contact with your former partner. They must of course feel and do the same. If each speaks well

of the other the child will feel secure as a result of this. This will lead also to a better relationship between yourself and your former partner since you do have in common the love for your child.

Illustration 2: Attempting to counteract potential negative influences and feelings leading to parental alienation

With the previous approach having taken place, we continue with a session with a parent who is more resistant to accepting the role of the other non custodial parent and who has already begun, to some degree, programming the child against that parent. It has to be said that many custodial parents are not so easily convinced that it is in their child's best interest, or their own best interest, to encourage positive contact between that child and their former partner.

The dialogue which follows between the present psychologist and the alienating parent demonstrates how the alienator feels and behaves in order to prevent positive contact between their child and the other parent. It also includes the direct and subtle resistance which the psychologist encounters in his effort to convince the custodial parent that they are already programming the child against the non resident parent. The custodial parent is undermining the non custodial parent subtly, and sometimes unconsciously. This is not in the best interest of the child. It will also do much to cause problems for that child in the future.

The custodial parent R could be either the father or the mother, P is the psychologist.

P: I believe there have been some problems about your former partner having contact with your mutual child?

R: That has nothing to do with me. I have never stopped my child (*it may be noted that 'my' is used instead of 'our' by the alienator*) from having contact. I can't force the child to do so and I don't intend to force them.

P: Why do you believe the child does not want contact?

R: I don't know. You will have to ask the child.

P: What do you think the child would say?

R: Probably that they did not behave as they should have behaved towards me and the child and that's why they want nothing to do with them, and feels very angry, with them.

P: So you are blaming your former partner for the fact that the child is so hostile towards him?

R: What other reason could there be? *(Here we may note the denial that the custodial parent is doing anything to prevent contact. This is where modelling is seen to be acting.)* I haven't done anything to stop the child from having contact. So don't blame me, which you are doing, because I know about your work on parental alienation and parental alienation syndrome.

P: Do you not believe that a parent sometimes tries to turn a child against a former devoted parent intentionally or even without meaning to do so?

R: Sure it exists, but I would never do such a thing even though I hate my former partner after what they have done to us.

P: You say 'us' don't you mean 'you' . . . what your former partner has done to you? Your partner has not really done anything to the child.

R: You have to ask my child.

P: What do you believe the child would say?

R: My *(note the constant use of 'my')* child does not like my former partner just as I don't.

P: But why . . .?

R: I know what you are trying to get me to say . . . That I influenced the child in some way.

P: Well have you?

R: Of course not. Why should I do that? I have always considered there should be the same contact with my ex-partner. *(One may note the denial here that the partner is doing anything to prevent contact).*

P: But how much? How much contact do you think the child should have?

R: That's up to the child. My child should have some say in the matter. *(Here again the power of the child is put in the frame. The child is to make the decisions rather than the mother or father. The custodial parent empowers the child totally when in fact the parents should be proactive in encouraging contact with both parents. The custodial parent is in fact pretty certain that the child will reflect the custodial parent's views and reject the other parent, now the alienated parent. Normally the custodial parent is a pretty dogmatic person but in order to appear 'fair' steps out of character and allows, and even insists that the child make the decisions in this instance.)*

P: Don't you realise you are putting an excessive amount of responsibility on the child?

R: My child has a right to decide what they want and I believe they can handle it.

P: Do you give your child that kind of freedom of choice about when to go to bed or when to get up, or how much television to watch, and whether the child needs to see a dentist or go to school, or whether to wear warmer clothes in the winter time etc.?

R: That's different . . . Very different.

P: What do you say to your child about being with your former partner?

R: I say that they want to see the child next weekend and ask if they want to go.

P: What if the child says, 'No, I would rather do other things such as being with my friends or playing games or watching television? What then?

R: What can I say? The child has a mind of their own and I can't and won't force them to go if they don't want to go. *(R neither encourages nor puts any pressure on the child to have contact with the other parent.)*

P: But you could insist that they see . . . let's say . . . a dentist and would insist on it, or . . . go to school, wouldn't you?

R: That's different. You do have to insist on a child going to school and seeing a dentist, but to be with a parent is not the same, especially if the child already doesn't want to do so.

P: Don't you see what could happen if the child rarely, or never sees the other parent?

R: I don't see what I can do about that and anyway why should that be harmful to the child not to be with the other parent, especially if the child says they do not want to be with that parent but prefers to do other things.

P: So you feel that the child not being with the other parent is not really that important? So you won't insist the child should go with their other parent who doesn't live with them anymore?

R: What can I do? I already told you that if the child doesn't want to go I can't do anything about it.

P: You could encourage . . . You could insist . . . You could say how important it is that they are with the other parent. You could do this for the sake of your child. You could even go out together perhaps with the child and the other parent providing that there are no arguments.

R: I can't do any of those things. My ex-partner wouldn't like it also.

P: Have you tried it . . . Have you discussed it with the other parent? Might not that be good for the child and also improve your relationship with the other parent?

R: No. Neither of us would like to be together in the company of the child. Anyway, it would just increase the chance of us quarrelling.

P: You seem very negative about possible ways to improve the situation between yourselves and your former partner.

R: You don't know what they are really like or you wouldn't suggest such an idea.

P: You seem very negative and pessimistic about all and everything I suggest. Don't you believe your child would benefit if you and your former partner could agree, most especially about good contact between the child and the other party? Isn't that what you would want if things were the other way around and your former partner had custody and not you?

R: Well that is not the case now is it. Besides that, I would do anything to have my child want to be with my former partner, but I have heard them say how much they dislike and even hate them, probably as much as I do.

P: So your child has heard you say that about your former partner?

R: I may have said it a few times. I was being honest. I can't help it. Should I have lied?

P: You could have said to the child, that your former partner loves them as much as you do and that they have always been a good parent to them. The other partner equally should say the same to the child. Both you and your former partner could emphasise the importance of the child showing 'respect and love' for both parents.

R: You really want me to help my former partner have contact and for me to be friendly towards them?

Here the mother or father has shown their true feelings. At this point the interview is at an end although it could go on without perhaps much being achieved. It must be admitted that those who are pathological alienators are not easily convinced that they should not directly or subtly programme a child against the absent parent. A former hostile relationship and acrimonious parting is often sustained and leads to parental alienation. It also leads to the prevention of contact between the child and the former grandparents and other relations of the absent parent. It can lead to insults by the child against the alienated parent which was not the case before the acrimonious parting between the adults.

In these cases, the expert witness (psychologist or psychiatrist) must rely on the judicial system

to enforce contact with the absent parent, even if this is against the 'apparent' wishes of the child. It could and should lead to a change of residence if all else fails to achieve its objective. Only in that way can there be the possibility of reversing the harm that has already been done to the child in the short and in the long term. It is unfortunate that at present the judiciary is rarely willing to act on behalf of what is best for the child but will only act as if the child's views are sacrosanct. What is lacking here is a failure to identify what the real needs are of the child and not what the child states, having been influenced by others in some way. It is very unfortunate that many psychologists or psychiatrists have an attitude of being 'child-centred' and by this they mean that they believe what the child says rather than what the child needs and what is best for the child in the short and long term. It is the view of this psychologist that, providing there has been no abuse of the child and there is unlikely to be any abuse of the child, both parents have a vital role to play in continuing having positive and good contact with the child over many years.

Summary

There is considerable research now that modelling and classical conditioning may be responsible for fear and hostility reactions in children towards an alienated parent where previously there had been a good relationship. These children have identified with the programmer who directly, or subtly, causes a child to develop animosity combined with fear towards a previously loved and caring parent. The process of alienation has produced a product or reaction in the child which is virtually pathological and can only be removed by changing custody for the child temporarily or permanently, or by intense treatment, or a combination of the two, so that the child will recollect positive moments with the alienated parent and resume the relationship which formerly existed. Obviously the process of alienation and identifying with the programming parent must be halted before this can solidify into total rejection of the non custodial parent. Only the psychological treatment combined with the court's appropriate reaction to this situation can lead to a resuming of a favourable relationship between the alienated parent and the child in question.

Part Two
The Role of the Judiciary

Chapter Eleven

Introduction: real justice for non custodial parents

In the findings of the Court of Appeal by Dame Elizabeth Butler-Sloss, Thorpe and Waller (June 19th 2000) I have been described in my one and only case before the committee as:

> ... at the one end of the broad spectrum of mental health practitioners and of the belief in the existence of PAS (Parental Alienation Syndrome).

The judiciary were right in stating that PAS has not as yet been recognised by such august bodies as the American Psychological Association or the American Psychiatric Association or indeed the British Psychological Society etc. One must intrude here to say that it was equally not recognised that women should have the vote during the period of the suffragette movement!

Even if PAS in a legal sense can be negated, the existence of parental alienation cannot be denied legally or realistically. It goes on as any rejected parent will verify. Until PAS (parental alienation syndrome) has been accepted, I will therefore reluctantly use only the term PA or parental alienation. It is unfortunate that my report at that time was rejected even though it was supported by a Court Welfare Officer. When the case went to appeal I was unfortunately not given the opportunity to argue in support of this report personally as I was never invited to do so. One might say I was sidelined, much as rejected parents are sidelined.

This particular appeal related to several cases where the fathers wished for direct contact. In each case a father's application for direct contact had been refused by the judge, 'against a background of domestic violence between the parents'. The court considered the report of the Children Act Sub-Committee of the Advisory Board on Family Law on parental contact in domestic violence cases, and a joint expert report prepared by two child psychiatrists for the Official Solicitor. In the case of **real** domestic violence, the decision for no direct contact is easy to uphold, but even here each case must be judged on its specific merits.

For example, domestic violence often occurs following severe provocation and often with both parents acting violently, although one parent only is held responsible (Lowenstein, 2005). Children should naturally not be exposed to such events. Once the parties have separated, there could be a case for allowing the non resident parent to have direct contact with the child even though there had been domestic violence, since the two parents are no longer associated or together. It is, of course, important that the inimical parents be kept apart, especially when change over of contact is being considered. There is therefore the need for an independent intermediary to convey a child from one parent to the other.

Unless the absent parent has in any way or form been abusive to a child, there is no reason for that parent not having close and regular contact with the child, especially if there has been a close and warm relationship with that child in the past. Later I will discuss the scenario of what should happen when the child no longer wishes to have direct, or any contact, with the previously much loved parent.

Suffice it to say, it is my view that the peremptory dismissing of the four appeals was wrong and should in time be reversed. The important or paramount factor at issue is 'the likely risk of harm to the child' (page 2 of the report Court of Appeal Dame Elizabeth Butler-Sloss P, Thorpe and Waller, LJJ 19 June 2000) in this I agree totally with the Court of Appeal's findings. Children should always feel and be safe. In that case, the judiciary found in favour of the mother who did not wish her former spouse to have direct contact. Although there was a background of violence during the marriage and it remained a factor which, the judge found, 'had left its mark on the mother, unlike the other appeals before us, violence does not appear to me to be the main cause of the refusal of contact by the mother.' One could well ask what was the main cause for not allowing the father contact, when the child was the most likely beneficiary?

I was jointly instructed by the mother and the father and gave my opinion that therapy should be instituted as soon as possible with the purpose of improving the likelihood of good contact with the other parent as the result of such therapy.

This, as with a number of my other cases, was refused.

The Court Welfare Officer was also in favour of my recommendation. A complaint made by the mother against the Court Welfare Officer led to that officer not wishing to appear before the court despite being asked to do so. As already mentioned, I was not invited in the original court hearing to appear to give evidence of the vindictive parental alienation that occurred which influenced the child against having contact with the father. Had I been asked, I would have happily given evidence and been cross examined in support of my own report and the Court Welfare Officer's views also. I was not aware at the time that the case had gone to appeal. I would likewise have been happy to support my position and the contents of the written report.

It is unfortunate that the parent who has custody will sometimes make unwarranted allegations against an expert whose views are contrary to their own. This happened in the case of the Court Welfare Officer. It could just as easily happen towards anyone including myself! This will, however, in no way dissuade me from giving evidence in the future which I believe to be both just and right.

The child, with the intractable hostility towards an absent parent and even the parent's extended family, will often express the view that they do not wish contact with the father or mother. These must always be viewed as individual cases. Children do not become hostile and wish no contact with a parent for no reason, especially if there has been a good relationship in the past. What one must seek to ascertain is what the **real reasons are for avoiding contact!** Such in-depth analysis of the child's motivation rarely occurs. It is therefore vital to examine the child's rejection of a parent at greater depth via therapy. This again rarely occurs. The child not wishing contact with a parent is accepted as sacrosanct. This is not being child centred, it is being duped by a child's superficial response.

It is not enough to accept what the child claims are the reasons. We must look **beneath their reasons** and *how they could have originated*. The phrase 'possession is nine tenths of ownership' has been used to claim justified ownership of objects. The custodial parent's claim of a child is very much the same. The child is claimed as theirs and theirs alone. That cannot be right, and yet at present that is exactly the case. The child may be said to have changed their view toward the absent parent for a reason!

Having viewed recent cases in the High Court, the expertise of two psychiatrists have been accepted as sacrosanct. Their view has been that the child, who does not wish direct or any contact with the parent, must be respected and acted upon. This conclusion is reached in the four cases that have appealed to the Court of Appeal for contact. I have waited long to respond to the decision of Dame Elizabeth Butler-Sloss and her colleagues. I have in some way responded indirectly by my articles on PA, both published and unpublished. The current response is more direct and is based on numerous cases where I have acted as an Expert Witness. My failures are not based on a parent having no justification for contact with a child but the precedent reached by Dame Butler-Sloss and her colleagues. These precedents must be altered and the right of the non custodial parent considered as equally important as that of the custodial parent. This is to the benefit of the child. This is a real illustration of being 'child centred'. The child really prefers both parents to be involved with them once the alienation process has been overcome. Again, one must ask oneself why were such unfair decisions reached by the highly learned and respected judges. It was not reached in the name of what is 'right' and 'just'. It was not reached in considering what is best for the child. It was reached for three main reasons:

1. Because the child 'wishes it' by reason of unjustified influences.
2. Because of the difficulties involved in seeking to reverse what the child wants following the alienation that the child has undergone.
3. Because of failing to understand **why** the child is intractably hostile to one parent. It must be remembered this was not the case in the past, when the parental relationship was relatively intact.

Let us remember that the child who now refuses contact or wishes for only supervised or indirect contact had previously been extremely happy with the currently alienated parent who is now the rejected parent. That rejection is based on something that has occurred in the interim, while that caring non custodial and loved parent has been absent. The reasons have been well documented in the current writers previous published and unpublished papers currently on the website www.parental-alienation.info.

Many parents who love their child find it difficult and sometimes impossible to accept supervised or indirect contact. They are humiliated by such proposals. They feel, and rightly so, that they have done nothing to deserve this kind of limitation of contact. The fathers feel, and often experience, that it does not lead to direct contact.

The problem, however, remains for the judicial system as how best to deal with the issue of a child refusing direct contact with a formerly loving parent and a formerly loved parent. My views are well known on how to make a custodial parent comply and insist that a child has contact with the absent parent. It is more often than not that the custodial parent has brought about the situation of a child's unwillingness to be with a parent by direct or indirect statements and actions which led to the child's antagonism towards the absent parent.

If the parent does not or will not reverse the alienation they have been instrumental in creating, then some justified action is required. This is both just and fair. Such parents will, of course, argue that they have done nothing to influence a child! As I have already said in courts on many occasions, the child is forced to wash, put on clean clothes, go to school, see a doctor or dentist (an especially unpleasant experience at times) but cannot be encouraged or made to see the other parent! Does this smack of reality or rational thinking? I think not.

I have always emphasised the value of therapy and/or mediation when this occurs. My preference is for cognitive behaviour therapy. This is also often opposed by the court and the custodial parent. They consider this unnecessary and even damaging to the child's emotional state! The opposition by a parent is seen, at present, as the right of that parent to refuse mediation and treatment to identify and reverse the process of alienation. What about the right of the non custodial parent? What about the right of the child to have contact with both parents which deep down without the alienation would have been the case? Unfortunately, at present, the right of the non custodial parent, as well as the child's **deeper needs**, are ignored.

Sometimes, it occurs that a parent 'plays along' with the therapy and mediation recommended. When the report by the expert and therapist is written and rational decisions are reached that go against the custodial parent, the report is often thrown out. Sometimes the expert is even viewed as prejudiced and being in favour of the non custodial parent. They are even disgraced or

discredited for having suggested that a parent must co-operate or that a parent should lose custody of their child if they fail to encourage the child to be in contact with the previously loved parent. The basis of such action is again in the best interests of the child. It should be remembered when a child rejects a good parent it is not the child speaking. The child is, in fact, repeating and expressing the views of the alienator.

Two well regarded psychiatrists used the child's right not to have direct contact with a parent as sacrosanct. This is despite the judiciary making the following statement:

I would however like to express some sympathy for the father, whose attempt to revive contact were found by the Judge to be genuine and well motivated. It may be that, if he perseveres in keeping in touch with G by interesting letters, postcards, cards and presents, when G is a little older he may express a wish to be in touch with his father.

Unfortunately by that time the important role of that parent has been destroyed.

In the interim, much harm is likely to occur due to the restrictions based on a loving parent not having positive contact with a child. Lack of contact by a good parent with a child goes against the views of Lord Woolf MR (and many others) in the case of (*Contact: Stepfather's Opposition*) [1997] 2LFR 579 where it is stated '. . . the general policy of this court that contact between a child and its natural parent is to be maintained wherever possible'. Lord Woolf has failed to understand that the phrase 'wherever possible' relies so much at present on the child's own unsubstantiated wishes or superficial wishes based on the alienation.

Of paramount importance is the welfare of the child. One cannot help but agree with this, rather than the rights of either parents for contact. The two issues are however linked; that is, good, positive, caring parenting leads to safety and security for the child. This view is also contained in S1(1) of 1989 Children Act:

'The welfare of the child is the paramount consideration of any court concerned to make an Order relating to the upbringing of a child. It cannot be emphasised too strongly, that the court is concerned with the interests of the mother and the father only in so far as they bear on the welfare of the child.'

How can this view be stated so clearly by Lord Woolf and others, including the House of Lords, in *S v M (Access Order)* [1997] 1FLR980 but in reality the reverse often occurs when parents separate in an acrimonious manner? The answer is that when a child does not wish contact, this is taken very seriously and acted upon by the judiciary. No effort, or very limited effort, is made to unearth the **real basis** for the child's stance and frequent implacable hostility to one parent, usually the absent father, although it could be the good mother also. Even when expert witnesses discover that the process of alienation has taken place, the judiciary believe they are acting in the best interests of the child by refusing to insist on the child being made to have contact, or making a Contact Order which could force the custodial parent to change the view of the child regarding contact. This is often sufficient if there is also pressure on the custodial parent that if they fail to do so they will lose the child in their care. Courts, however, are very reluctant to make such statements and even more to enforce such decisions. They consider it will be worse for the child if this occurs. I do not agree. The damage, long and short term created by a child's lack of opportunity to have contact with two parents is a much worse scenario.

It should be remembered that the child in many instances has had a close and positive relationship with the non custodial parent and it could be resurrected providing the child has contact with that parent on a regular basis without the interference or alienation of the custodial parent. Something has undoubtedly happened to change the views and feelings of the child towards the absent parent. Should whatever that is not be targeted for remediation? The reason for such change of attitude and behaviour in not wishing contact with a good but absent parent is almost certainly a process of programming, by the alienator.

Even if the child unfortunately has witnessed a scenario of domestic violence between the parents when they lived together, and this is not always the case; this has been resolved by the absence of one of the parents from the home. Sometimes the allegations of domestic violence have been exaggerated or have been mutual, or have indeed been unsubstantiated by independent and honest witnesses.

Lord McCluskey *S v M (Access Order)* [1997] FLR 980 stated the importance to the child of both parents having contact. In his view the link between the child and each of the natural parents is so important in itself that, unless there are very strong reasons to the contrary, it should be preserved.

The Tavisock Clinic has a similar view: '. . . There is no doubt where parents have separated . . . that for most children their mental health, their emotional, psychological and social development are enhanced by regular contact with their parents and extended family' (Dowling and Gorrell-Barnes, 1999). Hence virtually everyone agrees on the importance of contact for the absent parent with the child under positive circumstances. The area of uncertainty and disagreement is, however, how to interpret a child's statement of unwillingness to have contact with the absent parent despite a history of a good relationship. My own view here is that it is vital to **establish the real reasons for a child feeling this way** and to assess and study it. Frequently, it is due to the absent parent having done nothing wrong although this has been interpreted differently by the alienating parent to the child. It is more likely therefore, that an attitude of this kind is formed due to the influence of the custodial parent. This is sometimes termed 'programming' or even 'brainwashing'.

The result is that a good parent has been alienated, often permanently. Here something must be done to reverse this process. Sturge and Glaser would accept the right of the child to refuse contact with a parent and they consider it best to act upon this. I would strongly disagree. It is not the child giving the opinion here but the alienator! It must be remembered that the child is under the total control of the custodial parent (Lowenstein, 2005). **It must be necessary to look beneath what the child claims is a decision for not wishing contact with a parent.**

Sturge and Glaser prefer a slow, gradual process, sometimes commencing with indirect contact, to supervised contact leading by slow steps to direct contact. This approach is unlikely to be effective since during all this time, the alienation process continues unabated. Using the Sturge and Glaser method the child's views are not altered and cannot be altered. The child's attitude and behaviour often becomes worse. This is exemplified by having witnessed how the non custodial parent suffers when thrown together in a supervised situation. Such parents are humiliated, called names and worse during such contact meetings. This is especially the case if the custodial parent is present and the child has an audience and ally. Here the child is showing the custodial parent how falsely they feel about the non custodial parent. Emails and ordinary letters and telephone calls are equally unsatisfactory, and frequently do not bring the child closer to the non custodial parent. It must be remembered that the alienator still has total control of the child physically and psychologically. If anything the unwarranted animosity of the child towards the non custodial parent gets worse! Such behaviour is encouraged, directly or subtly, against the now hated former partner.

If there is more than one child, then the older child will often influence the younger ones to reject the father or mother. They will even influence the very young who have had little or no contact with the alienated parent before the acrimonious parting of the ways by the parents. The only answer should be to influence the alienator through strong sanctions to reverse that process and to sincerely and directly influence and encourage the child to seek good contact with the absent parent. Such behaviour must be **sincere** and not pretence. This can lead very often, however, to lip-service and the parent claiming that they can do nothing to 'change the views' of the child!? As has already been stated children are made to do many things i.e. going to the dentist, than meeting a loving parent.

It must be made clear to such a parent that if they are unable to alter the child's views then someone else must do so via therapy or mediation. This must always be with the backing of the court. If this fails, change of residence could be determined as a last resort. Often the threat of this likelihood to follow is sufficient for the custodial parent to do all they can to resolve the matter and to make certain that the child has contact with the absent parent. I would hasten to add that this is not primarily for the benefit of the sidelined parent, but for the child. The child has and will suffer as a result of being deprived of one parent in the short and even more in the long term (Lowenstein, 2005, article 20). The author is therefore equally child-centred since contact with two loving parents is of the greatest benefit to the child.

At the present time, the plight of the good and caring absent parent is being rejected by an alienated child and often by an alienated court which fails to see the reason for the lack of desire for contact that is the true reason. The softly, softly approach advocated by Sturge and Glaser and accepted by the judiciary at present does not work. Absent parents without contact with their children continues unabated. Absence does not make the 'heart grow fonder' towards the alienated parent. It is just the reverse. The absence of contact widens the gulf until it can no longer be bridged. Most alienated parents, after years of struggling against the legal odds as well as the deluded expert witnesses, 'throw in the towel'. They seek no further contact. This is a tragedy for the present and for the future of the child.

In the current situation, it is important to gather evidence via a survey of professional experts as well as from non custodial parents. It is important to obtain real evidence as to the percentage of success or failure of current acceptable methods to bring about direct contact. Are current procedures successful in leading to contact in the first instance? The answer is likely to be, no. The aim for direct contact between the absent parent and the child or children fails under the current conditions.

The survey (in preparation for publication) which is at the end of this article seeks to obtain for the first time, **objective evidence** as to whether the current recommendations of Dr J. G. Sturge, Consultant Child Psychiatrist, and Dr D. Glaser, Consultant Child Psychiatrist, are valid. By valid is meant whether it leads to direct positive contact between the absent parent and the child following indirect and supervised contact as stepping stones to full contact. The hypothesis is that this does not work, due to the continuing parental alienation practised by the custodial parent. This leads the child to adopt the intractable hostility and view that no direct contact with the non custodial parent is desired. This is viewed by current experts Sturge and Glaser as a child centred approach. Decisions therefore are likely to be made on the basis of what the child wishes 'superficially'. This then is wrongly linked to 'what is in the best interests of the child'.

In relation to the refusal of a child to see a parent, Sturge and Glaser (2000) state in Family Law, 615–621:

(i)   the child must be listened to and taken seriously;

(ii) the age and understanding of the child are highly relevant;

(iii) the child, and the younger and the more dependent, either for developmental or emotional reasons, if in a positive relationship with the resident parent will inevitably be influenced by:

- that parent's views;
- their wish to maintain their sense of
  security and stability within that
  household.
(iv) Going against the child's wishes must
  involve the following.
    - Indications that there are prospects of the
      child changing their view as a result of
      preparation work or the contact itself, for
      example, there is a history of meaningful
      attachment and a good relationship;
    - the non-resident parent has child-centred
      plans as to how to help the child to
      overcome their resistance;
    - there are some indications of ambivalence
      such as an adamant statement of not
      wanting to see that parent accompanied
      by lots of positive memories and affect
      when talking of that parent.'

The validity of their view and it being acted upon
by the court has never been proven as valid, and
yet it has been recognised in the UK by Dame
Elizabeth Butler-Sloss P, Thorpe and Waller LJJ
(19 June 2000) as the way matters should be dealt
with. It is time this approach should be verified
by objective evidence.

As an expert witness attending courts, dealing
with numerous child contact and custody
disputes, I have been witness to considerable and
unwarranted injustice to one or both parents. This
is most especially the case over parental contact
with one parent who is no longer in the
relationship with the other, but has done nothing
wrong in relation to the child. This occurs when
there has been an acrimonious parting between
the previously close parents. The children are
frequently brought into the hostility. They take
sides. The side they take is based on that parent
who has total control over their mind-set.

The custodial parent who does not wish for the
child to have good contact with the absent parent
directly or indirectly (subtly) does everything
possible to discourage contact of a favourable
kind between the now absent parent and the
child. The absent parent tends to be the father
more often than the mother. I have always striven
for real justice for both fathers and mothers. At
present, neither what is 'right' or 'just' is being
done. I believe strongly that our legal system, and
its code of laws or rules, prevent either justice or
right winning the day. It is time, high time, that
there is a change of thinking and judicial action
needs to be taken in this respect. Laws need to be

changed so that **both** parents have access to
justice. The chief casualty is always the child.

My contact with the courts leave me in despair!
I have had to witness both mothers and fathers in
distress, as well as their children losing contact
with a loving parent. I have had to witness a
parent seeking good contact with their child over
months and years and not being able to achieve
this. The courts have hardly been helpful. The
custodial parent usually programmes or
brainwashes the child to reject the now absent
parent. The absence of the parent is through no
fault of their own. The term parental alienation
falls on deaf ears in Courts of Law. The term
parental alienation syndrome or PAS fares even
worse because it has not yet been recognised by
the American Psychiatric or Psychological
Association and the British Psychiatric or
Psychological Association. Hence it cannot be
used as an argument in the courts.

PAS or parental alienation syndrome are
merely symptoms that occur together that lead a
child to reject, and even despise a worthy parent.
There are eight symptoms to be considered
which will be discussed later. Everyone knows
that programming against the parent exists and
leads to the rejection of that worthy parent and
yet the courts do not accept that this occurs.
They merely believe and act upon the child
rejecting one parent. It is my view, and others,
including Tony Coe from the organisation called
Equal Parenting Council (EPC), that the practice
of turning a child against a non residential
parent is an act of hostility, not only to the
absent parent but to the child in the short and
long term. Everyone knows that a child is likely
to identify more often than not with the views of
the custodial parent in showing the same
animosity towards the now absent father or
mother, the non custodial parent. Everyone
knows that there are other symptoms of this act
of programming the child such as exaggerating
or creating frivolous criticisms of the absent
parent. Everyone knows that this is wrong and
the child's comments about the faults of the
absent parent should not be accepted or taken
seriously. The child has in such cases been used
by a vindictive parent to carry on the hostility
which existed between the adults.

Despite this, the courts will act and make
decisions based on what the child wants, or what
they 'say' they want. This superficial and wrong
decision of judges needs to be reversed. Such
decisions are based on superficial face value

thinking. These need to be reversed by looking **beneath** what the child says and wants and why the child says what they say. This is more so now that so many relationships increasingly end in a hostile manner. Are we prepared for children growing up with one parent in an inimical environment and the other parent being viewed as bad or worse? Are we not depriving them thereby of an absent but caring parent? One should remember this is against a background of no domestic violence or the physical, sexual or emotional abuse of a child.

In time, many parents, usually the father, and after years of seeking rightful contact with a child give up the battle against an unjust legal response. Dame Elizabeth Butler-Sloss P is known for upholding the law when she states that PAS cannot be used as an argument against a brainwashing parent on the one side, and the rejection of the worthy parent on the other side.

Sometimes the child will wish to have no contact whatsoever with a parent with whom that child had previously enjoyed a close and warm relationship. Sometimes, for no good reason, based on the child's alleged wishes, the court allows only supervised contact, often with the parent present who has done the alienating! This is unlikely to be the right way forward. It is likely to be a humiliating experience for the loving, yet rejected parent, who has done nothing to deserve such treatment. Despite this, the court orders that this be done because of the child's alleged wishes. Let us look at what has formed these wishes:

1. The family of the child has already been broken up once.
2. The child has already possibly witnessed and felt the animosity between their two parents.
3. The sympathy of the child already lies possibly with one parent, often the mother, whom they have seen in a state of distress because they are the resident parent, due to the alienation felt between the two parents.
4. The child therefore often blames the absent parent for all the distress caused at the time of the break up of the parent's relationship, and continues to blame the absent parent for the continuous effort they make whilst trying to gain access to them.
5. All this happens before the custodial parent has had a chance to alienate the child against the non resident parent.
6. Often the children are forced to take sides. Who do you think they will side with? Yes, it is obvious that they will choose the custodial parent who is trying to provide for them and their needs.
7. This is a good ground for the alienator in which to sow the seeds of animosity. This is where the innuendos and emotional blackmail can be scattered subtly or directly. The child may observe the pent up anger of the alienator against the absent parent, poverty is claimed by the alienator because the absent parent is not contributing to the upkeep of the child, visible emotion is expressed about contact visits with the absent parent or over telephone calls etc, and the child may be used as an ally, friend or confessor by the alienator.
8. If there is a great deal of animosity and anger from the custodial parent toward the absent parent then children are often pawns in the game with the custodial parent using them as ammunition against the absent parent.
9. What therefore is the child to think? Of course they choose to remain and side with the custodial parent. Of course they want the security of staying with the one parent of the marriage on whom they now totally depend. Who is counselling them about the situation and what they are possibly doing to the other parent? No-one. So the situation continues unabated. Therefore when they are interviewed by the CAFCASS officer what is the outcome?
10. Yes, they wish to remain with the custodial parent and to get rid of, often totally, the other parent who they see as making a nuisance of themselves against the custodial parent and causing them stress or anger.

There has to be another way of measuring or determining what is best in the child's interest despite what they say. As a court expert and clinical expert of many years I abhor many of the court's decisions, based on a false impression gained from a child that has been brainwashed. Frequently, psychologists, psychiatrists and others feel they are helpless, and therefore they do not even consider changing the view of the child, so they go along with the system and the law. These professionals readily, though sometimes reluctantly, make decisions which further sideline one parent. In my view this is but short-term thinking. It is likely to have short and long-term unfortunate consequences for the child and obviously for the rejected parent. Sometimes in later years the alienating parent also pays the price for their nefarious activities, when the child, now an adult, realises they have been used.

What is required is to re-establish the relationship between the alienated parent and the child. This is unlikely to be achieved by further separation or by limited contact between the child and the absent parent. It must be remembered, that while PAS does not as yet have legal status, it is nevertheless real. It exists in the form of a cruel rejection of a caring parent for unfounded reasons who wishes for nothing more than to help, care and guide their child, as was the case before the separation or divorce. The child or children's brainwashing must not be accepted but be reversed.

Richard Gardner cites the following as signs of alienation:

1. The child is aligned with the alienating parent in a campaign of denigration against the target parent with the child making active contribution.
2. Rationalisations for the deprecating of the target parent are often weak, frivolous or absurd.
3. Animosity towards the rejected parent lacks the ambivalence normal to human relationships.
4. The child asserts that the decision to reject the target parent is their own, also referred to as the 'independent thinker phenomenon'.
5. The child reflexively supports the parent with whom they are aligned.
6. The child expresses guiltless disregard for the feelings of the target or hated parent.

7. Borrowed scenarios are present i.e. the children's statements reflect the themes and terminology of the alienating parent.
8. Animosity is spread over the extended family and others associated with the hated parent.

Children who have thus been used by an alienator must have contact with the other parent or must be treated sensitively but firmly until this is achieved. Absence from the alienated parent does not solve the problem. Only prolonged contact can achieve the re-establishment of the former caring and loving relationship.

It is my view that the law concerning the alienation of one parent and their being sidelined by the programmer, must and will change. This is because it is both unjust and unfair. It is also extremely harmful to the child. Those in power must accept the injustice of the current situation and not allow it to continue. It is not unlike the plight of the suffragettes many years ago, who were deprived of the vote because they were of the female gender. The law stated at that time that they should not have the vote. That law was changed. Equally slavery and the employment of young children in factories and mines was done away with. The same must be the case for those parents who have been alienated. Both political and judicial changes are necessary.

In the meantime I will continue to do what I can, despite the current laws, without accepting the 'status quo' which is currently the case. The programmer will not be victorious for long but at the moment one must sadly accept that this is the case.

Dear visitor,

We invite you to participate in our worldwide survey on parental alienation.

The purpose of this survey is to make the information that has been obtained available for the judiciary, psychological and psychiatric services worldwide for the purpose of reviewing current approaches to parental alienation. The information will also be made available to the general public on my website www.parental-alienation info and will be sent to my mailing list.

Of course your input will be treated with confidentiality and we will not use your name or email address, nor that of your 'loved ones', 'loved once' or any other party involved.

Thank you for your participation and best regards,

Dr. Ludwig Lowenstein

If you would like to receive a warning when this happens, please leave your e-mail address here:

_____

A. Some questions about you

1. What is your gender? male
   female

2. What is your age? _____ years

3. In what country do you live? _____

4. What is your occupation? _____

5. What is your relation to the child? parent
   grandparent
   other relative
   other non relative

B. Some questions about the parent related to you

6. What is their gender? male
   female

7. What is their age?   years

8. In what country do they live? _____

9. What is their occupation? _____

10. What is their relation to the child? parent
    grandparent
    other relative
    other non relative

C. Some questions about the other parent

11. What is their gender? male
                              female

12. What is their age? _____ years

13. In what country do they live? _____

14. What is their occupation? _____

15. What is their relation to the child? parent
                                          grandparent
                                          other relative
                                          other non relative

16. Who is the custodial parent? Father
                                  mother
                                  other

D. Some questions about the relationship between the two parents

17. What kind of relationship did the parents have before the break up?
     married
     living together
     living apart together (i.e. each has their own household)
     friends
     other
     none

18. Has there been violence during the relationship between the parents?
     no
     yes, from the custodial parent against the non custodial parent
     yes, from the non custodial parent against the custodial parent
     yes, there has been mutual violence between the parents

19. How did the relationship end? friendly
                                   acrimoniously
                                   other

20. Please specify how your relationship ended:
     _____
     _____
     _____

21. How is the relationship at the moment? non existent
                                            friendly
                                            neutral
                                            hostile
                                            violent

E. Some questions about the children

22. How many children are involved? _____

23. How often did you see the children before the end of your relationship?
    never
    sometimes
    regularly
    often
    every day
    I nurtured my children

24. How was your relationship with the children before the separation?

    _____
    _____
    _____

25. Do you still see your children? yes
    no

26. **How** is your contact arrangement? Are you satisfied with this? How would you like it to change?

    _____
    _____
    _____

27. In what year did you see the children for the last time?
    _____ (0 for never)

F. Some questions about the quest for contact

28. Who sought access through the Courts? non custodial parent
                                          custodial parent
                                          grandparents
                                          nobody

29. How much (estimation) money did you spend on legal fees?
    less than $15,000
    $15,000–30,000
    $30,000–45,000
    more than $45,000

30. Has indirect contact been used? (Indirect contact is when you are only being allowed to telephone or send letters, cards or emails to your children). yes
    no

31. Has it led to direct contact? (Direct contact is when you see the children on your own without anyone supervising or being present at the contact unless you have asked for this presence). yes
    no

32. Has supervised contact been used? (Supervised contact is when you are only able to see the children whilst being supervised). yes

no

33. Has it led to direct contact? yes

no

Most of the questions so far have been brief ones. Eight open questions follow, which may take some time to answer but they are very important for the survey. We welcome your concerns and suggestions. Good luck.

34. What are your main concerns experienced in seeking direct contact?

_____
_____
_____

35. What criticism do you have of the legal system when one seeks direct contact?

_____
_____
_____

36. How could matters be improved?

_____
_____
_____

37. Have you achieved direct contact? yes

no, but I think I am likely to do so
no
uncertain

38. How was direct contact achieved?

_____
_____
_____

39. What caused no contact?

_____
_____
_____

40. Have you any advice to a parent regarding seeking direct contact?

_____
_____
_____

41. What suggestions do you have to improve the current situation of obtaining direct contact between children and their non custodial parent?

_____

_____

_____

Here are the final three questions:

42. What allegations have been made against you by the child?

_____

_____

_____

43. What allegations have been made against you by the other parent?

_____

_____

_____

44. In your opinion are these true or false? true

                                 some of it is true

                                 some of it is false

                                 false

45. If there is anything else you would like to share with us, please submit this below:

_____

_____

_____

Chapter Twelve

PAS: what the legal profession should know

Introduction

I have been involved in and out of the legal system with the process of PAS, and propose to answer the questions outlined, in the most simple terms. I will try to explain (PAS) to those faced with cases of marital disharmony, marriage guidance, divorce proceedings, the legal system and the evaluation of children and adults involved, and suggest how to reverse some of the tragic consequences before they reach a court of law or during the proceedings in a court of law.

Using interview to evaluate the effect of PAS

A shortened version of a hypothetical session with the child is set out below (P = psychologist; C = child):

P: Now tell me how you feel about your father?
C: I never want to see him again.
P: Why is that?
C: I don't want anything to do with him . . . he stinks and he's nasty to my mother.
P: Why, what did he do?
C: He makes our mother's life unhappy and now we don't have to do what he says.
P: How?
C: Making us come here to see you and having to go to the court.
P: Your father wants to spend time with you and loves you.
C: Well I don't love him. We are better off without him. He's trying to make trouble for Mum . . . trying to get her put in prison maybe.
P: Why do you say that?
C: Mum told us and we believe her. She is the only one who really cares about us.
P: How do you know your father doesn't care about you?
C: Why, after all he's done?
P: What has he done?
C: The way he's treated us, especially Mum.
P: Didn't you ever feel close to him or love him at all?

C: No . . . well yes, but that was a long time ago before he and Mum quarrelled and split up.

Interviews between the alienated parent and children are especially important and often indicate the extent of the programming which has taken place by the alienator against the alienated party. Again the dialogue which follows has been abbreviated to present merely the highlights of PAS and its effects (C = child; F = father):

F: You know I have always loved you. Remember the good times we had when I used to read to you and play games with you.
C: I don't remember any of that, I only remember you used to shout at mum and how you always criticised her (*note the selective memory*).
F: I'm sorry about that but I've always loved you despite that.
C: It's too late just to be sorry. We're better off without you (*note sign of brainwashing having taken place*).
F: Don't you miss me at all?
C: No! You're a horrible man. My sister hates you too.
F: Do you really mean that? What can I do now?
C: Just leave us alone. If you give us money, mum told me we can manage without you altogether (*note the request for money comes from the programmer*).
F: But I'm your father and love you and want to spend time with you.
C: Mum says you have a funny way of showing it and we don't have to obey you any more (*note again the influence of the programmer*).
F: And you believe I don't love you when I always have loved you.
C: I believe mum.
F: And you don't believe me?
C: How can I believe both of you. Mum says she will never lie to me (*again we have selective believing based on the mother's brainwashing*).

It is important to know what is happening on the basis of such interviews and avoid taking one side or the other in the parental alienation struggle. Hence the children will learn best how to resist being programmed by becoming more independent in their thinking. They also need to learn not to feel guilty about what has happened, and understand they have not produced it themselves. Some children even blame themselves for the parental battle. They should be encouraged to develop their own confidence in a future life wherein they are in control, such as in their studies, peer relationships etc. Such increased independent thinking might well reduce the efforts of one or both parents to programme against the other parent. Therapists may be able to provide all encompassing, or at least helpful, responses which the child can use when efforts of brainwashing are in progress such as:

> *I will not hear about anything bad about either you or . . . I intend to make up my own mind as to how I see things. If you want to fight with . . . don't use me as a weapon against . . . I love and need you both and I don't want to become involved in your arguments etc.*

This undoubtedly is a hard thing to achieve. These would naturally be ideal responses for the child to make towards a programming adult. Here, the child is aware of the brainwashing efforts being made and stands up to it in a critical manner against the programmer. If the child is very young and/or not sufficiently insightful or assertive, such responses will be unlikely. The child may be too influenced by the programmer due to age and pacificity and will fail to evaluate the motives and techniques employed. A psychologist, once involved, should encourage understanding as to why and how the programming occurs, and communicate this to the child.

Often PAS occurs in the absence of contact or very much reduced contact with the alienated parent. The child is therefore overwhelmed by 'one side of the story'. Re-education by the therapist sometimes helps and of course the increasing of contact with the other party is vital. Sadly, sometimes the brainwashing has been so overwhelmingly effective, that nothing further can be achieved to reduce the impact of the brainwasher. The child has been so thoroughly turned against the other parent that only legal action by the embittered alienated parent has any chance at all. Unfortunately by this time, the children are often older and having failed to receive support from the other parent, becomes totally and habitually inflexible as a product

of the indoctrination process from the programmer.

If it has not gone this far, the evaluator or psychologist when speaking to the child must do so in a very sensitive manner, to both establish and maintain a good rapport with questions such as the following being asked:

> *Tell me something about both of your parents and their good qualities.*
>
> *Tell me how you heard about . . .*
>
> *Tell me how you know about this . . .*
>
> *What makes you think . . . ?*
>
> *Could there be any other explanation for . . . ?*
>
> *Is there anything you and I could do to make you feel different about the parent you now dislike?*
>
> *What would you like to see happen now and why?*

When interviewing the brainwasher, efforts must be made to show them up, despite the fact that they may already know the following:

> *Are you feeling vengeful against . . . ?*
>
> *Do you think that what you do is the best way of handling the situation?*
>
> *How will your child benefit from what you are doing now and in the future?*
>
> *Do you want your child to come through this process without suffering . . . ?*
>
> *What could be done to improve the situation?*
>
> *Do you think your accusations against . . . are totally correct?*
>
> *Please tell me why you feel as you do . . . what are your goals?*
>
> *Do you want me to help you and your child in this matter?*
>
> *Would you do what you can for the benefit of your child now and in the future?*

If the answer is yes, the programmer may be open to suggestions of a more rational nature and this could be beneficial to reverse the process of negative programming. Great care must be taken by the deprogrammer to appear to be as 'neutral' as possible, while at the same time reducing the effects of the unhealthy and destructive effects of brainwashing which have been carried out.

What does research say about PAS in the UK?

There is a considerable amount of research in the US on PAS, as published by Gardner and by Clawar and Rivlin (*Child Held Hostage*, 1998) a book previously mentioned. There has, however, been very limited research in the UK. As already mentioned about 75 per cent of cases of PAS indicate the mother to be the alienator with about a quarter being the father.

Table 1 shows both the sex and the severity of the alienation derived from a study of 60 consecutive referrals involving alienation of some kind by one of the partners.

Table 12.1 Severity of alienation by sex

	Male alienators	Female alienators
Mild	11	8
Moderate	5	19
Severe	1	16
Total	17	43

In the case of mild, we refer to occasional negative comments made by one partner or another. Moderate refers to disparaging remarks made at least 2–3 times per week. In the case of severe, we refer to daily, or more negative, comments about the alienated parent to children.

Table 2 refers to the kind of negative or disparaging statements made. In most cases there is a reference to more than one descriptive phrase (1–6) as to why the alienated partner is disparaged to the children. Hence, for example, 9 women stated that the male failed to provide financially. The males only state 3.

Table 12.2 Specific reasons given to children by alienating parent, by sex

	Against male	Against female
Failure to provide financially	9	3
Lacking in love or aggressive and lack of care	12	13
Disloyal and unfaithful	11	12
Drug or alcohol abuser	8	7
Immoral or mentally unstable	19	22
Accusations of physical abuse incest or sexual abuse	14	1

Table 3 indicates the variety of reactions of children to the alienating process being waged by a parent. It will be noted from Table 3 that virtually all the children suffered one way or another including gender identity problems from the alienating process. Some became psychologically disturbed by withdrawing into themselves. Others showed behavioural symptoms such as aggression, lowered school attendance and performance. There are also the long-term effects of failure to realise educational-vocational potential. Finally, although the data is incomplete, there is evidence that some youngsters eventually turned against the instigator of the alienation process. This could well be a warning to those who alienate by programming or brainwashing children against another parent!

Table 12.3 Types and frequency of reaction of child to alienation

Type	Frequency
Confusion: this includes frustration and not knowing what to believe	57
Becoming alienated towards one parent	53
Later failing to develop educationally, vocationally their potential	45
Becoming withdrawn and depressed, having sleep disorders, regressing, developing suicidal ideation, obsessive compulsive behaviour, enuresis, anxiety, daydreaming, psychosomatic disorders etc.	41
Turning elsewhere for stability to grandparents peers, etc.	38
Problems with sexual identity	37
Becoming a behaviour problem with lack of impulse control with siblings and in school	37
Lack of school attendance and deterioration in school performance	36
Later turning against alienator and the process of alienation	11
Partly ignoring alienation process i.e. becoming more independent	4

Conclusions and recommendations

1. The legal profession, and most importantly the courts, must be aware of the insidious influence of PAS, how it functions and what should be done to counteract it.
2. Having understood that PAS is unfair, unjust and detrimental to the present and future of

brainwashed children, appropriate action should be taken by the courts.

3. The court, in conjunction with an experienced expert witness in PAS, who ideally should be appointed by the court rather than by one of the solicitors on one side or the other, should be empowered to take steps to reduce the impact of PAS.

4. All evidence indicates that children who have contact with both stable parents, even if they are separated, are better adjusted now and in the future than those who are alienated from one of their parents due to the effects of PAS.

5. It is the role of the expert witness to help the child to understand the way PAS works and to encourage the child not to be influenced by it or to become embroiled in it. Loyalty and love to both parents is the order of the day. This will benefit the child in the short term and even more in the longer term.

6. There are both short and long term effects of PAS. This includes poorer adjustment in future years to a partner in another relationship, due to identification and identity problems including one's own sexuality. Children who have been subjected to programming are more likely themselves to practise this kind of behaviour when they become adults and embroiled in marital difficulties. The process of alienation becomes perpetuated.

Recent research into parental alienation syndrome (PAS)

Until the 1980s there was minimal research on the subject of PAS. One of the earliest to consider it was Palmer (1988) who addressed the legal remedies to the parental alienation syndrome in the context of divorce proceedings.

Plumb and Lindley (1990) suggest that PAS occurs when parents cannot settle or will not settle the matter of their children's wellbeing on their own. It becomes of paramount importance that they are given the opportunity, with the aid of appropriately ethical and impartial professionals, to settle the matter of their children's' welfare. In this way such professionals can dramatically reduce the psychological and psychophysiological damage typically resultant of adversarial litigation. Once, under current law, the parents have experienced the painstaking Family's Team evaluation process recommended

in this book, they need not remain passive in deciding custody for themselves. The Family's Team approach has the advantage of providing substantial data and recommendations to the court in its decision making. The book by Plumb and Lindley, *Humanising Child Custody Disputes: The Family's Team*, is written for parents who wish to become more informed as to the criteria and method for objective child custody and visitation recommendations. However, this present book is useful for legislators who, after considering the ideas, methods, and rationale contained therein, should recognise that custody matters are not best dealt with in adversarial courts where the participants are often mis- and uninformed victims of not only their own pain and vindictiveness, but also victims of the court's unpremeditated insistence that there be winners and loser. This book offers a more humane and efficient process for future dispositions of custody or visitation litigation.

Guidelines for using mediation with abusive couples were constructed by Geffner (1992) who focused on techniques and issues concerning couples during and after separation or divorce. A questionnaire was presented to identify abusive relationships. It was important that the wife and children were safe during mediation, since research showed that more batterers murdered their wives during the period when divorce was imminent. Since the balance of power was unequal in the relationship, mediation had to be modified so that the situation became neutral. Issues facing mediators in these cases also involved living arrangements, conversion changes in children, financial support, joint custody and parent alienation problems.

Efforts were made to expand the parameters of PAS by Cartwright (1993). He suggested, through new evidence, that PAS was provoked by other than custodial matters, that cases of alleged sexual abuse were often hinted at and the slow judgement by courts exacerbated the problem of prolonged alienation of the child. This could trigger a number of mental illnesses. The author also suggested that too little is as yet known of the long-term consequences to alienated children and their families.

A number of reviews were carried out in assessing current assessment methods used in child custody litigation and mediation. Hysjulien et al. (1994) used psychological tests, semi-structured interviews and behavioural observations of parents and children. The related issues of child abuse, sexual abuses, domestic violence and PAS were discussed. There was little empirical evidence to support the efficacy of methods typically used by professionals in making recommendations to the court.

Of foremost interest is the work of Richard Gardner (1992; 1998) in his book *Parental Alienation Syndrome*. In addition to the book, there have been Addendums (in November 1996 and September 1997) providing recommendations for dealing with PAS. Gardner divides PAS into three categories depending on the severity: mild, moderate and severe. He has provided legal approaches as well as psychotherapeutic approaches to deal with each in turn. He considers the primary symptomatic manifestations to be:

1. A campaign of denigration.
2. Weak, frivolous or observed rationalisation for the deprivation.
3. Lack of ambivalence.
4. The independent thinker phenomenon.
5. Reflective support of the loved parent on the parent control.
6. Absence of guilt.
7. Borrowed scenarios.
8. Spread of animosity to the extended family of the hated parent.

Detail on interviewing techniques as well as treatment approaches was suggested by Gardner. Some of these may seem severe and yet no one has provided a more comprehensive and realistic approach.

The work of Clawar and Rivlin (1991) in their book, *Children Held Hostage*, provides considerable information on the symptoms of PAS and what needs to be done to correct these problems. The book is outstanding in providing meaningful and useful techniques and is part of the section of 'Family Law' by the American Bar Association.

Turkat (1994) described the problem of child visitation interference; acute interference PAS, and divorce related malicious mother syndrome. He considered the associated difficulties in handling this problem in the legal system.

An experience with conducting child custody evaluation was explored by Stahl (1994). He explored the professional issues and techniques involved in child custody evaluations. Domestic violence, drug and alcohol abuse, supervised contacts, mental illness, parental alienation

syndrome, relocation of one or both parents, and the need for ongoing updated evaluations were considered. The book was intended for evaluators and other mental health professionals, solicitors and judges.

Sixteen selected cases formed the basis of an article by Dunne and Hedrick (1994). Their analysis of 16 divorcing families in which one or more of the children aged 0–24 years had rejected one of the parents was termed parent alienation syndrome. The cases were taken from the caseloads of clinicians working with the families. The cases met the majority of Gardner's criteria, including an obsessive hatred of the alienated parent on the basis of trivial and unsubstantiated accusations and complete support for the alienating parent. Although the cases showed a wide diversity of characteristics, Gardner's criteria were useful in differentiating these cases from other post divorce difficulties. PAS appeared to be primarily a function of the pathology of the alienating parent and that parent's relationship with the children. PAS did not signify dysfunction in the alienated parent or in the relationship between that parent and child.

Mapes (1995) studied child eye witness testimony in sexual abuse investigations. This book was written for psychologists, social workers, guidance counsellors, child welfare workers, physicians law enforcement personnel and solicitors, to whom a child may have disclosed allegations of sexual abuse, or those who may be responsible for the investigation of children's allegations. Current research and thinking on such topics as symptomatology, psychotherapy, repressed memories, Dissociative Identity Disorders, hypnosis, cults, the Parent Alienation Syndrome, and the non-leading-leading continuum of investigative techniques was presented. The reader was introduced to the sexual abuse investigative process and discussions of practical issues, such as the use of anatomically detailed dolls, where interviews should be conducted, the use of medical evaluations and psychological testing. A step-by-step process for assessing credibility and validity was explained following a four step decision making process.

A therapist's view of PAS was carried out by Lund (1995). She explored the different reasons why a child might reject one parent in a divorced family and the ways of helping such families. Cases in which a child resisted contact with a parent were not always, but quite often, linked to

PAS. The reasons for parental rejection were mainly due to the following:

1. Developmentally normal separation problems.
2. Deficits in the non custodial parent's skills.
3. Appositional behaviour.
4. High conflict divorced families.
5. Serious problems, not necessarily abuse.
6. Child abuse.

Lund considered Gardner's recommendations of legal and therapeutic interventions based on whether the case was assessed to be one of mild, moderate or extreme parental alienation. Success in the treatment of PAS cases had to be defined as the maintenance or removal of some contact between parent and child.

Rand (1997) considered the spectrum of PAS in two articles published in 1997. He reviewed Gardner's work and concluded that PAS was a distinctive family response to divorce in which the child becomes aligned with one parent and preoccupied with unjustified or exaggerated denigration of the other target parent. In severe cases, the child's once love bonded relationship with the rejected/target parent was destroyed. Testimony on PAS in legal proceedings sparked debate. Closely associated were high conflict divorce and the involvement of the legal system.

Finally, Johnston and Roseby (1997) concentrated on a developmental approach to understanding and helping children of violent, disputed divorce. They examined the immediate and long-term effects of high conflict divorce on children and especially traced the development of problems affecting very young children, through adolescence, with special attention to the impact of family violence and the dynamics of PAS. They described the clinical interventions that had proven to be most effective in their work with individual families and groups along with principles for custody decisions making and service programmes in the courts and communities that helped manage the conflict.

Medico-Legal Journal, 1999, 66: 4, 151–61

Chapter Thirteen

Family courts: where have courageous and just judges gone?

Judges vary in their capacity to be hard (strong) and compassionate (softer). The latter type often tend to administer lighter sentences for the same or similar offences compared with harsher sentences by less compassionate judges. Hence advocates will often ask who they are facing when defending or prosecuting. All this indicates that the administration of justice can be highly subjective. Barristers as well as alleged offenders are clearly aware of this difference between the judges they may face.

Judges are influenced by many elements before them in the court including evidence, witnesses, the appearance of the alleged offender, and the manner in which matters are communicated in connection with the alleged offender. Justice may therefore be dependent on many different criteria. It is accepted that the legal system is imperfect, but on the whole 'as good as it can be'. Life is after all also imperfect as well as frequently unfair. The courts of law are merely a reflection of this.

Many judges are also aware of how they will be regarded by society, and the mass media, in the verdicts they produce. It is this area that concerns me most as a practicing forensic psychologist who often works within the family court system. I, as all who are concerned with seeking justice for those facing the traditional system feel there is room for improvement. I feel there is a need for robust and also compassionate sentencing and verdicts depending on the situation. This difference of dealing with cases can never be obviated.

Family courts differ from criminal courts in that decisions are required about those who have not committed criminal acts in most cases. They instead deal with serious controversies between former close partners in a relationship who are now in a state of acrimony if not 'war' which often affects children. Children are in the middle of their parent's powerful acrimony towards one another. My role and experience with this type of situation has been as an expert witness appointed either by one side in the conflict or by the court as a single joint expert to try to sort matters out and advise the court on what can be recommended, in

order to proceed in a way that is fair to all parties. Unfortunately, children become involved when parents are in conflict and the situation is usually that alienation has been practiced against the non custodial parent which tends to be the father. Fathers and sometimes mothers (who are not the custodial parent) seek regular harmonious contact with their children. This can cause difficulties and the non custodial parent seeks redress through the courts. However, this does not always happen in a fair and just way.

Opposition to contact often occurs as a result of a desire for revenge by the custodial parent for having been rejected, or displaced. Hence the conflict between the former partners is ongoing after the relationship has ended. My own position, which I consider to be independent, encourages both parents to play a part in the lives of their children whenever possible. There are exceptions to this when either mother or father are a danger to children. It is essential that children be protected from physical, sexual and emotional abuse. That is a priority.

Unfortunately false allegations are often made against one parent or another primarily to deny them access to a child. The most vicious and unjust allegation is the allegation of sexual abuse when it has not in fact ever occurred. This is primarily directed by mothers towards fathers although I have had such false allegations also made against mothers.

Once such serious allegations have been refuted, the embittered alienator will seek other unjustified ways to discredit the fitness of one parent in order to deny them contact or provide them with limited contact. The next step is to alienate the children against an innocent, loving parent who is unable to reverse the programming of brainwashing being systematically conducted openly or subtly. This influences children adversely. It occurs despite the fact that these children have often experienced love and care from the now disparaged parent.

In time the children believe what they have been told about the alienated parent and behave in a rejecting manner. This is of course satisfying to the alienator who will tend to deny that they have done anything to bring the situation about. The result is that such children identify totally with the alienator. When courts and judges are involved, they are faced with the consequences of alienation. Now the children claim that they want no further contact or rare contact with the absent parent.

Judges and minions of the court process are influenced by the 'child's decision' to no longer be engaged with the sidelined parent. What judges are hearing actually is the voice of the alienator who has won over the mind of the child. That is often the end of the matter for some judges. Others agree to a process of mediation in an attempt to get the child round to having some contact with the absent parent, usually the father. If this is ineffective, which it often is, then judges claim that on the whole that they can do nothing more but to follow the views of the child. The views of a child are unlikely to have changed due to the fact that the process of alienation is ongoing and continues even during the mediation process against the non custodial parent.

It is unfortunate that judges frequently do not take this fact into consideration. Judges tend to make some 'status quo decision' of no contact or supervised contact for the absent parent who deserves better than this. This is normally a humiliation to the caring and loving parent, who previously to the vicious alienating process, had a warm and loving relationship with the child.

Most of the victims are fathers, and of course the child and children involved. It is therefore not surprising that some militant type organisations such as 'Justice for Fathers' have developed. They have, in often unorthodox ways, attempted to influence the legal and political system which limits their involvement with their own children. Other fathers opt out sooner or later in seeking any further contact via the courts that have essentially made unjust decisions. The traditional system, it would seem, has accommodated the perpetrator of alienation and been punitive against the victim of the process of alienation. One must ask oneself is that the justice we should expect from the judicial system?

What the judiciary should do when alienation leads to implacable hostility

It has often been said, by many, that it is easier to criticise than to find just and fair solutions in cases of parental conflicts affecting children. It is this very thing I should like to do now. It must be accepted that most alienators are mothers. From time to time I have also encountered fathers who are the programmers against mothers. This, however, is comparatively rare. There is a long tradition of judges being more sympathetic toward mothers than fathers in parental alienation type conflicts. This is often denied by judges who claim their main concern is only the child.

Mothers, on the whole, gain custody of a child. Most do not alienate children against the father. This is for the benefit of all concerned; most especially the child. The child thereby recognises and in time accepts that mummy and daddy no longer live together or love one another, but, both parents love and care and are devoted to the child they have created. In these situations both parents support the other parent in the eyes of the child. This unfortunately does not occur in the case of the process of alienation.

In the case where alienation is practiced, it is usually the mother who carries out this highly damaging activity but it does not matter who alienates. Whoever carries out this activity is wrong, and it should be determined that they are wrong by the court! Judges should not be influenced by the sex of the parent who alienates the child against the other parent. They should not be influenced by the parent who has custody since it is most always given to the mother. They should not be only influenced by what a child says, but why a child says what it does.

It should be understood that whoever programmes the child against the other parent, is abusing the child emotionally and is abusing their position by the fact that they have custody and are taking advantage of this to brainwash the child. Hence when the child states that they do not want anything to do with a parent with whom they previously enjoyed a warm and loving relationship, the court must realise from where the rejection of one parent originates. It is usually the mother that carries out the process of alienation. The mother then claims that it is the child who has made the decision to seek little or no contact with their father. This, unfortunately, is more often or not believed by the court. Such errors of judgement need to be rectified and rectified as soon as possible.

The court must act against the parent who is in the wrong. This, in most cases, is the mother. She must be made aware that a child is not only hers to mould as she sees fit against the father. She must be made aware that if the child does not have regular contact with the father then she will certainly lose custody of the child because she is responsible for the child making such a decision. The child will then be placed with the father or a member of the father's family. Such a threat often suffices for some mothers at least to see sense, and some will then encourage the child to have a relationship with the father. The others who fail to accept the decision should feel the full force of the law by losing custody of the child.

Judges are loath to act in this way. Perhaps they do not see the injustice they are perpetuating? Perhaps they are concerned with how society or the media would view such a decision? Perhaps they consider, wrongly, that it is in the best interest of the child to have the security of being with the mother and the side lining of the father is therefore acceptable? Taking the easy way out is not justice, it is not fair and it is not good for the child!

Alienating parents should not be allowed to be in opposition to seek justice. This should be done whatever the sex of the alienator. Father and mothers both deserve justice and fair play and most of all, the child deserves this. The answer also doesn't rest in the prolonged legal actions that usually follow. Once it has been established by a qualified psychologist that there has been alienation by one parent against the other, a report by that professional, who has investigated the matter thoroughly, should lead to action and it should be the action indicated by the findings of the psychologist. This would reduce some of the current activities of fathers in the effort to seek justice.

The judiciary would also, in time, be viewed as showing the courage of their convictions. There will be no further need for articles such as the present one asking the question: 'Where have courageous and just judges gone?'

Recent changes in the PAS approach by the judiciary

There have recently been some remarkable cases that have highlighted the importance of judging parental alienation in the courts. Judges are becoming bolder in insisting that all things being equal, both parents have the right to contact with their children. The exceptions are, of course, when one or both parents have proclivities towards violence or paedophilia, to name but a few negative features which must be considered.

The case of *Cox v Cox* (1990) in Family Law, was one of the first to impose the sentencing and imprisonment of parents who refused access to fathers for contact with the child. This was done by a highly courageous judge, who truly believed in 'justice for all', even though there was considerable embarrassment in having to put a mother into prison. This was despite the likelihood of also being castigated by the press for sending the mother into a prison cell. What is often not mentioned are the efforts made beforehand to gain the assent of the obdurate parent for such contact before such an action is taken and by threatening less stringent means than imprisonment. In most cases of lack of co-operation of a parent regarding contact rights, it is the mothers refusing fathers. Sometimes, following an acrimonious separation or divorce, the alienating parent, who is usually the mother, will claim there to be serious causes for concern about the father, such as being excessively punitive, permissive, being a substance abuser, and even being a paedophile. In most cases such allegations are unfounded.

In cases such as this fathers are often considered guilty by allegation alone and need to prove their innocence rather than the alienator having to prove the guilt of the alienated father! It appears therefore, in cases of PAS, justice often seems to stand on its head, rather than the head being used to achieve justice and equality for all!

Judges are naturally averse to imprisoning mothers for failing to honour the contact arrangements with fathers. This is because mothers usually are responsible for the day to day care of the children. As already mentioned, judges are not unaware also of the adverse publicity which follows imprisoning a mother in cases such as this kind.

There are alternatives, however, that could have been used, but they often fail to achieve what is desired with the alienating parent, that is, to comply with offers of mediation such as recommended by one psychologist (Lowenstein, 1999a–d). By having the threat of punishment, including the possibility of imprisonment hanging over the head of an uncooperative parent, like the sword of Damocles, there is a possibility that such mothers can be brought to the 'negotiating table'. Mothers and fathers who alienate children, much as anyone else, must stand before the law as either innocent or guilty of such an offence. Failing to adhere to the judgement of a court must be considered as breaking the law, with threatened punishment following.

Parents who thus fail to observe their legal responsibility to co-operate, are likely to suffer from severe and often unfounded hostility towards the other parent. Such hostility can, and often does, reach pathological proportions. The possible solutions are:

1. In extreme cases imprisonment must be threatened, until the parent is willing to co-operate with the law.
2. Accepting some form of mediation and treatment by a qualified psychologist over a prescribed period, normally two weeks to a month, in order to resolve the impasse.

3. Failure by the alienating parent to co-operate must lead to punishment including imprisonment as a final alternative only. It could also result in the alienated parent being given custody of the children temporarily or permanently.

Most alienating parents would and should learn to co-operate under such strictures and resolve the matter of parental alienation syndrome. It is hoped that future legal procedures will find it easier to deal with such cases and follow the courageous footsteps of earlier pioneering judges. These judges were not deflected from doing the just and right thing, despite the criticism from individuals and the mass media.

Part Three
Treating PAS

Chapter Fourteen

Introduction: treating families in turmoil

Mr and Mrs X had been married for 14 years. They were strict Catholics. Despite this however, they were divorced as each accused the other of being unfaithful. Mr X also accused his wife of not keeping the house tidy. He had always said, however, that she was a good mother. She, in her turn, accused her husband of being bad-tempered, especially in relation to the children and sometimes being 'physical' with them.

Mr X had, for six years, attempted through the courts to gain contact with his four children. Such contact had been denied by the mother, rather than the courts. The court appointed the present psychologist on the recommendation of the judge. The judge had read some of the articles written by the psychologist on mediation involving families in conflict.

Mrs X and her four children, aged six, eight, ten and twelve, were adamant in not wishing to have any contact with the father. The reasons given by all, who seemed to be in total agreement, were that:

1. Father had a bad temper.
2. He sometimes smacked them when they were naughty.
3. He did not give them much of his time when they had been with him after the parents separated.
4. He failed to provide financially for them after the divorce when contact had been denied, according to the mother.

Mrs X, when first interviewed by the psychologist, stated that she had always encouraged the children to be with their natural father. It was the children who refused to see him for the reasons already mentioned. 'What could I do? Should I force the children to be with their father against their wishes?' She had, in the meantime, developed a relationship with a partner, who the children, after six years, regarded as 'their father'.

At this point it was explained to the mother, after accepting her version of events, that considerable harm could result to the children, if they failed to have some kind of relationship with their natural parent. When she requested to know what harm could occur, the psychologist told her in some detail and gave her one of his articles on this subject, which involved dealing with children who had been alienated and who suffered as a consequence now and in the future. Finally, the remainder of the session sought to establish a good relationship with her and, through her, with the children. She was encouraged to do all she could to get the children to have some kind of contact with their father, but only after the psychologist had counselled the father on how he should behave towards the children. The meeting went extremely well, both by showing warmth and using understanding and humour to break down some of Mrs X's defensiveness and antipathy towards her former spouse. She also indicated that she was tired of, time after time, having to appear in court.

Additionally, she complied in taking two personality tests; one an objective test, the Eysenck Personality Inventory, and the other a projective technique, the Rorschach Test. The psychologist promised to let her know the result of these tests in due course. She became increasingly co-operative, especially when it was indicated by the psychologist that he did not anticipate at this time recommending unsupervised contact with the children by their father. Perhaps three to six months afterwards this may be considered, but not at the present time. This reassured the mother considerably. She was also informed that as a result of such contact, which was initially supervised, he would need to agree to provide some funding for her to deal with her children.

The next step was to see the children. It was vital to establish a good relationship with them as quickly as possible and also to depend to some degree on the mother talking to the children about co-operating. The children were then interviewed individually to ascertain their feelings in relation to possible contact with their father after so many years. They were not at all well disposed to any contact initially with their father. They were encouraged to say why they felt that way. They were also provided with an objective personality test, the Junior version of the Eysenck Personality Inventory, and a projective personality test. The projective test consisted of them drawing a picture of themselves and their family doing something. This established their position in the family, their relationship with their mother and their step-father. As was expected, the children drew a picture of their mother and partner and then labelled the male in the group, their 'dad'. They also indicated verbally that they now regarded the partner as their 'father'. The man played a fairly passive role, according to the children. He never disciplined them. He very wisely left that to the mother. The children saw this father as a 'kind' person. In direct contrast, they viewed their natural father (from their memory of him) as strict, with a bad temper.

Each child, following several short meetings on the same day, was encouraged by the psychologist, as well as by the mother, to regard the natural father as deserving of another chance for contact. They ultimately accepted that they would co-operate with supervised contact. Later it was decided that such supervised contact would occur on alternate Sundays. It was also to be carried out during the afternoon under the supervision of the catholic priest of the church where they attended.

The personality testing was important to ascertain the mental and psychological state of the children at the present time. Prior to making any decision, the father had been interviewed and counselled on three occasions during the day for short periods. He was also submitted to the objective and projective personality testing, identical to his ex-wife. The result of this testing was duly explained to him. He was made aware of his problems and also why his children wished to avoid having contact with him and how this could be reversed by changes in his own attitude and behaviour towards them.

The full facts of why the children no longer desired contact with him had a most salutary effect on him. At first he denied that he was or had been overly strict with them, but gradually accepted this. He, however, took notice of what would be required of him should he wish the supervised contact to work and to lead eventually to all he desired, i.e. unsupervised contact and the children being able to visit his own parents.

The final session was between the psychologist and the couple 'in conflict'. This could only be carried out after the initial sessions had led to an agreement between them on certain issues. This agreement was written down for each individual. One agreement was then put forward to them, to make certain that they both agreed once again with the arrangements which would lead to unsupervised contact. They were then asked to sign the statement. Mother even agreed to let father write down the actual agreement, obviously checking it afterwards to see it was correct.

There was a need for silence from time to time, when one or other of the parties brought up past grievances. It was then emphasised, and they agreed, to consider only those aspects which could be viewed at present and in the future, and which ultimately would improve their relationship regarding the children. The firm handling of this final interview showed each party what they had to gain by sitting down together and agreeing on areas of financial and emotional support for the children and both parents being involved in the parenting role.

The case went forward with a full report and the judge made orders based on the agreement which had been reached between the adult parties and also involving the children. Further progress was contemplated, including eventually unsupervised contact if all worked well with the supervised contact.

The initial success achieved may be attributable to three important aspects working together:

1. The role of the psychologist in leading the adults and the children towards co-operating with each other.
2. The 'court weariness' experienced by both parties.
3. The pressure of the court eventually backing the mediation process of the psychologist.

Summary of similar cases

A summary of cases which involved mediation, where there had been no contact between the parents and the children for six months to six years was carried out involving 24 males seeking contact and nine females seeking such contact. The table which now follows summarises the result which followed the process of mediation previously analysed through the case study.

Table 14.1   Number of cases assessed and treated and their outcome (initial)

	Indirect contact	Supervised contact	Contact unsupervised	No contact
Fathers (24)	6	9	5	4
Mothers (9)	3	1	2	3

Table 14.2   Type of contact – results following mediation

	Led to indirect contact	Supervised contact	Contact unsupervised	No contact
Fathers (24)	2	11	7	4
Mothers (9)	1	2	3	3

Explanation of tables

Although the result of the mediation is not perfect, it must be noted that no contact whatsoever had been accepted or achieved by the non-custodial parent, despite numerous appearances in court before the intervention of the mediator. In the case where no contact was achieved (in seven cases) between parents and children, this was due to the inaction of the courts in failing to deal effectively with the non-co-operating custodial parent.

It may be noted that the figures in Table 2 showed the changes from indirect contact to supervised and unsupervised contact. Hence, among fathers there was eventually a shift from six who had indirect contact to two; with supervised contact increasing from nine to 11. This again was due to mediation procedures.

Unsupervised contact was eventually increased from five to seven in the case of fathers. In the case of mothers, the number with indirect contact was reduced from three to one. The others had supervised contact. Mothers also had more unsupervised contact with their child/children after a period of time, this being from two mothers having unsupervised contact to three. Unfortunately, no changes could be achieved in the no contact group where, in four cases, fathers never had any contact with their children and equally so for mothers, as already stated, due to the failure of the court to ensure that the custodial parent co-operated with the mediator.

Justice of the Peace, June 8th 2002, 166: 23, 4442–224

Chapter Fifteen

How can one overturn PAS?

How can one overturn the programming of a child against the parent?

The ingredients necessary for the therapist to have are: determination, resilience, frustration, resourcefulness and single mindedness. This is the only way that parental alienation can be reversed.

Few expert witnesses, be they psychiatrists or psychologists, take on cases such as parental alienation. This is because the methods which often need to be employed for overturning a child's animosity towards an alienated parent are strewn with dangers! It provides a minefield of visible and hidden dangers to the therapist to deal with such problems.

The chief dangers are the child and the alienator, who are opposed to the efforts of the therapist and will do almost anything and everything to sabotage these efforts. They attend mediation sessions and assessment sessions merely because it has been ordered by the court. They will go so far as to discredit the expert and the manner in which he works as he seeks to change the thinking and behaviour of the alienated child. Whatever happens, one side or the other will be critical of the therapist. Behind the main antagonists, and opposed to the efforts of the parental alienation therapist, are legions of family members on the alienators side, solicitors, even Guardians ad Litem who are frequently very child-centred. The court itself may also believe totally what the child has to say about the alienated parent.

The court and the thinking of others is likely to be as follows: 'Why would a child say such things about her father or mother if it were not true?' In this of course they are totally wrong in their thinking, unless such views can be confirmed by other, truly independent sources. The therapist is in the middle, attempting to discover three important aspects:

1. Are the allegations of abuse about a parent true, false or exaggerated?

2. If untrue, and only if untrue, can the thinking and behaviour of the alienated child be reversed? The alienator is unlikely to change in their views towards the programmed parent. Hence work with the alienator is not likely to bear much success as many have found.

3. If the allegations against the alienated parent are true, such as when sexual, emotional or physical abuse has occurred, then the expert witness therapist should not be involved further, except under very specific circumstances.

Before commencing on how the present psychologist works and seeks to overturn the true effect of parental alienation we must consider the following:

• Why does the 'programmer' carry out the process of alienation?
• What are the psychological aspects involved in knowing that parental alienation has been carried out by the 'programmer' and what are its effects on the child?
• What therapy can be used to overcome the effects of parental alienation?
• How can rational emotive responses and methods be used to combat parental alienation?
• A case illustration

Why does the 'programmer' carry out the process of alienation?

Sometimes, a parent who instigates accusations against another parent, for example accusing the alienated parent as having abused a child sexually, physically or emotionally, are correct in this declaration. However, more often than not, such accusations or allegations are wrong. Their allegations are frequently based on hostility towards a former partner. This can lead to one of two pathological reactions:

1. The accuser believes what they are alleging to be correct. That is, they are deluded in their thinking or dangerously paranoid.
2. The accuser does not believe in the accusations that they are making but makes them nevertheless out of conscious hostility and the seeking for vengeance against a former partner.

In both cases, acrimony and hostility are the basis for such false accusations. There is even a middle position between these two extremes. Let me illustrate this by an actual conversation I have had with an alienating mother who could be said to be 'stretching the truth' of 'insinuating the worst scenario':

Dr. L: So you think your daughter does not want to be with her father because he once made her go to bed with him?

Mother: Yes, I don't think a father should ask a daughter to come into bed with him, not at the age of 10.

Dr. L: What do you think happened when the daughter got into bed with her father?

Mother: I really don't know, but I don't think.Do you think it is appropriate?

Dr. L: I'm asking you what you think about it. Never mind what I think about it. If you really do want to know, I don't think or see anything personally wrong with a child getting into bed with her father as indeed with her mother, providing they are having a cuddle and nothing more.

Mother: Well I think it is totally wrong especially if the child does not want this.

Dr. L: I do agree that if the child does not want to be in bed with her father he should not insist on it. You obviously believe the child did not want this and father did want her to get into bed with him.

Mother: Yes, and I don't think it's right, and goodness knows what could have happened or perhaps did happen.

Dr. L: You think perhaps she was sexually abused in some way by being touched?

Mother: I don't know but I wouldn't put it past him. Even if it didn't happen it could have happened.

Dr. L: So you think your former partner might be a sexual abuser of his daughter?

Mother: I wouldn't go so far as that. I don't really think he would do that, but you never can tell.

As one may note no precise accusations have been made but 'insinuations' are often sufficient for a claim of this kind to stick and the need for further investigations to be carried out in relation to it. It is often the accused who will need to prove their innocence, instead of someone needing to prove his guilt.

Paranoid ideations are infectious. A deluded parent, or one filled consciously with hate for the former partner, can lead to an effort by that parent (the alienator) to control a child totally and to inculcate certain ideas that the former partner and parent is somehow dangerous to the child. This could lead to the next development which is that the alienated parent may eventually be considered repulsive and worthy of denigration and rejection. Children will often act out this hatred for a parent, especially when the 'programmer' (the alienator) is present. The child will seek to please that parent by taking on, or accepting the views of the alienating parent.

Paranoid ideation is illustrated when the child states that the father or mother have somehow, in general terms, done the wrong things, or been evil or lied etc. Here the child is 'parroting' what the mother or father has said about the alienated parent. This is because the child has identified with the alienator and custodial parent, and the alienated parent eventually becomes the 'scapegoat' for all and any wrongs ever perpetrated against the alienator and 'ipso facto' those wrongs which the child feels has been done to them. This is in contrast with the programming parent who is idealised by the child as being both 'all good' as well as 'all powerful'.

This occurs because a child feels, having lost one parent due to the acrimony of separation and brainwashing, that there is a danger of losing the other parent as well. This fear is of a traumatic nature, leading to deep insecurity. The alienator senses this insecurity and works on the child, making it clear that 'I am all you have now. Forget about your father/mother. They are no longer to be relied on.'

What are the psychological aspects involved in knowing that parental alienation has been carried out by the 'programmer' and what are its effects on the child?

There are a number of ways in which psychological aspects come into play in the alienation process. Among the methods which will be discussed are: reaction formation, identifying with the aggressor and the strong person i.e. the custodial parent, identifying with an assumed ideal or perfect parent, a way of releasing hostility, and the child identifying with the power of the alienator.

The reaction formation

When deep love formerly felt for a parent is turned to hatred for purposes of disguising that love, this is not true rejection. True rejection is being indifferent to the parent, not hating that parent. Where there is hate there has been love and love can be rekindled. Alienated children do not so much love the alienator but fear losing the alienator by showing affection towards the alienated parent.

Identifying with the aggressor

Here the child backs the more powerful parent, the one who has custody of the child, and the one who is likely to be present more often than the alienated parent. The weak or alienated parent has been sidelined totally or partly. This is based on fear of a strong alienator.

Identifying with an idealised or perfect parent

Children who have been alienated cling desperately to the alienator. A common experience of a young child is 'My mother/father is perfect. I don't need a father/mother. My mother/father is perfect in every way.' This is especially when the alienating parent vilifies the alienated parent regularly, directly or more subtly, making that parent appear to be despicable to the child. Alienators cannot tolerate 'ambivalence'. One parent has to be always good and the other perfectly evil.

Releasing hostility

Most individuals have reasons for feeling hostile at different times. This is due to accumulated rage from other sources for which the alienated parent often becomes a ready target. The child therefore develops the same power as the alienator who can attack the alienated parent with impunity. The child will do this as well verbally, physically and by rejecting.

The child identifies with the power of the alienator

Hence the child feels free to attack and humiliate a father/mother (depending on who the alienated person is). They will call them horrible names, spit at them, and even strike them, knowing they have the protection of the alienator or anyone who is present at this particular interview. The alienated parent is helpless to counteract this except by talking kindly and often with tears in their eyes.

What therapy can be used to overcome the effects of parental alienation?

There are a number of ways of attempting to reverse the process of alienation.

Firstly it is to appeal to the child's intelligence or rational thinking

This could be difficult for the reasons already quoted. Such children are often so brainwashed that their rational thinking is totally at odds with reality.

Encouraging a child to confront the alienator

This is difficult to achieve due to the likelihood of the child identifying with the 'programmer' (alienator) and therefore fearing what the 'programmer' will do if the child is friendly towards the alienated parent.

Investigating specifics of pejorative remarks made about the alienated parent

One must be cautious about the remarks made by the child about the alienated parent. Such remarks made as 'father is nasty, evil, stupid, abuses me etc. etc.' This will be illustrated in the last section.

Making the child realise father loves them

This can only be done eventually when father/mother and child are together. This is sometimes difficult to achieve, especially when through the courts or some other restraint, access to the child is barred to the expert witness, and to seeing the child and the alienated parent together.

To break down absurd or frivolous criticisms towards the alienated parent

It is vital to spend as much time as possible initially listening to the child's complaints about the alienated parent before 'hammering home' the absurdities, unfairness and cruelty the child is expressing. This includes phrases like, 'Father is always bribing me to be with him'. This is an example of a 'borrowed scenario' since mother could well have used this term to describe the alienated parent who gives the child presents or money. If that parent did not give the child presents or money the borrowed scenario from the mother could well be 'He is such a mean man, never gives me anything'.

It is important to explain to the child how frivolous, absurd statements and borrowed scenarios come about and how it must be 'hammered home' as originating not with the child, but with the alienator. This will not always be accepted by the child as the child thinks they are thinking 'independently' of the alienator.

The child lacks ambivalence towards the alienating parent or the alienated parent. The alienating parent is 'all good' while the other is 'all evil'. There is not one good thing about the non-custodial parent and not one bad thing about the 'programming parent' in the child's mind.

The term 'independent thinking phenomenon' coined by Gardner is also of vital importance. Children must be shown how they have been alienated in thought and behaviour against the targeted parent by the programmer. Such children then consider such thoughts and behaviours as originating in their own thinking rather than originating from the alienator. They fail to understand that because of the alienator such ideas are in their minds. Children who are directly or individually being programmed, cannot admit this. Firstly they do not want to blame the programmer to whom they appear to be 'devoted'. They will claim the alienating

thinking and behaviour is based on their own independent thinking rather than emanating from the alienated parent. This is a delusion and hence difficult to nullify strictly by rational methods. This is why in the following section emotional approaches will be used in combination with rational methods.

How can rational emotive responses and methods be used to combat parental alienation? (A case illustration)

The present author has found it useful in a number of cases to combine vigorous and dramatic emotional responses with rational procedures. This has at least produced a breakthrough when the child who has had little or no contact with an alienated parent will, at least during the discourse within the therapeutic setting, re-enact a warmer relationship with the alienated parent. Unfortunately, very often the child will return to the custodial parent who will re-use any and all programming methods to reverse this tendency. It does however, indicate how even brief therapeutic approaches of 6–10 sessions can, for a time at least, change the child's thinking, until the child returns to the programming and custodial parent. The child should be seen in combination with the alienated parent whenever possible. It may be the very first time for a considerable period that both have been in the same room. The therapist at first sits between the two and later when some contact occurs, such as eye contact, the therapist will sit opposite the two. Still later, when some progress has been made via interaction verbally and otherwise between the child and the alienated parent, the psychologist briefly leaves the room and gradually extends the periods of absence. It will be noted that the psychologist becomes from time to time emotional to bring the child into reality thinking. The language tends to be 'down to earth', firm, rigorous and meaningful. The main objective is to make an impact on the brainwashed child, however difficult this may be.

Case illustration

This will be a summary of a number of sessions carried out with a child and their father. When collected the child very frequently clutched the alienator tightly. The child eventually went with the psychologist. Initially, the child entered the room hesitantly, fearing to leave the alienator. The father was waiting in the room while the child was being brought in by the psychologist to be with the father for the first time. The child on the whole tended to avert her eyes so that no contact could be established. The father in the meantime looked at the child somewhat despondently but greeted them in a friendly and caring manner. Frequently the father would remind the child of happy times together. This was reinforced by pictures or videos which had been brought along by the alienated parent to demonstrate how actually the alienated child behaved in the past when she was with her father. The dialogue went as follows:

Psychologist: This is the first time that you and your father have been together for some time hasn't it?

Child: *Does not answer*

Psychologist: I would like you to speak to me even if you don't at the moment speak to your father. This is the first time you have been in the same room with your father for some considerable time isn't it?

Child: It's not because I want to. I'm being made to do it.

Psychologist: *(speaking to the father)* Can you remind *(child's name)* of some of the happier times you were together by showing her some pictures of the past, or maybe some of the letters that she wrote to you before all this occurred.
> *Father then showed the child some pictures, and videos. The child averted her eyes in order not to look at these reminders of the past and happy times.*

Psychologist: I would like you to look at those pictures even if you don't look at your father so that you can see how things were in the past and why things have gone wrong in the meantime and this we will discuss later.
> *The child then turned her eyes to look at the pictures without looking at the father.*

Child: I can't remember these pictures being taken. I was probably only pretending to be happy when I was with my father. I have never really been happy with him at all.

Psychologist: Well these pictures don't indicate this at all. You seem to be smiling and cuddling your dad and generally showing signs of happiness. Can all this be pretence?

Child: Yes. I was only pretending. The only person I want to be with and love is my mother. She only needs me and I only need her. I don't need a father.

Psychologist: Don't you think your father loves you and deserves for you to be nice to him when he always tries to be nice to you. I believe he tries to telephone you regularly but you don't want to speak to him and hang up on him. Is that right?

Child: Yes. I don't want to speak to him. I don't want anything to do with him any more.

Psychologist: Why is that? What are the reasons you have? I want specific answers why you don't want any contact with your father. I don't want general remarks like 'I don't like him' or 'He is horrible to me'. I want to know exactly what he does wrong in your eyes to make you wish to reject a loving father who cares for you.

Child: I can't think of anything now but he always tries to make me go to places I don't want to go to and he sometimes asks me to come into the bed with him. I don't like that.

Psychologist: And what else?

Child: He shows me off to other people and tells them how clever I am and I hate that. Also he always tells me what to do and makes me eat things I don't want to eat. He makes me go on holiday with him and do things I don't like doing. He makes me sleep on a dirty bed which he has in his house.

Psychologist: Is there anything else?

Child: There are many other things I don't like. I don't even like being in the same room and talking to him.

Psychologist: Again I want you to be civil and nice to your father. OK? He is one of the few people in this world who will give anything to help you in any way he can, and I don't think it's fair that you should treat him in this way. Do you?

Child: *Silent, says nothing at first. Then says:* You don't have to be with him like I have to be with him. You don't know what he is really like.

Psychologist: No I don't really know. I am not always with him as you were in the past. There must be something good about your father that you enjoyed doing with him.

Child: *Thinking, then says,* Nothing.

Psychologist: There must be something that you remember that was good about him.

Child: *Thinking, then says,* He used to make some nice meals for me when I was with him. Nothing else. Anyway he could probably hit me from time to time if I was with him.

Psychologist: Has he ever hit you?

Child: *Answers,* No.

Psychologist: Has he ever hit you?

Child: *Answers,* No.

Psychologist: What makes you think he is going to hit you then?

Child: He could hit me. He's the sort of person who would do that sort of thing.

Psychologist: What makes you say that?

Child: Look at him, he is big and strong and he could hurt me.

Psychologist: But has he ever done so?

Child: *Reluctantly says* No.

Psychologist: If all these things you dislike about him and how he is with you were changed would you want to be with your dad after that?

Child: They could never be changed, and anyway even if they were changed I wouldn't want to be with him.

Psychologist: So there is no sense in changing anything is there?

Child: That's right. I just don't want to be with him.

It is clear from this interchange that there has been no breakthrough of any kind while the father has been in the room demonstrating pictures and videos from time to time to show how the past had been and how happy the child had been in the father's company. It is now felt that a more emotional and direct approach is required. This approach could well be criticised by those who believe in pure therapeutic approaches of an orthodox nature. The current psychologist however, has found that these methods are totally ineffective with an alienated child who is obdurate about wishing any contact with a former affectionate, caring and loving parent. The psychologist from time to time therefore uses fairly emotional and direct expressions, and also the tone of his voice is louder to be emphatic to the child. Essentially, it is a way of 'shocking' the child to reality:

Psychologist: Now I am going to say something that has been on my mind for some time having read everything you've said about your father, and having talked to your father for a long period of time to find out how he feels about you. I think you have treated him abominably. I think you have been a horrible little girl. You have been too powerful for your own good. What right have you got to reject a father who loves you and cares for you and wants to do everything for you? You should be ashamed of yourself. Don't you feel guilty at all about the way you have treated him all this time by not even looking at him, by not talking to him, by hanging up on him on the telephone? What has he really done that is so terrible for you to behave in this way? I think you have virtually thrown your father into the rubbish pile. If that is what you want to do then so be it. I think your father is very, very caring or he would not persist in wanting to be with you and wanting to have contact with you, and wanting to show his love for you. I'll tell you one thing, many fathers would have given up and not bothered any more, and not bothered even contacting you or wishing you a happy birthday or a good Christmas, or providing for you financially. Many fathers would have given up and just said to themselves that this was the end and I am not having any more to do with this child.

At this point very frequently the child will develop thinking. The emotional tone of the therapist or psychologist will in many cases have 'hit home.' Sometimes one has to go on in this vein using very emotional expressions and very 'down to earth' expressions defending the father and drawing attention to the good times that the child has had with the father which have been substantiated by the pictures and other information provided by the father. The important thing is not to accept what the child says and how the child behaves since it is based on considerable programming or brainwashing. It is vital to continue to try to break through that barrier and very frequently one does break through.

Eventually, in the case quoted above the child did look at the father, having seen the pictures and seen what an impact this had on the father. It was then the chance of the father to talk to the child in a caring, loving manner and remind the child of the good times they had together in the past.

It is at this point that the psychologist would best leave the room for a short period to provide an opportunity for interaction between the two parties. It is surprising, very often, when the psychologist returns after the first or second time being away from the two how much closer the chairs are between the two parties and how their eye contact has improved and how they are now speaking to one another. Sometimes the child will even hold the parent's hand and even at a later stage give that alienated parent a cuddle (often for the first time in years) or a sign of physical warmth. Sometimes it takes a number of sessions of this kind before this can be achieved. Powerful emotional language is vital in order to break through the barrier that has occurred due to the alienation process. The child then begins to think again for themselves rather than repeating the phrases and thoughts of the alienator.

It must also be said that the child feels safe interacting with the alienated parent as the mother is not present. Were the mother in the same room, the child could be very reluctant to allow a breakthrough of this kind, as they would be worrying about the views of the alienator. The child would be concerned with the disapproval of the alienating party if the child is too friendly to the alienated party. It will take a considerable effort to redeem the damage that has been done to the child over a period of months or years in which the programmer (alienator) has 'hammered home' their own prejudices and the child has identified with these prejudices.

Once the psychologist has completed the process of mediation there is a need for a report to go to the court. The court will either accept or fail to accept the views of the expert witness. In the extreme it will ignore all the views by the psychologist and retain the situation as it was before, with the child living with the custodial, programming parent. It is hoped more and more courts in future will, in extreme and prolonged cases of programming, consider the possibility of a change of custody, at least for a period of time, so that the alienated parent can have the opportunity of healing the wounds of the past. Only time will tell what occurs in the future.

Chapter Sixteen

PAS: a two step approach towards a solution

Background literature

The main pioneer in the area of alienation syndrome, frequently termed parental alienation syndrome, was Richard Gardner (1992; 1995). He drew attention to the gross injustice that frequently occurred, mostly in relation to fathers, being rejected from the family as a result of separation or divorce. His two books, *True and False Accusations of Child Sex Abuse*, and *Protocols for Sex Abuse Evaluation* are landmarks in the area of parental alienation syndrome. He has worked for many years as a forensic psychologist dealing with cases in the courts in the United States.

He has also written an Addendum UI entitled *Recommendations for Dealing with Parents who Induce a Parental Alienation Syndrome in their children* (1996). Virtually all subsequent work carried out has taken heed of his own investigations and most importantly, his evaluations of the alleged child victim, the accused and the accuser. He broke down the various aspects related to alleged child sexual abuse into various criteria. This has resulted in myself (1993a, 1993b) developing an inventory and interview procedure based on his work and dealing with the alleged victim of sexual abuse, the alleged abuser and the accuser. Although from time to time matters are reversed and the alienation syndrome refers to the mother being left out of the family conciliation, most often it refers to fathers, since the courts and western societies tend to favour mothers as custodians of their children and, unfortunately, frequently as sole custodians.

Among the evaluation aspects of males accused of sexual abuse (Gardner, 1995) were numerous factors. These included:

1. History of family influences conducive to the development of significant psychopathology.
2. Long standing history of emotional deprivation.
3. Intellectual impairment.
4. Childhood history of sex abuse.
5. Long standing history of sex abuse.
6. Impulsivity.
7. Narcissism.
8. Coercive dominated behaviour.
9. Passivity and impaired self-assertion.
10. Substance abuse.
11. Poor judgment.
12. Impaired sexual interests, in age appropriate women.
13. Presence of other sexual deviations.
14. Psychosis.
15. Immaturity or regression.
16. Large collection of child pornographic materials.
17. Career choice that brings him in contact with children.
18. Recent rejection by female peer or dysfunctional heterosexual relationship.
19. Unconvincing denial.
20. Use of rationalisation and cognitive distortion to justify paedophilia.
21. Utilisation of seductivity.
22. Attitude towards taking a lie detector test.
23. Lack of cooperation in the evaluative examination.
24. Duplicity unrelated to the sex abuse denial and psychopathic tendency.
25. Moralism.
26. Numerous victims.

Studies by Clawar and Rivlin (1991) in a book entitled, *Children Held Hostage*, reviewed some of the methods used, usually by mothers, to induce the alienation against the fathers. These include:

1. Intimidation and threat.
2. Guilt induction.
3. The 'buy-off'.
4. Playing the victim.
5. Suggesting the child or parent will experience loneliness and fear.
6. Parental promise to change themselves or conditions.
7. Parental over-indulgence and permissiveness.
8. Telling the 'truth' to the child about past events.

The authors emphasise that 'brain-washing and programming' are used by parents seeking to alienate their children from another parent.

Other recent literature on the Parental Alienation Syndrome (PAS) and reaction to separation and divorce were covered under the subject of: (A) Problems associated with divorce and especially acrimonious relationships between parents; (B) the role of mediation by professionals as an alternative to legal sanctions.

We will now look at each of these in turn.

Problems associated with divorce and especially acrimonious relationships between parents

This section deals with those who refuse mediation as opposed to those who accept such approaches. Buchanan et al. (1991) examined adolescents' feelings of being caught between parents to see whether this construct helped to explain:

- Variability in their post-divorce adjustments.
- Associations between family/child characteristics and adolescent adjustment.

522 subjects aged 10.5–18 years from 365 families were interviewed after their parents' separation. Feeling caught between parents was related to high parental conflict and hostility and low parental cooperation. Being close to both parents was associated with low feelings of being caught between. The relation between time spent with each parent and feeling caught in the middle depended on the co-parenting relationship. Subjects in dual residence were especially likely to feel caught up when parents were in high conflict. Feeling caught was related to poor adjustment outcomes.

Problems associated with divorce and causing legal confrontations were noted by Johnston and Campbell (1993). They reported data on allegations of domestic violence in two samples of high conflict families in child custody disputes. Sample 1 comprised 80 divorcing parents disputing custody and visitation of their 100 children, aged 1–12 years, and sample 2 comprised 60 divorcing parents with 75 children aged 3–12 years. Five basic types of inter parental violence and corresponding patterns in parent-child relationships were indicated:

- Ongoing and episodic male battering.
- Female initiated violence.
- Male-controlling interactive violence.
- Separation-engendered and post-divorce trauma.
- Psychotic and paranoid reactions.

It was hypothesised that children's adjustment was more disturbed in divorcing families litigating custody where the domestic violence had been more severe and repetitive, and where it was perpetrated predominantly by men compared with women. The results supported this hypothesis. Also, the long term effects of parental divorce on parent-child relationships, adjustment and achievement in young adulthood was studied by Zill et al. (1993). Longitudinal data from the National Survey of Children was examined to investigate whether effects of parental divorce were evident in young adulthood. Among 18–22 year olds from disrupted families, 65 per cent had poor relationships with their fathers and 30 per cent with their mothers. 25 per cent had dropped out of high school, and 40 per cent had received psychological help. Even after controlling for demographic and socioeconomic differences, youths from disrupted families were twice as likely to exhibit these problems as youths from non-disrupted families. A significant effect of divorce on mother-child relationships was evident in adulthood, whereas none was found in adolescence. Youths experiencing disruption before 6 years of age showed poorer relationships with their fathers than those experiencing disruptions later in childhood. Overall, remarriage did not have a protective effect, but there were indications of amelioration among those who experienced early disruption.

The effects of family composition, family health, parenting behaviour and environmental stress on children's divorce adjustment was considered by Ellwood and Stolberg (1993). The subjects, aged 8–11 years included 18 children whose parents remained married, 46 whose parents were divorced, and 17 whose parents divorced and subsequently remarried. Custodial parents completed questionnaires regarding family functioning, occurrence of stressful life events, and child's psychosocial adjustment. Children completed the Children's Report of Parent Behaviour Inventory and a self-perception profile for children. A trained examiner conducted a diagnostic interview of the child.

Family composition had a significant effect on occurrence of stressful events and change in income but not children's adjustment. The most powerful predictors of child adjustment were family competence variables. Higher levels of family functioning were associated with families where parental hostility was low and parents displayed few rejecting behaviours while practising consistent and appropriate discipline.

Parental Alienation Syndrome was studied in 16 selected cases by Dunne and Hedrick (1994). They analysed 16 cases of divorcing families in which one or more of the children, aged 0–14 years in the family had rejected a parent after divorce, in order to validate the work of Richard Gardner, previously mentioned. Cases were taken from the caseloads of clinicians working with the families. The cases met the majority of Gardner's criteria, including an obsessive hatred of the alienated parent on the basis of trivial or unsubstantiated accusations and complete support for the alienating parent. Although the cases showed a wide diversity of characteristics, Gardner's criteria were useful in differentiating these cases from other post-divorce difficulties. PAS (Parental Alienation Syndrome) appeared to be primarily a function of the pathology of the alienating parent and that parent's relationship with the children and PAS did not signify dysfunction in the alienated parent or in the relationship between that parent and the child.

Expanding the parameters of parental alienation syndrome was the work of Cartwright (1993). PAS, as we know, results from the attempt by one parent to alienate a child from the other parent, but, because PAS was newly recognised and described, it had to be defined and redefined as new cases were observed and the phenomenon became better understood. New evidence suggested that PAS was provoked by other than custodial matters, that cases of alleged sexual abuse were hinted at, that slow adjustments by courts exacerbated the problem, that prolonged alienation of the child triggered other forms of mental illness and that too much remained unknown of the long-term consequences to alienated children and their families.

Turkat (1994) studied child visitation interference in divorce. This was to raise an awareness of the problem among psychologists seeking to find solutions to these difficulties. From the clinical and legal literature, there appeared to be at least three types of situations related to child visitation interference: acute interference, parental alienation syndrome, and divorce related malicious mother syndrome. The associated difficulties in handling this problem in the legal system were considered.

Amato and Rezac (1994) tested the hypothesis that children's contact with non-resident parents (NRPs) decreased children's behaviour problems when inter-parental conflict was low but increased children's behaviour problems when inter-parental conflict was high. Data was analysed in 1,285 children aged 5–18 years of single parent families from the National Survey of Families and Households. The subjects, resident parents, reported on the frequency of interaction between the child and NRP and the conflict between the resident and NRP. When the resident parent reported little conflict with the NRP, boys who had a high level of involvement with the NRP were said to have fewer behavioural problems. However, when the resident parent reported to have conflict with the NRP, boys who had a high level of involvement with the NRP were said to have a larger number of behavioural problems. No support for the hypothesis was found among girls, regardless of the family background.

A therapist's view of parental alienation syndrome was studied by Lund (1995). She explored different reasons why a child might reject one parent in a divorced family and the ways of helping such families. Cases in which a child resisted contact with a parent had or had not to fit Gardner's theory of Parent Alienation Syndrome (PAS), which emphasised the psychopathology of alienating parents. The reasons for parental rejection were many according to this investigator. They could be due to:

- Developmentally normal separation problems.
- Deficits in the non-custodial parent's skills.
- Oppositional behaviour.
- High conflict divorced families.
- Serious problems, not necessarily abuse.
- Child abuse.

Gardner recommended legal and therapeutic interventions based on whether the case was assessed to be one of mild, moderate, or extreme parental alienation. Success in the treatment of the PAS cases was to be defined as the maintenance of some contact between parent and child.

The impact of parental divorce on the attainment of the developmental tasks of young adulthood was considered by Johnson et al. (1995). They assessed the impact of parental divorce on the development of 125 undergraduates (88 women) aged 19–53 years, who completed a demographic questionnaire, the Personal Authority in the Family System Questionnaire (college version), and the conflict sub scale of the Family Environment Scale. The results indicated that parental divorce and family conflict significantly interfered with developmental tasks attained. The interactions between sex and age and family structure, i.e. single parents or step family were also significant predictors of post-divorce task attainment. Therapists needed to help these individuals attain 'emotional middle ground' by separating and individuating from their family without emotionally cutting off or only remaining connected through anger.

The role of mediation as an alternative to legal sanctions

Kelly (1991) compared the interactions and perceptions of two groups of divorcing parents using different dispute resolution processes at final divorce and at one and two years post-divorce. The effectiveness of a comprehensive divorce mediation process was contrasted to the more customary two attorney adversarial process. The mediation sample at two years post-divorce consisted of 52 subjects, and the adversarial sample consisted of 73 subjects. The subjects in the divorce mediation group reported less conflict, more contact and communication, and a more positive attitude towards the other parent at final divorce. The majority of differences favouring the mediation intervention continued through the first year after divorce and disappeared by the second year post divorce data collection.

Following a contested custody case, parents who had won custody of their child appeared to need a particular kind of psychological help to prevent the development of the problems to which children of divorce were subject (Solomon, 1991). The critical time was between the third and sixth month after the court had awarded custody of the child to the parent with whom the child had been living. Three case studies illustrated the nature and timing of the necessary interventions. The therapeutic interventions:

- Made the parent aware of the changes in their perception of the child and the reasons underlying these changes.
- Furnished the parent with several bodies of information.
- Made the links between these factors and events occurring in their family.

Lowenstein (1992) was concerned with the manipulation which parents carry out in seeking child custody. It was vital to weigh up the removing of children from the home and the danger to the child in placing them with one or other parent without making adequate contact provisions for the other parent who was capable of playing an important role in the child or children's lives. He emphasised the importance of carrying out what he termed a group diagnostic interview, which was capable of leading to further meetings, leading eventually to cooperation and the avoidance of continued disputes and legal actions. The fact that PAS occurred, in which the controlling parent frequently accused the parent seeking contact of sexual abuse, needed to be properly investigated. Allegations of sexual abuse need not necessarily with certainty, signify that this has occurred. Unfortunately, very often this is the case and very often fathers, particularly, lose contact with their children due to false accusations of sexual abuse carried out by (usually) the mother in seeking to prevent children having contact with their rightful father. It is the role of psychologists carrying out tasks of mediation to help the antagonists find a solution which, at least in part, provides what they seek.

Geffner (1992) focused on techniques and issues concerning mediation of abusive couples both during and after separation or divorce. A questionnaire was presented which was used to help identify abusive relationships. It was important that the wife and the children were safe during mediation, since research showed that more batterers had murdered their wives during this time period when divorce was imminent. Since the balance of power was unequal in the relationship, mediation had had to be modified so that the situation became neutral. The mediator had to model ways of dealing with intimidation. Other issues facing mediators in these cases involved living arrangements, conversion changes in children, financial support, joint custody, and parent alienation syndrome.

Mediation strategies discussed by Bonney (1993) proposed that the focus of child custody evaluation and mediation was to be broadened beyond custody arrangement to consideration of the range of factors that had an impact on post-divorce relationships. The amount of conflict between parents, parental agreement on access, use of support, parental well-being, and parent-child relationships were factors associated with children's post-divorce adjustment. Strategies for involving parents in drafting agreements to guide relationships with each other and with the children were offered. These included communication, consistent discipline, warmth and support, encouraging a relationship with the other parent, and listening to the feelings and sharing values.

Kurkowski et al. (1993) used a brief educational intervention to reduce the number of times divorced parents put their children in the middle of parental conflict. A cohort of 98 9th–12th graders were divided into two groups: a 49 member intact family group and a 49 member divorced group (subjects from divorced or separated homes). An intervention group consisted of 45 of the 49 subjects, who were located for post-intervention assessment. The subjects completed a questionnaire, which rated the frequency and stressfulness of 32 situations into which a parent had put them 'in the middle', within the past month. Parents of the intervention group were mailed the subjects' averaged responses and an explanatory letter. The same 32-item questionnaire was given about one month after the mailing as the intervention evaluation. The subjects in the intervention group improved more than the two control groups combined.

Lowenstein (1994b) considered the Child and Child Sex Abuse Allegations. These were serious allegations which needed to receive a thorough examination by anyone investigating them. It was felt, however, that allegations were frequently considered to be valid, even if disproved eventually. In these circumstances both the victim of alleged child sexual abuse as well as the alleged perpetrator had to be protected so that truth and justice be done to both. It was felt, therefore, that what was urgently required was an objective assessment of allegations of child sexual abuse in the interview situation and the use of more sophisticated psychological tests or inventories specifically constructed to assess children as well as the accused and the accuser.

Lowenstein (1993a, 1993b) developed a Sexual Abuse Personality Inventory (LSAPI) which was as yet unpublished, and had restricted use by the author only. Lowenstein (1994b) also considered that many interviewers of children were leading them in the direction of assuming that sexual abuse had taken place and provided an actual illustration of this in his paper. The use of Gardner's paper (1992b) and his true or false accusation interview and process were recommended.

Peterson and Steinman (1994) described the development, goals and preliminary evaluation of the Helping Children Succeed After Divorce (HCSD) Seminar mandated by the domestic relations court of Franklin County, Ohio. The programme was designed to educate divorcing parents about the effects of divorce and parental conflict on their children. HCSD was a two and a half hour seminar presented by two mental health professionals. It covered the adult's and child's divorce experience, co-parental relationship building, and problem solving. An evaluation involving 600 initial HCSD participants, indicated that response to HCSD was favourable; following HCSD participation, the majority of the parents were more aware of their children's divorce experience, the importance of a continued relationship with their former spouse, and options available for resolution of child-related disputes.

A view of the methods used in litigation and child custody evaluations was carried out by Hysjulien et al. (1994). They reviewed the current assessment methods used in child custody (CC) litigation and mediation and discussed their reliability and validity. Existing outcome studies concerned CC evaluations and were presented. Psychological tests, semi-structured interviews, and behavioural observations of parents and children in CC disputes were reviewed. The related issues of child abuse, sexual abuse, domestic violence and parental alienation syndrome were discussed. There was little empirical evidence to support the efficacy of methods typically used by professionals in making recommendations to the court. This view was not shared by Lowenstein (1997a) in his unpublished work, *The Law and Protecting the Child and Accused from False Sex Abuse Allegations* and his work in the area of shared parenting after divorce (Lowenstein, 1997b), an unpublished study.

Parent Alienation Syndrome – A two step approach towards a solution

Introduction

The case which follows illustrates one of a dozen other cases which have involved me in seeking to find a solution to long term acrimonious parents. It involves a two-step approach to finding a solution. The first step is obviously the one which is preferred because it involves the voluntary cooperation of both parents in finding a solution which is mutually satisfying.

Frequently, adversarial approaches have gone on for a long period and have failed to resolve the essential issue. This is whether an alienated parent will be allowed to have contact with the children which may result in better times for the children through the improved parental relationship. The second approach essentially establishes who is cooperative and who is uncooperative as a parent and takes issue with the uncooperative parent by depriving that parent of autonomy in deciding on the matter of who shall take part in further contact with the children involved in the relationship.

Needless to say, anyone dealing with warring parents will note that each one attempts to portray the other in the most dismal or black light as possible vis a vis their behaviour and attitudes. Little can be achieved through this approach and certainly those who suffer the most as a result are likely to be the children who are confused by warring parents, or who are poisoned by one parent against the other. Usually the parent who has contact, initially on a total basis with the children, is able to portray the other parent as evil and unworthy of playing a parental role. Most cases involve mothers, who have contact with their children, and fathers who seek such contact, but who have been prevented from playing a parental role by the mother.

Each parent attempts to portray the other as being unfit to play the part of a parent, and in the most severe cases allegations such as sexual abuse are made. Alternatively a parent may be said to fail to provide sufficient support, care, guidance or discipline.

In my experience the adversarial system lends itself splendidly towards being manipulated by one or both parents and there is a failure to find a solution. Frequently an impasse is reached where the parent who currently has control of the children retains such control, despite the fact that the other parent could play an effective role in the parenting arrangement. In later years the children themselves acknowledge the fact that they have been poisoned against the other parent unjustifiably and both parents suffer, especially the parent who has sought to keep the other out of the parental rearing arrangement.

Now follows the kind of scenario which supports the importance of having the two-step approach previously mentioned.

The case of X versus Y

Step 1

As a consultant psychologist trained in forensic, clinical and educational psychology, I have found it useful to involve both parents in a discussion which could lead to a solution in front of a judge. The approach commences as follows: The psychologist sees each of the partners separately, gaining insight into what each feels about the situation, and seeking any common ground that may exist between the two warring factions. It is made clear to both parties that the partner who fails to cooperate with the psychologist in seeking a true, positive and constructive solution is likely to fail to benefit from the decision of the court. It is, of course, imperative that the psychologist has the mandate through the court to be able to engage both parents, initially separately, in discussions to find a solution to a problem which, in many cases, has lasted for a long period of time.

Once it has been established that some form of rapport exists between the psychologist and both members, having seen them separately, then the two parties in the dispute are brought together by the psychologist for a mutually valuable positive and constructive engagement to find a solution which will be agreeable to both, although not totally agreeable in every way to both sides. It is frequently necessary in this situation that past acrimonies and the hurt of both members of the dispute are not brought into the open, but rather the finding of a solution to the problem becomes the primary objective.

Once a decision has been reached by the psychologist in line with what he has found from both parents, this is then brought before the court for a decision to be made on a legal basis, having, as already stated, obtained the consent to this decision by both parties.

Table 16.1   Mediation approach and adversarial approach: time taken to achieve a solution

	<6 months	1	1–2	2–3	3–4	4–5	5–6	6–7	7–8
Adversarial	—	—	—	1	2	5	3	4	1*
Mediation	9	3	2	2	—	—	—	—	—

*This case was ultimately settled via mediation.

Table 16.2   Degree of ultimate satisfaction after mediation (52 children–32 parents, 32 cases)

	Very satisfied	Satisfied	Less than satisfied	Very unsatisfied
Children	33	14	5	—
Parents	22	9	1	0

Table 16.3   Degree of ultimate satisfaction without mediation (16 families, 49 children, n=32)

	Very satisfied	Satisfied	Less than satisfied	Very unsatisfied
Children	1	3	31	14
Parents	7	1	11	13

Should one or other of the parties fail to cooperate, it would then be necessary to go to Step 2 which follows.

Step 2

The court will have witnessed the cooperation or lack of cooperation of one or both members of the dispute in earlier sessions and will have mandated the psychologist to seek to find a solution which it will be possible for the court to implement in due course. The court's reaction will be at least partly dependent on the evidence obtained from the warring factions on their desire or willingness to cooperate in finding a solution or the reverse tendency. Unless the case is proven against one or other of the parties that there have been serious derelictions in parental responsibility, and in the extreme form, that this has been proven to be sexual abuse, it must be considered that both parties have a right to the responsibility of caring for their children, be it the father or the mother. The degree of the responsibility and the degree of contact must be decided upon by the court, perhaps with the advice of the mental health workers such as the psychologist or others.

The fact that both parents are aware that the law will take a hand if they fail to be cooperative as in Step 1, should incline them to seek a solution together rather than have it imposed upon them by the actions of the court. There are, however, situations where one or both parties fail to respond in a voluntary sense and hence it is vital to have Step 2 available, this being dependent on the reaction to Step 1.

Comparing the Adversarial Legal Approach to Mediation Approaches in Parental Alienation Syndrome

What follows is the result of a study over 10 years in dealing with 16 cases which used a purely adversarial approach and 16 which relied virtually totally on the mediation method.

Table 1 illustrates the time taken by the adversarial approach without necessarily achieving a resolution of the problems and a mediation approach in PAS type cases.

Summary of research

The pioneer in the area of Parental Alienation Syndrome and false allegations as well as true allegations of sexual abuse must be Dr. Richard Gardner (1992; 1995). He was one of the first writers to draw attention to the injustices committed by alienating parents. Included in this book I (Lowenstein, 1993a; 1993b) have attempted to develop an Inventory and Interview Technique to identify true and false alleged sexual abuse of victims, the accuser and the accused. I was guided by Gardner, 1994 and his own factors are involved in true and false accusations mostly associated with parental alienation syndrome. Clawar and Rivlin in their book *Children Held Hostage* also allude to the serious associated problems of parental alienation syndrome.

Numerous investigators have discovered the problems associated with divorce and the estrangement between formerly close parents and how this affects the children following an acrimonious ending of the relationship between them. All investigators indicate the importance of parents developing a way of dealing with their resentment for the benefit of their children as well as for one another.

Frequently, alienation occurs and strategies are used by one or both partners to denigrate the role played by the other partner in the relationship, most especially in their conduct towards their own children. False allegations frequently result which hamper the capacity of those seeking to find a solution to an on-going problem. Where litigation is continuous and acrimony particularly rampant, children tend to develop various reactions including neuroses and behavioural difficulties as well as educational problems. These children also tend to have poorer relationships with adults once they themselves have matured.

Psychologists and others must distinguish between pathological relationships between one partner and the children, as well as with the alienating partner and recognise when this is manufactured for the purpose of controlling children and preventing the alienated partner from having contact with their children. Alleged sexual abuse is just one of the strategies used by a partner to eliminate the other from having contact with the children who are their joint offspring. Most research has concluded that inter-parental conflict reduces the likelihood of children developing normally.

The recommendation by Gardner that both legal and therapeutic intervention is vital to obviate further harmful consequences for the children, cannot be over-emphasised. Following a successful outcome there is a greater likelihood that PAS is reduced or eliminated altogether. With one in three or four marriages leading to divorce or separation, there is a great urgency to

develop plans to make certain that both parents can continue to play a role in the lives of their children.

The role of mediation performed by psychologists and other mental health workers produces the positive and constructive result which is desirable for all concerned. It is important to link the benefits of this to children in both the educational and therapeutic process wherein the parents must be involved. As a result of such approaches, litigation plays a lesser role and mediation a greater one.

Conclusions and recommendations

1. It is urged that mediation play a larger role in cases of parental alienation syndrome. Those agents most likely to be effective in helping parents, and eventually their children, are psychologists, psychiatrists and other professional mental health workers.
2. There is also considerable evidence that mediation approaches are found superior to adversarial approaches although a combination of the two cannot be ruled out.
3. Judges and magistrates must take heed of the most recent research which psychologists and others have carried out to indicate the role played by themselves in seeking to repair pathological relationships that have developed due to parental alienation syndrome.
4. It is vital to have the court and its power overseeing that the mediation process occurs effectively. It is especially important for the court to take cognisance of any parent who fails to cooperate in the process and to take appropriate action. This may well mean that the parent who fails to cooperate, after ascertaining that both parents have done nothing pathologically wrong in relation to their children, will be duly dealt with through the court's action.

Discussion

It will take a considerable period of time and the pioneering spirit and courage of British justice to heed the advice which has been given in this article. Judges may come to see their role as more than perpetuators of previous cases and seek new ways of dealing with difficult issues such as parental alienation syndrome and probably other cases. The adversarial system does not lend itself particularly well to such issues, albeit it is ingrained in British justice as the method forward and the most fair way of dealing with a variety of offences and problems faced by members of society. Furthermore, the methods advocated for bringing in expert witnesses to deal with such cases as marital problems and other issues such as parental alienation syndrome does not dilute the power of the court for it still retains the option of a ruling, in the final analysis, as is noted in Step 2. Step 1 provides the court with an additional way, which is always preferable when the parties concerned in the dispute can be helped to solve their problems without the teeth of judicial decisions being immediately utilised.

It is now vital to consider the importance of appointing expert witnesses by the court to act as intermediaries between the parents and the court and to seek reconciliation of some kind by deliberately focusing on the positive aspects of the relationship between the former partners. This is the best way forward, whereby children will benefit and parents equally will be able to play a positive and constructive role in rearing such children. At the present time, through the adversarial system, there is often the use of two expert witnesses, one on each side, and their loyalty may well be to their 'camp' rather than in seeking a solution which is favourable, or as favourable as possible, to both parties rather than merely seeking the advantages for their own side. Any person attempting such work must be highly experienced and qualified to carry out this important work for the individual concerned, be they a psychiatrist or a psychologist, and they must be able to win the confidence of both parents, if possible, and thereby seek their cooperation after often highly acrimonious periods which have resolved nothing between the parents and the judicial system in seeking to find the most appropriate solution.

Chapter Seventeen

Mediation: the way forward

The concept of mediation

Mediation is an important way of seeking to rectify hostility between parties. There are actually two aspects which indicate whether mediation is likely to be successful:

1. That the parties concerned agree to participate in such a process with an expert in the area of mediation, preferably a clinical psychologist.
2. That they co-operate in the mediation process and not merely pay 'lip-service' to the fact that they wish mediation to occur.

Parties in dispute often require considerable help to assist them in developing greater harmony where there is currently severe conflict. The author has carried out a considerable amount of research in this area and has also practiced mediation for many years and reported this mediation to courts and others. As already stated the outcome of mediation depends on the co-operation of the parties concerned as well as the skill of the mediator.

The process in action consists of seeking to understand each of the parties involved and obtaining information as to their willingness to give as well as take in the process. Only after this has been established can parties be brought together. Failure to complete the initial part could lead to mere 'slanging' matches between the antagonists, which is totally unacceptable and unlikely to lead to a conclusion to the problem.

It is vital that the parties be informed that, whoever makes the decision, such as the court, their co-operation would be measured on the basis of what they do rather than what they say. The mediator must work hard to remove the obstacles that lead to entrenched positions by each of the parties concerned. It is obvious that the mediator must be viewed as an independent person eager to solve the problem rather than favouring one side or the other. Unless those in conflict understand and accept this little can be achieved. The way forward, however, is that mediation is a positive and constructive way of solving problems between hostile parties.

The way forward

We hear a great deal today about confrontation and most especially the number of divorces and separations between what were initially, apparently, well-adjusted and harmonious couples. Having dealt with several hundreds of such unfortunate people, I have come to certain conclusions; that many marital problems, divorces and separations and also acrimonious relationships that remain together, could be spared such ordeals, if timely intervention occurred through mediation procedures. It is unfortunate, however, that most of the problems to come to psychologists, psychiatrists and counsellors, are situations where the acrimony, hatred and the apparent dissolution of relationships have gone too far or can only be mended with great difficulty.

We will review the literature (1996–1997), comparing different therapeutic approaches by therapists and considering the general value of mediation today. We will go on to discuss the causes and associated features of marital problems including gender links, infidelity, power struggle, violence in the family and other problems. This is followed by diagnosing the problems of marital and relationship disharmony and finally dealing with treatment approaches. At the end of the chapter we will look at one therapeutic centre's approach to treatment.

Recent research literature

Family therapy researchers were criticised by Clark and Serovich (1997) for failing to address themselves to the extent to which marriage and family therapy does not recognise the importance of gay, lesbian and bisexual issues.

The literature by Kelly and Halford (1997) attempted to redress the balance in a psychological study of couple relationships by focusing on what is known about emotion in relationships. Emotional processes in couple relationships were significant in understanding the quality of the relationship, and the effect of the relationship on the partner's psychological and physical health. Most research on emotion within couple relationships had been cross-sectional in nature, comparing distressed and non-distressed couples, and these findings were reviewed in the first half of the article by these researchers. While such research described differences in emotional processes between distressed and non-distressed couples, it gave no information on how these emotional processes developed over time. In the second section of the article, the authors discussed the implications of these lines of inquiry for therapy and research. Questions regarding the availability, use and application of emotion data in clinical settings were addressed. Current knowledge about how traditional behavioural marital therapy impacted on emotional distress in couples was reviewed, and several possibilities for improving traditional behavioural marital therapy were considered.

Another research study by Bennun (1997) discussed the literature on systemic marital relationship interventions with one partner only. Increasingly, marital therapists and agencies offering services to distressed couples were seeing just one marital partner and needed to consider methods of treating relationships distress within this mode. Some of the empirically established methods were described, as were general clinical issues.

General values of mediation

Whether there is any value in the mediation process is difficult to establish as there are rarely studies which contain a control group wherein no mediation occurs and hence comparisons can be made. Welter (1995) contended that each marriage had its beginning and its ending and a primary meaning of marriage that was often overlooked by marriage counsellors was the story of the marriage. The counsellor needed to obtain a family history or the antecedents of the marriage story from each of the spouses, then the story of their marriage. Each partner was to provide information in connection with these questions and then comparisons were to be made between the two versions.

In the case of divorce mediation and the resolution of child custody disputes, Dillon and Emery (1996) examined the long-term effects of using mediation to resolve such problems. 25 parents who chose mediation and 28 parents who chose litigation to resolve child custody disputes

were followed up nine years after the dispute was first brought to court. Parents were asked whether the child involved in the dispute had experienced difficulties in adjustment, and whether psychological treatment was given. Frequencies of both direct and indirect contact between the child and the non-resident parent were assessed, and parents rated inter-parental cooperation and conflict. Non-custodial parents assigned to mediation reported more frequent current contact with their children and greater involvement in current decisions about them. Parents in the mediation group also reported more frequent communication about their children during the period since dispute resolution.

Following a decade of divorce mediation research which had focused on outcomes such as settlement rates, cost efficiency, client satisfaction, effect on levels of conflict and cooperation, psychological adjustment and compliance, Kelly (1996) still felt that research on the mediation process and mediation behaviour had received very limited attention. The main determinants of divorce settlement negotiations between divorcing spouses and their lawyers, according to Hochberg and Kressel (1996) was a favourable settlement outcome which led to cooperative negotiating between the parties. It therefore followed that psychological adjustment was for all concerned.

The role of children in mediation was studied by Lansky et al. (1996). They examined the actual practice of 324 practitioner members of the Academy of Family Mediators focusing on the inclusion or exclusion of children during the mediation process. 31 per cent of respondents were attorneys, 46 per cent had graduate-level mental health backgrounds, and an additional 7 per cent had both legal and mental health backgrounds. The survey instrument revealed that 77 per cent of the respondents included children, either following settlement to discuss the parenting plan or during mediation as a source of additional Information. Respondents reasons for including children (i.e. requests by the parents or children to avoid impasse due to divergent opinions among parents) or excluding them (i.e. to avoid pressure or loyalty conflicts) were outlined.

The training of therapists was considered by Latz (1996). She studied the administration and outcome of an experiential exercise for training beginning marital and family therapists in language skills, which aimed to sensitise individuals to the possibility of their own and clients' idiosyncratic application of words. The exercise consisted of two parts: Part 1 required individuals to interpret what they had heard from the audio of a film clip. All those participating had heard the same sounds and conversation, but each made a unique interpretation. They expressed frustration and discomfort at having to interpret only the audio portion. In the second part, the same individuals were shown the visual clip along with the audio and asked to share their descriptions. The multiplicity of meanings and flexibility of actions that was noticed in the first part of the exercise, disappeared in the second part.

Different kinds of mediation processes were compared by Vansteenwegen (1997). Differences in the verbal behaviour of two experienced couple therapists were studied in a videotaped intake session with the same couple (two professional actors, trained on a real case). One therapist worked from an experiential viewpoint (client-centred, Rogerian) and the other worked from a communicative approach (directive, problem-oriented). The therapists were both male, 40 years of age, and had over 12 years of experience as psychotherapists. For all verbal interventions the instrument utilised was the Pinsof Family Therapist Coding System. The results suggested that the communication therapist was more direct and his interventions were more directed towards the couple rather than towards the individual partners. At the same time many similarities were found between the two models.

A number of therapists have found that divorce mediation was a difficult prospect especially when arguments arose within the meetings. Greatbatch and Dingwall (1997) analysed the management of arguments between disputants in 121 divorce mediation sessions recorded in 10 agencies in England. It was found that the disputants did not always rely on mediators to initiate exits from their arguments. Instead they initiated exits on their own, often closing their argumentative exchanges without the mediators' assistance. The practices used to exit arguments in the sessions were prevalent in ordinary conversation, but their use here exhibited an orientation to conventions associated with mediation. This limited both the duration of arguments and the intensity of verbal conflict. These findings raised important questions about the interactional organisation of mediation sessions.

Finally, Worthington et al. (1997) founded an approach termed strategic-hope focused relationship enrichment. They used a brief eclectic research based programme to enhance couples' relationships. 51 couples (16 married, 24 cohabiting, 11 engaged) completed five sessions of enrichment counselling. Couples who received enrichment counselling had higher relationship satisfaction and quality-of-couple skills at post-test and at the three week follow-up than did written assessment only (control) couples. Conditions did not differ in terms of quality of overall attraction or two measures of commitment. It was concluded that relationship enrichment using this programme was effective, powerful and cost-effective.

Prevention

There were relatively few studies in the recent literature dealing with the prevention of relationship problems. Meyerstein (1996) found the joining of families through re-marriage was a complex process, particularly when children were involved. A host of ambivalent feelings, role changes, marital adjustments, and new challenges had to be faced. The format of brief systemic pre-remarital counselling offered family members an opportunity to address the feelings and multiple issues of transition. Within the counselling framework, therapeutic ritual had been found to be a useful adjunctive technique.

The prevention of marital breakdown was studied by Clulow (1996). He discussed three preventative paradigms commonly used for preventing divorce. These were policing, medical and educational. A fourth paradigm was suggested, a consultative approach, which implied a cyclical rather than a linear view of life experience. The consultative paradigm had the potential to integrate – not only the preventative paradigms but also the concepts of prevention and cure that so often were pursued as if they existed in separate compartments.

Finally, Fraenkel et al. (1997) studied the rationale for a preventive approach to helping couples in marriage. While divorce rates were high and many other couples remained together, but miserable, this was surely not what couples desired from the outset. The conflict and breakdown of these crucial relationships contributed to mental and medical health problems for adults and children, behavioural disturbances in children, problems in worker productivity, and serious economic difficulties for families and societies. Too many couples sought help only after significant, often irreversible, damage had occurred. It did not have to be that way. A variety of approaches were available that were capable of being used to teach couples the skills, behaviours and attitudes of good relationships before they encountered damage to their union. Here, one particular cognitive behavioural approach was used, along with a review of the research on the effectiveness of such approaches and a description of some of the strategies of this model. A list of common roadblocks to the work of prevention was discussed, along with a couple of brief case examples. It was felt that there was reason to believe that couples could benefit a great deal from prevention.

Causes and associated features of disharmony

In this section we will discuss the causes and associated features with marital disharmony and the need for mediation. These included:

- gender links
- infidelity
- power struggles
- fertility problems
- work addiction
- violence between partners
- physical handicap
- alcohol mis-use
- lack of communication

Gender links

Several studies allude to gender links as important aspects in mediation processes. O'Donohue and Crouch (1996) discussed whether communication training programmes in marital therapy had been sufficiently sensitive to gender-linked factors in communication, through a research review. Communication was often a treatment target in marital therapy. Although existing data indicated that individuals tended to hold stereotypes of gender differences in language, many of these differences had not been supported in empirical investigations. Gender

influences variables such as amount of conversation elicited, length of utterance, use of qualifying phrases, swearing and compliment style. Effective communication therapy had to be facilitated by evaluating each partner's gender-based expectations of their own communication behaviour and those regarding communication of the other partner. It was felt that a number of personality and situational variables moderated some of these effects, and need to be considered in therapy.

Gregory and Leslie (1996) examined the effect of the race and gender of 63 clients and therapists, aged 20–40 plus years, on their male (aged 21–52 years) and female (aged 21–57 years) partners' assessments of an initial and subsequent family/marital therapy session. The individuals, belonging to black and white families, evaluated the first and fourth therapy sessions using the Session Evaluation Questionnaire, which evaluated therapy smoothness. A strong effect for race was found, with black females rating the first sessions with a white therapist more negatively than white females. Black males had a more positive response than whites to the first session, regardless of the therapist's race. The therapist's sex had no significant effect on the client's session assessment. The effect of the therapist's race decreased over time. Only the black females with white therapists experienced an increase in smoothness over time.

A comparison was carried out between levels of sexism and feminism in the clinical decisions made by marriage and family therapists who had no training in gender issues with those who had such training, either through a separate course or by integrating gender issues throughout the curriculum (Leslie and Clossick, 1996). 150 entry-level marriage and family therapy students or therapists (aged 21–64 years) were assessed for the type of gender training received and whether the gender course was taught from a feminist perspective. Levels of feminism and sexism in clinical assumptions and interventions of the individuals were evaluated using clinical vignettes. Of the 102 individuals with some gender issue training, 64 per cent had received it from a feminist perspective. Though gender training alone did not influence levels of sexism and feminism in clinical decision making, levels of sexism were significantly lower for individuals who had received gender coursework from a feminist perspective.

Finally, Stabb et al. (1997) found differential treatment by gender had been an on-going area of concern and uncertainty both in society at large and in clinical research. In this investigation, the attributions of a 50 year old white male marriage and family therapist were coded and analysed over the course of therapy for three different married couples to determine if cause for positive and negative events was assigned differentially to females and males.

Additionally, the stability and globality dimensions of the therapist's attributions about the couples were examined for stereotypical gender-related patterns. The results indicated no gender differences in locus of causal attribution but some gender-related patterns in stability and globality dimensions.

Infidelity

Despite the commonness of infidelity in marital problems only two studies in recent years existed. Atwood and Seifer (1997) discussed the socio-cultural definitions of extramarital sex that influenced the reasons couples constructed for involving themselves in extramarital sex. Information was presented on their typical psychological reactions, taking into account current research. The article presented a review of what was known and the research on extramarital sex and then concentrated on marital meaning systems – their development and maintenance – focusing on social constructionist themes and therapy which served to shift the focus of a problem-oriented approach towards a search for the strengths of the extramarital sex couple. A four-stage constructionist therapeutic model was proposed. The stages included:

- Joining the family meaning systems.
- Inviting the couple to explore their present meaning systems.
- Inviting the couple to expand their meaning systems.
- Stabilising the new meaning systems.

This approach allowed the couple to construct new meanings around the extramarital sex issue so that they were able to find a workable solution.

Using cross-cultural perspectives to understand infidelity in couples, Penn et al. (1997) found that all marital therapists encountered a couple who had been or who were

affected by infidelity. The literature on infidelity lacked an understanding of its impact on cultural perspectives. This article discussed the ways in which infidelity was viewed within the context of three ethnic minorities in the United States: African Americans, Hispanic Americans, and Asian Americans. The authors provided an overview of infidelity according to religious traditions.

Power struggles

Only one study referred to power struggles, this being of Gray-Little et al. (1996). It examined the association of marital power type to marital adjustment, and response to behavioural marital therapy. A behavioural measure was used to classify 53 distressed couples into egalitarian, husband-dominant, wife dominant or anarchic power patterns. Marital adjustment was assessed by measures of marital satisfaction, desired relationship change and two communication indexes. At pre-treatment, egalitarian couples showed the best overall marital adjustment and anarchic couples showed the worst; at post-treatment, egalitarian and wife-led couples reported the highest marital satisfaction, and anarchic couples reported the lowest. Wife dominant couples improved the most, reporting increased marital satisfaction and demonstrating improved communication. The discussion considered the special treatment needs of anarchic couples for whom improved communication occurred in a context of continued marital dissatisfaction.

Fertility problems

Only one study, that of Jones and Hunter (1996) concerned itself specifically with infertility experiences. they studied three couples experiences of fertility problems in the early stages of investigation; men and women were interviewed together and separately and their accounts of infertility were analysed using a discourse analytic approach. The method involved examining the narrative text for theses relevant to the question, identifying accounts used by participants to explain their experiences and hypothesising about the functions of these accounting practices. The participants reported that non-conception was not always a problem to them, but that this varied depending on time, biology, life plans, relationships within which it was being discussed. The subjectivity of people with fertility problems appeared to be less consistent and more contextually contradictory than expected.

Work addiction

With the increased tendency towards the work ethic, work was considered an important aspect of marital problems by Robinson (1996). He studied the relationship between work addiction and family functioning. A theoretical model was presented which suggested that a relationship existed between work addiction, family of origin, and family functioning in adulthood. A review of the pertinent literature was presented followed by a case example and clinical implications for the practice of marriage and family therapy.

Violence between partners

Although a common issue, violence within the relationship only received one piece of research over the past years. Ehrensaft and Vivian (1996) used questionnaires and clinical interviews to reveal that over 6 per cent of couples seeking marital therapy experienced physical violence in their relationship. However, fewer than 10 per cent of these couples spontaneously reported or identified the violence as a presenting problem. Spouses' explanations for not spontaneously reporting couple violence were examined in 116 clinic couples. The top three reasons were as follows:

- It was not a problem.
- It was unstable or infrequent.
- It was secondary to or caused by other problems.

There were no gender differences in this regard. Further, there were no differences regarding explanations offered for failure to report partner violence versus own violence. However, differences were found between mildly and severely aggressive spouses and between husband to wife and wife to husband violence.

Physical handicap

Speziale (1997) examined the changes in couples living with multiple sclerosis (MS), particularly when sexual, cognitive and affective functioning had been affected. Two case studies of couples in whom the female partners had MS were presented and clinical intervention, divorce and extramarital relationships among couples living with MS were discussed. The author recommended a prerequisite clinical assessment of how the intrusion of MS disrupted the roles, rules, and boundaries of the marital and sexual relationship, and the larger social systems in which partners participated (including personal and familial histories of physical and psychosocial losses, life crises, stigmatised social identities, and socioeconomic hardship, It also included unresolved grief, depression, shame, and family secrets. The author suggested that the partners benefited from knowledge about MS, prescribed drugs and symptom management techniques.

Alcohol mis-use

Again only one study in recent years discussed the importance of alcohol mis-use leading to marital disorders (Rotunda and O'Farrell, 1997). Clients with alcohol and other substance use disorders were routinely encountered by practitioners in various treatment settings. This article traced the rationale for using marital and family therapy with alcoholics and described an ongoing behavioural marital therapy programme that exemplified an integration of clinical practice and research in this area. Specific treatment suggestions were offered and practical considerations for therapists working with families struggling with alcoholism were discussed including the role of self-help groups in family treatment, the danger of having preconceived notions about 'alcoholic families', and the necessity for clinics and clinicians to possess the capacity to assess and treat comorbid psychological disorders as well as addictive behaviours.

Lack of communication

Deterioration in communication patterns had been empirically linked to eventual separation and divorce in married couples (Ross and Estrada, 1997). This article drew on this research in describing a clinical intervention for use with couples in conjoint therapy. The intervention involved the use of a brief videotaped interaction task, which was completed by the couple at the outset and repeated periodically through the course of marital therapy. The potential utility of this intervention as both a clinical assessment and treatment tool with a wide range of couples was discussed and a brief case example of the intervention was provided.

The question of what makes relationships last or not last was considered by McCarthy (1997). Rather than an indication of lifetime commitment, the predominant form of marriage in western societies had become 'companionate'. It was held together by personal and emotional consideration rather than by traditional influences. The pursuit of personal satisfaction was an essential factor in marital relationships and, as a result, marriage had become less secure. One result of this was the growth of counselling services which aimed to assist couples through the process of negotiating relationships or in coming to terms with the emotional distress of failing to do so. This research attempted to address some of the concerns about the supposed lack of research on the impact of counselling. It focused on evaluation of marriage counselling provided by an agency operating in the field of relationship counselling. The evidence suggested counselling was able to help couples re-negotiate their relationships and help them through the personal anxieties connected with relationship problems. It clearly had a role to play in helping people through the complexities of companionate marriage, although it did not work for everyone and many couples who started counselling did not complete the process.

The diagnosis of marital mediation processes

It is important to not merely assess situations or problems relating to marital relationship difficulties, there should also be the assessing of individuals, especially in a relationship conflict (Lowenstein, 1994a). Marital mediation or therapy must involve the individuals and Lowenstein discussed the position of the big 'T' and little 't' i.e. those who seek thrills and are likely to be very extroverted personalities and those who do not seek such excitement and may be more introverted. Little 't' individuals are more eager for harmony and are conservative in their personality traits. While opposites attract in

a relationship, the more the individuals have in common, the more likely the marital relationship will work except in one area, that of seeking control or dominance. Areas where there are likely to be difficulties between big 'T' and little 't' individuals are in the rate of infidelity where big 'T' may predominate, also in sexual dissatisfaction and problems, attitudes to love, marital abuse and spouse abuse. Sometimes there are additional difficulties between extroverts and introverts or big 'T' and little 't's in relation to caring for children, dealing with household chores, division of labour, recreation interests, religious differences and the handling of money. It is vital when carrying out mediation processes to make each partner aware of their strengths and weaknesses and to discuss these individual differences in the diagnostic sessions.

Attributions and behaviour in functional and dysfunctional marriages were studied by Bradbury et al. (1996). The study examined whether spouses' attributions for partner behaviour were related to their own behaviour by assessing their attributions and observing the problem-solving discussions of couples in which:

- Neither spouse was depressed or maritally distressed.
- The wife was depressed and both spouses were maritally distressed.
- The wife was not depressed and both spouses were maritally distressed.

To the extent they made maladaptive attributions, wives displayed less positive behaviour and more negative behaviour. Husbands' attribution and behaviour were unrelated, and associations between attributions and behaviour were not moderated by marital distress and depression. These results highlighted the need to clarify how partner behaviour contributed to the attributions spouses made and to re-examine interventions designed to modify attributions in marital therapy.

Wilson and Wilson (1996) considered that there were multiple selves operating within relationships. They asserted that the issues presented by couples in relationship therapy were to be regarded as an example of negative (dysfunctional) multiple selves. The authors clarified the role of multiple dysfunctional selves and their influence on each partner within a relationship. It was proposed that this provided the therapist with specific information regarding the client's diagnosis and intervention strategies. This consisted of 10 selves (e.g. telic, paratelic, arousal-avoiding, excitement-seeking, the conformist, negativistic types). Finally, Bagarozzi (1997) suggested a Marital Intimacy Needs Questionnaire. He discussed the construction of the Marital Intimacy Needs Questionnaire which contained information on satisfaction with the intimacy in marriage which was thought to be an important aspect of a successful marriage. For many clinicians and family researchers, intimacy had been narrowly conceptualised as a unidimensional construct and unidirectiorial process. The author, however, conceptualised intimacy as a multi-faceted construct, and identified nine dimensions of intimacy, each having four inter-related components. Clinical assessments of these dimensions and components were accomplished by the use of the Marital Needs Intimacy Questionnaire.

Treatment approaches in mediation

The recent research suggested at least 11 approaches for the treatment of marital or relationship disharmony. They included the following:

- Role planning
- Developing empathy
- Pro-social development
- Eclectic psychodynamic approaches
- Cognitive behaviour therapy
- Solution focus tests
- Physical, emotional closeness development
- Family of origin approach
- Involving clergy
- Emotionally focused therapy
- Education-type therapy

Role planning

Cohen et al. (1996) assisted parents, by mediation, in the transition from being a nuclear family to a bi-nuclear family. During the process, the needs of the children were taken into consideration and the particular difficulties of the parents who no longer functioned as a couple, rather as two independent individuals jointly responsible for rearing their children. A way was proposed to create a common basis for discussion between the two spouses, who were in a conflictual situation,

in order to jointly plan their parenthood in terms of times, roles and content.

As a result in the dramatic increase in women's participation in the work force, more relationship therapists were seeing couples who were dissatisfied with how domestic labour was divided in their homes (Rasmussen et al., 1996). This paper was an effort to delineate some of the complex therapeutic issues such as engaging men in therapy, exploring emotional issues connected with house-work, and the mechanism of gatekeeping or the tendency of many wives to resist or manage their husbands' efforts to increase participation in the home. Also included was a therapeutic framework for addressing client concerns about domestic responsibilities.

Another study by Worthington (1996) considered health and productivity as important values in 20th century American society. As business companies had become more major players in delivery of mental health services via managed mental health care, the value placed on productivity had become even more important than in the past. Here the impact of managed mental health care on marital and family interventions was discussed. Implications for helping marriages and families were grouped as follows:

- Improvement of effectiveness and efficiency of marital and family therapies.
- Documentation of effectiveness and efficiency of marital and family therapies.
- Shift to more focus on health and prevention.
- Identity of providers of services that helped marriages and families.
- Training of providers of services to marriages and families.

Developing empathy

The inverse relationship between depression and intimacy was conceptualised as a function of the couple's affective experience, with empathising as the specific mediating factor. Depression, as a disorder of excessive self-focusing was amenable to treatment approaches that helped to shift the focus of concern from self to others, as found by Odegaard (1996). This shift occurred in couple treatment when the underlying negative affect of the caretaking partner was accessed and used to pull the depressed one out of self-absorption and into an empathy, other-focused experience.

Prolonged caretaking and chronic depression led to a breakdown in a couple's empathising capacity, as the caretaker's experience of fear, helplessness, or frustration activated old coping patterns of withdrawal or over-functioning such as use of control, while the depressed one slipped into further self-absorption. Unmasking the caretaker's despair activated the other's empathy, facilitating movement out of the self-absorption. Depression was in fact, in part, a consequence of under-utilised empathy.

Pro-social development

Rudd (1996) considered the communication effects on divorce mediation: how participants' argumentativeness, verbal aggression and compliance-gaining strategies were used in mediation. She investigated the relationship among participants' argumentativeness, verbal aggression and the use of compliance-gaining strategies and their level of satisfaction with the divorce mediation process. 87 couples who participated in court-related divorce mediation, specifically to settle child custody and visitation issues, were interviewed. The results of a stepwise regression analysis indicated that the more participants used prosocial compliance-gaining strategies the more satisfied they were with the mediation. Similarly Lowenstein (1998a) studied Parental Alienation Syndrome and saw a 2-step approach towards a solution. The first considered motivation towards participation in the mediation process was having hovering over them the possibility of legal or judicial sanctions if this could not be achieved through mediation. The second step was to use the court procedure for the purpose of settling those who were unable to benefit from the mediation process, and most especially that party which failed to cooperate in that process. In a later unpublished study, Lowenstein (1998b), the author presented the value of the expert witness in dealing with couples in a conflict situation, often concerning their children and who should have custody of them. He suggested several approaches including the sectarian approach and the expert witness as an independent arbitrator, and presented the results of mediation as compared with the use merely of the legal system and the courts. It was found, as many others had found, that of those who participated in arbitration and mediation, they achieved greater

satisfaction than those brought into the legal system, and the adversarial system most particularly, using only solicitors within the conflict situation.

Eclectic psycho-dynamic approaches

Schoenewolf (1996) in an article with the intriguing title, 'The Couple who fell in hate', studied couples in which the husband was passive and the wife aggressive who were a common sight in therapy clinics. Such couples were difficult to work with because they had become addicted to their ritual of hate, which offered each a secondary gratification. To work with them, therapists often needed to be creative and utilise eclectic approaches. In the case described, the therapist used a paradoxical behavioural approach combined with psychoanalysis.

Cognitive behaviour therapy

Cognitive behaviour therapeutic approaches in marital conflict were used by Cheung (1996). He used the problematic concept of attribution, which had received increasing attention in cognitive behavioural marital therapy. Research had found that the attribution dimensions of source, globality, stability, intent, and voluntariness were related to the marital distress and conflict behaviours. It was proposed that there were three levels of events for which a spouse had to make attributions: the episode level, the behaviour level, and the global relationship level. Different reattribution techniques needed to be employed to target attributional change at appropriate levels of conflict attributions.

Individual behavioural cognitive therapy in marital problems related to depression were used by Emanuels-Zuurveen and Emmelkamp (1996). 37 depressed individuals, aged 18–65 years, experiencing marital distress were randomly assigned to either individual behavioural cognitive therapy or marital therapy. The individual treatment condition focused on depressed mood, behavioural activity and dysfunctional cognitions, whereas in the marital condition the partner was involved in the treatment and the focus was on the communication process in the marital relationship. Multiple analysis of variance revealed that treatment led to statistically significant improvements in depressed mood, behavioural activity and dysfunctional cognitions, an increase in relationship satisfaction and improvement of communication in patients and spouses. A significant interaction effect was found, showing that marital therapy had more impact on relationship variables than the individual treatment.

Solution focus tests

Solution-focused therapy mediation was used by Franklin (1996). Processes of change were illustrated in a marital case study in which solution-focused therapy was being applied. This approach focused on stabilising semantics and politics at level one and on changing semantics and politics at level two. The individuals made progress in therapy as indicated by verbal reports and scores on standardised tests.

Physical emotional closeness development

Durana (1996) used quantitative and qualitative research methods to evaluate the impact of bonding (i.e. physical closeness and emotional openness) and catharsis in the bonding and emotional re-education. 73 adults were assessed by means of measures of marital adjustment, self-esteem, depression, anxiety, control and support. The results suggested that bonding and emotional re-education in marital adjustment led to greater affection, satisfaction and self-esteem. The study explored differences in changes for males and females. Exploratory findings indicated that the practical application of intimate relationship skills approach was useful for distressed couples and suggested that there was a gender difference associated with changes in marital satisfaction.

Family of origin approach

An example of this was by Kane (1996) who used an experiential approach to family of origin work with marital and family therapy students. The incorporation of a day workshop into an introductory course on marriage and family therapy for graduate counselling students was

described. In this workshop, participants moved through a series of experiential exercises that invited affective involvement with family of origin dynamics. However, because educators had to evaluate the work of trainees, they had to avoid engaging students in affective work for fear of entering into dual roles. By including a therapist whose only function in the programme was to facilitate the trainees' family of origin work, training programmes were to incorporate this component without blurring the roles of instructor and therapist,

A similar approach was used by Framo (1996). He presented a general technique for using the family of origin as a therapeutic resource for adults in marital and family therapy. Marital and family difficulties were viewed as elaborations of relationship problems of the spouses in their original families, so sessions with the family of origin were considered a possible basis for reconstructive changes in the present family setting.

Involving clergy

Weaver et al. (1997) examined the need for greater collaboration between clergy and marriage and family therapists. Several reasons for collaboration were outlined including that clergy are frequently asked to address marital and family problems and religion played an important role in family and marital coping and support strategies. This was not accepted by everyone concerned. In addition, marriage and family therapists acknowledged the highest rates of religious involvement of any mental health profession, placing them in a unique position to be involved in the continuing education of clergy. The authors stressed the need for therapists and clergy to use each other's resources for training purposes, clinical evaluative and referral skills, and information on domestic violence and child abuse, as well as other family issues.

Emotionally focused therapy

Hannah et al. (1997) examined the extent to which a brief, structured couples therapy programme based on Imago Relationship Therapy was associated with improvements in individual psychological functioning as well as on a measure of relationship satisfaction, the

Marital Satisfaction Inventory (MSI). Individuals were nine heterosexual couples, all aged 26–58 years, referred for therapy. An examination of pre to post treatment differences revealed statistically significant differences on three of the four COMPASS scales and all three MSI scales. The rate of improvement in individual distress per couple's therapy session was approximately equal to the improvement, found in previous studies, yielded by individual therapy. The results supported previous findings that couples therapy was likely to be effective for the treatment of intra-personal difficulties and suggested that both relationship and individual distress indices should be utilised in the evaluation of the efficacy of marital therapies.

Predictors of success in emotionally focused marital therapy were examined by Johnson and Talitman (1997). They examined client variables expected to predict success in emotionally focused marital therapy. The relationship of attachment quality, level of emotional self-disclosure, level of interpersonal trust, and traditionality to the therapy outcome variables, marital adjustment, intimacy and therapist ratings of improvement were examined. 34 couples, mean age 22–60 years participated. The couples were given 12 sessions of emotionally focused marital therapy. At the end of the treatment and at a three month follow-up, the couples' marital adjustment and intimacy level were assessed using various rating scales. Overall, therapeutic alliance predicted a successful outcome; the task dimension of the alliance in particular predicted couples' satisfaction. Couples who made the most gains at follow-up also indicated lower initial marital satisfaction and included males who indicated lower levels of use of attachment figure on the attachment measure at intake. The couples most likely to be satisfied after the 12 sessions of emotionally focused marital therapy and at follow-up were couples who made a positive alliance with the therapist and, more specifically, who saw the task of this approach as relevant to their problems.

Education type therapy

Arbuthnot et al. (1997) studied the patterns of relitigation following divorce education. Two groups of parents were tracked for two years following their divorce: a group of 89 who attended a mandatory divorce education class and a comparison group of 23 who did not. The two groups did not differ in any assessed demographic or family characteristics. At the follow-up assessment, the parents who attended the class had relitigated over all issues less than half as often than those who had not attended the class. Moreover, rate of relitigation was related to mastery of skills learned in the class. The results were discussed in terms of the needs for outcome evaluation and design of education programmes for divorcing parents.

Finally, Johnson (1997) commented on marital therapy and suggested that the new 'gold standard' for outcome in marital therapy was a 50 per cent success rate. The author contended that the 50 per cent success rate in marital therapy, whether success was defined as improvement or recovery, was in no way accepted by the leading proponents in the field as an acceptable or sufficient standard of success in this modality.

Summary of the research of mediation

Virtually all research into the process of mediation and most especially the process of mediation regarding warring partners and their relationship indicated positive or more positive outcome than that through legal channels. It would appear that the mediation process provides not merely the opportunity of individuals in conflict to solve their problems through this procedure but even when the relationship has ended, mediation can play an important part in developing harmony between the partners. This must be seen as essential especially in relation to the offspring which both partners share. Numerous mediators report that frequently individuals in a relationship come too late to the mediation process. This led to acrimony between the partners, with difficulties which were almost impossible to solve through mediation procedures. Even here, however, there is the possibility of achieving something or much more than through the legal process of the courts or through solicitors.

If nothing else, the mediation process, if used alongside the legal process in marital disharmony can prove to be effective in stabilising situations that exist between once close partners and their children. The research, of course, as always, indicates the importance of preventing parental or relationship splits by establishing or re-establishing communication links after a diagnostic approach to the marital relationship problem has been completed.

The mediation process viz a viz 100 consecutive referrals to a therapeutic centre

Problem

Couples often fail to realise they have relationship difficulties until it is too late or until there is no way back to the re-establishing of a relationship. Often, partners have sought others outside marriage or have been so disillusioned with the relationship that they deem it impossible to seek a reconciliation. There are, however, instances when some glimmer of hope still exists, wherein both partners, one often more than the other, seek for the benefit of themselves and even more for their children, to seek a rescue of their relationship. What follows will be the delineation of the causes of marital difficulty and how they were diagnosed and ultimately treated within one centre.

Representative causes among marital couples

The representative causes of marital disharmony and eventual abandonment of one partner or the other in the relationship are shown in Table 5. It will be noted that the causes are rarely singular but rather multitudinous. The most common is a general feeling of malaise or feeling that the relationship is over and that one or both partners no longer feel loved or love towards the other partner. This rather general view needs to be explored carefully in order to ascertain what are usually other specific causes related to the marital difficulty. Also important are frequent heated arguments and sulking within the relationship, poor or negative communication, sexual problems and infidelity.

Therapeutic approaches adopted

The most common therapeutic approach adopted was a combination of cognitive and behavioural approaches. Rarely were cognitive methods on their own or behavioural methods used or psychodynamic procedures. Couples tended to

need the feeling that there was a problem which could only be sorted out with the help of an expert. Often they relied too heavily on the expert to provide a solution to their problems and it was made clear to couples that without them having control ultimately over the situation and participating effectively with the guidance of the therapist, little could be achieved.

Most couples referred themselves for help, usually by one partner encouraging this. Others were referred by general practitioners or friends but generally the motivation towards having help was there, although it varied in intensity. Once it was made clear to the couples that there was no 'magic wand' that could be waved which would resolve all difficulties, but problems had to be worked at conscientiously, intensively and with the guidance of the therapist, better results were possible, although in some cases, no positive result was obtained. A number of couples, however, benefited from the sessions, even though their marriage could not be saved. They were able to resolve their conflicts and parted as amicably as possible. This naturally was beneficial to themselves as well as to any children who were present.

Results

The results are delineated in Tables 1–8.

Table 1 indicates that most couples referred themselves for help.

Table 2 shows that most marital problems occurred in the early years between 18 and 45. Socio-economic backgrounds tended to favour upper and middle class groups with working class couples being somewhat less likely to refer themselves or be referred for marital therapy (Table 3).

Table 4 indicates the motivation to participate in the mediation process was important, although some couples considered that the mediation process occurred too late or felt uncertain of its outcome. After the first session, however, there was an almost immediate change of view and more positive or optimistic notions were expressed as to how the process of mediation could work favourably.

The frequency of diagnosed causes or problems in the dysfunctional relationship showed that the initial number was much higher than the ultimate number when some success had been achieved (Table 5).

On the whole, there were relatively few treatment sessions for most clients. It was unfortunate that 15 of the clients dropped out before the completion of the sessions, which might have improved the results indicated in Table 17.8, 'Immediate outcomes'. Ten per cent

Table 17.1 Source of referral

Self referral	69
G.P. or other Professional	23
Others e.g. friend	8

Table 17.2 Ages of clients

Ages	
18–25	21
26–35	39
36–45	20
46–55	17
56+	3

Table 17.3 Socio-economic background

Upper and middle class	59
Working class	34
Out of work or retired	7

Table 17.4 Motivation to participate in mediation process

	Initially	After 1st session
Very motivated	16	37
Hopeful	27	34
Unsure	36	16
Expressed feeling it might be too late	21	13

of the couples had a relationship which was dissolved with remaining conflicts while a good number also had a dissolved relationship with little outcome conflict remaining. About half of the individuals were able to rescue their relationship.

Table 17.5 Frequency of diagnosed cause (problem) of relationship dysfunctions*

	Initially	After 1st session
Generally feeling of being out of love	83	27
Frequent heated arguments, sulking etc.	71	23
Poor or negative communications	59	21
Infidelity	26	11
Alcohol or other substance abuse	19	17
Mental health problems (depression, paranoid behaviour, manic behaviour etc.)	12	11
Physical illness or its effects on relationship	16	9
Financial problems	29	18
Child rearing difference	14	9
Sexual problems	67	14

*Most couples and individuals gave a number of reasons.

Table 17.6 Method of treatment employed

Cognitive behavioural	77
Cognitive	21
Behavioural	1
Psycho-dynamic	1

Table 17.7 Number of treatment sessions required

1–5 sessions	42
6–10 sessions	24
11 + sessions	19
Dropped out of treatment before completion	15

Table 17.8 Immediate outcomes

	Immediate outcome	Follow-up outcome 1 year later
Relationship very much improved	19	22
Relationship somewhat improved	37	34
Relationship dissolved with little outcome conflict	34	35
Relationship dissolved with remaining conflict	10	9

Conclusions

The mediation process has a valuable role to play in the dynamics of resolving marital problems or relationship difficulties between couples.

Even when marriages or relationships are over, mediation processes can do a great deal to make a reduction of conflict possible between the individuals in the former relationship.

Chapter Eighteen

Mediation and the legal profession

As an expert witness working with the legal system, and a forensic psychologist, I have for many years acted as mediator in a variety of areas – way before it was in vogue! There are probably as many techniques, procedures and strategies on how mediation actually works as there are mediators.

The following chapter explains my own approaches which may be of value to other mediators or those considering using this approach now and in the future. Table 1 considers the kind of problems wherein I have found mediation to have a place. Table 2 sets out the rate of success achieved and the steps involved in the process of mediation.

Table 18.1 108 Consecutive mediation cases

Type	No.
Marital or relationship conflicts	84
Industrial or work related disputes	15
Other conflicts	9

As may be noted from Table 1, most of the mediation which I practice has been in the area of marital or relationship conflicts. This is followed by industrial or work-related disputes, either between members of the management team or between employers and employees. The third group has been in the form of other conflicts, usually conflicts between neighbours, parents and children, etc.

Table 2 demonstrates that mediation has had a good result in most cases. It must be stated that the selection of cases for mediation bear a large reason for such successes. This will be noted in the next section.

Selection for mediation

It is important to understand the criteria for accepting cases which involve mediation. Some clients are not at all willing to accept mediation. In such cases, there must be a very powerful incentive and punitive alternatives to encourage

Table 18.2 Rate of success

	A	B	C	D	Total
Marital or relationship conflict	61	15	4	4	84
Industrial or work related disputes	11	2	1	1	15
Other conflicts	5	2	1	1	9
Totals	77	19	6	6	108

Key: A – Very successful; B – Moderate improvement; C – Temporary improvement; D – No improvement.

participation in the mediation process. This group will, despite everything, be the least likely to have beneficial results or a positive outcome. Next are those who are willing to participate, but have fixed, inflexible or intransigent positions from which they are unwilling to move to any degree. These clients are also unlikely to respond positively. Lastly, the largest group, who expect to adopt a more 'give and take' approach. They expect to have some of the issues resolved in their favour and they are able to accept that issues will also be judged in favour of 'the opposition'. This group is likely to have the best prognosis for a more lasting and successful outcome. In the case of the largest group (marital and relationship problems) it is of the utmost importance to accept only those clients who agree on the following:

1. The mediation process is not a vehicle to 'have it all their own way'.
2. They are willing to view the issues as 'problems' that they wish to resolve with the help of the mediator.
3. They will be willing to adhere to the decisions made by the mediator with the assistance of the factions in conflict.
4. Each faction wishes to find a solution, even if this means giving in more to their adversary and their demands.

The last point is the most difficult on which to reach agreement, and yet if the other three areas are acceptable, mediation still has a place. It is virtually impossible to achieve success through mediation when at least three of the above are not attained.

The mediation process

Before mediation between conflicting parties can take place, it is vital to ascertain what the conflict is all about. This can be carried out as follows:

1. Seeing those in conflict individually to ascertain:
   - The reason for their grievance.
   - What they wish to achieve through the mediation process.
   - How much each one involved in the conflict is willing to give way.
   - How much power for decision-making they will allow the mediator.
   - Assessing the position of each, using standardised relationship forms.
   - Getting each party to take an objective and projective personality test.
2. Further:
   - See areas of agreement with individuals concerned in the conflict.
   - Ascertain areas of disagreement with the individuals concerned in the conflict.
   - Discover areas towards which each of the parties are willing to be shifted with the help of the arbiter.
3. Decide whether there is sufficient common ground but leave areas of disagreement for the time being.
4. Move the process forward and engage the individual parties in conflict to view only areas of agreement that have been established by the individual meetings with the arbitrator.
5. Meet individuals in conflict to seek to shift some of the issues of disagreement.
6. Meet again with the adversaries to discuss additional areas of agreement.
7. Continue the process of eliminating those areas of conflict still remaining and to encourage each of the adversaries to make further concessions.
8. Only after there is agreement obtained by individual meetings should areas formerly in conflict be presented to both parties when they meet together.
9. Future meetings should be arranged by both parties agreeing to these meetings and the times that they are to be held.
10. Both parties must agree when the mediation process is to end, either because there has been a successful resolution of all or most of the issues in conflict or because no further progress can be made.
11. All parties in conflict should be encouraged to solve future problems, if possible, on their own.
12. Failing (11) parties should have access to further help from the mediator if this is necessary, and they both accept such help.

Long-term effects of mediation

One is frequently asked, 'What are the long-term effects of mediation?' The answer depends on what one means by long-term and what one means by success. In the case of warring adults who have had, or still have, a relationship through marriage or cohabitation, positive results may follow successful mediation, but this is not to say that there will be no future conflicts. Having once been counselled in conflict resolution, those in further conflict often try to solve future difficulties on their own by putting into effect what they have learned from the mediation process. Sometimes this leads to success; at other times, they may be in need of further involvement of the mediator. The same can be said for conflicts in business, industry or between neighbours, etc.

Summary

It has been shown how important the selection process is and which individuals are likely to respond to mediation and those who may not.

The success rate is encouraging when one considers the difficulties involved in resolving three areas of conflict, i.e. between couples in a relationship, industrial disputes and other conflicts such as those between neighbours. My personal experience of the mediation process demonstrates considerable success in more than 50 per cent of cases over a 20-year period. It must, however, also be accepted that mediation is not a panacea for all problems, and many instances and issues cannot be resolved by mediation alone.

Mediation is currently in the limelight as an alternative to the increasing litigation costs and time involved in trying cases before the courts. It is felt, and rightly so, that many conflicts between individuals and groups can more effectively be ameliorated through mediation. The most recent inaugural lecture by the Lord Chancellor, Lord Irvine of Lairg, emphasised the importance of mediation. The Legal Aid Board has also decided to allow mediation to be covered by legal aid. Seeking mediation as a viable alternative to litigation has also been supported by the Academy of Expert Witnesses, the Law Society and the Bar Council.

In the case where mediation fails, there is still recourse to litigation; however, the fact that litigation remains as the final option may in itself encourage solutions via mediation.

It must be understood that mediation and the processes involved is dependent, to a large extent, on the individual carrying out the task. Although skills can be learned, personality factors and motivation play a part in the success of the individual carrying out the 'art' of mediation. Among the most important personality traits in the successful mediator are optimism, conviction, confidence, and perseverance. Additional attributes include patience, tolerance, and the ability to gain the respect and support of the parties involved in mediation.

Justice of the Peace, 4 Sept. 1999, 163: 709–10

Chapter Nineteen

The value of mediation in child custody disputes

Introduction and abstract

What follows will be set out into the following categories:

- Diagnosing child custody disputes.
- Policies and strategies dealing with child custody disputes.
- Favourable outcomes through mediation.
- Mediation in cases of domestic violence.

Virtually all research indicates that the role of mediation should be increased in custodial disputes between parents following divorce or separation. There is considerable evidence now that mediation is superior to litigation. Despite this however, litigation and adversarial approaches continue in connection with disputes between parents over their children. Not all cases lend themselves to shared parenting type decisions. Such shared parenting is certainly the ideal for which to aim, whenever possible. The crux of the matter appears to be seeking to have parents view their conflict as secondary to the care and future development of their children. This is where mediation could play an important role with the support of the courts and the litigation process. It is the view of the author that any parent who fails to co-operate with the aims of the mediator in putting children first in any dispute should be forced, by the court, to co-operate or else lose a degree of custody over children.

Diagnosing child custody disputes

Psychological diagnostic tools are rarely used in the diagnosis of parents and their children who are involved in child custody disputes. Heinze and Grisso (1996) reviewed the following instruments of parenting capacity that are currently used in child custody evaluations. These are: The Ackerman-Schoendorf Scales for Parent Evaluation of Custody, the Bricklin Perceptual Scales and Perception of Relationships Test, the Child Abuse Potential Inventory (CAPI), the Parent-Child Relationship Inventory (PCRI) and the Parenting Stress Index (PSI). These instruments were reviewed by obtaining the test manual and published and unpublished research on the instruments. Each measure was described, as well as research on the measures, norms, reliability, validity and generalisability. The measures were discussed with regards to their approach in processing parental effectiveness and principles of test construction. The results indicated that the CAPI, PCRI, and PSI were all useful measures that could be utilised in child custody cases and in divorce mediations.

Attempts were made to develop standardised tests for mediation assessment by others including Mathis and Yingling (1998a). The objective of such tests was to measure competent, discordant, disoriented, and chaotic parenting. One criteria of this assessment was to select good candidates for mediation as opposed to those who were unlikely to benefit from it. Emery (1999) suggested a way to help mental health professionals carry out child custody evaluations was to change the system for deciding custody in divorce, by promoting mediation procedures and adopting a new legal standard guiding child custody determinations.

The views of children always need to be considered when making decisions regarding parenting. This is emphasised by Ramirez et al. (1999). This Spanish study considered children's responses and beliefs towards parental separation and divorce. The parents were undergoing some form of mediation during separation and the divorce process. The results were evaluated according to age and sex, and also sex of the custodial parent, judicial or family mediation divorce/separation process, time since the divorce/separation, parental visitation regularity, and the children were questioned as to their perception of the source of parental conflict. Social policies on easing inter-parental conflict were discussed by Emery (2001). The social policies explicitly designed to reduce interpersonal conflict were often limited to:

- Divorce, especially child custody mediation.
- Legal interventions in spousal violence.

- Various educational programmes, particularly pre-marital counselling and educational programmes for divorcing parents.

Emery suggested that whilst these social policies might only have a limited effect on reducing inter-parental conflict and increasing co-operation, the policy might produce substantial effects over time as one of many contributors to shaping cultural views of conflict and the co-parenting relationship. Finally, Ackerman (2001) thought a step-by-step guidance approach to be of value, through a process of interviewing, performing behavioural observations, and collecting collateral information. The author used a wide variety of psychological tests designed specifically for evaluation of parental fitness for custody. These tests provided guidelines for evaluating the behaviour of parents and presented practical steps to take in determining whether alleged abuse between parents or parents and children had actually occurred.

Policies and strategies dealing with custody disputes

Those who carry out the procedures of mediation with divorced or separated couples must learn to assist them through mediation. Mediators should develop a strategy for dealing with children changing from a nuclear family to a bi-nuclear family. Any mediation technique must propose a method for developing a common basis of discussion between the two spouses. Such parents are often in conflict and find it difficult to plan their parenthood jointly in terms of times, roles and content (Cohen et al., 1996). One study concerned itself with mediation when one of the parents was gay. Here Campbell (1996) emphasised the importance of the mediator to interpret matters for both children and the parents. In the case of non-married couples Raisner (1997) reviewed the research and found that non-married parents had a higher no-show rate for purposes of mediation than that of divorcing parents. However, when non-married parents did appear for court ordered mediation, they reached agreements at the same rate as divorcing parents. The author found, surprisingly, that non-married parents with a history of violence were more likely to appear for appointments and reach agreements.

A Canadian study by Carruthers (1997) discussed the first legislatively based child protection mediation programme in Canada which was implemented in the Province of Nova Scotia in 1993. This programme had been criticised for not saving children from neglect and abuse. In Nova Scotia, there is, however, a growing interest and implementation of mediation programmes which is now passing throughout Canada. In a Norwegian study by Ekeland and Myklebust (1997) mandatory divorce mediation was discussed involving 456 male and female Norwegian adults who were either married with children aged 16 years and under, or unmarried adults with custody disagreements. These subjects were surveyed concerning conflicts in, and characteristics of, divorce proceedings and custody disagreements immediately before and after mediation and one year later. The success of mediation in solving conflicts was measured. The influence of custody decisions such as joint custody and the amount of visitation on amount and type of conflict was examined. The effect of these factors on the children's mental health was also assessed. The process of mediation led to considerable success.

Enforcing mediation however, can be a problematic matter as found by Kandel (1998). To avoid this it was found useful to have an affirmative obligation for mediation requested by the court and mediators to carry out child custody procedures, under a judicial sanction.

A nation-wide survey of 253 practitioner-level mediators was conducted to determine their views on the effectiveness of divorce, education programmes for parents on both the process and the outcome of divorce mediation. Arbuthnot and Kramer (1998) found that three-quarters of the respondents reported that divorce programmes were available in their communities. These programmes were run by the local court or by an independent non-profit organisation, and over half were mandatory. Over half the mediators reported that they covered formal divorce education with clients at least sometimes. The chief impact on the mediation process and outcome included greater focus on the children, more co-operation, and better communication skills between the parents. There should also be a minimum of custody and parenting plans and a trend towards less time required to reach agreement. Mediators believed that divorce education was appropriate for highly conflicted and power-imbalanced couples, but less so for couples involved in substance or spousal abuse. Just over two-thirds of mediators believed that divorce education should be made mandatory for all divorcing couples with children.

Solicitor's opinions concerning child custody mediation were reported by Lee et al. (1998a, 1998b). Psychologists who conducted divorce mediation or child custody assessments needed to understand the context of such professional practice and the views of other professions involved such as lawyers. In this study, family lawyers (n = 161) completed a questionnaire about mediation and assessment of custody disputes, indicating positive attitudes toward mediation and recognition of its favourable effects on the family. Lawyers viewed assessment as a desirable alternative to litigation but did not associate it with enhanced family functioning. Lawyers strongly endorsed the need for abuse screening prior to mediation.

A further favourable result of the value of mediation was reported by Kruk (1998), Lamb et al. (1999) and Austin (2000). Another study emphasised the importance of kinship care especially with individuals of African background who are involved in resolution disputes (Wilhelmus, 1998).

The emphasis by Wallerstein (1998) was that society has an important task in protecting the millions of children who have suffered from the father's emotional and economic abandonment, often in favour of commitment to new children in subsequent marriages. Allegations of substance abuse and physical, emotional and sexual abuse by spouses are sometimes involved in custody disputes as noted by Pruett et al. (2000). Here again court family service mediators are likely to play an important role to differentiate true from false allegations.

There have been a number of books written for couples to guide them on how best to deal with divorce or separation. Kranitz (2000) provided some practical information in resolving issues that arise when people who have lived together decide to separate. It is unfortunate that there are still a considerable number of custody battle 'burn-outs', where parents give up their role as carers due to the difficulties involved in legal custody battles (Turkat, 2000). In order to prevent this, another book which has had great influence in offering divorcing parents a way of avoiding custody battles is that of Stahl (2000). Many recent pieces of research emphasise the importance of increasing the non custodial

parent's access and visitation with their children (Keoughan et al., 2001; Hyden, 2001).

Favourable outcomes through mediation

Reference has already been made to the value of mediation by countries and states and local areas. The reviews of literature concerned with how children from divorced families adjust under different custodial arrangements is carried out by Twaite and Luchow (1996). The level of inter-parental conflict present in the family before and after divorce appears to be a powerful mediating variable that affects children's adaptation to different custodial situations.

It was concluded that custodial decisions needed to be made on an individual basis, with no presumption that custody should be awarded to either the mother or the father. It was clear, that regardless of the decision regarding custody, the parents should be educated regarding the importance of avoiding overt hostility in establishing a workable co-parenting relationship. Problems with communication in divorce mediation were noted by Rudd (1996). Also noted were a participant's argumentativeness, verbal aggression, and the need for compliance-gaining strategies during mediation.

The long-term effects of divorce mediation and resolution were studied by Dillon and Emery (1996). They found that of the 25 parents who chose mediation and the 28 parents who chose litigation to resolve child custody disputes, the mediation parents reported better communication between themselves and their former partner concerning the children. Non-custodial parents assigned to mediation reported more frequent current contact with their children and greater involvement with decisions about them.

Kelly (1996) discovered that after a decade of divorce mediation research which has focused on outcomes and settlements, as well as cost efficiency and client satisfaction, most studies reported mildly favourable to very positive results for the use of mediation. Kelly felt that research on the mediation process and mediator behaviours had received very limited attention and should be focused upon in the next decade of research to elevate the mediation field to a more sophisticated, effective level of practice.

Considering such a result it is clear that mediation is still the least used area of expertise, the preference being for solicitors to deal with disputes on a litigation basis. The questioning by Lee et al. (1998) of 161 family lawyers aged 25–59 years about mediation found there was a difference by gender and experience. Female attorneys held stronger views than did their male counterparts. There were few differences among the opinions of lawyers based on their years of experience or their own training in mediation. Compared to non-mediators, mediators rated the positive effect of mediation more highly. Mediators, however, differed as to their intervention, some preferring complete intervention and others non intervention (Smoron, 1998). Whatever methods were used, however, mediation was found to be effective in changing parents' views regarding adoption when there were crises between the partners (Heath, 1998).

In the case of parental alienation syndrome Lowenstein (1998) discussed the steps involved in mediation before, or while legal action occurred. The courts intervened only to enforce a solution recommended by the mediator. This is to prevent often tragic, acrimonious human interactions between former partners. He also advanced the proposal that mediation played a much larger role in cases of parental alienation syndrome in Britain than was previously recognised. Fathers and sometimes mothers gave up the battle to have regular contact with their children because of the custodial parents' intransigence and the court failing to act justly.

Professionals such as qualified psychologists or psychiatrists should be able to offer a full course of mediation, ideally before partners begin divorce proceedings or decisions regarding the placement of children with one party or the other are made. A 10-year study involving 16 cases provided evidence that the initial use of mediation might well be superior to the initial use of the adversarial system. Long-term and short-term satisfaction with mediation was strongly correlated according to Jones and Bodtker (1998). Returning to the earlier theme of parental alienation syndrome Vestal (1999) found that through mediation it was possible to detect this situation and remedial plans could be made to offset it and to restore the relationship of the non custodial partner with the children.

Most importantly the need for medication was significantly reduced by relying on mediation more than is currently the situation as noted by Jones and Bodtker (1999). They hypothesised that mediated child custody cases would have high rates of agreement and agreement maintenance. They also found that disputants in mediated child custody cases were more satisfied than disputants in non-mediated child custody cases; and that mediated child custody cases would have lower incidents of re-litigation or recidivism than non-mediated child custody cases. The results confirmed all hypotheses. Similar results were obtained by Hahn and Kleist (2000) in their study of a review of 10 years of divorce and custody mediation research. Alternative dispute resolution (ADR), similar to mediation, was analysed by Ezzel (2001). He concluded that this approach, favoured by judges as well as attorneys in domestic relationship disputes was beneficial and should be used in all domestic relation cases aside from those involving disputed child custody.

Perhaps most conclusive of all is a very recent study by Emery et al. (2001) who carried out a long-term follow-up on families who had been randomly assigned to mediate or litigate their child custody dispute. In comparison with families who litigated custody, non-residential parents who mediated were more involved in multiple areas of their children's lives. They also maintained more contact with their children, and had a greater influence in co-parenting 12 years after the resolution of their custody disputes. The increased involvement of non-residential parents who mediated did not lead to an associated increase in co-parenting conflict. Parents who mediated also made more changes in their children's living arrangements over the years. For the most part, the changes apparently reflected increased co-operation and flexibility. Satisfaction declined for parents (especially fathers) in both groups over time, but fathers remained much more satisfied if they mediated rather than litigated custody. Few differences in satisfaction were found between mothers in the two groups. The 12-year follow-up data indicated that, even in the contested cases, mediation encouraged both parents to remain involved in their children's lives after divorce without increasing co-parenting conflict.

Mediation in cases of domestic violence

There was some hesitancy to involve mediators when there has been definite violence between the adults. Mathis and Tanner (1998b) studied a sample of 149 couples who were assessed for spouse violence prior to family court mediation. Standard mediation was conducted without the participants or mediators knowing who was classified as violent or non-violent. The 65 couples who reached full agreement were grouped according to whether they had ever had a violent dispute during their relationship.

Violent couples who reached agreement chose terms granting wives significantly more power in terms of control over custody and visitation than the non-violent couples chose. This suggested that wives of violent husbands were empowered sufficiently during standard mediation to negotiate somewhat more powerful, safer terms for themselves than was necessary for wives of non-violent husbands.

Nevertheless, 57 per cent of all agreements between violent couples specified a form of shared custody which was felt to promote too much future contact between the violent ex-spouses. This tendency for violent spouses to choose shared custody was interpreted to mean that wives needed violence screening and special protective intervention measures to successfully negotiate, safer, more restrictive sole custody agreements.

Mandatory mediation of custody in face of domestic violence was also studied by Maxwell (1999). He found that as a process that required a balance of power between participants, mediation was not an appropriate method to resolve domestic violence disputes, a phenomenon that reflected profound disparities in power between the perpetrator and the victim. There was, however, the tendency now for alternative dispute resolution (ADR) to be increasingly used by social workers in cases of domestic violence (Imbrogno and Imbrogno, 2000). Finally, Sachs (2000) emphasised the importance of placing children in the custody of that parent who was more nurturing rather than the 'superior litigator'. This would also protect the child more and prevent injuries to the child by an aggressive parent.

Summary

Virtually all research currently and in the past emphasised the best form of post-divorce or separation strategy was 'joint parenting'. When this was not possible it was always due to the conflict between parents relentlessly continuing. Parental hostility led to conflict between themselves, but also to serious psychological and behavioural consequences for the children, immediately and in years to come.

Since the ideal of joint parenting prevents children suffering, one may well ask why do parents not acknowledge this and become better parents by developing harmony between one another? The answer is fairly obvious. Parents often refuse to acknowledge that joint parenting is in the best interest of their children because of their animosity towards one another. Such hostility feeds upon itself and creates a denial that a former parent has anything of value to contribute to the rearing of children.

Such parents cannot have any positive communication with one another, cannot be flexible about arrangements on sharing strategies, and almost always favour the adversarial legal approach. They see no value in the process of mediation, since mediation seeks to resolve the entrenched and hostile position which one or both parents have adopted.

Mediators work to promote co-operation for the benefit of children and the former partners. Mediators can often achieve little to help highly stressed and hostile parents unless the legal system via the courts backs their efforts towards harmonious shared parenting and punishes parents for failing to co-operate.

With the help of the court, mediators can do much to resolve conflicts between former partners. The mediators major role is to get parents to be committed to working together harmoniously for the benefit of children. At present sole custody arrangements are often accepted by the courts because of the inability of parents to work together. This can never be viewed as an ideal solution. One parent is forced to give in to the pressure or power of the other parent often with the backing of the court. This is based on the reluctance of most courts to insist that parents must co-operate with the mediation process or suffer the consequences of losing the custody of the children. What judge would be seen to imprison a mother for failing to co-operate with the father and his visitation rights or any other working arrangement via the mediator? The answer is obvious . . . few if any. Such decisions are hard to make and yet such decisions are sometimes necessary because they are fair and just. In most cases the threat of removing a child from the sole custody parent is sufficient in forcing co-operation. The law must always be fair and just. It must also sometimes arrive at decisions that may seem harsh, in order to achieve both fairness and justice.

The mediators role is to:

1. Help each parent to value the contributions made by the other parent.
2. Encourage parents always to put the children first.
3. Avoid allowing one parent's hostility and mistrust towards the other parent to undermine the main required objective – to promote the physical and psychological health of their children now and in the future.

Justice of the Peace, 2000, 166: 739–44

Chapter Twenty

The role of mediation in child custody disputes

Clinical psychologists have, for some years, been involved in child custody disputes, and most especially in the assessment of parental fitness. Disputes may arise in the following cases:

- Parental divorce or separation. One-third of children live with a stepfamily and more than half in a single parent home (Bray, 1991).
- Where there is concern as to the treatment of children within the family by one or both parents.

Problems arising from custody disputes

It has been found that homosexual or lesbian parents seeking child custody or adoption continue to be marginalised by the general public and the legal system (McIntyre, 1994). Yet this is despite research on gay parenting and children raised by gay parents, which documents that same-sex couples are as effective as mixed-sex couples. In addition, studies have failed to show differences between children raised by lesbian and heterosexual mothers. Many approaches have been employed by the courts to evaluate the fitness of homosexual parents (Fowler, 1995) including the 'per se', the 'middle ground' and the 'nexus' approach. Examples of rationales put forward by the courts when denying custody include: possible damage to the child's psychological development; societal stigmatisation, harassment or intolerance; an alleged inability of gay people to be good parents; the threat of AIDS; and potential exploitation or molestation of children by gay parents. Mediation was used most successfully in cases of gay parenting where the mediator attempted to interpret the sub-culture of the gay lifestyle which is essentially different from the heterosexual equivalent – the purpose being to encourage understanding between participants that will allow them to continue parenting tasks together whilst developing very different personal lives (Campbell, 1996).

During times of friction between spouses, the risk of domestic violence increases. Newmark et al. (1995) studied 293 families disputing custody or visitation rights: 80 per cent of the women and 72 per cent of the men reported experience of abuse during the dispute period. Similar reports were provided by Sorenson et al. (1995) where judges appeared responsive to allegations of abuse with regard to awards of primary physical residence, despite the lack of substantiated evidence. Allegations of maltreatment had no apparent impact on awards of shared, versus sole, custody.

During custody battles, there is a danger of child abduction by one or other of the parents. Johnston and Girdner (1998) carried out in-depth interviews with, and administered psychological tests to, 70 parents; half were abductors and the remainder were the non-abducting parents. The major distinguishing characteristics were arranged into six profiles of risk for serious custodial interference. Family court councillors then randomly assigned 50 families to either 10 or 40 hours of free counselling service. At the nine-month follow-up session, the at-risk parents, as a group, were substantially more co-operative, expressed less disagreement, and were more likely to have resolved disputed custody issues with their ex-partner compared to baseline (time of referral to the project).

Types of child custody

Due to the disputes resulting from marital breakdown, child custody evaluations are conducted by specialists such as psychologists, psychiatrists and social services. It is usually the parents who are considered best able to meet the legitimate needs of the child who are granted rights of custody (Wall and Amadio, 1994; Smoron, 1998). Joint custody resolution, although a positive solution, is less frequently decided upon and, more often, one parent is awarded sole legal custody while the other is granted varying degrees of visitation rights.

In the rare case where joint custody occurs, one parent has 'physical' custody and the child spends most of their time with that parent. The parents share parental rights and decisions relating to the education and care of the child. The main differences between joint and sole custody are:

- In joint custody there is more interaction between the child and either parent. This is positive, providing any controversy is minimal.
- There is obviously more association between parents – again to the benefit of the child, providing the interaction is mainly harmonious.
- There can be more flexibility as to who is caring for the child at a particular time, which can be of value to either parent, should one need to be away from home or be unable to care for the child (Clingempeel and Repucci, 1982).

Evaluating parental fitness for custody

Evaluation occurs when there is some doubt as to whether either of the parents is fit to have custody or visitation or whether visitation is to be supervised. Parental competency is not easy to assess and, on the whole, unless there is serious concern – the possibility of sexual, emotional or physical abuse – the natural parents retain their right to custody (Azar and Benjet, 1994).

Gardner (1997) describes the *Parental Discipline Technique Self-Report Instrument* for objective comparison by examiners of parents' ability to use disciplinary techniques when conducting a child custody evaluation. Evaluators assess each parent's assets and liabilities and then compare the two to ascertain which parent would be more suitable for the child to live with.

One of the most difficult issues faced by the courts and expert witnesses involved is when children refuse to visit a parent. Courts are often confronted with children who, regardless of court orders, refuse to visit their non-custodial parent (Murray, 1999).

Baker (1997) summarises the most important principle when dealing with parental custodial disputes: the welfare of the child is paramount. Hence, the emphasis must be on the child's rights and parental responsibility. It is vital that children be protected from 'external abuse' whilst under the care of the parent, i.e. physical, sexual and emotional abuse. The parent with custody rights must be able to protect the child from abuse within and outside the family circle. A parent who is not competent in this provision, for

whatever reason, may have to relinquish the custodial role temporarily or even permanently.

In custodial disputes parents are often hostile to one another and to the authorities involved. Outsiders, including social services, are often viewed as unnecessary 'meddlers'. Yet, failure of the authorities to become involved can result in tragic consequences. The primary task of the expert witness in such cases is to help decide on the best possible course of action which will benefit the child, whilst considering the parents who may be in an acrimonious relationship. It is the role of the expert witness to assess:

1. Family interactions and lifestyle.
2. The competence of both parents and relations or unrelated witnesses. (Questions may be asked regarding the sexual orientation of either parent.)
3. The effect of divorce or separation of the parents on the child.

Experts may well come under attack and be criticised by the parents or various individuals, whatever decision they reach. Criticisms may relate to the following:

1. Their expertise and the clinical tests or methods used to reach their decision.
2. The personality or character of the expert witness, or alleged unethical approaches used in carrying out the evaluation.

Fees or payments may be withheld due to disagreement with decisions made, although other excuses will be given for non-payment. Currently the court often appoints the expert, although the solicitors representing the parties in dispute may agree on the appointment (Weissman, 1991).

Approaches used in decision-making

Among the essential components on which psychologists' definite or interim decisions are made are:

- The social history and mental status of the parents or others caring for the child and the child's needs or wishes.
- The standardised objective tests of parents and children, e g the Eysenck Personality Inventory or the Minnesota Multi-Phasic Personality

Table 20.1   Recommendations

Recommendations	Mean % time actually recommended
Single parent custody without visitation	4.6
Single parent custody with visitation	30.4
Limited child custody	42.8
Joint custody	21.7
Other arrangements including foster home or placement with other relations	0.3

Inventory (MMPI). There may also be included projective techniques which are not standardised on norms, such as the Thematic Apperception Test (TAT) or the Children's Apperception Test (GAT).

- Observations of parental interaction and child/parental interaction.
- Observation and interviewing of other relations, neighbours, general practitioners, teachers, etc.
- Research of various documents from different sources, including medical records, police files, etc.

The collection of information and evidence, as above, is ideal but not always possible. Evaluation is an exhaustive exercise in compiling and sifting through information (Ackerman, 1995). Only then can conclusions or verdicts be reached upon which decisions can be made. Despite the even-handed approach, one party or the other will often challenge decisions. However, a variety of different custodial arrangements and visitation rights can result.

Although, in a perfect world, the child remains with both parents in a harmonious relationship, the next best alternative is for parents to interact in a positive manner following divorce or separation, and to share joint custody. Unfortunately, such ideals are rarely possible. Sometimes a constructive solution can be achieved with the efforts of an expert witness, such as a psychologist or psychiatrist, through mediation. Keilin and Bloom (1986) drew up Table 20.1, indicating preference for custodial recommendations.

It is generally considered that joint custody is of most benefit for the child, providing that the parents are in a relatively harmonious relationship. In this way, children can maintain close contact and family cohesion exists (Crosbie-Burnett, 1991; Stiller, 1986; Wolchik et al., 1985).

There are also sex differences to be taken into account in custody decisions: Crosbie-Burnett found that girls are more upset by sole custody decisions, whilst boys express more anxiety in joint custody families. Poor adjustment occurs when there are continued signs of hostility and conflict between the parents, irrespective of the type of custody arrangements (Emery, 1982, Hetherington and Arasteh, 1988).

The Role of mediation

The role of the expert witness as mediator cannot be stressed too highly when custody disputes arise between parents (Grych and Fincham, 1992; Kelly, 1991; Lowenstein, 1998, 1999a–d). Mediation is beneficial to both parties – especially fathers and, to a lesser degree, mothers (Emery et al., 1991, 1994). A study by the present author found that mediation was far more successful in developing harmony between parties than the litigious approach.

An analysis of mediation procedures was carried out by Evans and Havercamp in 1994. They analysed the discrepancy between the conceptual ideals of mediation and the actualities of child custody mediation practices. Twelve assumptions that may threaten mediation processes and strategies included: pre-mediation interview; involving the child as decision-maker; the spacing and sequencing of sessions; games, simulations and trust exercises; and the use of written agreements through the mediation process. An analysis of 32 cases of custody mediation revealed two contrasting styles of enacting the mediator role: the settlement orientation style (SOS) and the problem-solving style (PSS). The SOS mediators were primarily concerned with securing a settlement and remaining neutral. The PSS mediators were more focused on understanding the causes of the conflict through persistent questioning, and were willing to part from strict neutrality in cases where the conflict was being fuelled by particularly destructive behaviour in one of the parents. SOS was the mediator style in 59 per cent of cases, and PSS in 41 per cent. Compared with SOS, PSS produced a more structured and vigorous approach to conflict resolution during mediation, more frequent and durable settlements, and a more favourable attitude towards the mediation experience (Kressel et al., 1994).

Schwartz (1994) discusses the legal procedures in divorce that can adversely affect children, including the negative impact of litigation, children's lack of legal representation, and mandated joint custody arrangements. The need for evaluation of parental interaction, the importance of expeditious decision-making regarding living arrangements, and the role of mental health professionals in custody decisions also come under discussion. Recommendations include educating legal professionals in matters of child development and children's rights and empowering children in the custody decision-making process.

It has been established that during mediation, disputants accuse each other of a particular offence. Most of the alleged offences involve perceptions of specific behaviour instead of non-negotiable character flaws. Disputants frequently rebuke their former spouses rather than simply asking for an explanation. In general, partners tend to respond to these aggravating approaches with equally aggravating account forms; these are followed by rejection of the account or by mediator intervention (Manusov et al., 1994). On the whole, couples are more likely to reach custody agreements when mediators intervene after reproaches, when discussion over behaviour is avoided, and when the reproachers are allowed to use direct rebukes.

Mediation is not universally accepted, but is widely respected and the evidence points in its favour. One review of assessment methods in custody cases (Hysjulien et al., 1994) states that there is very little empirical evidence to support the efficacy of methods typically used by professionals in making recommendations to the court. This view is in the minority. Most of the research indicates a positive or favourable impact from the employment of mediation techniques (see Burrell et al., 1994; Emery et al., 1994).

Donohue et al. (1994) examined the impact of mediators' interaction management on client satisfaction during mediation of child custody visitation and support disputes. Transcripts of 22 one-hour mediation sessions revealed that mediators who ignored disputants' relational concerns experienced more difficulty bringing them to agreement. A follow-up study by Kitzmann and Emery (1994) found that custody settlements promoted on-going contact between parents after divorce and this resulted in both reward and risk: children gained when the parents' relationship was co-operative, but suffered when parents continued to fight.

In their comparison between mediation techniques and litigation, Emery et al. (1994) discovered that for fathers it was significantly more satisfying to mediate than to litigate. The mediation approach also led to greater compliance of fathers, and satisfaction amongst mothers. The factors influencing success in mediation were studied by Depner et al. (1995). Characteristics indicative of a good outcome included the attributes of the father – particularly relating to educational influences – and whether the parents decided on shared parenting.

An examination into the long-term effects of mediation in custody disputes was carried out by Dillon and Emery (1996). Twenty-five parents who chose mediation and 28 who opted for litigation were followed up nine years after the dispute was first brought to court. Parents were asked whether the child involved in the dispute had experienced difficulties in adjustment and whether psychological treatment had been given. Frequency of direct and indirect contact between the child and the non-resident parent was assessed, and the parents rated inter-parental co-operation and conflict. Non-custodial parents assigned to mediation reported more frequent current contact with their children and greater involvement in current decisions about them. Parents in a mediation group also reported more frequent communication about their children during the period since dispute resolution.

The work of the present author (1998) discusses the steps involved in mediation, which should be carried out before or during legal action but prior to the court's enforcement of a solution through the law. It is proposed that mediation play a far larger role within the justice system, especially in cases of parental alienation syndrome. With at least one in three marriages leading to separation or divorce in the UK, there is a greater urgency to co-ordinate a plan of action with the legal system to make certain that both parties in custody cases continue to play a role in the lives of their children. Professionals such as qualified psychologists or psychiatrists should be able to offer a full course of mediation before partners begin divorce proceedings or consider decisions regarding the placement of children with one party or another.

Justice of the Peace, 2000, 164: 14: 256–62

Chapter Twenty-One

Treating the alienator

Introduction

The treatment of the alienator is the most difficult of all. The trilogy of our alienator, child and victim of the alienation are the three involved in the process of Parental Alienation (PAS). The difficulty results due to the alienator feeling totally justified in the programming being carried out. Sometimes, but rarely, the alienator would not even be able to admit that they are programming a child against the target parent. This is commonly termed 'denial'.

Most alienators know exactly what they are doing and are prepared to avoid any form of treatment in order to continue doing what they are doing. This is because they feel totally justified in their action of seeking to destroy any possible relationship between a child in their care and the targeted parent. Normally, in order to reduce the resistance of an alienator and to get them to participate in therapy, there must be a court resolution and pressure by the judge that parental alienation syndrome or programming must be eliminated.

The treatment process has three objectives:

- To prepare the alienator for the treatment itself.
- To treat the alienator.
- To monitor the effects of the treatment vis a vis the child who has hitherto been programmed.

Preparation for treatment

The therapist must be prepared for resistance from the alienator. The attitude of the alienator will reflect the following types of thinking when verbalised:

There is nothing wrong with what I am doing. I don't need any treatment.

I am only coming along to the treatment as you call it because the court has forced me to do so.

There is nothing wrong with me that needs treatment. It's . . .

With this kind of attitude, treatment involving a change in attitude seems far from simple. It is, however, important to repair step by step this tragic destructive interaction by convincing the alienator that there is much to be gained by co-operating with the therapist and by accepting the irrationality of their demeanour. This needs to be emphasised as being so for two main reasons:

- The alienator would benefit via a better relationship with the alienated partner including, possibly greater financial help, care and support, and even friendliness from the alienated parent.
- One must appeal to the good sense of the mother. The mother must realise, and the father for that matter, the benefit the child would have in the short and long term if contact of some kind were established with the alienated parent.

The treatment

The treatment will initially have to be played by ear. It is vital to win the confidence of the alienator. It must be stressed that one is concerned with the resident parent, that is the alienator, as much as with the targeted parent. It is important to listen carefully and sensitively to the grievances of the alienator and to sympathise with their feelings of hurt, anger and having been betrayed in some cases. It is similar to when one is involved in a hostage situation. One must develop a positive relationship with the hostage taker.

The treatment must not only be concerned with the past but planning a way forward of hope for the alienator. They have been living, one can only term it, through their hatred of the alienated partner. The way forward must be to collect one's resources within oneself and seek to establish a new relationship, if this is required, or support from friends. One should also help the alienator to develop new interests or pursuits which have a positive aspect and can eliminate or counteract those negative feelings which tend to originate totally within the person. One might say that the alienation process is obsessive, compulsive and habit forming.

Promoting and guiding the alienator to develop a personal hope for the future does much to reduce or remove the often pathological animosity towards the targeted parent. This has become the very centre of the alienators 'modus vivendi'. It can only be counteracted by an attitude of looking outwards. It means being optimistic and rebuilding a life and thereby putting behind them the hurt that has led to the process of alienating the child against the perceived perpetrator of acts of evil and betrayal.

The therapeutic intention is to change simultaneously the attitude and behaviour of the alienating individual. The kind of treatment adopted is cognitive plus behavioural. The success of this therapeutic approach can only be ascertained via two interacting factors: changing the hostility of the programmer towards the targeted parent and the child being encouraged to have contact with the alienated parent and actually spending positive time with that parent. This obviously means requiring the child or children to be involved in the treatment, once the alienating parent has shown the necessary signs and actions of co-operating with the efforts of the therapist.

Monitoring the effects of the treatment against PAS

In order to prepare fertile grounds for the anti-PAS therapeutic success the therapist must be involved in a positive reintroduction of the child with the targeted parent. This can only be achieved with the full agreement and co-operation of the previously alienating parent.

The alienated parent must also be prepared in how best to deal with the initial likely difficulties of having contact with the child that has hitherto been adversely programmed and hence inimical to the targeted parent. If possible, there may be a need to establish positive and workable ways whereby some communication takes place between the alienator and the targeted parent.

A form of mediation should take place between the two adults with the help of the therapist. This is in order to develop agreement between them which can then lead to some kind of co-operation in the initial and ongoing process of re-establishing a harmonious relationship between all concerned in a family which was once united. This must initially be done individually rather than as a couple. Once there are sufficient signs of agreement, the couple can be seen together.

The therapist must ascertain with great care, each step of the way, how much further they can go, or what further can be achieved, to advance the process of harmonising the formally acrimonious relationship as far and as much as this can be achieved.

Success in reducing the acrimony inherent in the PAS situation can only be measured in degrees. The success depends both on the skill of the therapist and the sincere willingness of the alienator to co-operate in the process of reducing or removing the PAS. Much again depends on the support of the court as to whether the treatment of the PAS has the desired successful outcome. Without such support, little if anything is likely to be achieved.

Outcome of PAS treatment when ordered by the court

It has been well established that very few courts of justice endorse putting pressure on the alienator to be involved in treatment to counteract the PAS. This is because judges on the whole, consider it counter-productive, or even unlikely, that any form of treatment will be successful. Judges therefore rarely order an alleged perpetrator of PAS to participate in and benefit through therapy. The outcome of therapy in a relatively few instances when it is ordered to take place and accepted, is surprising. The table which follows indicated what can be achieved via

Table 21.1   Result of treatment for PAS

Outcome	Targeted and former PAS parent	Relationship with child
Has led to effective harmony being developed	7	6
Some positive contact established	3	5
No effective change	1	0

the therapeutic intervention of just one psychologist who has for some time specialised in severe or recalcitrant cases of PAS.

Discussion of results

The results of this rather small study indicates what can be achieved through a form of mediation and therapy with those individuals involved intensively in programming a child or children against another parent. Parental alienation syndrome is a process which has been occurring over time and is much more common than is realised. It occurs not only in acrimonious separations and divorces but also in often unhappy marital relationships, or where one of the partners seeks almost total control over a child or children at the expense of the other partner.

In a happy or loving relationship between partners this is much less likely to occur as each will seek to involve the other partner in making decisions concerning children and in dealing with them. It also means they will adopt a unified approach to the rearing of children and most especially to the application of discipline which is necessary from time to time. In dealing with PAS we are however, not concerned with parents of that ilk who are loving and caring, towards their children and one another, but with parents that are opposite to this. PAS parents often feel and express a great deal of antagonism, hatred and hostility towards the other partner and will do anything they can to cause damage to the partner, who they feel has let them down in one way or another.

In extreme cases alienation becomes pathological where the individual virtually thrives on his/her antagonism and animosity towards the other party. Unfortunately the victim is not only the alienated parent but the children themselves involved in the trilogy.

Judges, as it has been stated, are reluctant to pressurise the recalcitrant programming parent to participate in therapeutic efforts to change this pattern. They realise there is so much hatred and antagonism that forcing anyone to participate in treatment against their will is likely to fail. This, however, is not always the case. The previous table indicates that when judges are strong in their desire to resolve the alienation process, much can be done by psychiatrists and psychologists to deal with the alienation and to reduce or even remove it altogether.

It is important for the judiciary to realise their responsibility and potential power to change PAS. Failing to comply with the order of a court must incur punishment. This includes both parents having responsibility for the rearing of their children. PAS must be viewed as an injustice to the alienated parent and also to the child in question. Judges therefore, must adopt a much more firm approach to alienators who fail to comply with court rulings and who may require some form of severe punishment, threatened and carried out if necessary. Among the punishments could be imprisonment or passing the child or children on to the alienated parent or relatives of the alienated parent who have hitherto not had these children in residence. These are extreme measures which should only be applied if there is a total lack of co-operation from the alienating parent with the court ruling. In order for rulings to be made they must have 'teeth' and this provides a favourable climate and strong therapeutic pressure for the participant who is the alienator to seek to benefit from the treatment being carried out. It can also lead to better relationships eventually between the alienator and the former targeted parent. There is much to be gained but the course of action is not easy and relies heavily on the commitment and strength of the judiciary system supporting the therapeutic process. It also relies greatly on the wisdom, sensitivity and skill of the therapist.

Chapter Twenty-Two

Dealing with the treatment of PAS

Johnston et al. (2001) described goals and strategies for family focused counselling and therapy when children are alienated from a parent after separation and divorce. The confidential intervention takes place within a legally defined contract and is based upon a careful assessment of the dynamics of the multiple factors that contribute to the alienation and how the child's development is affected. Strategies for forming multiple therapeutic alliances with often reluctant, recalcitrant, and polarised parents are discussed together with ways of helping the child directly.

It has already been indicated how important it is to diagnose the problems associated with possible parental alienation or parental alienation syndrome. Lee and Olesen (2001) describe in-depth child custody evaluations which are critical in forming an accurate understanding of families in which alienation of children is a concern. By integrating interviews and psychological test data of parents and children along with collateral information, the evaluator can differentiate an alienated child from children with other forms of parental rejection and can form a thorough understanding of the multiple contributing factors in the alienation process. This comprehensive and integrated understanding is then used to develop a clear and specific intervention plan.

Cases entering the family court with an alienated child require intensive and coordinated case management to intervene effectively (Sullivan and Kelly, 2001). It is critical to link the authority of the court with the delivery of mental health services to address the complex systemic factors that may entrench the child's unwarranted rejection of a parent. Similar results were obtained by Gardner (2002) who considers that it is vital that the psychologist or psychiatrist involved in these cases adopts a very different attitude to the usual therapeutic methods practised by these two professionals. Efforts were made, for example, by Bernet (2002) to summarise the procedures as to how a mental health professional such as a psychologist or psychiatrist should conduct a child custody evaluation. The article addressed the format for the evaluation including the initial conference with both parents, the individual meetings with each parent, the meetings with the children, outside information that should be collected, psychological testing, and the 'wrap up' conference with the parents and their attorneys. The current psychologist adopts a different approach of never seeing all the individuals together initially but always individually before commencing treatment (Lowenstein, 2005). The article by Bernet also lists the discussions and the critical factors considered in drawing conclusions and making recommendations, such as a child's attachment to the parents, the child's preference, and the possibility of indoctrination and parental alienation.

A number of case studies were presented by Vassiliou and Cartwright (2001). They examined five alienated fathers and one alienated mother's perceptions of parental alienation syndrome (PAS). The data was collected via semi-structured open-ended interviews and questionnaires to identify whether there were shared characteristics among alienated families, or common issues in the marital conflicts that contributed to the marriage dissolution. An attempt was made to understand the nature of the participant's reports of alienation and what things an alienated parent might do differently. Overall, these findings indicate that there are several possible attributes, such as changes in relationships among family members, the roles of mental health and the legal professionals, as well as custody arrangements. These may be precursors or indicators of PAS.

A way of preventing parental alienation and the dire condition to which it leads was suggested by Thayer and Zimmerman (2001). They examined the conflict, divorce, and the children involved. This guide showed how to avoid the hot spots and the common traps of hostility, inflexibility, and constant squabbling. It also developed ideas on how to promote skills to sustain a co-parenting partnership based on love and concern for the children. Children of divorced parents benefited best from two parents living separately but working together. Their book offers families a solution and a chance to move beyond the high-conflict divorce experiences and suggests a parenting system that allows the children to keep their family despite it being in the reconstituted manner.

The authors focus on co-parenting the children even after the divorce, indicating that parents can learn to put their issues aside and deal directly and fairly with one another for the good of the children. New rules and communication styles were capable of being developed by the parents to accommodate the change in their marital status. It was also felt by the authors that parents can learn to undo the past errors, regroup, and restructure their post-divorce parenting so the children can grow up in a loving environment in both parents homes. This rather idealistic approach, while necessary, is unfortunately not always successful.

Gardner (2001) comments that there has been a significant amount of controversy among legal and mental health professionals in regards to the question of whether the courts should order children with PAS or PA to visit or reside with their alienated parent. Gardner describes 99 PAS cases in which he was directly involved, cases in which he concluded that the court should order visitation with or transfer of primary residential custody to the alienated parent. The outcome when such orders were implemented was compared with the outcome when this recommendation was not followed. Unfortunately the premature death of Richard Gardner in 2005 may result in no further information being provided concerning this important question. Other investigators need to verify Gardner's views regarding change of custody.

A great advocate of joint custody and shared parenting is Lowenstein (2002). The question of whether there should be sole custody or split custody (one child with one and another with another parent), after separation or divorce has in recent days given way to a preference for 'joint custody' and 'shared parenting'. This eliminates the need for visitation rights and unsupervised or supervised contact for the non-custodial parent, and is preferable whenever possible. Lowenstein focused on four main issues:

1. The problems and advantages associated with joint custody.
2. What should be done if joint parenting and custody does not work.

3. What happens to the children when there is alienation and hostility between the parents.
4. The role of judges and the courts.

Novick (2003) in reviewing Gardner's book on PAS appears to agree with the conclusion that the process of alienation must be reversed to prevent it becoming an ongoing way of life. Novick suggests that the strength of the book rests in Gardner's clinical experience and expertise and that it is useful for clinicians to study Gardner's clinical style and manner in dealing with most difficult individuals. Meister (2003) concurs that Gardner's book is undoubtedly of great assistance to therapists in how to deal with parental alienation problems. Meister considers that Gardner has effectively placed parental alienation treatment 'on the map' especially in high conflict family cases.

Other authors have commented on the pioneering work of Gardner including Goncalves and de Vincenzi (2003). The authors note that when there is a 'war' between parents it often leads to PAS. Different interventions and techniques are described, inspired by that of Gardner. They stress that there are some potential traps and that there is the need to coordinate therapeutic interventions with the courts involved in custody decisions.

The objective of such therapy is to prevent children and adolescents as well as adults suffering in later life from the parental alienation syndrome process. Drieu (2004) reviewed recent research into the involvement of parents in the treatment of adolescents with social alienation disorders. Characteristics of adolescents with alienation disorders often have the potential for violence. Here, there is value for parental consultation in determining causes and treatment for alienation. It was felt vital to open good communication between the parents so that they may work together more effectively.

Drieu illustrates the importance of involving parents in the treatment process with a case study of a 17-year-old male adolescent in France with drug dependence and internet addiction. It is unfortunate that sometimes, therapists are alienated in the process of attempting to heal or forestall parental alienation conflicts (Garber, 2004). This results when there is an impasse or rupture in the psychotherapeutic relationship between the psychologist and the patient dyad. There is therefore the need for the therapist to be both sensitive in preventing this from occurring while at the same time standing firm as to their findings observed between the parent in conflict.

In the United States a programme funded by the Health and Human Services has been developed (Neff and Cooper, 2004). It was introduced in Phoenix, Arizona and has served more than 1,000 families in several jurisdictions. Whereas other programmes dealt with entrenched, high conflict cases and were found to be time consuming requiring an intensive two to six months, this was a programme of four hours for the less serious alienation cases. Good results were reported.

Another study concerned itself with the evaluation of the efficacy of structural and therapeutic interventions for interrupting parental alienation towards the severe end of the spectrum (Rand et al., 2005). Follow-up was obtained on 45 PAS children from a custody evaluators practice. The child's adjustment and relationship with both parents at evaluation and follow-up were compared. Children who had enforced visitation with the target parent or were in target parent custody, maintained relationships with both parents unless the alienator was too disturbed. In the completed alienation outcome group, the alienating parent had custody before and after the evaluation, and was able to violate court orders with impunity. Therapy as the primary intervention was ineffective and sometimes made things worse. There are several possible reasons for this including the lack of involvement of the court to make definite decisions of possibly changing custody and the lack of skill of the expert witness in providing the courts with the necessary information to act more decisively.

Perhaps the best way forward is advocated by Boyan and Termini (2005) who recommend that over time divorced parents who experience moderate to severe levels of parental conflict, should be ordered by the juvenile court, family court, and superior court judges to participate in parent coordination programmes. Attorneys, mediators, guardians ad litem, custody evaluators, physicians, and psychotherapists have referred parents to such a programme. Some parents include the services of parent coordination in their settlement agreement. Two areas critical to the ongoing development of parental coordination are psychotherapists, working as parent coordinators, and the need for unique training and professional support in order to provide competent assistance to these challenging families.

One thing is clear from all the information on therapeutic intervention by alleged experts, and that is the need for further research into the effects of a variety of approaches in curtailing and possibly reducing the level of alienation practised against children. Needless to say the most important ingredient in all this is the need for a close working relationship between the expert carrying out assessments and treatment, and the court listening to these experts.

Chapter Twenty-Three

How to make child custody parenting work effectively

Introduction

I will make no distinction between joint or shared custody and joint parenting. These are but words but they mean virtually the same as that both parents are involved whenever possible in the rearing of children that they have created. It is important to remember that we cannot own a child, but we can rear, nourish and guide children.

Four areas will be covered in this chapter. These include:

1. What is the value of joint custody?
2. What must be done to make joint custody work effectively?
3. When will joint custody not work?
4. What can and should be the role of the court to establish chances of success in joint custody decisions?

The value of joint custody

The value of joint custody has been discussed and debated over many years. There is little doubt that two parents have a better chance of raising children effectively and this is to the benefit of the children concerned whenever this is possible (Kelly, 1991). The statement is frequently made: 'Are custody decisions made for the benefit of the children or their parents?' The answer is a simple one. It is made or should be for both, since they coincide in every way. Happy or effective parents make for the chance of happy and successfully reared children. Hence, what is in the best interest of the child is also in the best interest of the parents and vice versa. This also makes certain that from the point of view of society that families should, and do endure. There may be a change in relationship between the adults or parents concerned but a relationship between themselves and the child should be as warm, caring and effective as before the separation or divorce between themselves. This is possible when both parents co-operate and put first and foremost the welfare of their children. Unfortunately, marriages do not break up unless

there is much hostility between the parents and even domestic violence (Lowenstein, 1999e). This hostility is likely to continue unless such parents are provided with the help of a mediator responsible to the court, with the court having the 'teeth' to strengthen the position of the mediator and what they are attempting to do.

There is considerable research commencing with Wallerstein and Kelly (1980) which suggests that once divorce or separation has occurred it is important for the parents to stop the hostility between themselves and concentrate on how best to rear their children. Children by nature are attached to both parents but not necessarily equally and ideally would have liked them to remain together. This not being possible, the next most important issue is how the parents can work together to bring up the children, in the most harmonious way. To do this they need to work together and not merely to avoid hostility but a more insidious hostility such as parental alienation syndrome (PAS) (Gardner, 1992; 1998; 2001) (Lowenstein 1998; 1999a–c; 2000; 2001).

Frequently one of the parents have their eye on the custody of the child. More frequently than not it is the mother who has had the predominant share in rearing the children due to the separation of roles between the parents, one being the 'bread-winner' while the other is the 'carer of the home' and children. This separation of roles should not in any way dictate that the custodial parent should have sole input or custody of a child. Joint custody is yet the best way of assuming that the child will have the benefit of two parents rather than one providing these parents co-operate and put the welfare of the child first. The child therefore has the best chance of developing normally, or as normally as possible.

It is unfortunate that as there is frequently a great deal of antipathy, if not direct hostility, between the parents, one parent who has a 'superior' position vis a vis the child, is the one that has been caring for that child i.e. the custodial parent. Joint custody however, emphasises the importance of both parents playing as vital a role as possible in the lives of their children. The courts frequently make an unjust decision based on the 'status quo' or power of a custodial parent to dictate the terms, rather than what is justice for both the parents. Sometimes it is the mother and sometimes it is the father who dictates that the other should have as little as possible contact with the child, or certainly not a large share of contact.

This is a wrong manner of proceeding. It is however, the view frequently expressed by certain investigators like Goldstein et al. (1973) who considered that this is the natural state and that little can be done by the courts to interfere with this state of affairs. The current author does not feel as such and it is vital that both parents are involved, all things being equal. We will discuss later when joint custody will not work and when such joint custody is not possible. It should be remembered that in the short as well as the long-term, children benefit from having both parents play a role in their lives, and as equally as possible. It is unlikely, however, that such divisions can be made on a strictly 50–50 basis. The father or mother who is employed cannot spend a large amount of time caring for young children and there may be other reasons for selecting a less than 50–50 position.

What must be done to make joint custody work effectively?

It is often for mediators, dealing with warring parents to promote through mediating, goals for successful joint parenting. There are certain criteria which will make for effective joint parenting. These are as follows:

1. That both parents accept the importance of being eager for joint custody to be an effective way of rearing their children and that both parents wish the other, as well as themselves, to play an active role in the lives of their children.
2. The parents have an understanding and are convinced of the importance of joint custody or parenting and why it affects children beneficially. They are therefore willing to discuss any differences remaining between themselves as parents in order to establish a good working relationship with their children.
3. The important thing is for these parents to consider the needs of their children as well as

their own needs in making arrangements with their children and how best to work together as parents despite their separation or divorce. This requires some degree of flexibility.
4. The parents who can make joint custody work effectively, are those who despite their anger in the past, or even current anger, can stop this affecting their common sense of caring and wishing for the good future of their children.
5. Joint custody is also likely to be an effective way of bringing up children when there is a good capacity for positive communication between the parents and the desire to co-operate for the benefit of the children.
6. Due to the fact that children will be living from time to time in two different homes it is important to establish some tolerance or flexibility between the parents so that they may agree on who should have the children, when there are some uncertainties which have not been planned for in the formal arrangements.
7. It is important for each parent to appreciate and respect the role that the child has in the relationship with the other parent, despite the failure of the marriage or relationship between the parents.
8. Avoiding an intense and continued hostility and conflict between one another, and attempting to control or assuage the anger which one spouse might feel against the other, for the benefit of the child. The child, especially the older child may plan to be with friends or wish to change arrangements. This can cause problems for the one parent who wishes to be with the child. There may also be a need for changes to parental needs. Thus parents must accept (Hodges, 1986) that no steadfast, absolute rules can ever hold for ever. In other words, in time, changes will need to be made in arrangements as situations change and children develop, as well as the parents and their own needs require changes. This could require the help of a mediator to assist in making such changes if the parents cannot agree.

When will joint custody not work?

Joint custody is unlikely to be effective if one or both of the parents involved fail to consider their predominant obligation to the child and are more concerned with their animosity towards one another. Sometimes this is one parent who feels particularly aggrieved, but in some cases it is both. This can, in due course, be overcome with effective mediation as well as the backing by the courts (discussed below). There are also other factors which relate to joint custody not being effective. This is when the following exists:

1. There is a history of one or both parents being addicted to drugs or alcohol, making them ineffective and even dangerous parents.
2. There has been, and is likely to continue to be, violence between the partners, or when one or both partners commit child neglect, abuse or sexual interference with the child.
3. It is unlikely to have been an effective way of dealing with child care if one or both parents suffer from mental illnesses, or extreme instability.
4. It is also likely to be an ineffective way of dealing with children if one or more of the children oppose one of the parents, or indeed both parents, as carers for themselves. This is often as a result of parental alienation and one must be careful to distinguish between parental alienation procedures and an actual parent being a danger to a child.
5. Sometimes joint parenting or joint custody is a difficult alternative when parents live geographically at great distance to one another.

What can and should the courts do to establish joint custody of children

Leaving aside the areas where joint custody is unlikely to be effective due to some deficit of an extreme nature in one or both parents, we must now consider what the courts can and should do to make certain that the 'ideal' of joint custody is possible, with the important addition of flexibility in the arrangements being made.

It is the role of the court to encourage the parents to co-operate with one another for the benefit of the child or children. It is the view of the author of this paper, that any child that is neglected, or treated in an abusing manner, by either parent or both parents, that that child should be removed from that setting. Therapeutic efforts should be made to help such a parent whenever possible but certainly no child should be placed in the situation of being abused or neglected. In the case where parents are at odds

with one another and have extreme animosity towards one another, it is vital to develop a scheme of mediation, which should help these parents come to terms with their primary obligation, the care of their child or children 'jointly'. This could do much to prevent one parent returning again and again to court to gain some access to a child and thereby being considered a nuisance (Coe, 2001).

With the help of the mediator the court should act in accordance with which parent is most co-operative in seeking a solution to the problem of animosity between the parents. It is the parent who considers the welfare of the child first and foremost who should have custody of the child, irrespective of who has initial custody, due to pressure or 'status quo' situations. Hence, a mother who fails to provide adequate care for a child should not have this responsibility. The same must be said when failing to allow the other parent to play an appropriate role in the rearing of a child. No parent should prevent the child from having two parents who are equally responsible for their welfare except when situations exist as mentioned in the previous section. Any parent who fails to include an appropriate other parent in the rearing of a child should not have custody of that child. One might say that parent is depriving that child and hence abusing the child by preventing contact with a potentially caring and responsible parent who wishes such contact (Gardner, 2000).

As already mentioned, parental alienation is practised, by both males and females, who seek to oust the other parent from playing an important role in the process of child care. In that case mediation should be the procedure for altering this situation. If mediation, however, is unsuccessful in gaining the co-operation of one or both parents, then those children should not be in the care of such a parent. Both parents, all things being equal, have the right and the responsibility in sharing in the caring of their children.

The alternative is to remove the child from the home-setting where such parental alienation occurs. In the case where both parents are practising abuse, there is little that can be done except to remove the child through social care agencies, hoping thereby to heal the rift between the parents through mediation so that they yet may play an appropriate caring role towards their children. Failure of either or both parents to co-operate with the mediation process ordered by the court, means that the children should remain in care until this changes. It must be accepted that research indicates that the only young children who did well in joint custody were those whose parents' central motive was a deep commitment to the child, and from this also a strong desire to involve the other parent.

This may seem a harsh action but the alternative is equally damaging to the child concerned. It is also an injustice to deprive a good parent of the right to parent and it is also a loss for the child. Failure of the parents to co-operate with the court, and in so doing, failure to co-operate with what is best for the child, can only do harm to that child. Children are vulnerable and will tend to go with whatever parent has the dominance over the other. This should not be the principle whereby decisions are made by a court. It is for the courts to act to prevent the one parent seeking sole custody through a power struggle, and then to 'sideline' the other parent by using that child by a process of alienation.

The preferred term 'shared parenting', is now in use instead of 'shared custody'. This concept eliminates the difficulty of each parent wanting a 50 per cent share of the child, often for the wrong reasons. It must be understood, and it is sensible that on the whole, one parent will have a significantly greater share of care for the child. Hence a fair balance can mean an unequal portion of time spent with one parent in caring for the child. This may be due to the fact that one parent may not be available to spend as much time with a child due to the need to work, or for other reasons. This is not dissimilar to non-separated parents spending unequal periods of time with their children. It is often for the mediator to develop the best way for children to

be cared for by parents and each case is different. The importance of good communication between the parents must always be emphasised as must the importance of both parents putting the children first. Additionally, flexibility in the manner in which parenting occurs is a vital aspect of good post-divorce relationship and parenting.

The decision very much depends on not merely general principles of favouring joint parenting or custody, but also the individual situation involving the parents and the child. Previous to the relationship break-up there may have been situations which favour custody being given to one or both parents. These have already been mentioned such as if there has been abuse of a child, or a child is particularly averse to contact with a particular parent. This should not alter the basic principle that what is best for the child and indeed for parents, is for both parents to continue to have contact either the same or better than when the relationship was intact. What should never take precedence is the acrimony between the parents being allowed to be involved in decisions made in connection with the child, this often leading to the custody of the child by one parent only. This is to be deplored under most circumstances. Providing both parents wish to be involved in the rearing of the child, and the child is happy with this involvement, this should continue in the best possible manner. Unless the child has been alienated by one parent or both parents towards the other, there is no reason why that child should not wish to retain contact with both parents in the manner in which it can be arranged. This could be on a 50–50 basis or on a 25–75 basis or a variety of arrangements where both the parents are joining in the important task of caring for and rearing the children.

Chapter Twenty-Four

The psychological treatment of children who have suffered from PAS

Introduction

It is unfortunate that the symptoms of children who suffer from Parental Alienation Syndrome (PAS) are rarely given over to treatment procedures (less than 10 per cent are involved in this). Their response varies but on the whole the mere fact that they are receiving treatment and are accepting such treatment frequently leads to good results. The remainder of children involved in the PAS situation fail to receive treatment. Much of this is due to the alienating parent influencing the children to refuse treatment. In combination with this are the courts who frequently do not recommend that treatment is to be carried out. In a case of PAS, where the alienating parent is caused to defend her behaviour and the courts find in favour of her, they tend to side with the defending solicitors and barristers who seek to avoid any form of treatment, influenced by their client who is usually the alienating parent. Judges on the whole tend to back such an approach of non-treatment since there are so many obstacles involved in overcoming the resistance of the resident parent in allowing this treatment to take place. One cannot help but suspect that less than 10 per cent of children who are being treated were those least damaged by the programming of the alienating parent. Before any form of treatment can commence it is vital to assess or diagnose such children carefully. This is done through in-depth interviews as well as psychological personality testing. It is also valuable whenever possible to at the same time seek to deal with the alienating parent and also the targeted parent of the alienation. The objective of the treatment procedure is to deprogramme children who have been turned against the target parent. It is also important to make the alienating parent aware of the damage that has been done and to seek their co-operation in deprogramming such children.

For the most effective result through treatment it is important for one therapist to work not merely with the whole family but also with the guardian ad litem or anyone else associated with the court procedures involving PAS children. Psychologists must have the backing of the court in order to have any chance of effectively reducing the effect of PAS. What follows now will be the approaches taken in dealing with children who have been alienated.

It will noted that efforts have been made to reduce and eliminate, if possible, the hatred and paranoia that has been created in the child towards the alienated parent. This has in turn led to the denigration of the targeted parent. It is also important to develop independent thinking in the child so that the child is not influenced by one party, the alienating parent, and is able to see matters from an autonomous or independent point of view. Finally it is vital to develop some form of shame or guilt in the child for what has been done and seek thereby to alter their feelings towards the alienated parent. Eventually, through such treatment, the child will be more amenable to make contact with the alienated parent to re-establish a positive and loving relationship which was destroyed through the alienation process.

Needless to say if the alienated parent has been involved in emotionally, physically or sexually abusing the child the process of treatment towards rehabilitation should not be carried out. It would be wrong to return a child to a parent who has in the past mis-treated the child, and is likely to do it again, without having made some effort to treat that parent before such a reunion is to be considered. On the other hand, the alienated parent may have done nothing to deserve such treatment by the child and the alienator. All efforts must be made to change the child's point of view and how the child sees the targeted parent. The therapist who carries out this work must be aware that the alienator will be working constantly behind the scenes against the efforts of the therapist. This is why it is vital that the court appoints a therapist, the therapist has the backing of the court, and will report back to the court should an attempt be made by the alienator to sabotage the treatment being carried out. This, in turn, should result in some form of punishment by the court of the alienator.

Dealing with hatred and paranoia

The child who practices hatred towards a previously well regarded parent does so with the power of the alienator behind that child, encouraging this. This may be done directly or very subtly. Direct dialogue between the therapist and the child needs to ascertain not only the strength of the paranoia which has developed, but the reasons for it and to counteract the arguments that the child has been given and identified with, which leads to such antagonistic behaviour towards the parent.

It must be accepted that the child's 'thinking for himself or herself' is extremely limited by the impact of the alienation process. The child therefore must be questioned as to why this hatred is shown for the parent, and the arguments used by the child, which are usually a reflection of the alienator, must be demolished through rational and logical arguments from the therapist.

The paranoia and hatred which forms it must be viewed as a delusion and therefore of no substance. Those practising paranoia and inculcating it in the child will frequently feel as if they are themselves prosecuted by the alienated parent, when in fact this is not occurring at all. When there is a real prosecution by the alienated parent then this is not a case of paranoia.

Children who have developed a strong hatred and paranoia are difficult to influence through logic and reason. This, however, must form the efforts of the therapist. They must question why the child feels as they do towards the alienated parent and what evidence (real evidence) there is for behaving as they do towards the alienated parent.

Gardner points out this paranoia through an example given in his work *Therapeutic Intervention for Children with Parental Alienation Syndrome.* (2001) It is worth quoting here:

Gardner: I am very sorry to hear that your grandfather died.
Billy: You know he just didn't die. My father murdered him.
Gardner: *(Increduously)* Your father murdered your grandfather, his own father?

Billy: Yes I know he did it.
Gardner: I thought your grandfather was in hospital. I understand he was about 85 years old and that he was dying of old age disease.
Billy: Yeah, that's what my father says.
Gardner: What do you say?
Billy: I say my father murdered him in the hospital.
Gardner: How did he do that?
Billy: He sneaked into the hospital, at night, and did it while no-one was looking. He did it while the nurses and the doctors were asleep.
Gardner: How do you know that?
Billy: I just know it.
Gardner: Did anyone tell you such a thing?
Billy: No, but I just know it.
Gardner: *(Now turning to the mother who has been witness to this conversation)* What do you think about what Billy has just said?
Mother: Well, I don't really think that my husband did it, but I wouldn't put it past that son of a bitch!

One may note it would take a considerable argument to be able to redress the paranoid impression which the child received undoubtedly through the mother, of his own father being a party to murdering his grandfather.

The child identifying with the alienator

Children upon whom alienation is practised will take the side of the alienating parent against all the evidence or past experiences with the parent who is now no longer present. In order for therapy to be successful such an identification with the alienator must be broken down. In other words, one must try to provide evidence for the child for viewing the alienated parent in a more favourable light or at least a more realistic light. One must ask the child whether there were any times in the past when the child felt different about the alienated parent and why the changes in views have taken place. It is vital to make the child aware of the fact that they have been the instrument of alienation and prejudice.

Confronting the child by providing evidence from the child themselves as to what favourable aspects there are about the alienated parent may mean a more balanced view could be developed in the child. Children must be made aware of the fact that they are merely repeating the views expressed by the alienating parent and are not thinking independently. Such independent thinking must be inculcated so that the child is made aware that all is not negative or bad about the alienated parent. Children who have suffered a reasonably long period of indoctrination by an alienating parent find it difficult to deal with confrontation type therapy, which involves the child and the alienating parent, in an attempt by the therapist to make the child realise what has been done to them, in the presence of the alienating parent. It becomes even more difficult with a very young child. This is mainly because the child has lost one parent and does not feel it is possible to lose yet another through being confronted with the idiosyncratic and damaging realisation that they have been the victim of indoctrination and brainwashing against the other parent. Older children, however, may be more amenable – but then a longer period of indoctrination has usually occurred in their case.

It is important to reiterate that the child of parental alienation is a victim, but does not realise that they are a victim. Any love they may have had for the beleaguered alienated parent has been destroyed and it becomes difficult to reverse this. The other victim is, of course, the targeted parent. In many cases judges administering alleged fair and just decisions find it difficult to deal with seeking to reverse such powerful indoctrination against one of the parents. They will frequently, instead, accept the situation as it is and often also provide little opportunity for contact between the alienated parent and the child, especially if the child offers resistance against such contact.

Children show their animosity to the alienated parent if they come and visit them at all by reporting back almost as a secret agent to the alienating parent about what has happened, and often lying about what has occurred. They may even carry out acts of stealing from the targeted parent. Children often return to the alienating parent carrying objects and money from the targeted parent as a proof of their animosity towards that parent.

Attention must be drawn to such behaviour by the therapist to show that it is not merely disloyal to behave in this way but also it is a criminal act which is likely to be perpetuated in the future by anti-social behaviour ranging from delinquency to criminality.

Even if the child has met and not found anything favourable about the alienated parent it is the role of the therapist to do all that they can to engage the child in more favourable attitudes towards the alienated parent by bringing forth arguments that support such a claim. Most importantly, the child must be made aware of the fact that they have been used in the armoury of alienation as a weapon against the alienated parent.

It cannot be repeated too often that without the power of the court behind the therapeutic effort little can be achieved with recalcitrant alienating parents or their offspring. It must be the objective of the therapist to get the child to think independently and not respond and co-operate with the vilification of the father or mother.

Children deep down realise that they are depriving themselves of a parent but they don't want to realise it on the surface, and will do almost anything to avoid contact with the alienated parent for that reason. More must be done therapeutically to encourage such contact despite this opposition.

It is important to convince the child of the sacrifices the alienated parent would be likely to make if that child required help merely to survive. Gardner (2001) emphasises how an alienated parent could well give up a kidney for the child to survive which an ordinary stranger or even another member of the family more distant to the alienated parent would be unlikely to do. Gardner (2001) in his book on the treatment of therapeutic interventions for children with parental alienation syndrome terms the alienators approach as a campaign of denigration of the targeted parent. It is this denigration which the therapist needs to reduce or eliminate. Without the court behind one the therapist is on an uphill struggle. Obviously, if the alienated parent has indeed been abusive or difficult or has neglected the child, the job of the therapist becomes even more difficult. This, however, is rarely the case, or indeed if it does exist it has been exaggerated by the alienating parent.

The children thus alienated must view the situation from the point of view of rational and logical thinking. The child must learn not to please the programmer at the cost of the targeted parent. This is somewhat easier with older children, but as already stated these have often been put through the process of alienation for longer periods. Younger children are more difficult to influence due to the total control of the alienator and the relatively undeveloped capacity for rational thinking of very young children. Due to the process of alienation children are often exaggerating what has happened to them while the targeted parent was still living in the same home. Hence the child eating their dinner and refusing to eat vegetables when encouraged to do so by the alienated parent will claim that they were 'forced' to eat the vegetables against their will. Precise information therefore must be obtained from the child as to why they feel so acrimonious towards the alienated parent and seeks to denigrate that parent for that reason.

Even as adults, children who have been programmed against one of the parents will remember this, and even attend therapy to rid themselves of the process of alienation. One such case involved an adult woman who, as a child, complained that her father teased her, as did her brother, about her not eating meat. This later became a massive exaggeration of the father's terrible and insensitive behaviour towards his young daughter. This as a whole shows a lack of unity between the parents and leads to children using one parent against the other in order to get their own way. It is therefore vital to get underneath to the true reasons as to why a child feels a parent has all the negative traits possible. The therapist must work hard to get the child to be rational, to think clearly and to provide information which, in the end, can lead to the right reasons, if there are any, as to why the child feels negative towards a particular parent after having been programmed to be as such. From the cognitive and attitude changes in thinking the child must then be encouraged to behave appropriately towards the alienated parent. This can only be achieved, however, when the child feels that their initial attitude towards the alienated parent was faulty.

Many alienated parents are placed in a no-win situation whereby if they do something they are criticised and if they do nothing, they are equally criticised. A good example of this was when a father was asked to come to a football game and the child indicated to the mother that the father was unwanted. Had the father not offered to come it would have showed rejection, however, the fact that he comes indicates that he might do something to embarrass the child in question by his being there.

Needless to say, therapists vary in their approach to the problem of PAS. Some will actually view the situation from the child's current thinking and not attempt to alter that thinking in any way. This prevents PAS from being reduced or eliminated and in fact encourages it to continue. Therapists who are likely to do any good to reverse the PAS situation must be well versed in logic and reason and be sensitive to the indoctrination process of alienating parents and the helpless plight in which the targeted parent finds themself.

In order to change the child's view of the world and of the alienated parent it is sometimes necessary to resort to what may be termed anti-psychological approaches such as making a child actually feel guilty for the way the child behaves towards the alienated parent. Such feelings of guilt can have a positive effect in removing the alienator's influences on the child.

The process of de-alienating or deprogramming a child may be viewed from the dialogue which follows:

Dr L: Now tell me why is it you don't want to see your mother at all anymore?

Child: She was cruel to me once and even hit me. She made my father's life hell when he was still alive and I preferred to be with my grandmother for that reason.

Dr L: I did speak to your mother about what you have said and she has admitted to me that she did hit you once, but that was to prevent you from doing something that could be dangerous to you. Do you remember?

Child: I only did what other children do, that is to want to stay out late at night and not come home if I felt like doing so.

Dr L: Do you think it is a parent's role to let children do what they like even if it is bad for them?

Child: Parents have no right to tell me what to do. My grandmother never tells me what to do and I can stay out and do what I like for as long as I like.

Dr L: Do you think the parent has no right or duty to try to protect you from a life outside the home that could be detrimental to your welfare now and in the future?

Child: I know what I am doing I am now fifteen years old and I should be able to do what I want to do.

Dr L: Tell me exactly what you specifically dislike about your mother and be as specific as possible.

Child: She's just no good, she's nasty to me and she's not nice to my grandmother. She has never done anything for me of any value.

Dr L: Do you really mean that? She has never done anything for you at all? Think about what she might have done for you in the past that you have forgotten.

Child: I can't think of anything good she has ever done for me.

It is statements such as these which may need to be investigated further and points brought out as to what the mother has done in the past which made the child happy and which have now been forgotten consciously or unconsciously disowned. It is, of course, vital for the therapist to have developed a close relationship, with respect from the child towards the therapist, in order to convince the child that their thinking against the alienated parent has no foundation or has been exaggerated due to the programming process. The therapist must do all they can to rid the child of the total negative attitude and resulting behaviour towards the alienated parent and the alliance of a total nature again between the child and the alienator. The therapist must help the child to see both the negative and positive aspects of both the alienating parent and the alienated one. It is vital to develop such independent thinking in the child, albeit difficult.

Children, although they may not show it, frequently welcome the fact that a court of law has been involved in their unhappy family relationships, since through the court, the child can feel that they must now follow the instruction of a superior force; even more superior than the alienating parent, and thereby have an excuse for giving some time and possibly affection to the alienated parent. Confronted by the alienating parent the child is able to say, 'I am only doing this because the court demands it and I don't want to get into any trouble.'

As has also already been mentioned the child often feels ashamed and even guilty about the manner in which they have treated the alienated parent despite no really good evidence being present for such treatment. Children who denigrate such a parent are faced with deep feelings of guilt which they tend to hide through cruel actions against the denigrated parent. The process of feeling guilty can lead to a change in attitude and behaviour. Another term for guilt is conscience and this has not been a term

denigrated even by psychologists. The super-ego, as Freud termed it, is often responsible for right actions.

It has long been known that broken homes create instability in the child and can often lead to psychological problems, delinquency and other serious difficulties. When a relationship break up is more harmonious so that both partners seek to love the child and also encourage the child to love both parents and respond to them effectively, and when parents are unified in their approach, many problems can be avoided. It should always be made clear to any child involved in a marital break up that the love for the child has not been lost and the friendship between the parents can be maintained for that reason. Children then realise that they have two parents who both care for them even though they cannot live with each other in harmony. They may even choose another partner but this does not in anyway reflect on both parents seeking to continue their support, love and care of the child. This is the very opposite of parental alienation. It is the aim of the therapist to develop such a relationship if this ideally is possible. In this way, the child's future may be assured rather than put into jeopardy.

Children who turn against one parent are developing a process leading to serious consequences. This is due to the fact that they have renounced one parent and frequently feel a sense of guilt thereafter especially if that parent dies or is no longer available for other reasons. It is vital in such children to engender both a feeling of guilt for wronging the alienated parent and a sensitivity towards that parent. Changing behaviour relies on changing the attitude or cognition of the child but equally important is changing the behaviour of the child towards the programmed against parent. It should be remembered that both parents can practise PAS, one as the initiator and the other as the reactor by seeking to demolish the value of the alienated parent. It must be remembered that children can suffer in the long term from the alienating process emotionally, educationally and in future relationships that may develop and could themselves in the future become the alienator.

Chapter Twenty-Five

Identifying and treating false accusations of sex abuse

In what follows I shall examine the subject of the psychological aspects of parental alienation. I will discuss: How and why parental alienation processes lead to sexual abuse accusations; getting at the truth; and what can be done to reverse false accusations of sexual abuse, concluding with a clinical case illustration.

How and why parental alienation processes lead to sexual abuse accusations

It is vital to be certain in the first instance that no sexual abuse has occurred. If it has occurred, parental alienation processes and its identification and treatment are very different from that which follows. Hence it is vital to establish that before seeking to break the deadlock of a child and alienator making such allegations against an alienated parent, that sexual abuse has not actually occurred. Parental alienation is usually preceded by an acrimonious relationship and the targeted member, usually the father, having left the home. It is most important to protect children from the trauma resulting from sexual abuse and this cannot be stressed too greatly. It is equally important, however, that we protect children from an emotionally abusing adult programming them against the other parent.

As is almost always the case false sexual abuse allegations originate from the alienator and are supported by the supposed victim and possibly other members of the family. Sometimes such abuse has been:

- Exaggerated, such as a the result of an inadvertent or innocent touch of a genital area.
- With no such basis whatsoever for the allegations having occurred.

The child supports the alienator, mainly the mother, because the child:

- Has identified with the parent and in so doing also with the attitudes and allegations made against the alienated parent.

- Some of the signs that a child is lying or exaggerating may be noted as due to brain-washing and the programme of alienation the child has received.

A number of ways to identify whether the child is telling the truth or not will be gone into the next section in connection with the following:

- The phrases and words used, especially by a very young child, which have been borrowed from the indoctrinator: 'He sexually abused me ... He seduced me ... He sodomised me ... He molested me ... He had penile intercourse etc, etc.' 'He makes me watch pornographic films.' Sometimes such statements are known to be suspect such as when the father does not even have a video player.
- Sometimes the child will inadvertently reveal that the very source of the allegations made came from the mother. 'I don't feel safe with my father ... He could hit me ... Mummy told me'.
- Frequently, the alienator will reveal a precise 'litany' on what has allegedly occurred, this being repeated word for word by the child. Often the child does not understand the meaning of the words used such as the father being 'controlling', 'authoritarian', 'permissive' and other statements already noted above. They merely 'parrot' what is heard from the alienator, such as: 'My father did not cuddle me until I was two years old.' One could well ask how the child could know this unless they had been told by someone, possibly the mother.
- Some children will write directly to the court and judges with sexual abuse complaints instigated by the alienator who addresses the very envelopes and posts the letter. Frequently the mother actively writes letters and then attributes them to the child. They are dictated by the mother as to what the child should say, such as father being: 'a paedophile ... not sufficiently protective ... being too much of a disciplinarian ... or not providing discipline.'

- The children asked to define the terms used are likely not to be able to do so. They are merely repeating what they have heard from the alienator. Sometimes they will even admit that the alienator used such words to them about the parent who is being vilified.

While these signs do not directly discount the possibility that some form of sexual abuse has occurred, they demonstrate the general tendency which results when a child is programmed against an absent parent in order to discredit them. It can also lead, in the case of sexual abuse allegations, to the prosecution of an innocent parent and if found guilty the imprisonment of that parent. The courts and the law unfortunately do not always get it right. Such injustices can never be rectified, even when the child later recants the accusations made.

Getting at the truth

It is the task of the psychologist to get at the truth as to whether sexual abuse has occurred in the first instance. It must be understood that sex abuse allegations are often a spin off of the parental alienation process. This is not to say that parents do not commit acts of sexual abuse against their children but one must be suspicious, however, when such allegations are made once parents are separated, when the separation is acrimonious, and when no such allegations have ever been made while both parents lived together.

Should sexual abuse actually have taken place, as established via an 'independent investigator' then it is necessary:

- To treat the child for its effects.
- To treat the perpetrator within or outside the prison system.
- To allow only supervised contact between the child and the sex abuse offender at some point in time, usually after therapy has been completed and been successful.
- An attempt must be made to rehabilitate the family if at all possible.

Allegations of sexual abuse frequently occur in cases of parental alienation and for these there is often no foundation, and thus false. They are attributable to the implacable hostility of the alienator towards the targeted parent. Here the alienator will use each and any strategy to keep the other parent from having contact with the child. This is done from hostility and instils in the child the notion that the absent parent is of evil intent, dangerous or otherwise unworthy of playing any role in their lives.

False accusations of sexual abuse are strewn with signs which are easy to ignore. This occurs when one has already preconceived notions that if a parent and child state that it has occurred it must have happened. This is why it is so important that the investigator be totally independent, impartial, skilled and dedicated in getting at the truth of such dangerous allegations. These allegations include in summary:

- The language used by the child when speaking of the abuse.
- Inconsistencies in the stories of the child.
- Borrowed scenarios from the alienator.
- Elaboration of the abuse that does not make sense.

Through individual interviews with the alienator, alienated parent and the child, and also in various combinations, the objective is to note both the consistencies and inconsistencies in the information obtained.

It must be emphasised that interviewing and gathering information concerning whether sexual abuse took place is both an art and a science. Those who are likely to be sexual abusers usually have from an early age shown signs or histories of abusing. They may themselves have been sexually abused as children.

The author of this paper has written a book which contains a test and interviewing procedure which is still being revised. It is important never to depend on one or more pieces of evidence before making any decisions. Decisions must be based on past research in the personality and history of sexual abusers, interviews with a variety of individuals and using a variety of personality tests.

While sex abusers are devious and deniers, so are those who make false allegations as a result of the parental alienation phenomenon. Furthermore there are, as already mentioned, psychologists, psychiatrists, social workers and organisations who consider a child's statement sacrosanct. They will then seek further evidence to corroborate the fact that sexual abuse has occurred according to what the child has said, instead of impartially seeking for the truth. As has already been made abundantly clear, children do not always tell the truth.

What can be done to reverse false accusations of sexual abuse?

There are a number of ways in which children can be made to tell the truth and to reverse their very dangerous allegations that sexual abuse has been practised upon them due to the alienation of a hostile parent:

1. Promoting shame and guilt felt towards the alienated parent for having made false accusations of sexual abuse. Children who are being alienated, or have been alienated are in a conflict situation. Here the promotion of guilt plays an important part as well as feelings of insecurity. Let me elaborate on this view. Children who have been programmed by a parent against the other non-resident parent fail to develop what can only be termed, a balanced sense of guilt. They will make accusations, even of having been sexually abused, at the instigation of a hostile programmer.
2. They develop, by reason of programming, a feeling of responsibility of duty towards the parent with whom they currently reside, usually the mother. The parent who is no longer there by reason of an acrimonious separation, receives comparatively little concern. The longer the separation, the less positive the child feels towards the absent parent, often blaming that parent for the absence, even when there has been a close loving relationship with that parent and that parent's family. This is because absent parents lose their capacity to influence events. This is not the case for the custodial parent who has the capacity and often does use that capacity to influence the thinking and emotions of a child towards the absent parent. This is especially the case when the absent parent has developed a new relationship. There is much jealousy here by the alienating parent towards the new relationship. This feeling is passed on to the child by the alienator.

There are many reasons why parents separate. It is usually because all is not well with the relationship as experienced by one or both parents. A good, healthy and otherwise positive relationship results in both parents seeking to support the child. Both parents and the child have a balanced memory of good time together. Thereby parental alienation is prevented. Such parents do not need the help of the psychologist. They are demonstrating their love for the child and providing that child with what is in their best interest, to feel loved by both parents.

It is the programmed child against a parent who needs to be helped to view the situation realistically, that is, the one parent is absent but still loves the child. The child should continue to feel the same towards the absent parent and this can only be done by encouragement by the potentially alienating parent. Such children are fortunate as they will have the chance for a good start in life and therefore a good future.

Only alienating by the programming parent can prevent such positive results. When the alienation process occurs, the child is initially in a conflict as to who should be rewarded for their continual love and affection . This situation does not last long when the brainwashing is effective, combined with the absence of the targeted parent. Hence the conscience and loyalty easily becomes one sided in the direction of the custodial and programming parent. This is partly due to the need for security by the child, the programming, and the absence of the targeted parent having any influence on the child. One might well say that in this situation 'absence does not make the heart grow fonder'. Instead the absence towards the vilified parent leads in time to partial, or eventually, total rejection.

There appears to be, at least on the surface, no involvement of the conscience in the child about the alienated parent. As already mentioned, and it will continue to be mentioned, the alienator becomes 'all good' while the alienated parent is 'totally evil'. The child identifies therefore totally with the custodial parent and their views relative to the vilified absent parent.

One might say that the child has destroyed, or put to sleep, any conscience in regard to the alienated parent, for the reasons already mentioned of identifying with the alienator totally. There is therefore no room for ambivalence of feelings. This term is constantly referred to by Gardner (2001). Such parents inculcate a lack of empathy and sympathy for the victim of parental alienation. As a psychologist one is often asked by the court: 'How will this affect the child now and in the future?' Such experiences are likely to influence children all their lives unless they can be deprogrammed as quickly as possible. It will also influence the future adult in the manner in which they conduct themselves with other people. Empathy, conscience and morality are learned early in life by positive contact with caring, loving and firm parents.

Because children have been alienated against a parent they could well develop psychopathic personalities, demanding but never giving. They will lie and cheat and take what they want when they want it irrespective of the feelings of others. This is very much in the way that the programmer has behaved towards the targeted parent and children learn from this. Such individuals who programme children against others never appear to give but always seek to take and always provide the vilification of the absent parent. The child, having no contact with the absent parent, is directly or subtly discouraged from thinking for themselves and for adopting ethical and moral ways of living. An alienated parent will often fight for years to have contact with a child. They fight for this in court at great expense. Courts however, do not always see or want to see what the alienation process has done. Courts and the minions who help to make decisions make several mistakes. They are nevertheless understandable but legally and morally reprehensible:

- They believe what the child says and wants, instead of looking beneath the reasons for the child's assertions of not wishing contact with the targeted parent. They fail to see what was done to promote these reasons.
- Courts therefore often inevitably side with the custodial parent as this is the easier way out of a tangled and complex situation, instead of punishing those responsible for the alienation.

Such decisions do little to prevent the negative short and long-term effects on the child, by depriving the child of contact with the loving non-custodial parent and others. It does not even, in the end, benefit the programming parent when the child grows up and understands what has been done to prevent another loving parent being involved with their life, so that the child turns against the alienator.

The estranged parent, often after years of attempting to seek a relationship with the child, finally gives up. The reason is that the courts have not listened to the vilified parent or the true views of the child. Such alienated parents then start, if they have not done so already, to seek a new partner and further children. The result is that the child has been deprived of the valuable relationship with the father or mother. Such contact could have helped the child in future to promote relationships with others and become socialised. It also teaches the child, ultimately, that the courts are both unfair and unjust but they are powerful. What legacy is that for the new generation!?

Clinical case illustration

What follows is based on an actual case, considerably disguised so as not to reveal the individuals who actually participated. The case concerns a child who has made a sexual abuse and other allegations against her father. The dialogue between the child and the psychologist, as well as the mother and the psychologist, are both to identify whether sexual abuse has occurred and also to seek to treat it by deprogramming the child who has been alienated, in this case against the father over a long period of time. It should be made absolutely clear that this is a clinical example and not an actual case. It is, however, typical of many of the cases that this psychologist and others have dealt with in the past and will continue to do so. It will also be made clear the dangers that psychologists are facing when attempting to get at the truth and to deal with that truth following it having been revealed. The first part deals with the interview with the alienating mother, the second with the child, and the third the interview with the psychologist, the father and the child together.

Interview with the mother

As she enters the room it is with a bearing of authority.

1   **Psych:** 'Would you tell me again what your eight year old daughter told you about getting into bed with the father.'
    Mother: 'He touched her in an inappropriate way between her legs.
2   **Psych:** 'Would you show me exactly what your daughter said he did'.
    Mother: *(She demonstrated by running both her hands along the side and then between her*

inner thighs close to, but not actually touching the private parts).

3 **Psych**: 'Did he touch her private parts at any time?'

Mother: 'It looks that way to me, doesn't it to you?'

4 **Psych**: 'You demonstrated and you showed that he was near but not actually at the exact area of her private parts.'

Mother: 'You will have to ask my daughter. She will show you exactly what he did do. Anyway do you think it's right for a grown up man to have a little girl in bed with him, touching her the way he did?'

5 **Psych**: 'She is his daughter, isn't she? Have you never been in bed with your daughter?'

Mother: 'Of course I have. We are both of the same sex. I was only giving her a cuddle. Anyway he's not living with us now. He's with some slut who already has three children.'

6 **Psych**: 'Why did your relationship break up?'

Mother: 'What has that got to do with his molesting my daughter by asking her to get into bed with him?'

7 **Psych**: 'I would still like to know why you and your husband decided your relationship was over between you.'

Mother: 'If you want to know. I told him to go. He was an overbearing man and I told him one day that the marriage was over.'

8 **Psych**: 'Was there any other reason, remember you created a child between the two of you.'

Mother: 'And that's the only good thing to come out of our relationship. It's all I ever wanted.'

9 **Psych**: 'You wanted the child, but no longer did you want your husband, the man who incidentally gave you that child.'

Mother: 'I had enough of him and his ways. Yes one day I just told him it was over.'

10 **Psych**: 'When he came back home I believe you had changed the lock of the front door.'

Mother: 'Yes, I didn't want any more to do with him.'

11 **Psych**: 'I understand, you did want to have your daughter, but you didn't want your husband to have anything to do with your mutual daughter that you created together, is that right?'

Mother: 'It's my daughter and not I who stopped her seeing him anyway. You will have to ask her why she doesn't want to see him. She has a mind of her own you know. I can't do anything about the way she feels.'

12 **Psych**: 'You have of course said you tried to get her to visit her father and to be with him and to answer telephone calls from him?'

Mother: 'Of course, I said you should see your father, and she refused. What do you expect me to do, force her to see her father? I can't do that, nobody can do that. And anyway he shouldn't have asked her to go into bed with him. She told me everything. My daughter and I are very close. You saw how she clings to me in the waiting room. She didn't want to go in to see you, you know? But I insisted, I had to: why couldn't you have me in the room when you were talking to her? That's what she wanted. Remember you are a stranger to her.'

13 **Psych**: 'You know very well that I need to see her on her own, and I will be seeing her again later to discuss the points you made about her father sexually abusing her while in bed with her.'

Mother: 'I don't know whether he was doing that, but that's what my daughter told me. You will have to ask her yourself. No-one should be calling a little girl into bed with him to do with her what he did. If that isn't sexually abusing a child then I don't know what is. That's why she doesn't want anything to do with him. She won't even talk to him on the telephone now.'

14 **Psych**: 'You and your daughter have made a very strong allegation against her father. You realise that if what you are insinuating is true, he could be prosecuted and if found guilty he could he imprisoned. He could be in prison for a very long time. It will also affect his career as a medical doctor. He could easily be struck off by the British Medical Association. He would therefore be unable to practise medicine. This means that he would have no income and no financial support for you and for your daughter. It would mean that you would have to rely totally on your own job. Fortunately, you are in a fairly powerful position, you are I believe a

director of an IT firm which has over one thousand employees?

Mother: *(Mother thinks deeply for some time).* 'I hadn't imagined how it would affect him or us in the way you have described it. Well, I'll just have to provide for everything and I would be willing to do this just to get rid of him for good.

15   **Psych**: 'I suppose you don't really need your husband's income to support your way of life. You are the director of your own firm and you are therefore in a powerful position yourself.

Mother: 'And I hope you realise I did it all by myself. It is still not easy for a woman to do what I did in a man's world' *(Here it is clear her resentment against the 'male' is very powerful as she considers the male to be in a more powerful position compared with women.)*

16   **Psych**: 'Now that is about as far as we can go and I now need to see your daughter'.

Interview with the child

The protagonists are the psychologist (psych) and the child (child).

17   **Psych**: 'I hear you are an intelligent girl getting high marks in school. Is that right?'
Child: 'I suppose so.' *(Very much on the defensive.)*

18   **Psych**: 'You know why you are here with me, don't you?'
Child: 'It's about my father. I don't want to see him. I don't want to speak to him. Nobody can make me.'

19   **Psych**: 'I would like to know what happened to make you feel that way. I believe you were once very close to your father.'
Child: 'What makes you think that? I was never close to him.'

20   **Psych**: 'He showed me some pictures when you were with him and you seemed to be very much enjoying yourself in his company.'
Child: 'I was only pretending to enjoy myself. I really hated being with him, and that woman she is nothing but a slut.'

21   **Psych**: 'Well I think you looked very happy in the picture your father showed me. By the way what do you mean by the word 'slut'?'

Child: 'It's someone who has *(hesitating)* sex with lots of men.'

22   **Psych**: 'How do you know if she has had sex with lots of men? Have you seen or heard of her sleeping with lots of men?'
Child: 'I don't know, but she has three children and she and her husband are divorced.'

23   **Psych**: 'Are they all his children and hers?'
Child: 'I suppose so. How do I know?'

24   **Psych**: 'I believe she and your father have been together for a few years. Has your father ever said she was a 'slut'?'
Child: 'No, but how does he know what she gets up to when he's at work?'

25   **Psych**: 'I believe she works as a social worker doesn't she? That would appear to give her very little time to have sex with lots of men. By the way how did you hear about the word 'slut'?'
Child: 'I don't know. I just heard it.'

26   **Psych**: 'From whom?'
Child: 'I don't . . . I can't remember. Why do you keep asking me such stupid questions?'

27   **Psych**: 'I need to get at the truth, the real truth why you said your father had touched you in an inappropriate place. That's what you said isn't it?'
Child: 'Yes I did and I'm not changing my mind. You won't be able to talk me out of it. Mum said you would try.'

28   **Psych**: 'I'll do nothing of the kind, I want only to get at the truth of what actually happened. I need to know exactly what your father did do.'
Child: 'He wanted me to get into bed with him. Isn't that enough? He is a grown up man and I'm only a little girl.' *(A borrowed scenario.)*

29   **Psych**: 'Father said you were happy to get into bed with him.'
Child: 'That's not true, he made me go into bed with him.'

30   **Psych**: 'How did he do that. Did he pull you or carry you into his bed?'
Child: 'No, not exactly. He just said come and get into bed with me.'

31   **Psych**: 'For a cuddle, yes?'
Child: *(She does not answer.)*

32   **Psych**: 'You are a pretty strong-willed young girl, very much like your father and mother, they are both strong adults. You could have said: No I don't want to get into bed with you.'

Child: 'I could have, yes'.

33 **Psych**: 'But you didn't did you?'

Child: 'No I didn't, but he would have made me get into his bed!'

34 **Psych**: 'How do you know he would have made you do that?'

Child: 'That's the kind of man he is. He would have forced me, even hit me.'

35 **Psych**: 'Has he ever hit you or forced you?'

Child: 'No, but he could have . . . For instance he forced me to eat fruit every day and he made me do my homework before I could watch TV.'

36 **Psych**: 'Isn't that very much a sign of a good parent to want his child to be healthy in the food she eats and to do well in school by getting her to do her homework?'

Child: 'He still didn't have to do that. Mum never forces me to do anything I don't want to do.'

37 **Psych**: 'She doesn't insist you see your father does she?'

Child: 'She says it is up to me and I don't want to. How much longer do I have to sit here with you. I want to go back to my mother. This is all such a waste of time.'

38 **Psych**: 'We are not finished yet. We have a long time, maybe to get to the real truth about what your father is supposed to have done when you were in bed with him.'

Child: 'Not again, I told you already that he touched me where he shouldn't have and I told you, and I told my mum and she must have told you.'

39 **Psych**: 'Yes she told me but I want to know what happened exactly and not generally, but specifically what your father is supposed to have done while you were in bed with him.'

Child: 'I've already told you he touched me inappropriately.'

40 **Psych**: 'I want to know exactly where and for how long he touched you. Please show me exactly what he did.'

Child: (*She demonstrates being rubbed in the outer area of her waist, legs and thighs but nowhere near her private parts.*)

41 **Psych**: 'Is that it?'

Child: 'He touched me very near my private parts.'

42 **Psych**: 'But you showed me he did not actually touch them did he?'

Child: 'No but he was very close. He could easily have done so he is that kind of man!'

43 **Psych**: 'You keep saying that phrase 'he is that sort of man'. You say he could but he didn't actually force you to go into bed with him; you said he could have hit you, but then you say he never did hit you; you say he touched you inappropriately, but he never did touch your private parts. Do you know that you have caused a lot of trouble for your father saying what you said about what he was supposed to have done with you in bed.'

Child: 'It's the truth. I didn't lie.'

44 **Psych**: 'I don't like to call anyone a liar, but you really stretched, bent, or otherwise gave an impression that your father is a sex abuser of his own daughter whom he loves very much and desperately wants to do everything for you. You make him sound like a paedophile, a pervert, who uses his own little girl for his own sexual gratification.'

Child: 'I never said he was all those things.'

45 **Psych**: 'Maybe not in so many words you didn't say it, but you and your mother intimated that your father was a horrible man who took advantage of his own daughter and who used and abused his own daughter sexually. Your father could easily have been prosecuted and given a long prison sentence and lost his profession. Did he deserve that for what he did when he was only giving you affection and love?' You virtually threw your father in the rubbish.

(*This statement needs to be repeated a number of times with an increasing emotional aptitude.*)

Child: (*She sits quietly. She is beginning to have tears in her eyes*) I didn't mean to do all that you say. I didn't.'

46 **Psych**: 'Your father has in all truth been a good father to you hasn't he? He doesn't deserve the treatment you have given him, such as hanging up when he calls you.'

Child: (*Remains silent.*)

47 **Psych**: 'Now it's time to get your father in the room so that you can tell him in your own words how you feel. Your mother won't be here and once I see you talking to him, not pretending but really wanting to speak with him I will go and leave you with him. I know now for certain that your father never sexually abused you. You know it also.'

Child: 'I don't want to see and be with him on my own.'

48   **Psych**: 'Oh yes you do and you will.'
      Child: (*When the father enters the room the child looks in the opposite direction.*) At this point a part of the previous dialogue, certainly from 37 onwards is repeated and emphasised especially number 43. Eventually the child began to look at the father first at the pictures he showed her when she was happy in his company with his family. At this point the psychologist left the room for several minutes returning only to observe and encourage this positive contact to continue. By the end of several times leaving the room and noting the friendly and verbal intercourse with the father the psychologist called an end to the session. After poor or no contact for several years father and daughter were once again on friendly terms.

There could be one of two endings here. The first and hoped for ending would be that the daughter continued to have contact with the father and their relationship grew in time and that the father was allowed to have a valued relationship with his daughter. The court upheld his right to have contact and agreed the child should receive further treatment to undo the harm done to her by the alienating parent who was ordered not to interfere with the father/daughter relationship. The alienator would be under threat from the court if she tried to influence the daughter in any way against the father.

The ending here, however, was not as happy as it all appeared. The girl in question once again repeated her previous denunciation of her father and refused further contact with him once she returned to her mother. She was once more under the influence of the alienator who had custody and residence of the child. The mother and daughter made a verbal and written complaint to the guardian ad litem that the psychologist had 'bullied' the child into having contact with her father.

The mother's solicitor took up the cause on her behalf suggesting that the evidence of father and daughter's rehabilitated relationship be struck off as unacceptable. There was even a veiled threat made that the psychologist would be reported to

his professional body, the BPS, for disciplinary action to be taken against him, for behaving in an unprofessional manner toward the child.

This kind of work is indeed a 'poisoned chalice' for the mediator which should be recognised by the court when appointing such mediation sessions between 'warring' factions, especially when parental alienation of a severe nature has occurred. In the US there is court support for the mediator from the judge and the hostility of the alienating parent recognised and curtailed. This does not happen as yet in the UK and needs to be taken into account as a matter of urgency if further mediation/treatment is to take place. Professional bodies should also be supportive to those carrying out the difficult task of treating parental alienation. Only in this way can the position be changed and justice be done for the alienated parent and the mediator who undertakes such a case, not merely as a fact finder but as someone who makes a difference to the often stalemated position of the case, and the entrenched position of the alienator who still continues to alienate from a powerful position.

Why go to court if there is to be no change? If the 'wolf has not teeth' what can be done? Each solicitor maintains the 'status quo' for their client whether or not they morally agree. There should be a meeting of all parties with the judge, not in a court situation, but in chambers to seek a solution to the way forward without the protagonists or the child being present. Being child centred is not the solution when parent alienation has occurred. Being fair and just with all parties is what will move the case forward.

Which is the best solution? I know which one I would wish to happen. This would also be in the **best interests of the child**.

It may be noted that the outcome of the investigatory committee meetings were that Dr Lowenstein had conducted his mediation process in a most acceptable manner being fair to all parties concerned and reaching a conclusion which was based on the evidence. They concluded that he showed no prejudice whatsoever towards either party but acted in an independent, professional manner.

Chapter Twenty-Six

Recent research into risk assessment of children

Introduction

Expert witnesses and others have always been concerned with how much risk can be taken, if any, in the concern for the safety of children. Safety of children should ensure that they are in no danger of physical, sexual or emotional abuse or neglect. The prediction of danger to children, though vital, can be problematic.

It is vital for those who assess risk to use any type of assessment, measurement, interview etc. likely to lead to the most accurate prediction. There is a tendency for many who assess dangerousness to over-estimate it, as it is better 'to err on the side of caution' than the reverse. This is despite the fact that only a few individuals are likely to be a danger compared to those who are not likely to act as such (Menzies et al., 1994).

There has been an increase in the use of the actuarial method for predicting that risk is minimal. Hence false positives may be prevented, i.e. people who are predicted to do something wrong but do not do so. False negatives are people who are not expected to do anything dangerous but do so; they must also be identified (Gardner et al., 1996)

Ackerman (1999) clearly indicates the factors likely to increase the risk of dangerousness or violence. These include:

- History of violence (Steadman and Robbins, 1998; Wrightsman et al., 1998).
- The use of substances such as alcohol and drugs (Steadman et al., 1998; Steadman and Robbins, 1998).
- Psychotic illness including hallucinations and delusions such as fear of being threatened (Melton et al., 1997).
- Being immature or under the age of 30 (Tardiff et al., 1997; Melton et al., 1997).
- Anti-social personality disorder i.e. psychopathy (Tardiff et al., 1997a, b; Harris and Rice, 1997).
- Failure to take psychotropic medication (Monohan and Steadman, 1994).

The most recent research into risk assessment of children has been divided into four parts:

1. Risk factors associated with children's welfare.
2. Problems associated with risk assessments.
3. Assessment methods for ascertaining risk to children.
4. Therapeutic approaches to reduce risk towards children.

1. Risk factors associated with children's welfare

Risk factors for physical child abuse were studied by Christmas et al. (1996). The review of the current literature in relation to this considers foremost a history of abuse in the past, the depression of one or both parents, single parenting, the socio-economic status of the family, social isolation, the maternal age with younger women being more vulnerable and partaking in substance abuse.

Mentally ill mothers who have killed in the past were studied by Jacobsen and Miller (1998). One proposal is to 'fast-track' cases involving parents with long-standing mental disorders by automatically terminating parental rights. This approach assumes that a severe and chronic mental disorder is incompatible with safe parenting. Three cases were studied where children were killed. The conclusion was evaluation of parenting competency of mentally ill parents is important. An American study carried out in the state of Massachusetts by Whitney and Davis (1999) considered the importance of an internal domestic violence programme better to identify and serve families where partner's abuse and child abuse overlap.

With child custody disputes there are particular dangers to children as well as to adults due to the acrimony which exists between the former partners. Austin (2000a) studied the relocation of child custody and its impact on children. Courts usually allow the child to move away with the residential parent, unless there is potential harm to the child. The forensic violence risk assessment literature provides an analogous conceptual framework for understanding the prediction of harm. Harm is likely to be exacerbated when comments are made by the resident parent towards a child to develop a condition commonly termed parental alienation syndrome (Lowenstein 1998a, b, 1999a–c, 2001; Gardner 1992, 1998, 2001).

Finally Gambrill and Shlonsky (2001) considered that risk assessment studies in child welfare have largely focused on identifying individual or family risk factors. This is often associated with future harm. These risks include, lack of proper assessment of service needs, inadequate linkage of available services to desired outcomes, and an agency culture that is reactive rather than pro-active in pursuit of risk reduction.

2. Problems associated with risk assessments

There are major problems in carrying out risk assessments. To carry out no risk assessment is obviously wrong, but to consider that risk assessments are always reliable is equally fallacious. A review of the literature up to 1996 by Lyons et al. (1996) of risk assessments included the examining of psychometric properties including reliability and validity and outcomes of the implementation as a response to the crisis of growing intakes of child protective services agencies. Risk assessment models and their evaluation were search based on two criteria: 1) the evaluation published or presented at a conference; 2) the evaluation conducted by an independent evaluator. The result highlighted the need for development and research into risk assessment procedures.

Kelly and Milner (1996) suggested that case conference decisions e.g. by social worker, were inherently more risky than those taken by professionals with 'individual responsibility' because of the way in which cases are framed in terms of losses. A different view was expressed by Milner et al. (1998). They stressed that despite the number of assessment techniques currently available, researchers and practitioners had few methods of clearly identifying risk and mitigating factors and that direct assessment techniques currently offer the best assessment strategies. Unfortunately, a child care worker was the poorest predictor of further risk.

Bell (1999) studied 22 local authorities in Great Britain and their social workers undertaking child protection investigation. He noted that while social workers were committed to being, and

believed their practice to be, participative, the dual tasks of making risk assessments for conferences and working in partnership with problem families created conflicts of interest and rights. The impact of this on social workers' engagement with family members, on their assessment, and on the decision-making process was explored. It was concluded that the difficulties identified were endemic and pointed out the need for a more broadly-based child care service to appropriately meet the welfare needs of the family. Also the contradictory nature of the conference task needed to be addressed by clarifying the legal base of the intervention and developing other models of decision making.

Drury-Hudson (1999) examined the process of decision making in child protection, particularly as it related to the decision whether or not to remove a child from home. A group of novice social workers was compared with expert practitioners, with particular focus on the types of knowledge that novices draw upon when making such decisions. A three stage qualitative methodology was employed. All parts of the study utilised a case vignette of a neglect scenario. Findings were reported in respect of the use of theoretical, empirical and procedural knowledge and suggested novices tended to lack a clear understanding of the factors associated with child maltreatment. While they have a superficial awareness of the concept of risk assessment, they failed to weigh factors appropriately and apply them to their practice. This supports the findings of the previous study.

An Australian study by Goddard et al. (1999) considered the practice of risk assessment in children via the protection services. It highlighted the complexity of the concept of risk as the basis for a future oriented assessment activity. The authors suggested that this change of time frame (from what has happened to what might happen) was likely to be detrimental to children. Through a critical review of the literature, the authors questioned whether risk predictions were possible and discussed limitations of risk assessment instruments which omitted some risk factors and may have totally ignored the perspective of the child. The authors therefore challenged the validity of risk assessment instruments in statutory settings and suggested that the protection of the organisation was likely to be the major objective in their implementation. This might be considered a kind of self-protection rather than risk assessment of children!

Houston and Griffiths (2000) argued that objectivist paradigms failed to provide valid and reliable measures of risk. Risk should be explored from an alternative subjectivist paradigm. They therefore advocated the reinstatement of the individual to the family and the relationship as the guiding rationale for social work intervention. This view is likely to be highly criticised by many social services, especially when there is a threat of child sexual or physical abuse.

Risk reduction interventions in the case of child custody relocation cases were considered by Austin (2000b). When a custodial parent chooses to relocate to a new community, the child of divorce faces a life transition that was potentially even more traumatic than the parental break-up. The courts generally allow the custodial parent to move away with the child. Divorce affects research into child risk assessments and a recent model of risk assessment for relocation suggested factors that predicted potential harm or protection for the child. Family mediators and psychotherapists had important roles to play in reducing the risk. (This will be discussed in the last section dealing with the therapeutic approaches to reduce risks for children.) It must be added that there are risks caused by the involvement of social services as noted in one study by DePanfilis and Zuravin (2001) which found that families with a previous substantiated report of child abuse were 22 per cent less likely to be open for services than families without prior substantiated reports. In cases substantiated for neglect they were 20 per cent less likely to be open for services than physical abuse cases.

intrusive and therefore less damaging to children and their families. This is in contrast to clinical interviews most often used by social services. It was, however, suggested that risk assessment should ideally use several procedures in a multi-dimensional approach to assessing child sexual abuse. This method was also favoured by Lowenstein (1998).

Baird et al. (1999) also found there were no 100 per cent reliable methods of risk assessment. It was only possible to reduce the risk in the end by using a number of methods, and monitoring the situation carefully and intensively (Lowenstein, 1998).

Assessing the credibility in allegations of marital violence in the high conflict child custody type situation was studied by Austin (2000a). The author states that forensic psychology had not systematically examined the problem of evaluating the credibility of allegations of marital violence in the context of a child custody case. A risk assessment approach to marital violence in the custody evaluation context must be viewed as a serious matter involving the children. The actuarial approach was considered to classify more accurately cases of risk (Baird and Wagner, 2000). Again the Washington State Risk Assessment Matrix was favoured by Camasso and Jagannathan (2000). Fuller et al. (2001) gave preference to the Illinois Child Endangerment Risk Assessment. Here results indicated that the age of the youngest child, single parent households and the number of child problems as well as type of maltreatment could be more effectively diagnosed as to risk.

3. Assessment methods for ascertaining risk to children

Notwithstanding the problems associated with risk assessment, risk must still be assessed albeit using imperfect tools. Jagannathan and Camasso used the Washington Risk Assessment Matrix and found three distinct risk profiles which made risks more likely. These were: children with behaviour problems were more likely to be at risk; as were children from disadvantaged households and children with an unemployed parent.

Psychological tests were particularly useful in the assessment of risk of children, who had been, and might yet again be, sexually abused. Babiker and Herbert (1998) found these tools to be less

4. Therapeutic and other approaches to reduce the risk towards children

Christmas et al. (1996) considered the most effective therapeutic method to be cognitive behaviour therapy especially when the parents suffer from depression. When dealing with parents who cause risks to their children also important were sex education, and instruction skills in anger management. On the whole a multi-faceted approach is to be preferred.

Fisher and Beech (1998) emphasised the use of a comprehensive assessment of sex offenders, using psychological methods and risk factors for offending, in families after sexual abuse has taken place. The emphasis needs to be on reducing social inadequacies and dealing with pro-offending attitudes in the case of sexual abuse and the denial which frequently accompanies this and relapse prevention.

A question to be answered as far as Turnell and Edwards (1999) were concerned was: 'How can child protection professionals build partnerships with parents where there is suspected or substantiated child abuse or neglect'. The authors felt there was a need for practical hands-on strategies for building a partnership with parents, which may, in the long run, prevent abuse and family dissolution. The emphasis was on family reunification practices supposed to be carried out following the identification of specific risks of re-entry of family members (Terling, 1999).

At present protection service agencies tend to be bureaucratic, technocratic, regulatory mechanisms for detecting and managing abuse and neglect. Krane and Davies (2000) suggested a 'mothering narrative', and thereby prevent risks to children emerging. Initially, however, it is important to filter out 'high risk' cases from the rest. A view, currently growing, is that there is limited empirical support for the wholesale adoption of managed care of children and their families (Embry et al., 2000). The focus it is felt, should be on the reduction of maltreatment risks between case opening and closing. A large study by Lyle and Graham (2000) consisting of 245 families with a total of 592 children resulted in significant decreases in risk scores from intake to case closing. Dealing with the whole family in the form of family therapy was a necessary approach according to Hohmann-Marriot (2001) rather than just an individual or individuals without the whole family.

Summary and abstract

Much must be done to improve the accuracy of risk assessment of children. Agencies and social services tend to err on the side of extreme caution rather than truly weigh the risks. This is undoubtedly due to the anxieties associated with the consequences, should tragic mistakes occur. Hence children are often unnecessarily prevented from being with their families. This could be considered an abuse in itself.

The best risk assessment techniques require a number of approaches including psychological testing, especially personality assessments, intensive monitoring of children at risk and interviewing members of families. More accurate specific methods including psychological tests are needed to assess and weigh risks more accurately.

Chapter Twenty-Seven

The psychological assessment and treatment of pathologically induced alienation (dealing with the phobic reaction)

Children who have been alienated frequently behave towards the alienated parent much as phobics react to the object of their fear. For example, despite a previous harmonious relationship with the now absent parent, these children often claim that this parent is a danger to them and therefore they feel hostile toward them. They therefore claim to be afraid of being alone with them. This is despite the fact that they are not in any way in danger.

Psychological treatment here involves changing both their attitudes and behaviour simultaneously. The changing of attitudes or 'mindset' involves cognitive strategies as well as behaviour changes. Let us begin with cognitive treatment.

Cognitive treatment

The child is reminded of the happy times spent with the alienated parent. Such memories sometimes re-awaken the child's positive feelings towards the now alienated parent and shakes the child from their determination to both hate and fear that parent. It is also necessary to engage the child's conscience in so far as how the child is upsetting the alienated parent without justification by their behaviour. This is sometimes effective, but not in severe and long-term alienation towards the targeted parent. One might say that these children are bereft of any guilt feelings. Instead they cling to the custodial parent even more for fear of losing that parent also. The child also fears to show any affection or care towards the absent parent especially when the alienator is present. The child fully realises that the alienating parent will look poorly on positive behaviour directed towards the alienated parent by the child. It is then that the child acts in the most unfriendly ways towards the absent parent by insulting, humiliating and even spitting at the targeted parent. The behaviour of the child often, but not always, changes when alone with

the targeted parent. Now there is no need to put on any acts of animosity towards the targeted parent since the alienating parent is absent. The therapist must be firm in overcoming the lack of conscience of the child towards the now absent parent. The ethics of psychological treatment with its generally softly, softly approach are unlikely to be effective.

One must also remember that whatever the psychologist achieves can easily be reversed by the continuing process of alienation when the child is once more with the programmer. It is for this reason, that alongside the cognitive process of therapy, there needs to be a behavioural therapeutic engagement.

Behaviour therapeutic approach

The major behavioural approaches are desensitisation, flooding and modelling. These approaches are collectively called 'exposure treatments'. We will look at each of these behavioural procedures in turn. These need to be used alongside the cognitive methods previously discussed.

Systematic desensitisation is used to relax the child while they are confronted with the object, real or imaginary, of the person allegedly feared. Since relaxation and fear are incompatible, the objective is to replace the fear with calming, and relaxing the child about eventually meeting the disparaged parent. This meeting should be under the conditions of relaxation about the encounter. Fear therefore needs to be replaced by calmness.

Fear is eventually dissipated utilising three phases; relaxation training, construction of a fear hierarchy, and graded pairings of the fear object (that is the alienated parent) and relaxation responses. The relaxation training programme seeks to release all tensions in the child's body. Next a fear hierarchy is constructed. This comprises a list of specific situations regarding the alienated parent. The fear situations are ranked in ascending order from thinking of the targeted parent in their own home, distant from the child, to eventually imagining that parent in the next street, the next room, and eventually in the same room as the child. This is termed 'covert desensitisation'. The first of these would result in only very mild fear, while the rest are likely to result in increased fear reactions. In each case, relaxation is paired with the fear-provoking situation, thereby dissipating each of the fear responses. At first this is done by imagining the situation. Later it is done via 'in vivo' desensitisation, that is with the alienated parent actually involved and present. Here again the child moves from the least to the most fearsome phase while undergoing relaxation. This is a typical type of treatment used with individuals who suffer from phobias of various kinds.

The second behavioural approach is termed **flooding**. The theory behind this method is that the child will stop fearing and being hostile to a parent by being exposed to that parent repeatedly and over longer and longer periods of time. This would make the child aware that they have no reason to fear or be hostile toward that parent. This technique forces the child to confront their fears without relaxation training being involved.

There is likely to be much opposition to this approach by some psychologists or psychiatrists who are 'child-centred' and who consider such an approach possibly 'harmful' to a child. Often the truth of the matter is obscured when allegations have been made of sexual, physical or emotional abuse of the child by the absent parent. Even when there is no proven truth to the allegations, the procedure is to consider such allegations 'possibly true unless proven otherwise'. Hence guilt is assumed merely because allegations are made by the alienator or an ally of the alienator.

This can result in no contact being permitted for the non custodial parent for months and even years. Supervised contact is also even disallowed, because the child claims to be afraid of, or hostile to the absent parent. What has been forgotten is that the alienated parent has often had a good relationship with the child before the alienation was carried out. It is the process of programming the child to feel hostile and fearful of the absent parent which leads to the avoidance or phobic reaction by the child.

The present psychologist cannot see any other therapeutic process likely to be effective in the long term other than the child being confronted face to face with the absent parent and thereby overcoming fears and other delusions felt towards the alienated parent. This is not advocated by others in the field of child and family problems. Some consider such an approach to be 'insensitive' to the child's state of mind. Unfortunately, putting off such direct confrontation destroys the chance of the child being 'healed' from the effects of the process of alienation. Only by actually seeing and being with the now absent parent who has been maligned, will the child see and experience the reality of the former loving individual. This will then trigger off the parent's association with happier times.

Sometimes it is helpful for the child to view the way the therapist, as an intermediary, engages with the alienated (allegedly feared) parent in what is termed 'vicarious conditioning'. Hence a child views the alienated and allegedly feared parent while in the presence of the therapist, whom the child trusts, and who encourages a friendly and non threatening relationship between the child and the parent. Hence the therapist proves to the child via his own interaction with the parent that the child has no grounds for their fears. Following such vicarious conditioning, while the child is interacting with the once feared parent, there eventually results a closer relationship, especially when the therapist eventually feels it is right to leave the room so that the child can interact more directly with the previously maligned parent. This can then lead to more direct interaction and bonding between the child and the once feared parent.

The third behavioural approach is termed 'modelling'. There is considerable research that indicates the effectiveness of reducing specific phobic reactions by the methods described (Wolpe, 1997; Wolpe et al., 1994; Emmelkamp, 1994). The key to success with a purely behavioural approach to eliminate specific phobias (objects or situations) is to have actual contact with the feared object (Hellstrom and Ost 1996; Emmelkamp, 1994; Arntz and Lavy, 1993). 'In vivo' desensitisation is also considered more successful than covert (imagined events) desensitisation. Similarly, 'in vivo' flooding is more effective in reducing or eliminating phobias than 'imaginal' flooding. 'Participant' modelling is also more useful than 'vicarious' modelling (Menzies and Clarke, 1993; Flynn et al., 1992; Ritchie, 1992). In the case where the fear or hostility is expressed by the child toward a non custodial parent, the evidence is still limited to single case studies. Single case studies of 'flooding' have produced good results, but unfortunately the success is often reversed when the child leaves the therapeutic environment and returns to the alienating influences of the programmer.

It is for this reason that it may be necessary to consider a change of residence temporarily or permanently. This could be to stay with the alienated parent for a specific time (e.g. a full summer holiday) or a non alienating neutral individual, while the therapeutic process continues. Courts are still, however, reluctant to do this. The reason for such reluctance is the child's apprehension to see the alienated parent and this fact weighs heavily on judges. The argument that the child was in the past happy to be with the now rejected parent is discounted due to the child's current reluctance to be with that parent.

All the arguments offered, that the child's reluctance is based on a process of programming which the child has endured, and that this is the reason for the phobic and antagonistic habituated reaction, are ignored. It is assumed that the child, previously so close in relationship to the absent parent, has somehow developed a fear and hostility due to some unknown event or experiences with the currently alienated parent. Judges often become convinced, irrationally, that the innocent alienated parent 'must have done something' to be thus treated with a combination of fear and hostility.

This type of 'rationalisation' makes it easier for the judicial system to maintain the 'status quo' that is, the custodial parent continues with having total control of the child and providing further opportunity to alienate the child. Judges are likely to consider that in due course the child, in later years, or even as an adult, will on their own volition make contact with the sidelined parent. The realities, however, are that in situations where contact has been completely severed – with the approval of the courts – the relationship is not likely to be salvageable. If the child finally meets the alienated parent, they can not return to the happy point before the rupture of the relationship; there are no significant shared moments of happiness they can memorise and relive, there are no photographs or videos of recently enjoyed happy moments. The relationship is destroyed and can no longer continue to build on shared experiences.

There is the stronger likelihood that the alienated parent and the extended family of that parent become permanently redundant due to the process of habituation. It must be said that judges, as well as expert witnesses, have much to be blamed for when they adopt the view that the child must always be believed, and that actions should follow on the basis of this fact. There is here a failure to assess in depth what actually are the reasons for the child's attitude and behaviour towards the absent parent. This is a most important factor mostly missed by those who are responsible for delivering justice for the child.

Conclusions

Children can develop various phobias during their childhood, and many are treated for this. The psychological properties of the phobic rejection of a parent by a child is an example of this. The treatment for this kind of behavioural deficiency is similar to the treatment of other phobias, being an 'in vivo' flooding and 'participant' modelling of the alienated parent to the child. Where these treatments are effective but become overindulging for a child due to the counteractive behaviour of a resident parent, then the child should no longer reside on a day-to-day basis with the parent who is continuing to imprint the phobia into the child.

Chapter Twenty-Eight

Is PAS a mental illness?

Introduction

There has been, and continues to be, some controversy as to whether Parental Alienation Syndrome should be accepted into DSM-IV and be considered a distinct mental illness. In its mild form it is not a mental illness. When symptoms of alienation are extreme and pathological, involving paranoia and delusions, an argument is made for its inclusion in DSM-IV, since its symptoms constitute a syndrome much as other conditions currently included in DSM-IV.

At present parental alienation syndrome (PAS) does not exist in DSM-IV classification. Despite this there are many who believe it should now be included in the *American Psychiatric Association Diagnosis and Statistical Manual of Mental Disorder*, 4th edn. (APA, 1994). The argument frequently put forward is that since it is not acknowledged to be 'registered' in DSM-IV, it ipso facto does not exist and should not be used as a term, especially within the legal system. What follows will attempt to convince the doubters that parental alienation should be considered a mental disorder and be included in DSM-IV.

DSM-IV has added mental disturbances over the years to its list, including such leading disorders associated with reading and mathematics; communication disorders such as phonological disorders and stuttering; pervasive developmental disorders such as Asperger's disorder etc. etc. DSM-IV has also deleted such conditions as homosexuality which is no longer deemed to be a mental illness. DSM-IV and those that preceded it therefore is a moveable feast, dynamic and not immutable to change. We might therefore ask and attempt to answer just why PAS has not as yet been included in DSM-IV.

Why is PAS not included in DSM-IV

There are various arguments as to both why PAS should and should not be included in DSM-IV. The first reason for not including it is because PAS or PA (parental alienation) can be mild in form as well as extreme, profound, or as Gardner put it, pathological and severe (Gardner, 1997).

Like many patterns of behaviour the alienation process is on a continuum with normal behaviour. The same, however, could be said about depression or feeling depressed. Depression only becomes a mental illness when it occurs in an extreme form and for long periods of time. Here the individual could be suffering from what is commonly termed also mild, temporary depression or severe depression, resulting in self-harming or even suicidal tendencies.

In the case of parental alienation, custodial mothers or fathers might make mild to moderate critical or derogatory statements about the behaviour of the absent parent e.g . . . spoke very nastily to me . . . always critical of me . . . was quarrelsome . . . was away a lot . . . was untidy . . . did not provide enough money for the family . . . etc. This cannot be deemed a mental illness or a pathology since it is only a mild form of what could be a very severe or pathological condition.

Whether true or false, therefore, these are relatively mild statements. They may even be exaggerations. This is not PAS or mental illness in any way or form, much as mild unhappiness or depression is not true depression. Let us contrast this with, 'They . . . are evil . . . are capable of killing you and myself . . . are capable of sexually abusing you children . . . could be extremely violent (when there is no actual evidence of this) . . . have always been a terrible partner and parent . . . should have nothing to do with you or any children because of being a danger to you and might even sexually abuse you . . . etc.' Here we see a more extreme form of parental alienation, approaching the position of being a delusion. Thus the child, being vulnerable, could easily believe and act upon these comments, and therefore wish no contact with the absent parent.

Gardner (1997) considered that those parents who practised severe (pathological) kinds of alienation inculcated it in the victim/child, via 'multiple, absurd rationalisations about the absent parent such as being totally evil with no ambivalence or guilt felt, or experienced by that programmer.' The hatred for the other parent is total and often fanatic and delusional. This results in the non custodial parent having no access to the

PAS symptoms or signs	Symptoms or signs of PMDD (Chase, 1993)
1. Paranoia – communicate to the child about the non resident parent.	1. Sad or hopeless feelings.
2. The campaign of denigration against the non custodial parent.	2. Tense or anxious feelings.
	3. Marked mood changes.
3. Weak, frivolous and absurd rationalisations for the depreciation of the absent parent.	4. Frequent irritability or anger and increased interpersonal conflicts.
4. Total lack of ambivalence, i.e. the targeted parent is totally evil and unfit to play the role as a parent.	5. Decreased interest in her usual activities.
5. Independent thinker phenomenon, i.e. the child identifies so much with the custodial parent that they do not think for themselves.	6. Lack of concentration.
	7. Lack of energy.
	8. Change in appetite.
6. Absence of guilt over cruelty committed against the targeted parent.	9. Insomnia or sleepiness
7. Presence of borrowed scenarios.	10. A subjective feeling of being overwhelmed or out of control.
8. Spread of animosity to extended family friends of the alienated parent.	11. The physical symptoms such as swollen breasts, headache, muscle pain, a 'bloated' sensation, or weight gain.

Figure 28.1   Comparison of symptoms or signs of *PMDD* with symptoms and signs of *PAS*

child and provocative behaviour being constantly presented towards the targeted parent often in the presence of the child by the custodial parent. The child in turn bonds (identifies) totally with the programming, paranoid and delusional parent. Hence the delusion is passed on to the child that the absent parent is to be hated and avoided.

Why extreme forms of PAS should be included in DSM-IV

There are good precedents of categories now included in DSM-IV that were at first not considered to be included, while others, already mentioned, were included, such as homosexuality, which have been removed as mental illnesses. The category 'premenstrual dysphoric disorder (PMDD)' had considerable difficulty in becoming listed in DSM-IV as a distinct kind of depressive disorder. Five to eleven symptoms had to exist during the week before the mensis. In the case of PAS, there are eight basic signs of symptoms. Both of these conditions will be presented alongside one another making it obvious that PAS as described by Gardner 1997, has as much right to the claim of being accepted by DSM-IV as the category premenstrual dysphoric disorder (PMDD).

In contrasting these two conditions one cannot help but note that PAS has similar signs and symptoms which are harmful to children and, of course, the non custodial parent. The result is that this parent is unjustly 'sidelined' from playing the role of an active, loving, caring parent. In viewing the criticisms made of the non custodial parent one must ask oneself whether the statements made are true about the non custodial parent. One must also ask why such statements are made and does the accuser truly believe that these statements are true. Finally, one must consider the impact on a child of such damaging negative statements being made about the absent parent.

If such statements are true, one would expect no or very limited contact between the child and that parent, or we would expect such contact to be carried out under supervised conditions. What if such statements were untrue, manufactured or highly exaggerated? Such statements in that case could only come from a very disturbed, evil or highly deluded individual. In either case, such a parent should not have responsibility for caring for vulnerable and credulous children. The reader must draw their own conclusions. In answer to one of the questions as to why such statements are made to the child, if untrue, one can only reason that that individual is either deluded or extremely evil and capable of doing a considerable degree of harm to the child, as well as the non custodial parent.

Whether the alienator truly believes what is being communicated or not, is irrelevant when such statements are clearly untrue, exaggerated or unverifiable. What does matter is the impact this has on the child. How will that child view that absent parent, who should act as a model for the purpose of identification with an appropriate adult. This is especially the case for boys in their attitudes towards their father if that father is portrayed in negative terms. One must consider what are the consequences in the short term as well as long term (Baker, 2005a, b). If the target of alienation is the father in the case of girls it will almost certainly develop in that girl a generalised view of the male gender which could lead to future problems towards that gender. The same can be said for boys who have been alienated against the mother by a programming father. Such boys are likely to have difficulties in their relationship with members of the opposite sex.

The author has already described elsewhere the tendency for alienators to suffer from delusions which lead to shared psychotic disorders. These delusions are inculcated in the child victim. Such youngsters are likely to develop, eventually,

adjustment disorders and relational problems especially with future partners.

Such dangerous repercussions are preventable early on by removing these vulnerable, victimised children from any damaging influences, as soon as PAS of such an extreme nature has been diagnosed. There is also an imperative need to provide therapy for the child on an intensive basis once that child has been removed from the abusive influence of the custodial parent. This is to rid the vulnerable child of the delusions which the child has been led to believe by the alienator. This form of child emotional abuse is all too common in the case of an acrimonious separation or divorce of partners and the implacable hostility which ensues. This leads to no or restricted contact between the absent parent and the children at the behest of the custodial parent.

Gardner (1997) (Addendum IV) recommends in the case of severe PAS that the legal approach should be:

- Court ordered transfer of primary custody to the alienated parent.
- Court ordered transition site with a therapist monitoring a therapeutic programme.

Chapter Twenty-Nine

The comparison of PA to the 'Stockholm Syndrome'

What follows is in great part fact; and what is not fact is based on supposition and the psychological assessment of how the Stockholm Syndrome develops and how it has worked in the case of Natascha Kampusch, recently reported in the press. She was abducted and kept in a prison in an underground cell without natural light, with air being pumped into her enclosure. The Stockholm Syndrome was coined in 1973 by Nils Bejerot, a psychiatrist, while working for the police. It occurred when there was a bank robbery and four bank clerks were taken hostage by an armed robber who threatened to kill them. To the surprise of the police, the hostages stated that they had no wish to be rescued, indicating that they felt sympathy for their captor.

It was assumed that the feeling of stress and helplessness and possibly a desire to survive led to this unlikely scenario. All the captives were eventually released without harm. The hostage taker himself must have been influenced by the behaviour of his victims as they were influenced by him. One can only wonder how this phenomenon occurred after such a short captivity. In the case of Natascha Kampusch her period of captivity of eight years probably brought about deeper psychological changes and more enduring ones.

As a specialist in the area of parental alienation and parental alienation syndrome where I have acted as a psychological expert in the courts, there appears to be a considerable similarity between parental alienation and the Stockholm Syndrome. The alienator in the case of the Stockholm Syndrome also needs to extinguish any desire in the victim's past which seeks to demonstrate any allegiance to anyone other than the powerful captor of that individual.

Here, too, is demonstrated the power of the alienator and the insignificance of the power of the alienated party. It is almost certain that Natascha Kampusch had an opportunity in the past to escape from her captor, yet chose not to do so. This was despite her initial closeness to her family. A combination of fear, indoctrination and 'learned helplessness', promoted the total loyalty and obedience of the child to her captor. This

captor was no longer viewed, as was the case initially, as evil, but as necessary to the child's well-being and her survival. A similar scenario occurs in the case of children who are alienated against an absent parent.

My forthcoming book and my website www.parental-alienation.info provides information as to why Natascha may have remained so slavishly with her captor for eight years of her young life. Why she decided finally to escape her enslavement will in due course be established. I will attempt to explain what might have occurred to finally induce her to escape.

A child who has had a good relationship with the now shunned parent will state: 'I don't need my father/mother; I only need my mother/father'. Such a statement is based on the brainwashing received and the power of the alienator who is indoctrinating the child to sideline the previously loving parent.

In the case of the Stockholm Syndrome, we have in some ways a similar scenario. Here the two natural loving parents have been sidelined by the work of subtle or direct alienation by the perpetrator of the abducted young girl. At age 10, the child is helpless to resist the power of her abductor.

To the question: 'How does the abductor eventually become her benefactor?', we may note the process is not so dissimilar to the brainwashing carried out by the custodial parent. This latter is done for the double reason of:

1. Gaining total control over the child and consequently its dependence upon them.
2. To sideline the other parent and to do all possible to prevent or curtail contact between the child and the absent parent.

The primary reason here for such behaviour is the intractable hostility of the custodial parents towards one another. This reason does not exist in the case of the abductor of a child such as occurred in the case of Natascha Kambusch. Nevertheless, the captor wished to totally alienate or eliminate the child's loyalty or any feeling towards her natural parents. Due to the long

period away from her parents and a total
dependence for survival on her captor,
Natascha's closeness to her family gradually
faded. She may even have felt that her own
parents were making little or no effort to find her
and rescue her. This view may also have been
inculcated by her captor.

Her captor's total mastery and control over her
eventually gave her a feeling of security. She
could depend on the man to look after her with
food, shelter, warmth, protection and hence led to
her survival. Such behaviour on the part of the
captor led over time not only to 'learned
helplessness' and dependence, but in a sense to
gratefulness. As he was the only human being in
her life this was likely to happen. She therefore
became a ready victim of what is commonly
termed the 'Stockholm Syndrome' or the victim
of 'Parental Alienation.'

This led even to her beginning to love her
captor. This view has been substantiated by the
fact that Natascha found it difficult to live and
feel any real closeness to her natural parents once
she was rescued or once she ran away from her
captor. She even pined for the loss of the captor
who had since committed suicide. Even her
speech had been altered from the native Austrian
or Viennese dialect to the North German speech
due to the fact that she only had access to the
outside world via radio and television. This
again, however, was carefully monitored by her
captor. He controlled what she could see on
television and listen to on the radio from outside
her underground cell. There was little in

Natascha's present life to remind her of her past
except for the dress that she wore when she was
captured.

While she developed physically from 10 to 18
years, her weight changed but little. Why did she
decide eventually to leave her captor? This is a
question that requires an answer. It is the view of
the current author that the answer lies in the fact
that she may have had a quarrel with her captor,
possibly over a very minor issue. The result was
her leaving her captor and then regretting doing
so, especially after she heard of his death. By the
time her captor, undoubtedly fearing retribution
by the law, had ended his life, she had pined for
him.

After eight years of living in close proximity to
his victim, some form of intimacy undoubtedly
occurred, including a sexual one. This led to a
mutual need and even dependence. It is likely
that the 'learned helplessness' of the victim
succumbed and eventually a caring, perhaps
even loving relationship developed. It is also
likely that the psychological explanation is that
attribution, helplessness and depression in the
victim for the loss of her parents quickly gave
way to seeking to make the best of her situation
while under the total domination of her captor.

Again the same scenario occurs in the case of
parental alienation where the power of the
dominant custodial parent programmes the child
to eschew or marginalise the absent parent. That
absent parent no longer appears to be important
and is even likely to be viewed as damaging to
the child's survival.

Conclusion

The Introduction has given two reasons for writing this book. As a result of its publication, it is hoped that there will be a change in two areas:

1. The judiciary showing greater depth of understanding of how parental alienation and parental alienation syndrome functions, and how a parent can manipulate the system causing tragic consequences to the children as well as the parents themselves. The chief victim is the child who sidelines an often caring and loving parent. The parent being alienated is another victim who is so often so unjustly treated by the judicial system.
2. That children will be protected from the tragic consequences of being alienated against a loving parent, and that both parents are treated fairly by the system. Good, non-abusive parents, as so often stated in the book, have a duty of care over their mutually conceived children. There is more that can be done to educate parents and to make them aware of the damage being done to one or both when they fail to understand that parental alienation or parental alienation syndrome has dangerous consequences to their children. I would go so far as to say that it is important to seek to prepare potential parents before the birth of children to recognise the danger of parental alienation.

Since 50 per cent of relationships break up, there is a chance that among those who have children many relationships will not last. Among these will be parents who are a danger to children as they will brainwash the children against an absent parent. All should be done that can be done to create an awareness in parents that a break up of a relationship could happen and what the dangers are of the children being alienated against one of the parents. Preparing parents at the time they have children could do much to prevent future generations of victims of abuse of parental alienation. What is required is a revolution in thinking and behaviour in how parents can be helped to play a positive role in bringing up children, despite the break up of the adult relationship, into a happier future.

References

Abdel Hameed Al-khateeb, S. (1998) Women, Family and the Discovery of Oil in Saudi Arabia. *Marriage and Family Review*, 274: 2, 167–89.

Ackerman, M.J. (1995) *Clinician's Guide to Child Custody Evaluations*. USA: John Wiley and Sons.

Ackerman, M.J. (1999) *Essentials of Forensic Psychological Assessment*. New York: John Wiley and Sons.

Ackerman, M.J. (2001) *Clinician's Guide to Child Custody Evaluations*. 2nd edn. New York: John Wiley and Sons.

Allen, D.W. and Brinig, M. (1998) Sex, Property Rights and Divorce. *European Journal of Law and Economics*, 5: 3, 211–33.

Allen, M. (2005) Parents Should Read the Fine Print of Divorce. *PsycCritiques*, 50: 1.

Amato, P.R. and Cheadle, J. (2005) The Long Reach of Divorce: Divorce and Child Well-Being Across Three Generations. *Journal of Marriage and Family*, 67: 1, 191–206.

Amato, P.R. and Rezac, S.J. (1994) Contact With Non-Residential Parents, Inter Parental Conflict and Children's Behaviour. *Journal of Family Issues*, 15: 2, 191–207.

Amato, P.R. and Rogers, S.J. (1999) Do Attitudes Towards Divorce Affect Marital Quality? *Journal of Family Issues*, 20: 1, 69–86.

Ancona, P. (1998) *Crisis in America: Father Absence*. Huntington, NY: Nova Science Publishers.

Anderson W.I. and Little, D.W. (1999) All's Fair: War and Other Causes of Divorce from a Beckerian Perspective. *American Journal of Economics and Sociology*, 58: 4, 901–22.

Andre, K.C. (2004) Parent Alienation Syndrome. *Annals of the American Psychotherapy Association*, 7: 4, 7–11.

Anthony, T. (2005) Calming the Family Storm: Anger Management for Moms, Dads and All the Kids. *Bulletin of the Menninger Clinic*, 69: 2, 180.

Arbuthnot, J. and Kramer, K. (1998) Effects of Divorce Education on Mediation Process and Outcome. *Mediation Quarterly*, 15: 3, 199–213.

Arbuthnot, J., Kramer, K.N. and Cordon, D. (1997) Patterns of Relitigation Following Divorce Education. *Family and Conciliation Courts Review*, 35: 3, 269–79.

Arntz, A. and Lavy, E. (1993) Does Stimulus Elaboration Potentiate Exposure in Vivo Treatment: Two Forms of One-Session Treatment of Spider Phobia. *Behavioural Psychotherapy*, 21, 1–12.

Atwood, J.D. and Seifer, M. (1997) Extramarital Affairs and Constructed Meanings: A Social Constructionist Therapeutic Approach. *American Journal of Family Therapy*, 25: 1, 55–75.

Austin, W.G. (2000) A Forensic Psychology Model of Risk Assessment for Child Custody Relocation Law. *Family and Conciliation Courts Review*. 38: 2, 192–207.

Austin, W.G. (2000a) Assessing Credibility in Allegations of Marital Violence in The High-Conflict Child Custody Case. *Family and Conciliation Courts Review*. 38: 4, 462–77.

Austin, W.G. (2000b) Risk Reduction Interventions in The Child Custody Relocation Case. *Journal of Divorce and Remarriage*. 33: 1, 65–73.

Azar, S.T. and Benjet, C.L. (1994) A Cognitive Perspective on Ethnicity, Race and Termination of Parental Rights, *Law and Human Behaviour*, 18, 249–67.

Babiker, G. and Herbert, M. (1998) Critical Issues in The Assessment of Child Sexual Abuse. *Clinical Child and Family Psychology Review*. 1: 4, 231–52.

Bagarozzi, D.A. (1997) Marital Intimacy Needs Questionnaire: Preliminary Report. *American Journal of Family Therapy*, 25: 3, 285–90.

Bailey, J.D. and Robbins, S.P. (2005) Couple Empowerment in Divorce: A Comparison of Mediated and Nonmediated Outcomes. *Conflict Resolution Quarterly*, 22: 4, 453–72.

Baird, C. and Wagner, D. (2000) The Relative Validity of Actuarial and Consensus-Based Risk Assessment Systems. *Children and Youth Services Review*. 22: 11–12, 839–71.

Baird, C. et al. (1999) Risk Assessment in Child Protective Services: Consensus and Actuarial Model Reliability. *Child Welfare*. 78: 6, 723–48.

Baker, A.J.L. (2005a) The Long-Term Effects of Parental Alienation on Adult Children: A Qualitative Research Study. *American Journal of Family Therapy*, 33: 4, 289–302.

Baker, A.J.L. (2005b) The Cult of Parenthood: A Qualitative Study of Parental Alienation. *Cultural Studies Review*, 4: 1.

Baker, E. (1997) Assessing and Managing Allegations of Child Sexual Abuse: an

Australian Perspective, *Family and Conciliation Courts Review*, 35: 3, 293–9.

Bandura, A. and Rosenthal, T. (1966) Vicarious Classical Conditioning as A Function of Arousal Level. *Journal of Personality and Social Psychology*, 3, 54–62.

Barlow, J.L. (1999) A New Model for Premarital Counselling in the Church. *Pastoral Psychology*, 48: 1, 3–9.

Bartholomae, S., Landry-Meyer, L. and Tishler, C.L. (2003) Mediation and Child Support: an Effective Partnership. *Journal of Divorce and Remarriage*, 38: 3–4, 129–45.

Batchy, E. and Kinoo, P. (2004) The Organisation of Children's Lodging When Parents Break Up. *Therapie Familiale*, 25: 1, 81–97.

Baum, N. (2004) Typology of Post-Divorce Parental Relationships and Behaviors. *Journal of Divorce and Remarriage*, 41: 3–4, 53–79.

Baum, N. and Shnit, D. (2003) Divorced Parents' Conflict Management Styles: Self-Differentiations and Narcissism. *Journal of Divorce and Remarriage*, 39: 3–4, 37–58.

Bell, M. (1999) Working in Partnership in Child Protection: The Conflicts. *British Journal of Social Work*. 29: 3, 437–55.

Bennun, P. (1997) Systemic Marital Therapy With One Partner: A Reconsideration of Theory, Research and Practice. *Sexual and Marital Therapy*, 12: 1, 61–75.

Bernet, W. (2002) Child Custody Evaluations. *Child and Adolescent Psychiatric Clinics of North America*, 11: 4, 781–804.

Binner, J.M. and Dnes, A.W. (201) Marriage, Divorce and Legal Change: New Evidence from England and Wales. *Economic Enquiry*, 39: 2, 298–306.

Blush, G.J. and Ross, K.L. (1987) Sexual Allegations in Divorce: The SAID Syndrome. *Conciliation Court Review*, 25: 1, 1–11.

Bonney, L.A. (1993) Planning for Post-Divorce Relationships: Factors to Consider in Drafting a Transition Plan. *Family and Conciliation Courts Review*, 31: 3, 367–72.

Booth, A. (1999) Causes and Consequences of Divorce: Reflections on Recent Research. In Thompson, R.A. and Amato P.R. (Eds.) *The Post Divorce Family: Children, Parenting and Society*. Thousand Oaks, CA: Sage.

Bougheas, S. and Georgellis, Y. (1999) The Effect of Divorce Costs on Marriage Formation and Dissolution. *Journal of Population Economics*, 12: 3, 489–98.

Bowling, T. (2005) Children of Divorce: Stories of Loss and Growth. *International Journal for The Advancement of Counselling*, 27: 1, 157–60.

Boyan, S.M. and Termini, A.M. (2005) *The Psychotherapist as Parent Coordinator in High Conflict Divorce: Strategies and Techniques*. Binghamton, NY: Haworth Clinical Practice Press.

Bradbury. T.N. et al. (1996) Attributions and Behaviour in Functional and Dysfunctional Marriages. *Journal of Consulting and Clinical Psychology*, 64: 3, 569–76.

Bray, J.H. (1991) Psychological Factors Affecting Custodial and Visitation Arrangements, *Behavioural Sciences and The Law*, 9, 419–37.

Brinig, M.F. and Allen, D.W. (2000) 'These Boots are Made for Walking': Why Most Divorce Filers are Women. *American Law and Economics Review*, 2: 1, 126–69.

Brooks, C. (2002) Religous Influences and the Politics of Family Decline Concern: Trends, Sources and US Political Behavior. *American Sociological Review*, 67: 12, 191–211.

Broyles, J. (2002) *An Examination of Religiosity and Attitudes Towards Divorce*. Southern Sociological Society.

Buchanan, C.M., Maccoby, E.E. and Dornbusch, S.M. (1991) Caught Between Parents: Adolescents' Experience in Divorced Homes. *Child Development*, 62: 5, 1008–29.

Burgess, S., Propper, C. and Aassye, A. (1997) 'I Want to be Alone', Transitions to Independent Living, Marriage and Divorce Among Young Americans. Centre for Economic Policy Research.

Burley, J and Regan, F. (2002) Divorce in Ireland: The Fear, the Floodgates and the Reality. *International Journal of Law Policy and the Family*, 16: 2, 202–22.

Burns, A. and Dunlop, R. (2000) Parental Divorce, Personal Characteristics and early adult Intimate Relationships A Longitudinal Australian Study. *Journal of Divorce and Remarriage*, 33: 1–2, 91–109.

Burrell, N.A. et al. (1994) Evaluating Parental Stressors of Divorcing Couples Referred to Mediation and Effects on Mediation Outcomes, *Mediation Quarterly*, 11: 4, 339–52.

Butler-Sloss, Dame Elizabeth, Thorpe and Waller, Court of Appeal LJJ 19 June 2000.

Calder, M.C. et al. (2000) *The Complete Guide to Sexual Abuse Assessments*. Lyme Regis: Russell House Publishing.

Caces, M.F. et al. (1999) Alcohol Consumption and Divorce Rates in the United States. *Journal of Studies on Alcohol*, 60: 5, 647–52.

Calder, M.C. et al. (2004) *Children Living with Domestic Violence: Towards a Framework for Assessment and Intervention*. Lyme Regis: Russell House Publishing.

Camasso, M.J. and Jagannathan, R. (2000) Modeling The Reliability and Predictive Validity of Risk Assessment in Child Protective Services. *Children and Youth Services Review*. 22: 11–12, 873–96.

Campbell, A. (1996) Mediation of Children Issues When One Parent Is Gay: A Cultural Perspective, *Mediation Quarterly*, 14: 1, 79–88.

Caplan, P.J. (2004) What is it That's Being Called Parental Alienation Syndrome? In: Caplan, P.J. and Cosgrove, L. (Eds.) *Bias in Psychiatric Diagnosis*. Lanham, MD: Jason Aronson.

Carrers, S. et al. (2000) Predicting Marital Stability and Divorce in Newly-wed Couples. *Journal of Family Psychology*, 14: 1, 42–58.

Carruthers, S.E. (1997) Mediation in Child Protection and The Nova Scotia Experience. *Family and Conciliation Courts Review*. 35: 1, 102–26.

Cartwright, G.F. (1993) Expanding The Parameters of PAS. *American Journal of Family Therapy*, 21: 3, 205–15.

Charton, L. and Wanner, P. (2001) Divorce in Switzerland: Impacts of Individual Factors, Partnership Formation and the Couple. *Schweizerische Seitschrift fur Sociologie/Revue Suisse de Sociologie*, 27: 2, 255–80.

Cheung, S. (1996) Cognitive Behaviour Therapy for Marital Conflict: Refining The Concept of Attribution. *Journal of Family Therapy*, 18: 2, 183–203.

Christmas, A.L., Wodarski, J.S. and Smokowski, P.R. (1996) Risk Factors for Physical Child Abuse: A Practice Theoretical Paradigm. *Family Therapy*, 23: 3, 233–48.

Clark, W.M. and Serovich, J.M. (1997) Twenty Years and Still in The Dark? Content Analysis of Articles Pertaining to Gay, Lesbian and Bisexual Issues in Marriage and Family Therapy Journals. *Journal of Marital and Family Therapy*, 23: 3, 239–53.

Clawar, S.S. and Rivlin, B. (1991) *Children Held Hostage: Dealing With Programmed and Brainwashed Children*. American Bar Association.

Clingempeel, W.G. and Repucci, N.D. (1982) Joint Custody After Divorce: Major Issues and Goals for Research. *Psychological Bulletin*, 91, 102–27.

Clulow, C. (1996) Preventing Marriage Breakdown: Towards A New Paradigm. *Sexual and Marital Therapy*, 11: 4, 343–51.

Coe, T. (2001) Notes Taken at Parent Education Class Run by The Superior Court of Maricope County, Phoenix, AZ: (03–08–01)

Cohen, P., Dattner, N. and Luxenburg, A. (1996) Planning Parenthood in The Divorce Transition – Through-Mediation. *American Journal of Family Therapy*, 24: 2, 181–8.

Coney, N.S. and Mackey, W.C. (1998) On Who's Watch? The Silent Separation of American Children from their Fathers. *Journal of Sociology and Social Welfare*, 25: 3, 143–78.

Criddle, M.N., Allgood, S.M. and Piercy, K.W. (2003) The Relationship Between Mandatory Divorce Education and Level of Post-Divorce Parental Conflict. *Journal of Divorce and Remarriage*, 39: 3–4, 99–111.

Crosbie-Burnett, M. (1991) Impact of Joint Versus Sole Custody and Quality of Co-Parental Relationship on Adjustment of Adolescents in Remarried Families, *Behavioural Sciences and The Law*, 9, 439–49.

Daly, M. and Wilson, M.I. (2000) The Evolutionary Psychology of Marriage and Divorce. In Waite. L.J. et al. *The Ties That Bind, Perspectives on Marriage and Co-habitation*. New York: Aldine de Gruyter.

Davila, J. and Bradbury, T.N. (2001) Attachment Insecurity and the Distinction Between unhappy Spouses who do and do not Divorce. *Journal of Family Psychology*, 15:3, 371–93.

Dember, C. and Fliman, V. (2005) Tailoring Parental Visitation Orders to The Developmental Needs of Children of Divorce. In Gunsberg, L. and Hymowitz, P (Eds.) *A Handbook of Divorce and Custody: Forensic, Developmental, and Clinical Perspectives*. Hillsdale, NJ: Analytic Press.

DePanfilis, D. and Zuravin, S J. (2001) Assessing Risk to Determine The Need for Services. *Children and Youth Services Review*. 23: 1, 3–20.

Depner, C.E., Cannala, K. and Ricci, I. (1995) Mediated Agreements on Child Custody and Visitation: 1991 California Family Court Services Snapshot Study, *Family and Conciliation Courts Review*, 33: 1, 87–109.

Dillon, P.A. and Emery, R.E. (1996) Divorce Mediation and Resolution of Child Custody Disputes: Long-Term Effects. *American Journal of Orthopsychiatry*. 66: 1, 131–40

Dobson, R. (2000) Children With Father in Family Have Head Start in Life. *The Sunday Times*, May 21.

Dolan, M.A. and Hoffman, C.D. (1998) Determinants of Divorce Among Women: A Re-examination of Critical Influences. *Journal of Divorce and Re-marriage,* 28: 3/4, 97–106.

Donohue, W.A., Drake, L. and Roberts, A.J. (1994) Mediator Issue Intervention Strategies: A Replication and Some Conclusions, *Mediation Quarterly,* 11: 3, 261–74.

Doucet, J. and Aseltine, R.H. (2003) Childhood Family Adversity and The Quality of Marital Relationships in Young Adulthood. *Journal of Social and Personal Relationships,* 20: 6, 818–42.

Dowling, E. and Gorrell-Barnes, G. (1999) *Working With Children and Parents Through Separation and Divorce.* Basingstoke: Macmillan Press.

Dremen, S. (2003) Family Cohesiveness, Flexibility and Maternal Anger: Boon or Detriment to Children's Adjustment? *Journal of Divorce and Remarriage,* 39: 1–2, 65–87.

Drieu, D. (2004) Therapeutic Progress in Parents of Adolescents Who Are Alienated From Their Social Environment. *Pratiques Psychologiques,* 10: 1, 39–50.

Dronkers, J. (2002) Does a Relationship Exist Between Divorce-risk and Intelligence in the Netherlands? *Mens en Maatschappij,* 77, 25–42.

Drury-Hudson, J. (1999) Decision Making in Child Protection: The Use of Theoretical, Empirical and Procedural Knowledge by Novices and Experts and Implications for Fieldwork Placement. *British Journal of Social Work.* 29: 1, 147–69.

Dunne, J. and Hedrick, M. (1994) The Parental Alienation Syndrome: an Analysis of Sixteen Selected Cases. *Journal of Divorce and Remarriage,* 21: 3–4, 21–38.

Durana, C. (1996) Bonding and Emotional Re-Education of Couples in The Pairs Training: Part II. *American Journal of Family Therapy,* 24: 4, 315–28.

Ehrensaft, N.K. and Vivian, D. (1996) Spouses Reasons for Not Reporting Existing Marital Aggression as a Marital Problem. *Journal of Family Psychology,* 10: 4, 443–53.

Ekeland, T.J and Myklebust, V. (1997) Brukarperspeltiv Pa Foredldremeekling Ved Samlivsbrot./ Customer Evaluation of Divorce Mediation. *Tidsskrift for Norsk Psykologforening.* 34: 9, 767–78.

Ellis, E.M. (2000a) Parental Alienation Syndrome: A New Challenge for Family Courts. In Ellis, E.M. *Divorce Wars: Interventions With Families in Conflict.* Washington, DC: American Psychological Association.

Ellis, E.M. (2000b) *Divorce Wars: Interventions With Families in Conflict.* Washington, DC: American Psychological Association.

Ellwood, M. and Stolberg, A.L. (1993) The Effects of Family Composition, Family Health, Parenting Behaviour and Environmental Stress on Children's Divorce Adjustment. *Journal of Child and Family Studies,* 2: 1, 23–36.

Emanuels-Zuurveen, L. and Emmelkamp. P.M.G. (1996) Individual Behavioural-Cognitive Therapy versus Marital Therapy for Depression in Martially Distressed Couples. *British Journal of Psychiatry,* 169: 2,181–8.

Embry, R.A., Buddenhagen, P. and Bolles, S. (2000) Managed Care and Child Welfare: Challenges to Implementation. *Children and Youth Services Review.* 22: 2, 93–116.

Emery, R.E. (1982) Interpersonal Conflict and The Children of Discord and Divorce, *Psychological Bulletin,* 92, 310–30.

Emery, R.E. (1994b) *Renegotiating Family Relationships: Divorce, Child Custody and Mediation.* The Guildford Press.

Emery, R.E. (1999) Changing The Rules for Determining Child Custody in Divorce Cases. *Clinical Psychology: Science and Practice.* 6: 3, 323–7.

Emery, R.E. (2001) Interparental Conflict and Social Policy. In Grych, J.H. and Fincham, F.D. (Eds.) *Interparental Conflict and Child Development: Theory, Research, and Applications.* New York, NY: Cambridge University Press.

Emery, R.E. (2005) Parental Alienation Syndrome: Proponents Bear The Burden of Proof. *Family Court Review,* 43: 1, 8–13.

Emery, R.E. et al. (2001) Child Custody Mediation and Litigation: Custody, Contact and Coparenting 12 Years After Initial Dispute Resolution. *Journal of Consulting and Clinical Psychology.* 69: 2, 323–32.

Emery, R.E., Matthews, S.G. and Kilzmann, K.M. (1994) Mediation and Litigation: Parents' Satisfaction and Functioning One Year After Settlement. *Journal of Consulting and Clinical Psychology,* 62: L, 124–9.

Emery, R.E., Matthews, S.G. and Wyer, M.M. (1991) Child Custody Mediation and Litigation: Further Evidence on The Differing Views of Mothers and Fathers, *Journal of Consulting and Clinical Psychology,* 59, 410–8.

Emmelkamp, P.M. (1994) Behaviour Therapy With Adults. In Bergin, A.E. and Garfiel, S.L. (Eds.) *Handbook of Psychotherapy and Behaviour Change.* 4th edn. New York: Wiley.

Enoch, D. and Ball, H. (2001) *Folie à Deux (et Folie à Plusieurs) Uncommon Psychiatric-Syndromes.* 4th edn. London, Arnold.

Ermisch, J.F. (1986) *The Economics of the Family: Applications to Divorce and Re-marriage. Centre for Economic Policy Research.* Discussion Paper 140. Not Available.

Evans, W.P. and Havercamp, M.J. (1994) An Analysis of Mediation Assumptions: Strategies to Help Mediators in Child Custody Disputes, *Mediation Quarterly*, 11: 3, 229–45.

Evans, M.D.R., Kelly, J. and Wanner, R.A. (2001) Educational Attainment of the Children of Divorce: Australia 1940–90. *Journal of Sociology*, 17: 3, 275–97.

Ezzel, B. (2001) Inside The Minds of America's Family Law Courts: The Psychology of Mediation Versus Litigation in Domestic Disputes. *Law and Psychology Review.* 25: 119–43.

Falco, E. (2003) Commentary: Children and Divorce. *Journal of The American Academy of Psychiatry and The Law*, 31: 2, 171–2.

Finnas, F. (2000) Ekonomiska faktoneroch aktenskaplig stabilitet i Finland. Economic Determinants of Divorce in Finland (with English summary). *Ekonomiska Samfundet Tidskrift*, 53: 2, 121–31.

Firestone, R.W. and Catlett, J. (1986) Displacement of Negative Parental Characteristics and The Development of a Victimised or Paranoid Approach to Life. In Firestone, R.W., and Catlett, J. (1986) *The Fantasy Bond: Structure of Psychological Defences.* New York, NY: Human Sciences.

Fisher, D. and Beech, A. (1998) Reconstituting Families After Sex Abuse: The Offender's Perspective. *Child Abuse Review.* 7: 6 (Spec Issue) 420–34.

Flynn, T.M., Taylor, P. and Pollard, C.E. (1992) Use of Mobile Phones in The Behavioral Treatment of Driving Phobias. *Journal of Behavioural Therapy and Experimental Psychiatry*, 23: 4, 299–302.

Fowler, J.G. (1995) Homosexual Parents: Implications for Custody Cases. *Family and Conciliation Courts Review*, 33: 3, 361–76.

Fox, D. (2001) Children of Divorce: is There a Personality Component? *Journal of Divorce and Marriage*, 35: 3–4, 107–24.

Fraenkel, P., Markman, H. and Stanley, S. (1997) The Prevention Approach to Relationship Problems. *Sexual and Marital Therapy.* 12: 3, 249–58.

Framo, J.L. (1996) Family of Origin as a Therapeutic Resource for Adults in Marital and Family Therapy: You Can and Should Go Home Again. *Therapie Familiale*, 17: 3, 367–90.

Franklin, C. (1996) Solution-Focused Therapy: A Marital Case Study Using Recursive Dialectic Analysis. *Journal of Family Psychotherapy.* 7: 1, 31–51.

Fredrikson, M., Annas, P. and Wik, G. (1997) Parental History, Aversive Exposure and The Development of Snake and Spider Phobia in Women. *Behaviour, Research and Therapy*, 35: 1, 23–8.

Friedberg, L. (1998) *Did Unilateral Divorce Raise Divorce Rates? Evidence from Panel Data.* National Bureau of Economic Research, Paper 6398, 17.

Fu, H. and Goldman, N. (2000) The Association Between Health-related Behaviors and the Risk of Divorce in the USA. *Journal of Biological Science*, 32: 1, 63–88.

Fuller, T.L., Wells, S.J. and Cotton, E.E. (2001) Predictors of Maltreatment Recurrence at Two Milestones in The Life of A Case. *Children and Youth Services Review.* 23: 1, 49–78.

Gagne, M.H., Drapeau, S. and Henault, R. (2005) Parental Alienation: an Overview of Research and Controversy. *Canadian Psychology*, 46: 2, 73–87.

Gambrill, E. and Shlonsky, A. (2001) The Need for Comprehensive Risk Management Systems in Child Welfare. *Children and Youth Services Review.* 23: 1, 79–107.

Garber, B.D. (2004) Therapist Alienation: Foreseeing and Forestalling Third Party Dynamics Undermining Psychotherapy With Children of Conflicted Caregivers. *Professional Psychology: Research and Practice*, 35: 4, 357–63.

Gardner, R.A. (1982) Joint Custody is Not for Everyone. *Family Advocate*, 5: 2, 7.

Gardner, R.A. (1987) *The Parental Alienation Syndrome and The Differentiation Between Fabricated and Genuine Sex Abuse.* Creskill, NJ: Creative Therapeutics.

Gardner, R.A. (1989) *Family Evaluation in Child Custody Mediation, Arbitration and Litigation.* Creskill, NJ: Creative Therapeutics.

Gardner, R.A. (1992a) *The Parental Alienation Syndrome: A Guide for Mental Health and Legal Professionals.* Creskill, NJ: Creative Therapeutics.

Gardner, R.A. (1992b) *True and False Accusations of Child Sex Abuse.* Creskill, NJ: Creative Therapeutics.

Gardner, R.A. (1995) *Protocols for Sex Abuse Evaluation.* Creskill, NJ: Creative Therapeutics.

Gardner, R.A. (1997) Addendum IV. In Gardner, R.A. (1992) *The Parental Alienation Syndrome: A Guide for Mental Health and Legal Professionals.* Creskill, NJ: Creative Therapeutics.

Gardner, R.A. (1997) Instrument for Objectively Comparing Parental Disciplinary Capacity in Child-Custody Disputes. *Journal of Divorce and Remarriage,* 27: 3–4, 1–15.

Gardner, R.A. (1997) *Therapeutic Interventions for Children With Parental Alienation Syndrome.* Creskill, NJ: Creative Therapeutics.

Gardner, R.A. (1998) *The Parental Alienation Syndrome.* 2nd edn. Creskill, NJ: Creative Therapeutics.

Gardner, R.A. (2000) Normal-Sexual Fantasy Consideration in Sex Abuse Evaluations. *The American Journal of Family Therapy,* 29: 2, 83–94.

Gardner, R.A. (2001) Should Courts Order PAS Children to Visit/Reside With The Alienated Parent? A Follow-Up Study. *American Journal of Forensic Psychology,* 19: 3, 61–106.

Gardner, R.A. (2001) *Therapeutic Interventions for Children With Parental Alienation Syndrome.* Creskill, NJ: Creative Therapeutics.

Gardner, R.A. (2002a) Does DSM-IV Have Equivalents for The Parental Alienation Syndrome (PAS) Diagnosis? *American Journal of Family Therapy,* 31: 1, 1–21.

Gardner, R.A. (2002b) Parental Alienation Syndrome versus Parental Alienation: Which Diagnosis Should Evaluators Use in Child Custody Disputes? *American Journal of Family Therapy,* 30: 2, 93–115.

Gardner, R.A. (2002c) Denial of the Parental Alienation Syndrome Also Harms Women. *American Journal of Family Therapy,* 30: 3, 191–202.

Gardner, R.A. (2002d) The Empowerment of Children in The Development of Parental Alienation Syndrome. *American Journal of Forensic Sciences,* 20: 2, 5–29.

Gardner, R.A. (2003) The Judiciary's Role in The Aetiology, Symptom Development, and Treatment of The Parental Alienation Syndrome (PAS). *American Journal of Forensic Psychology,* 21: 1, 39–64.

Gardner, R.A. (2004a) Commentary on Kelly and Johnston's The Alienated Child: A Reformulation of Parental Alienation Syndrome. *Family Court Review,* 42: 4, 611–21.

Gardner, R.A. (2004b) The Relationship Between The Parental Alienation Syndrome (PAS) and

The False Memory. *American Journal of Family Therapy,* 32: 2, 79–99.

Gardner, W. et al. (1996) Clinical Versus Actuarial Predictions of Violence in Patients With Mental Illness. *Journal of Consulting and Clinical Psychology,* 64: 602–9.

Geffner, R. (1992) Guidelines for Using Mediation With Abusive Couples. *Psychotherapy in Private Practice,* 10: 1–2, 77–92.

Goddard, C.R. et al. (1999) Structured Risk Assessment Procedures: Instruments of Abuse? *Child Abuse Review.* 8: 4, 252–63.

Goldstein, J., Freud, A. and Solnit, A.J. (1973) *Beyond the Best Interests of the Child.* New York: Free Press.

Goldstein, J.R. (1999) The Leveling of Divorce in the United States. *Demographics,* 36: 3, 409–14.

Goncalves, P. and De Vincenzi, A.G. (2003) Co-Parenting After A Conflicted Divorce: Growing From Enemy to Ally. *Therapie Familiale,* 24: 3, 239–53.

Gottmann J.M. et al. (2000) A Two-factor Model for Predicting When a Couple Will Divorce: Explanatory Analysis Using 14-year Old Longitudinal Data. *Family Process,* 41: 1, 83–110.

Gray-Little, B., Baucom. D.H. and Hamby. S.L. (1996) Marital Power, Marital Adjustment, and Therapy Outcome. *Journal of Family Psychology,* 10: 3, 292–303.

Greatbatch, D. and Dingwall, R. (1997) Argumentative Talk in Divorce Mediation Sessions. *American Sociological Review,* 62:1, 151–70.

Greeff, A.P. and Van Der Merwe, S. (2004) Variables Associated With Resilience in Divorced Families. *Social Indicators Research,* 68: 1, 59–75.

Gregory, N.A. and Leslie, L.A. (1996) Different Lenses: Variations in Clients' Perception of Family Therapy by Race and Gender. *Journal of Marital and Family Therapy,* 22: 2, 239–51.

Grych, J.H. and Fincham, F.D. (1992) Interventions for Children of Divorce: Toward Greater Integration of Research and Action, *Psychological Bulletin,* 111, 434–54.

Gunsberg, L. and Hymowitz, P. (Eds.) (2005) *A Handbook of Divorce and Custody: Forensic, Developmental, and Clinical Perspectives.* Hillsdale, NJ: Analytic Press.

Hahn, R.A. and Kleist, D.M. (2000) Divorce Mediation: Research and Implications for Family and Couples Counseling. *Family Journal of Counseling and Therapy for Couples and Families.* 8: 2, 165–71.

Haine, R.A. et al. (2003) Changing The Legacy of Divorce: Evidence From Prevention Programs and Future Directions. *Family Relations*, 52: 4, 397–405.

Hannah. N.T., Luguet, W. and McCormick, J. (1997) COMPASS as A Measure of The Efficacy of Couples Therapy. *American Journal of Family Therapy*. 25: 1, 76–90.

Harper, C.C. and McLanahan, S.S. (2004) Father Absence and Youth Incarceration. *Journal of Research on Adolescence*, 14: 3, 369–97.

Harris, G.T. and Rice, M E. (1997) Risk Appraisal and Management of Violent Behaviour. *Psychiatric Services*. 48:1168–76.

Hauser, B.B. (2005) Visitation in High-Conflict Families: The Impact on A Child's Inner Life. In Gunsberg, L. and Hymowitz, P. (Eds.) *A Handbook of Divorce and Custody: Forensic, Developmental, and Clinical Perspectives.* Hillsdale, NJ: Analytic Press.

Heath J.A. and Ciscel, D.H. (1996) Escaping the Fate of Sisyphus: Bargaining, Divorce and Employment in the Patriarchal Family. *Review of Radical Political Economies*, 28: 1, 1–19.

Heath, D.T. (1998) Qualitative Analysis of Private Mediation: Benefits for Families in Public Child Welfare Agencies. *Children and Youth Services Review*. 20: 7, 605–27.

Heiliger, A. (2003) Problems With Child Custody and Right of Access in Highly Controversial Cases. A Call for Decisions Enhancing The Child's Well-Being. *DISKURS*, 13: 3, 62–8.

Heinze, M.C. and Grisso, T. (1996) Review of Instruments Assessing Parenting Competencies Used in Child Custody Evaluations. *Behavioral Sciences and The Law*. 14: 3, 293–313.

Hetherington, E.M. and Arasteh, J.D. (Eds) (1998) *Impact of Divorce, Single Parenting and Step-Parenting on Children.* Hillsdalc, NJ: Erlbaum.

Hellstrom, K. and Ost, L.G. (1996) Prediction of Outcome in The Treatment of Specific Phobia. A Cross-Validation Study. *Behaviour, Research and Therapy*, 34: 5/6, 403–11.

Hilton, J.M. and Kopera-Frye, K. (2004) Patterns of Psychological Adjustment Among Divorced Custodial Parents. *Journal of Divorce and Remarriage*, 41: 3–4, 1–30.

Hochberg, A.M. and Kressel, K. (1996) Determinants of Successful and Unsuccessful Divorce Negotiations. *Journal of Divorce and Remarriage*, 25: 1–2, 1–21.

Hodges, W. (1986) *Interventions for Children of Divorce: Custody, Access and Psychotherapy.* New York: Wiley.

Hoem J.M. (1997) Educational Gradients in Divorce Risks in Sweden in Recent Decades. *Population Studies*, 51: 1, 19–27.

Hoge, H. (2002) *Women's Stories of Divorce and Childbirth: When the Baby Rocks the Cradle.* Binghamton NY: Haworth Clinical Press.

Hohman-Marriot, B.E. (2001) Marriage and Family Therapy Research: Ethical Issues and Guidelines. *American Journal of Family Therapy*. 29: 1, 1–11.

Houston, S. and Griffiths, H. (2000) Reflections on Risk in Child Protection: is It Time for a Shift in Paradigms? *Child and Family Social Work*. 5: 1, 1–10.

Hyden, M. (2001) For The Child's Sake: Parents and Social Workers Discuss Conflict-Filled Parental Relations After Divorce. *Child and Family Social Work*. 6: 2, 115–28.

Hysjulien, C., Wood, B. and Benjamin, G. (1994) Child Custody Evaluations: A Review of Methods Used in Litigation and Alternative Dispute Resolution. *Family and Conciliation Courts Review*; 32: 4, 466–89.

Imbrogno, A.R. and Imbrogno, S. (2000) Mediation in Court Cases of Domestic Violence. *Families in Society*. 81: 4, 392–401.

Insabella, G. et al. (2003) Family and Legal Indicators of Child Adjustment to Divorce Among Families With Young Children. *Journal of Family Psychology*, 17: 2, 169–80.

Jacobsen, T. and Miller, L.J. (1998) Mentally Ill Mothers Who Have Killed: Three Cases Addressing The Issue of Future Parenting Capability. *Psychiatric Services*. 49: 5, 650–7.

Jagannathan, R. and Camasso, M.J. (1996) Risk Assessment in Child Protective Services: A Canonical Analysis of The Case Management Function. *Child Abuse and Neglect*. 20: 7, 599–612.

Janssen, J.P.G. and De Graf, P.M. (2000) Heterogamy and Divorce: Lack of Similarity in Preference or Lack of Social Support? *Mens en Maatschappij*, 75: 4, 298–319.

Jenkins, S. (2002) Are Children Protected in The Family Court? A Perspective From Western Australia. *Australian and New Zealand Journal of Family Therapy*, 23: 3, 145–52.

Johnson, P., Wilkinson, W.K. and McNeil, K. (1995) The Impact of Parental Divorce on the Attainment of The Developmental Tasks of Young Adulthood. *Contemporary Family Therapy*, 17: 2, 249–64.

Johnson, S. (1997) A Critical Review of Marital Therapy Outcome. *Canadian Journal of Psychiatry*, 42: 3, 323.

Johnson, S.M. and Talitman, E. (1997) Predictors of Success in Emotionally Focused Marital Therapy. *Journal of Marital and Family Therapy.* 23: 2, 135–52.

Johnston, J.R. (2003) Parental Alignments and Rejection: an Empirical Study of Alienation in Children of Divorce. *Journal of The American Academy of Psychiatry and The Law*, 31: 2, 158–70.

Johnston, J.R. and Campbell, L.E. (1993) Parent-Child Relationship in Domestic Violence Families Disputing Custody. *Family and Conciliation Courts Review.* 31: 3, 282–98.

Johnston, J.R. and Girdner, L.K. (1998) Early Identification of Parental Risk for Custody Violations and Prevention of Child Abductions, *Family and Conciliation Courts Review*, 36: 3, 392–409.

Johnston, J.R. and Kelly, J.B. (2004) Rejoinder to Gardner's Commentary on Kelly and Johnston's The Alienated Child: A Reformulation of Parental Alienation Syndrome. *Family Court Review*, 42: 4, 622–8.

Johnston, J.R., Walters, M.G. and Friedlander, S. (2001) Therapeutic Work With Alienated Children and Their Families. *Family Court Review*, 39: 3, 316–33.

Johnston, J.R., Walters, M.G. and Oleson, N.W. (2005) The Psychological Functioning of Alienated Children in Custody Disputing Families: an Exploratory Study. *American Journal of Forensic Psychology*, 23: 3, 39–64.

Jones, K. (2004) Assessing Psychological Separation and Academic Performance in Non-Resident-Father and Resident-Father Adolescent Boys. *Child and Adolescent Social Work Journal*, 21: 4, 333–54.

Jones, S.C. and Hunter, M. (1996) The Influence of Context and Discourse on Infertility Experience. *Journal of Reproductive and Infant Psychology.* 14: 2, 93–111.

Jones, T.S. and Bodtker, A. (1998) Satisfaction With Custody Mediation: Results From The York County Custody Mediation Program. *Mediation Quarterly*, 16: 2, 185–200.

Jones, T.S. and Bodtker, A. (1999) Agreement, Maintenance, Satisfaction and Relitigation in Mediated and Non-Mediated Custody Cases: A Research Note. *Journal of Divorce and Remarriage*,32: 1–2, 17–30.

Kaganas, F. and Sclater, S.D. (2004) Contact Disputes: Narrative Constructions of 'Good' Parents. *Feminists Legal Studies*, 1: 1, 1–27.

Kandel, R.F. (1998) Situated Substantive Expertise: an Ethnographic Illustration and A Proposed Standard of Practice for Mediators. *Mediation Quarterly.* 15: 4, 303–19.

Kane, C.M. (1996) an Experiential Approach to Family of Origin Work With Marital and Family Therapy Trainees. *Journal of Marital and Family Therapy*, 22: 4, 481–7.

Kapinus, C.A. (2004) The Effect of Parents' Attitudes Toward Divorce on Offspring's Attitudes: Gender and Parental Divorce as Mediating Factors. *Journal of Family Issues*, 25: 1, 112–35.

Keilan, W.G. and Bloom, L.J. (1986) Child Custody Evaluation Practices: A Survey of Experienced Professionals. *Professional Psychology: Research and Practice.* 17, 338–46.

Kelly, A.B. and Halford, U.K. (1997) Couples in Therapy: Assessing The Heart of The Matter. *Sexual and Marital Therapy*, 12: 1, 5–21.

Kelly, J.B. (1991) Parent Interaction After Divorce: Comparison of Mediated and Adversarial Divorce Processes, *Behavioural Sciences and The Law*, 9, 387–398.

Kelly, J.B. (1996) A Decade of Divorce Medication Research: Some Answers and Questions. *Family and Conciliation Courts Review.* 34: 3, 373–85.

Kelly, J.B. (2000) Children's Adjustment in Conflictual Marriage and Divorce: A Decade Review of research. *Journal of the American Acadremy of Child and Adolescent Psychiatry*, 39: 8, 963–73.

Kelly, J.B. (2003a) Parents With Enduring Child Disputes: Focused Interventions With Parents in Enduring Disputes. *Journal of Family Studies*, 9: 1, 51–62.

Kelly, J.B. (2003b) Changing Perspectives on Children's Adjustment Following Divorce: A View From The United States. *Childhood*, 10: 2, 237–54.

Kelly, J.B. and Emery, R.E. (2003) Children's Adjustment Following Divorce: Risk and Resilience Perspectives. *Family Relations*, 52: 4, 352–62.

Kelly, J.B. and Johnston, J.R. (2001) The Alienated Child: A Reformulation of Parental Alienation Syndrome. *Family Court Review*, 39: 3, 249–66.

Kelly, N. and Milner, J. (1996) Child Protection Decision-Making. *Child Abuse Review.* 5: 2, 91–102.

Keoughan, P., Joanning, H. and Sudak-Allison, J. (2001) Child Access and Visitation Following Divorce: A Growth Area for Marriage and Family Therapy. *American Journal of Family Therapy.* 29: 2, 155–63.

Kiernan, K and Mueller, G. (1998) *The Divorced and Who Divorces?* LSE Centre for the Analysis of Social Exclusion. May, 40.

Kiernan, K. and Cherlin, A.J. (1999) Partnership Divorce and Partnership Dissolution Adulthood: Evidence from a British Cohort Study. *Population Studies*, 53: 1, 39–48.

Kim, J.Y, and Kim I.I. (2002) Stigma in Divorce and its Deterrence Effect. *Journal of Socio-economics*, 31:1, 31–44

Kim, S.W. and Hoover, K.M. (1996) Tridimensional Personality Questionnaire: Assessment in Patients With Social Phobia and A Control Group. *Psychological Reports*, 78, 43–9.

King, M. (2002) an Autopoietic Approach to 'Parental Alienation Syndrome'. *Journal of Forensic Psychiatry*, 13: 3, 609–35.

Kitzman, K.M. and Emery, K.E. (1994) Child and Family Coping One Year After Mediated and Litigated Child Custody Disputes, *Journal of Family Psychology*, 8: 2, 150–9.

Klein, A.J. (2005) The Rights of Parents and Stepparents: Toward A Redefinition of Parental Rights and Obligations. In Gunsberg, L. and Hymowitz, P. (Eds.) *A Handbook of Divorce and Custody: Forensic, Developmental, and Clinical Perspectives*. Hillsdale, NJ: Analytic Press.

Knight, T.A. (2005) Addressing The Fallout of High-Conflict Divorce: A Hopeful Model. *Psychcritiques*, 50: 30.

Knox, D. and Zusman, M.E. (2001) Marrying a Man with Baggage: Implications for Second Wives. *Journal of Divorce and Re-marriage*, 35: 3–4, 67–79.

Kraljic, S. (2005) Druzinska Mediacija. Uspesno Starsevstvo Kljub Neuspesnemu Partnerstvu./Family Mediation. Successful Parenthood Despite Unsuccessful Partnership. *Socialno Delo*, 44: 3, 223–8.

Krane, J. and Davies, L. (2000) Mothering and Child Protection Practice: Rethinking Risk Assessment. *Child and Family Social Work*. 5: 1, 35–45.

Kranitz, M.A. (2000) *Getting Apart Together: The Couple's Guide to A Fair Divorce or Separation*. Atascadero, CA: Impact Publishers.

Kressel, K. et al. (1994) The Settlement Orientation versus the Problem-Solving Style in Custody Mediation, *Journal of Social Issues*, 50: 1, 67–84.

Kruk, E. (1988) Practice Issues, Strategies, and Models: The Current State of The Art of Family Mediation. *Family and Conciliation Courts Review*. 36: 2, 195–215.

Kurkowski, K.P., Gordon,D.A. and Arbuthnot, J. (1993) Children Caught in The Middle: A Brief Educational Intervention for Divorced Parents. *Journal of Divorce and Remarriage*, 20: 34, 139–51.

Lamb, M.E., Sternberg, K.J. and Thompson, R.A. (1999) The Effects of Divorce and Custody Arrangements on Children's Behavior, Development, and Adjustment. In Lamb, M.E. (Ed.) *Parenting and Child Development in Nontraditional Families*. Mahwah, NJ: Lawrence Erlbaum Associates.

Lansky. D.T. et al. (1996) The Role of Children in Mediation. *Mediation Quarterly*, 14: 2, 147–54.

Latz, M. (1996) On an Exercise for Training Beginning Marital and Family Therapists in Language Skills. *Journal of Marital and Family Therapy*, 22: 1, 121–6.

Laughrea, K. (2002) Alienated Family Relationship Scale: Validation With Young Adults. *Journal of College Student Psychotherapy*, 17: 1, 37–48.

Lee, C.M., Beauregard, C.P. and Hunsley, J. (1998a) Lawyer's Opinions Regarding Child Custody Mediation and Assessment Services: Implications for Psychological Practice. *Professional Psychology: Research and Practice*. 29: 2, 115–20.

Lee, C.M., Beauregard, C.P. and Hunsley, J. (1998b) Attorney's Opinions Regarding Child Custody Mediation and Assessment Services: The Influence of Gender, Years of Experience, and Mediation Practice. *Family and Conciliation Courts Review*. 36: 2, 216–26.

Lee, S.M. and Olesen, N.W. (2001) Assessing for Alienation in Child Custody and Access Evaluation. *Family Court Review*, 39: 3, 282–98.

Leslie, L.A. and Clossick, M.L. (1996) Sexism in Family Therapy: Does Training in Gender Make A Difference? *Journal of Marital and Family Therany*, 22: 2, 253–69.

Lester, D. (1999) Regional Differences in Divorce Rates: A Preliminary Study. *Journal of Divorce and Re-marriage*, 30: 3/4, 121–4.

Lorandos, D. (Ed.) (2005) *International Handbook of Parental Alienation Syndrome: Conceptual, Clinical and Legal Considerations*. Binghampton, NY: Haworth Press.

Louw, D.A. and Scherrer, R. (2004) Children's Perception and Experience of The Family Advocate System. *International Journal of The Sociology of Law*, 32: 1, 17–37.

Lowenstein, L.F. (1992) The Psychologist's Role in The Courts. *Family Law*. 22: 32–4.

Lowenstein, L.F. (1993) *The Accused and Sex Allegations*. Unpublished Study.

Lowenstein, L.F. (1994a) Marital Therapy: The Importance of The Assessment of The

Individuals on Personality Tests. *Counselling Psychology Quarterly*, 7: 2, 99–104.

Lowenstein, L.F. (1994b) The Child and Child Sex Allegation. Links. No.3.

Lowenstein, L.F. (1997a) *The Law and Protecting The Child and Accused From False Sex Abuse Allegations.* Unpublished Study.

Lowenstein, L.F. (1997b) *Shared Parenting After Divorce.* Unpublished Study.

Lowenstein, L.F. (1998a) Parent Alienation Syndrome: A Two Step Approach Toward A Solution. *Contemporary Family Therapy*, 20: 4, 505–20.

Lowenstein, L.F. (1998b) Parent Alienation Syndrome: A Two Step Approach Towards A Solution. In *Paedophiles, The Sexual Abuse of Children: Its Occurrence and Treatment.* Able Publications.

Lowenstein, L.F. (1999) Parent Alienation and The Judiciary. *Medico-Legal Journal*, 67: 3, 121–3.

Lowenstein, L.F. (1999) Parent Alienation Syndrome: What The Legal Profession Should Know. *Medico-Legal Journal*. 66: 4, 151–61.

Lowenstein, L.F. (1999a) Parent Alienation Syndrome (PAS). *Justice of The Peace*, 163: 3, 47–50.

Lowenstein, L.F. (1999c) Mediation in The Legal Profession. *Justice of The Peace*, 163: 4, 709–10.

Lowenstein, L.F. (1999d) The Consequences Upon Victims of Violent Crime Including Domestic Violence. *Medico-Legal Journal*. 67: 4, 171–4

Lowenstein, L.F. (2000) The Role of Mediation in Child Custody Disputes. *Justice of The Peace*. 164: 258–62.

Lowenstein, L.F. (2001) A Review of Recent Research Into Risk Assessment of Childen. *Medico-Legal Journal*, 69: 3, 133–8.

Lowenstein, L.F. (2001) Joint Custody and Shared Parenting: Are The Courts Listening? *Justice of The Peace*, 165: 49, 963–6.

Lowenstein, L.F. (2001) Tackling Parental Alienation. *Justice of The Peace*, 165: 6, 102.

Lowenstein, L.F. (2001b) The Value of Mediation in Child Custody Disputes: Recent Research. *Justice of the Peace*, 166: 739–44.

Lowenstein, L.F. (2002) Joint Custody and Shared Parenting: Are The Courts Listening? *Family Therapy*, 29: 2, 101–8.

Lowenstein, L.F. (2002) Problems Suffered by Children Due to The Effects of Parental Alienation Syndrome (PAS). *Justice of The Peace*, 166: 24, 464–6.

Lowenstein, L.F. (2003) Tackling Parental Alienation: A Summary. *Justice of The Peace*. 167: 3, 29–30.

Lowenstein, L.F. (2005) Domestic Violence: Recent Research Parts 1, 2 and 3. *Justice of The Peace*, 169: 37, 715–7; 169: 38, 733–5; 169: 39, 758–761.

Lowenstein, L.F. (2005) The Psychological Effects and Treatment of Parental Alienation Syndrome Worldwide. In Gardner, R., Sauber, R. and Lorandos, D. (Eds.) *International Handbook of Parental Alienation Syndrome: Conceptual, Clinical and Legal Considerations.* Binghampton, NY: Haworth Press.

Lowenstein, L.F. (2005b) Causes and Associated Features of Divorce as Seen by Recent Research. *Journal of Divorce and Remarriage*, 42: 3/4, 153–71.

Lowenstein, L.F. (2005d) Parental Alienation Syndrome or Parental Alienation: is That The Question? (A Problem Crying Out for A Solution) Part 1. Being Considered for Publication.

Lowenstein, L.F. (2005e) Parent Alienation Syndrome and Its Impact on Children. Part 2. Being Considered for Publication.

Lowenstein, L.F. (2005g) Dealing With The Treatment of Parental Alienation Syndrome or Parental Alienation. Part 4. Being Considered for Publication.

Lowenstein, L.F. (2005h) How Can One Overturn The Programming of A Child Against A Parent? Being Considered for Publication.

Lowenstein, L.F. (2005i) How Does One Identify and Treat False Accusations of Sexual Abuse in Parental Alienation Situations? Being Considered for Publication.

Lowenstein, L.F. (2005j) Family Courts. Being Considered for Publication.

Lowenstein, L.F. (2005k) 'Real' Justice of Non-custodial Parents. Being Considered for Publication.

Lowenstein, L.F. (2006a) Long-Term Reactions as A Result of PAS. (Being Considered for Publication)

Lowenstein, L.F. (2006b) The Psychological Assessment and Treatment of Pathologically Induced Alienation (Dealing With Alienation Leading to an Induced Phobic Reaction.) (Being Considered for Publication)

Lowenstein, L.F. (2006c) Signs of PAS and How to Counteract Its Effects. *Journal of Parental Alienation*, 2(2), 26–30.

Lowenstein, L.F. (2006d) Real Justice of Non Custodial Parents and Their Children. (Being Considered for Publication.

Lowenstein, L.F. (2006e) Assessing The Treatment of Parental Alienation. (Being Considered for Publication)

Lowenstein, L.F. (2006f) The Types of Remedial and Therapeutic Methods Required in Parental Alienation. (Being Considered for Publication)

Lowenstein, L.F. (2006g) Overturning The Programming of A Child. *Journal of Parental Alienation*, 1(5), 1–12.

Lund, M. (1995) The Therapist's View of PAS. *Family and Conciliation Courts Review*, 33: 3, 308–16.

Lyle, C.G. and Graham, E. (2000) Looks Can Be Deceiving: Using A Risk Assessment Instrument to Evaluate The Outcomes of Child Protection Services. *Children and Youth Services Review*. 22: 11–12, 935–49.

Lyons, P., Doueck, H.J. and Wodarski, J.S. (1996) Risk Assessment for Child Protective Services: A Review of The Empirical Literature on Instrument Performance. *Social Work Research*. 20: 3, 143–55.

Mackinnon, D.P. et al. (2004) How Did It Work? Who Did It Work For? Mediation in The Context of A Moderated Prevention Effect for Children of Divorce. *Journal of Consulting and Clinical Psychology*, 72: 4, 617–24.

Mantle, G. and Critchley, A. (2004) Social Work and Child-Centred Family Court Mediation. *The British Journal of Social Work*, 38: 4, 1161–72.

Manusov, V. et al. (1994) Accounts in Child Custody Mediation Sessions, *Journal of Applied Communication Research*, 22: 1, 1–15.

Mathis, R.D. and Tanner, Z. (1998b) Effects of Unscreened Spouse Violence on Mediated Agreements. *American Journal of Family Therapy*. 26: 3, 251–60.

Mathis, R.D. and Yingling, L.C. (1998a) Family Modes: A Measure of Family Interaction and Organization. *Family and Conciliation Courts Review*. 36: 2, 246–57.

Maxwell, J.P. (1999) Mandatory Mediation of Custody in The Face of Domestic Violence: Suggestions for Courts and Mediators. *Family and Conciliation Courts Review*. 37: 3, 335–55.

Mazur, A. and Booth, A. (1998) Testosterone and Dominance in Men: *Behavioural and Brain Sciences*, 21:3, 353–97.

McCarthy, P. (1997) Mediating Modern Marriage: A Role for Marriage Counselling? *Sexual and Marital Therapy*, 12: 3, 275–87.

McIntosh, J. (2003) Enduring Conflict in Parental Separation: Pathways of Impact on Child Development. *Journal of Family Studies*, 9: 1, 63–80.

McIntosh, J. and Deacon-Wood, H.B. (2003) Group Interventions for Separated Parents in Entrenched Conflict: an Exploration of Evidence-Based Frameworks. *Journal of Family Studies*, 9: 2, 187–99.

McIntosh, J. and Long, C. (2005) Current Findings on Australian Children in Postseparation Disputes: Outer Conflict, Inner Discord. *Journal of Family Studies*, 11: 1, 99–109.

McIntosh, J., Long, C. and Moloney, L. (2004) Child-Focused and Child-Inclusive Mediation: A Comparative Study of Outcomes. *Journal of Family Studies*, 10: 1, 87–96.

McIntyre, D.H. (1994) Gay Parents and Child Custody: A Struggle Under The Legal System. *Mediation Quarterly*, 12: 2, 135–49.

McIsaac, H. and Finn, C. (1999) Parents beyond Conflict: A Cognitive Restucturing Model for High-conflict Families in Divorce. *Family and Concilliation Courts Review*, 37: 1, 74–82.

McKnight, M.S. and Erickson, S.K. (2004) The Plan to Separately Parent Children After Divorce. In Folberg, J., Salem, P. and Milne, A.L. (Eds.) *Divorce and Family Mediation: Models, Techniques, and Applications*. New York, NY: Guildford Publications.

McManus, P.A. and DiPrete, T.A. (2001) Losers and Winners: The Financial Consequences of separation and divorce for Men. *American Sociological Review*, 66: 2, 246–68.

Meister, R. (2003) Therapeutic Interventions for Children With Parental Alienation Syndrome. *American Journal of Family Therapy*, 31: 4, 321–4.

Melton, G.B. et al. (1997) *Psychological Evaluations for The Courts*. 2nd edn. New York: Guilford Press.

Menzies, R. et al. (1994) The Dimensions of Dangerousness Revisited. *Law and Human Behaviour*, 18: 1–28.

Menzies, R.G. and Clarke, J.C. (1993) A Comparison of in Vivo and Vicarious Exposure in The Treatment of Childhood Water Phobia. *Behaviur, Research and Therapy*, 31: 1, 9–15.

Meyerstein, I. (1996) Pre-Marital Counselling and The Problem Box Ritual. *Journal of Family Psychotherapy*, 7: 4, 63–70.

Miller, T.W. and Veltkamp, L.J. (1995) Clinical and Preventative Issues in Child Custody Disputes. *Child Psychiatry and Human Development*, 25: 4, 267–80.

Milner, J.S. et al. (1998) Assessment Issues in Child Abuse Evaluations. In Lutzker, J.R. (Ed.) *Handbook of Child Abuse Research and Treatment. Issues in Clinical Child Psychology*. New York, NY: Plenum.

Moloney, L. and McIntosh, J. (2004) Child-Responsive Practices in Australian

Family Law: Past Problems and Future Directions. *Journal of Family Studies*, 10: 1, 71–86.

Monohan, J. and Steadman, H. (1994) *Violence and Mental Disorder: Developments in Risk Assessment*. Chicago: University of Chicago Press.

Most, C.J. (2005) What About The Kids? Raising Your Children Before, During and After Divorce. *Psychoanalytic Quarterly*, 74: 3, 917–20.

Murray, K. (1999) When Children Refuse to Visit Parents: is Prison an Appropriate Remedy? *Family and Conciliation Courts Review*, 37: 1, 83–98.

Neff, R. and Cooper, K. (2004) Parental Conflict Resolution: Six, Twelve, and Fifteen Month Follow-Ups of A High Conflict Program. *Family Court Review*, 42: 1, 99–114.

Newmark, L., Harrell, A. and Salem, P. (1995) Domestic Violence and Empowerment in Custody and Visitation Cases. *Family and Conciliation Courts Review*, 33: 1, 30–62.

Nock, S. (2005) We're Still Family: What Grown Children Have to Say About Their Parents' Divorce. *Journal of Marriage and Family*, 67: 3, 784–6.

Novick, M.R. (2003) Therapeutic Interventions for Children With Parental Alienation Syndrome. *Journal of The American Academy of Psychoanalysis and Dynamic Psychiatry*, 31: 2, 418–21.

O'Donohue, W. and Crouch, J.L. (1996) Marital Therapy and Gender-Linked Factors in Communication. *Journal of Marital and Family Therapy*, 22: 1, 87–101.

Odegaard, P. (1996) Empathy Induction in The Couple Treatment of Depression: Shifting The Focus From Self to Other. *Families, Systems and Health*, 14: 2, 167–81.

Ogawa, N. and Ermisch, J.F. (1994) Women's Career Development and Divorce Risk in Japan. *Labor*, 8: 2, 193–219.

Ortega, D. et al. (2004) Judicial Efficiencies in Child Custody Disputes: Comparing Mediated and Litigated Outcomes. *Journal of Divorce and Remarriage*, 40: 3/4, 23–40.

Palmer, S.E. (2002) Custody and Access Issues With Children Whose Parents Are Separated or Divorced. *Canadian Journal of Community Mental Health*, Special suppl. 4, 25–38.

Papp, L.M., Cummings, E.M. and Schermerhorn, A.C. (2004) Pathways Among Marital Distress, Parental Symptomatology, and Child Adjustment. *Journal of Marriage and Family*, 66: 2, 368–84.

Pasley, K., Kerpelman, J. and Guilbert, D.E. (2002) Gendered Conflict Identity Disruption and Marital Instability: Expanding Gottman's Model. *Journal of Social and Personal Relationships*, 18: 1, 5–27.

Penn, C.D., Hernandez, S.L. and Bermuda, M. (1997) Using A Cross-Cultural Perspective to Understand Infidelity in Couples Therapy. *American Journal of Family Therapy*, 25: 2, 169–85.

Peterson, V. and Steinman, S.B. (1994) Helping Children Succeed After Divorce: A Court-Mandated Educational Programme for Divorcing Parents. *Family and Conciliation Courts Review*: 32: 1, 27–39.

Pinsof, W.M. (2002) Introduction to the Special Issue on Marriage in the 20th Century in Western Civilisation: Trends, Research, Therapy and Perspectives. *Family Process*, 41: 2, 133–4.

Poortman, A.R. and Kalmign, M. (2002) Women's Labor Market Position and Divorce in the Netherlands: Evaluating Economic Interpretations of the Work Effect. *European Journal of Population*, 18: 2, 175–202.

Price, C. and Kunz, J. (2003) Rethinking The Paradigm of Juvenile Delinquency as Related to Divorce. *Journal of Divorce and Remarriage*, 39: 1–2, 109–33.

Pruett, M.K., Insabella, G.M. and Gustafson, K. (2005) The Collaborative Divorce Project: A Court-Based Intervention for Separating Parents With Young Children. *Family Court Review*, 43: 1, 38–51.

Pruett, M.K., Nangle, B. and Bailey, C. (2000) Divorcing Families With Young Children in The Court's Family Services Unit: Profiles and Impact of Services. *Family and Conciliation Courts Review*. 38: 4, 478–500.

Raisner, J.K. (1997) Family Mediation and Never-Married Parents. *Family and Conciliation Courts Review*. 35E: 1, 90–101.

Ram, A., Finzi, R. and Cohen, O. (2002) The Non-custodial Parent and His Infant. *Journal of Divorce and Re-marriage*, 36:3/4, 175–202.

Ramirez, M. et al. (1999) Infantiles Sobre La Separacion Parental/ Children's Beliefs About Parental Divorce. *Psicologia Conductual*. 7: 1, 49–73.

Rand, D.C. (1997a) PAS. *American Journal of Forensic Psychology*, 15: 3, 37.

Rand, D.C. (1997b) The Spectrum of Parental Alienation Syndrome (Part II). *The American Journal of Forensic Psychology*, 15: 4, 1–13.

Rand, D.C., Rand, R. and Kopetski, L. (2005) The Spectrum of Parental Alienation Syndrome Part

III: The Kopetski Follow-Up Study. *American Journal of Forensic Psychology*, 23: 1, 15–43.

Rasmussen. K.S., Hamkins, A.J. and Schwab, K.P. (1996) Increasing Husbands' Involvement in Domestic Labour: Issues for Therapists. *Contemporary Family Therapy*, 18: 2, 209–23.

Read, L. (2003) High Conflict Family Court Cases: Working for The Child's Best Interests. *The Australian and New Zealand Journal of Family Therapy*, 24: 2, 95–101.

Regan, L. (2006) *Helping Mothers Move Forward: A Workbook to Help Provide Assessment and Support to the Safe Carers of Children who Have Been Sexually Abused.* Lyme Regis: Russell House Publishing.

Repetti, R.L., Roesch, S.C. and Wood, J.J. (2004) Divorce and Children's Adjustment Problems at Home and School: The Role of Depressive/Withdrawn Parenting. *Child Psychiatry and Human Development*, 35: 2, 121–42.

Ressler, R.W. and Waters, M.S. (2000) Female Earnings and the Divorce rate: A Simultaneous Equation Model. *Applied Economics*, 32: 14, 1889–98.

Ritchie, E.C. (1992) Treatment of Gas Mask Phobia. *Military Medicine*, 157: 2, 104–6.

Robinson, R.F. (1996) Relationship Between Work Addiction and Family Functioning: Clinical Implications for Marriage and Family Therapists. *Journal of Family Psychotherapy;* 7: 3, 13–29.

Ross, K.L. and Blush, G.J. (1990) Sexual Abuse Validity Discriminators in The Divorced or Divorcing Families. *Issues in Child Abuse Accusations*, 2: 1, 1–6.

Ross, S.A. and Estrada, A. (1997) An Empirically Driven Marital Therapy Intervention. *Journal of Family Psychotherapy*, 8: 4, 39–45.

Rotunda, R.J. and O'Farrell, T.J. (1997) Marital and Family Therapy of Alcohol Use Disorders: Bridging The Gap Between Research and Practice. *Professional Psychology: Research and Practice*, 28: 3, 246–52.

Rudd, J.E. (1996) Communication Effects on Divorce Mediation: How Participants' Argumentativeness, Verbal Aggression, and Compliance-Gaining Strategy Choice Mediate Outcome Satisfaction. *Mediation Quarterly*, 14: 1, 65–78.

Ruggles, S. (1997) The Rise of Divorce and Separation in the United States, 1880–1990. *Demography*, 34: 4, 455–66.

Rye, M.S. et al. (2004) Forgiveness of an Ex-Spouse: How Does It Relate to Mental Health. *Journal of Divorce and Remarriage*, 41: 3–4, 31–51.

Sachs, N.P. (2000) Is There a Tilt Toward Abusers in Child Custody Decisions? *Journal of Psychohistory*. 28: 2, 203–28.

Sauber, R. and Lorandos, D. (Eds.) (2005) *International Handbook of Parental Alienation Syndrome: Conceptual, Clinical and Legal Considerations.* Binghampton, NY: Haworth Press.

Sayer, L.C. and Bianchi, S.M. (2000) Women's Economic Independence and the Probability of Divorce: A Review and Re-examination. *Journal of Family Issues*, 21: 7, 906–43.

Sbarra, D.A. and Emery, R.E. (2005) Following A Divorce? Coparenting Conflict, Nonacceptance, and Depression Among Divorced Adults: Results From A 12–Year Follow-Up Study of Child Custody Mediation Using Multiple Imputation. *American Journal of Orthopsychiatry*, 75: 1, 63–75.

Schepard, A.I. (2004) *Children, Courts and Custody: Interdisciplinary Models for Divorcing Families.* New York, NY: Cambridge University Press.

Scherrer, R. and Louw, D.A. (2004) Family Advocates' and Family Counsellors' Perceptions and Experience of the Family Advocate System. *International Journal of The Sociology of Law*, 32: 3, 223–41.

Schoenewolf, G. (1996) The Couple Who Fell in Hate: Electic Psychodynamic Therapy With an Angry Couple. *Journal of Contemporary Psychotherapy*, 26: 1, 65–71.

Schoffer, M.J. (2005) Bringing Children to The Mediation Table: Defining a Child's Best Interest in Divorce Mediation. *Family Court Review*, 43: 2, 323–38.

Schwab, R. (1998) A Child's Death and Divorce: Dispelling the Myth. *Death Studies*, 22: 5, 445–468.

Schwartz, L.L. (1994) Enabling Children of Divorce to Win, *Family Conciliation Courts Review*, 32: 1, 72–83.

Segrin, C., Taylor, M.E. and Alman, J. (2005) Social Cognitive Mediators and Relational Outcomes Associated With Parental Divorce. *Journal of Social and Personal Relationships*, 22: 3, 361–77.

Shopper, M. (2005) Parental Alienation: The Creation of A False Reality. In Gunsberg, L. and Hymowitz, P. (Eds.) *A Handbook of Divorce and Custody: Forensic, Developmental, and Clinical Perspectives.* Hillsdale, NJ: Analytic Press.

Silveira, J.M. and Seeman, M.V. (1995) Shared Psychotic Disorder. A Critical Review of The

Literature. *Canadian Journal of Psychiatry*, 40: 7, 389–95.

Sirvanli-Ozen, D. (2004) Journal of Divorce and Remarriage, 41: 1–2, 137–57.

Smith, I. (1997). Explaining the Growth of Divorce in Great Britain. *Scottish Journal of Political Economy*, 44: 5, 519–44.

Smith, I. (1998). The Economics of the Grounds for Divorce in Great Britain. *European Journal of Law and Economics*, 60, 39–52.

Smoron, K.A. (1998) Conflicting Roles in Child Custody Mediation: Impartiality/Neutrality and The Best Interests of The Child, *Family and Conciliation Courts Review*, 36: 2, 258–80.

Smyth, B.M. and Moloney, L. (2003) Therapeutic Divorce Mediation: Strengths, Limitations, and Future Directions. *Journal of Family Studies*, 9: 2, 161–86.

Snow, R.J. (2003) Nonresidential Father-Child Involvement: Fathers' and Mothers' Perspectives in Acrimonious Divorce Relationships. *Dissertation Abstracts International*, 63: 9, 3359.

Solomon, C.R. (1991) A Critical Moment for Intervention: After The Smoke of The Battle Clears and Custody Has Been Won. *Journal of Divorce and Remarriage*, 3–4: 325–35.

Sorenson, E. et al. Judicial Decision-Making in Contested Custody Cases: The Influence of Reported Child Abuse, Spouse Abuse, and Parental Substance Abuse, *Child Abuse and Neglect*, 19: 2, 251–60.

Speziale, B.A. (1997) Couples, Sexual Intimacy, and Multiple Sclerosis. *Journal of Family Psychotherapy*, 8: 1, 13–32.

Spruijt, E. et al. (2005) Parental Alienation Syndrome (PAS) in The Netherlands. *American Journal of Family Therapy*, 33: 4, 303–17.

Spruijt, E., De Goede, M. and Vandervalk, I. (2004) Frequency of Contact With Non-Resident Fathers and Adolescent Well-Being: A Longitudinal Analysis. *Journal of Divorce and Remarriage*, 40: 3–4, 77–90.

Stabb, S.D., Cox, D.L. and Harber. J.L. (1997) Gender-Related Therapist Attributions in Couples Therapy: A Preliminary Multiple Case Study Investigation. *Journal of Marital and Family Therapy;* 23: 3, 335–46.

Stahl, P.M. (2000) *Parenting After Divorce: A Guide to Resolving Conflicts and Meeting Your Children's Needs.* Atascadero, CA: Impact Publishers.

Stahl, P.M. (2002) Child Custody Evaluations. In Van Dorsten, B. (Ed.) *Forensic Psychology: From Classroom to Courtroom.* New York, NY: Kluwer Academic/Plenum Publishers.

Stamps, L.E. (2002) Maternal Preference in Child Custody Decisions. *Journal of Divorce and Remarriage*, 37: 1/2, 1–11.

Stamps, L.E., Kunen, S. and Rock-Faucheux, A. (1997) Judges' Beliefs Dealing With Child Custody Decisions. *Journal of Divorce and Remarriage*, 28: 1/2, 3–16.

Steadman, H. and Robbins, P. (1998) *The Macarthur Violence Risk Assessment Study.* Paper Presented at The Competency, Coercion and Risk of Violence Conference, Marquette University, Milwaukee, WI.

Steadman, H. et al. (1998) Violence by People Discharged From Acute Psychiatric Inpatient Facilities and by Others in The Same Neighbourhoods. *Archives of General Psychiatry.* 55: 393–401.

Stewart, S.D. (2003) Non Resident Parenting and Adolescent Adjustment: The Quality of Non-Resident Father-Child Interaction. *Journal of Family Issues*, 24: 2, 217–44.

Storm, C.L., York, C.D. and Keller, J.G. (1997) A Genderist Philosophy Transforms an MFT Proqramme. *American Journal of Family Therapy*, 25: 2, 151–68.

Sturge, C. and Glaser, D. (2000) Contact and Domestic Violence: The Expert Court Report. *Family Law*, 615–23.

Sullivan, M.J. and Kelly, J.B. (2001) Legal and Psychological Management of Cases With an Alienated Child. *Family Court Review*, 39: 3, 299–315.

Sweeney, M.M. (2002) Re-marriage and the Nature of Divorce. Does it Matter which Spouse Chose to Leave? *Journal of Family Issues*, 23: 3, 410–40.

Szabo, C.P. (2002) Parental Alienation Syndrome. *South African Psychiatry Review*, 5: 3, 1.

Tardiff, K. et al. (1997a) Prospective Study of Violence by Psychiatric Patients After Hospital Discharge. *Psychiatric Services.* 48: 678–81.

Tardiff, K. et al. (1997b) Violence by Patients Admitted to A Private Psychiatric Hospital. *American Journal of Psychiatry.* 154: 88–93.

Taylor, R.J. (2003) Use of Change Theory in the Context of the Divorce Mediation Session. *Journal of Divorce and Remarriage*, 40: 1–2, 87–92.

Taylor, R.J. (2004) Therapeutic Intervention of Trauma and Stress Brought on by Divorce. *Journal of Divorce and Remarriage*, 41: 1/2, 129–35.

Taylor, R.J. (2005) Use of Nash Equilibrium in The Education and Use of Divorce Mediation. *Journal of Divorce and Remarriage*, 43: 1–2, 163–8.

Terling, T. (1999) The Efficacy of Family Reunification Practices: Re-Entry Rates and Correlates or Re-Entry for Abused and Neglected Children Reunited With Their Families. *Child Abuse and Neglect.* 23: 12, 1359–70.

Terling-Watt, T. (2001) Divorce and Poverty. In Peck, D.L. and Dolch, N.A. (Eds.) *Extrordinary Behaviour: A Case Study Approach to Understanding Social Problems.* Westport, CT: Praeger, 121–43.

Terling-Watt, T. (2001) Explaining Divorce: An Examination of the Relationship between Marital Characteristics and Divorce. *Journal of Divorce and Remarriage,* 35: 3–4, 125–45.

Thayer, E.S. and Zimmerman, J. (2001) *The Co-Parenting Survival Guide: Letting Go of Conflict After A Difficult Divorce.* Oakland, CA: New Harbinger Publications.

Turkat, I.D. (1995) Divorce Related Malicious Mother Syndrome. *Journal of Family Violence,* 10: 3, 253–64.

Turkat, I.D. (2000) Custody Battle Burnout. *American Journal of Family Therapy.* 28: 3, 201–15.

Turkat, L. (1994) Child Visitation Interference in Divorce. *Clinical Psychology Review,* 8: 737–42.

Turnell, A. and Edwards, S. (1999) *Signs of Safety: A Solution and Safety Oriented Approach to Child Protection Casework.* New York, NY: WW Norton.

Twaite, J.A. and Luchow, A.K. (1996) Custodial Arrangements and Parental Conflict Following Divorce: The Impact on Children's Adjustment. *Journal of Psychiatry and Law.* 24: 1, 53–75.

Van Gijseghem, H. (2005) Les Controversies Entourant La Notion De L'alienation Parentale. /Controversies Around The Notion of Parental Alienation. *Revue De Psychoeducation,* 34: 1, 119–29.

Vandervalk, I. et al. (2004) Marital Status, Marital Process, and Parental Resources in Predicting Adolescents' Emotional Adjustment: A Multilevel Analysis. *Journal of Family Issues,* 25: 3, 291–317.

Vansteenwegen, A. (1997) Do Marital Therapists Do What They Say They Do? A Comparison Between Experiential and Communication Couples Therapy. *Sexual and Marital Therapy,* 12: 1, 35–43.

Vassiliou, D. and Cartwright, G.F. (2001) The Lost Parents' Perspective on Parental Alienation Syndrome. *American Journal of Family Therapy,* 29: 3, 181–91.

Vestal, A. (1999) Mediation and Parental Alienation Syndrome: Considerations for an Intervention Model. *Family and Conciliation Courts Review.* 37: 4, 487–503.

Von Boch-Galhau, W. (2002) Parental Alienation Syndrome (PAS): Influence of Separation and Divorce of Offspring on Adult Life. *Revista Argentina De Clinica Psicologica,* 11: 2, 113–38.

Wakefield, H. and Underwager (1990) Personality Characteristics of Parents Making False Accusations of Sexual Abuse in Custody Disputes. *Issues in Child Abuse Allegations,* 2: 3, 121–36.

Walker, J. and McCarthy, P. (2001) Marriage Support Services and Divorce: A Contradiction in Terms? *Sexual and Relationship Therapy,* 16: 4, 329–48.

Walker, J. (2003) Radiating Messages: an International Perspective. *Family Relations,* 52: 4, 406–17.

Wall, J.U. and Amadio, C. (1994) An Integrated Approach to Child Custody Evaluation: Utilizing The Best Interest of The Child and Family Systems Frameworks, *Journal of Divorce and Remarriage,* 21: 3–4, 39–57.

Wallerstein, J.S. (1998) Children of Divorce: A Society in Search of Policy. In Mason, M.A. et al. (Eds.) *All Our Families: New Policies for A New Century.* New York, NY: Oxford University Press.

Wallerstein, J.S. and Blakeslee, D. (1994) Second Chances: Child Visitation Interference in Divorce. *Clinical Psychology Review,* 14: 8, 734–42.

Wallerstein, J.S. and Kelly, J.B. (1980) *Surviving the Breakup: How Children and Parents Cope with Divorce.* New York: Basic Books.

Walper, S. et al. (2004) Parental Separation and Adolescents' Felt Insecurity With Mothers: Effect of Financial Hardship, Interparental Conflict, and Maternal Parenting in East and West Germany. *Marriage and Family Review,* 36: 3–4, 115–45.

Warshak, R.A. (2000) Remarriage as A Trigger of Parental Alienation Syndrome. *American Journal of Family Therapy,* 28: 3, 229–41.

Warshak, R.A. (2001) Current Controversies Regarding Parental Alienation Syndrome. *American Journal of Forensic Psychology,* 19: 3, 29–59.

Warshak, R.A. (2002) Misdiagnosis of Parental Alienation Syndrome. *American Journal of Forensic Psychology,* 20: 2, 31–52.

Warshak, R.A. (2003) Payoffs and Pitfalls of Listening to Children. *Family Relations,* 52: 4, 373–84.

Waters, M.S. and Ressler, R.W. (1999) An Economic Model of Cohabitation and Divorce. *Journal of Economic Behaviour and Organisation*, 40: 2, 196–206.

Weaver, A.J., Koenig, H.G. and Larson, D.B. (1997) Marriage and Family Therapists and The Clergy: A Need for Clinical Collaboration, Training and Research. *Journal of Marital and Family Therapy*, 23: 1, 13–25.

Weissman, H.N. (1991) Child Custody Evaluations: Fair and Unfair Professional Practices, *Behavioural Sciences and The Law*, 9, 46.

Wells, A. et al. (1995) Social Phobia: The Role of In-Situation Safety Behaviors in Maintaining Anxiety and Negative Beliefs. *Behaviour Therapy*, 26: 1, 153–61.

Welter, P.R. (1995) Meaninq as a Resource in Marriage Counselling. *International Forum for Logotherapy* 18: 2, 109–13.

Whitney, P. and; Davis, L. (1999) Child Abuse and Domestic Violence in Massachusetts: Can Practice Be Integrated in Public Child Welfare Setting? *Journal of American Professional Society on The Abuse of Children*. 4: 2, 158–66.

Whittington, L.A. and Alm, J. (1997) 'Til Death or Taxes do us Part': The Effect of Income Taxation on Divorce. *Journal of Human Resources*, 32; 2, 388–412.

Wild, L.G. and Richards, M.P. (2003) Exploring Parent and Child Perceptions of Interparental Conflict. *International Journal of Law, Police and The Family*, 17: 3, 366–84.

Wilhelmus, M. (1998) Mediation in Kinship Care: Another Step in The Provision of Culturally Relevant Child Welfare Services. *Social Work*. 43: 2, 117–26.

Willbourne, C. and Cull, L. (1997) The Emerging Problem of Parental Alienation. *Family Law*, 807–8.

Williams, R.J. (2001) Should Judges Close The Gate on PAS and PA? *Family Court Review*, 39: 3, 267–81.

Wilson, R. and Wilson, L. (1996) Multiple Selves Operating Within Relationships. *Journal of Family Psychotherapy*, 7: 2, 41–51.

Winstock, Z. and Eisikovits, Z. (2003) Divorcing the Parents: The Impact of Adolescents' Exposure to Father-to-Mother Aggression on Their Perceptions of Affinity With Their Parents. *Journal of Emotional Abuse*, 3: 1–2, 103–21.

Wollinger, N.H. (2000) Beyond the Intergenerational Transmission of Divorce: How People Replicate the Patterns of Marital Instability they Grew up with. *Journal of Family Issues*, 21: 8, 1061–86.

Wolpe, J. (1997) From Psychoanalytic to Behavioral Methods in Anxiety Disorders: A Continuing Evolution. In Zeig, J.K. (Ed.) *The Evolution of Psychotherapy: The Third Conference*. New York: Brunner/Mazel.

Wolpe, J., Craske, M.G. and Reyna, L.J. (1994) *The Comparative Efficacy of Behaviour Therapy and Psychodynamic Methods in The Anxiety Disorders*. Unpublished Manuscript.

Wood, J.J., Repetti, R.L. and Roesch, S.C. (2004) Divorce and Children's Adjustment Problems at Home and School: The Role of Depressive/Withdrawn Parenting. *Child Psychiatry and Human Development*, 35: 2, 121–42.

Worthington, E.L. (1996) Speculations About New Directions in Helping Marriages and Families That Arise From Pressures of Managed Mental Health Care. *Journal of Psychology and Christianity*. 15: 3, 197–212.

Worthington, E.L. et al. (1997) Strategic Hope-Focused Relationship Enrichment Counselling With Individual Couples. *Journal of Counselling Psychology*, 44: 4, 381–9.

Wozchik, S.A., Brewer, S.L. and Sandler, L.N. (1985) Maternal versus Joint Custody: Children's Post-separation Experiences and Adjustment. *Journal of Clinical Child Psychology*, 14, 5–10.

Wrightsman, L.S. et al. (1998) *Psychology and The Legal System*. Pacific Grove, CA: Brooks/Cole.

Yilmaz, A.E. and Fisiloglu, H. (2005) Turkish Parents' Post-Divorce Adjustment: Perceived Power/Control Over Child-Related Concerns, Perceived Social Support, and Demographic Characteristics. *Journal of Divorce and Remarriage*, 42: 3–4, 83–107.

Zeag, Y., Schultz, T.P. and Wang, D. (1992) *An Event History Analysis of Divorce in China*. Yale Economic Growth Center, Discussion Paper 675, 34.

Zill, N., Morrison, D.R. and Coiro,M.J. (1993) Long-Term Effects of Parental Divorce on Parent-Child Relationships, Adjustment, and Achievement in Young Adulthood. *Journal of Family Psychology*, 7: 1, 91–103.

Zimmerman, D.K., Brown, J.H. and Portes, P.R. (2004) Assessing Custodial Mother Adjustment to Divorce: The Role of Divorce Education and Family Functioning. *Journal of Divorce and Remarriage*, 41: 1–2, 1–24.

Zirogiannis, L. (2001) Evidentiary Issues With Parental Alienation Syndrome. *Family Court Review*, 39: 3, 334–43.

Letters and Web Messages about PAS

Letters

Dear Dr Lowenstein

I have found some of your articles on the Internet, regarding PAS, very interesting.

I should like to know whether you have done any research or encountered any situation in which PAS may occur in the opposite direction. By this I mean whether you have come across cases in which the behaviour towards or statements about the custodial parent by the non-custodial parent was leading to PAS?

I have observed symptoms, very like the ones you describe as being exhibited by children in these cases, in my own children. I did not know that there was a name for this. I have been involved in an intractable court case over my children for four years. As a mother and as the custodial parent I realise that I may be perceived as the alienating parent. However I have tried to encourage good contact between my children and their father. Sometimes I have even given up my house for my ex husband to move in and have his contact with the children in my home, in order to make it more comfortable. Despite my best efforts, this has not been reciprocated. I find that my ex husband denigrates me with the children and encourages them to make unjustified complaints about my care of them to the authorities and to officials, to a degree that I believe is having a severe psychological effect on them, but in different ways. I find that my daughter refuses all contact with her father; whereas my son appears to be affected by what I can only call a type of brainwashing because after a holiday with his father at the beginning of which he went away from me happy, he came back very hostile towards me and would not meet my eyes. Apparently he had been told to behave badly at home so that he would get sent to live with his father; and he had been encouraged to make complaints about me by phoning the NSPCC. I recognise something very like your PAS in my children. However I have had little success in making the courts understand that these symptoms exist and have a real psychological impact. I think it is serious. However I am the custodial parent and the mother so I think that I am the one being perceived as difficult. I think that my description of these happenings are merely looked upon as feeble excuses for asking contact to be supervised.

I left my husband initially because he was abusive, mainly emotionally, but also physically towards me. We had both been sent to a psychologist previously who did a risk assessment for the court which concluded that my ex husband posed a real emotional and psychological risk to the children and to me, given his attitudes. However, as you seem to stress in your articles, it is very hard to get the courts to take account of such attitudes. What worries me, although I think your research is valid, is what if a mother has genuine concerns about the children because a process of denigration is going on by the father towards the mother? What has surprised me is how little time it takes for a child to show hostility and this strange behaviour. In the space of two weeks my son, who went *away* happy and joyful for his Christmas holiday with his father, came back hostile towards me, angry, withdrawn, and unable to meet my eyes. I fear that if my ex had prolonged contact with our children, this would happen on a bigger scale. It can take a lot of work to get a child back emotionally who has been programmed against you. I assumed because I am the custodial parent that this would have little impact on my children but I was wrong. It can have a big impact in a short period of time.

I fear being one of those mothers who is penalised or sent to jail by the court. The trouble about advocating such a penalty is that the court would have to be damn sure it was jailing the right parent. How is a court to judge that? Judges have no psychological expertise and neither do the CAFCASS officers who carry out interviews and assessments on behalf of the courts.

I should very much like to know whether you have done any research or considered the question of whether PAS can occur in this way, with the alienating parent being the non-custodial parent. If you have any such articles I should be interested to read them.

Yours sincerely K.J.

Please understand I am not sure what I am doing is working. I have spoken to you before and things have not improved.

My question today is what ethical responsibility does a person of the psychological profession have if being aware of child abuse and discussing the cause and possible outcome a parent acts on their advice things get worse for children; and when asked to confirm his advice to child protection services then says he doesn't want to get involved (even though it was his advice that has led to even more abuse and the deterioration of that child's well-being in front of his very eyes on a almost daily basis).

Please respond soon my children are being turned against me by my wife who possibly may have an anti-social disorder.

Jeff Opperman, a 49-year-old corporate-communications officer in Seymour, Connecticut, got the first gut-churning clue of how ruinous his divorce was going to be to his relationship with his younger son the night it became clear he and his wife, Anne, had to part.

They'd been married for 17 years, but it hadn't been going well. 'We were fighting and drifting apart,' says Opperman, 'and the more we fought, the more we drifted apart, and the more we drifted apart, the more we fought'. They decided to hold off telling Alec, just 11, until he'd finished camp that summer. But the marriage was so rocky that Jeff and Anne arrived in separate cars to take him home, leaving it to Alec to choose which car to ride home in. He picked his mother's – a fateful choice, as things turned out. 'God knows what she said to him in that car for an hour and a half', Opperman says.

The next night, when he and Anne 'got into it' in their bedroom, she burst out the door and raced down to Alec's room, where she yelled, Opperman recalls, 'the most horrid, disgraceful things, calling me a liar, a cheat, a son of a bitch, just everything'. Tears streamed down Alec's reddened face, but he didn't try to defend his dad. Instead, to Opperman's astonishment, he started to chime in, feebly parroting some of his mother's charges though he'd always been close to his father.

When Opperman tried to give the boy a reassuring hug, Anne abruptly stepped between them claiming that Jeff was going to hurt the boy, threatened to call the police if he came any closer. Opperman backed off, not wanting to risk a bigger scene in front of his son. 'Alec cried his eyes out', Opperman recalls. 'Just cried and cried'.

That was six years ago, but it established the dynamic by which Jeff became the designated ogre parent and Alec became Anne's exclusive possession. Jeff acknowledges that he hadn't been a perfect husband. 'When a marriage breaks down, both parties are at fault, and ours was no different'. But regardless of who was responsible for the divorce, Jeff feels his ex should have protected Alec from the negative aspects of the relationship. Instead, he claims, she burdened their son with her pain and sense of betrayal – and Alec responded by aligning himself fully with his mother; emotionally cutting off his dad.

Although Opperman was granted joint custody and lives just 10 minutes away, he has since seen his son only for the briefest intervals – despite repeatedly taking his ex to court over custody violations. 'The court adopts this tough-talking John Wayne attitude', Opperman recounts. 'You will take child to counselling. You will allow the child to maintain relations with the father. You will, you will'. But my ex doesn't do any of it – and nothing happens'. Despite all Opperman's efforts the court has been both reluctant to force Alec to spend time with a father he wants nothing to do with and unwilling to compel Alec's mother by threat of jail time.

All this leaves Opperman out in the cold. His Christmas and birthday presents to Alec go unacknowledged. When Opperman calls, Alec will occasionally pick up, but when he hears that it's his father on the line, he won't speak. All Jeff hears is Alec's breath in the receiver before he sets the phone down. Last summer, Opperman came to the house to pick up his older son, Alec's brother. There were lights on in Alec's bedroom, and Opperman could see the back of Alec's head as he stared at a computer screen. Jeff honked the horn, hoping to get Alec's attention. 'I was sure he hear me', Jeff recalls. 'But Alec never even turned his head'.

Opperman's desperation is hardly unique. About 40 percent of children living with their mother don't see their fathers so much as once a year. Even allowing for fathers who are at war, in prison or otherwise unavailable, statistics like that force the question: Are there really that many men out there who simply don't care about their kids and vice versa? Or is something more sinister at work?

Dear Ludwig,

Thank you for your offer of assistance re my request via FNF (regarding a PACT project). I hope you are still keeping well. I include a brief overview of PACT projects at the end of this e-mail. Approximately three years ago we spoke on the telephone at a time when I tried to persuade a Judge to order the appointment of an expert.

My own family law case (involving severe parental alienation of all three children) has taken an unexpected but welcome turn (my persistence caused a legal guardian to over-react which in turn caused the Judge to react) and now requires the identification of experts – the Judge (HHJ Darwall-Smith sitting in Bristol) has ordered the following:

An adult psychologist to perform an assessment of both parents and produce a report for the Court.

A child psychiatrist to perform an assessment of all papers and produce a report for the Court.

If the child psychiatrist recommends an assessment of the children then that will be ordered too.

Note that the Judge wants 'highly-regarded' experts, preferably attached to hospitals (e.g. the Maudsley).

My ex-wife's lawyers oppose your appointment (I think because of your knowledge of parental alienation) so in case the Judge fails to support my proposal, could you possibly recommend other experts?

PACT have several projects either planned or in progress that I am assisting with. Any information that could help me with these would be very welcome! The projects are:

1. Identification of all research material regarding Parental Alienation (Syndrome), to be used as baseline for further research (by a prominent academic institution).
2. Survey of and report on parental alienation within the U.K. population (by the academic institution).
3. Persuade a British TV company to broadcast the 'Victims Of Another War' documentary.

There is also a second documentary in production, featuring 'left-behind-parents' in cases of international parental abduction (which involve severe parental alienation).

Also, a wealthy individual based in the U.S. (who has been bequeathed a fortune and has been affected by parental alienation and abduction) wants to make a movie in Hollywood to dramatise the reality of parental alienation/abduction.

Thank you for any help you can give, Best wishes,

Andrew

I have spoken to you regarding Parental Alienation due to Shared Psychotic Disorder (folie à Deux).

My daughter spoke with her solicitor, and she said because she had contact with her son, so they may not recognise that the above was happening, also the cost involved may not be granted. The headmaster asked my daughter and her partner to take Steven to the doctor to get a referral to CAHMs as he was worried about his behaviour, and he may be excluded from school. Can you tell me, does CAHMS have the experience and expert knowledge to recognise (folie à Deux).

Regards

L.S.

I came across this site quite by accident. I am a stepmother and both my stepchildren refuse to see their dad (my husband). My stepson has not come over in two years, and my stepdaughter walked out on us this week, vowing not to return. When I read through the articles light bulbs went on in my head with each line. YES YES YES – to everything I have been feeling, noticing, seeing, etc. over the past few years. We are the classic textbook case. It doesn't change our situation, but at least it gives me some comfort that we aren't alone, and more importantly that can help assuage any guilt that we have done something wrong to cause this alienation. Thank you.

Hello my name is Salvador S.
I got divorce two years ago in Arizona USA. When have one child ll y and 9 m old girl. The court grant us joint legal custody, being mother the primary residential parent. I have a new family with two kids 12 y boy and 8 y girl. We get along petty good all of us five. My daughter has a good time with everybody. We went on vacation last year, the five of us. We were getting ready to go on vacation again but now mother won't let us see her or talk to her, saying that I say bad things about mother to child, and she doesn't want too see nobody from my side of family. Gave child a mobile phone that she gave back saying that she didn't want it any more. Child was very happy because she was going to go on vacation with us, now she does not want anything to do with us. What is going on or what can I do. Please help. Thank you . . . we fear for her.

Hello,
I am a victim of PAS, and currently do not see my children for two months now (daughter 13, son 11). Their mother is exhibiting all characteristics as described on your website. I would like to receive advice on how best to tackle this increasingly difficult issue.
　Kind regards,
　B.P.

My children's father and I have been separated for 3 ½ years, now divorced. After a long custody dispute, our children (7 year old boy and 6 year old girl) live with me the majority of the time. (We have joint custody). Their father is unable to see them as agreed upon (judgment) so he sees them at his convenience, but doesn't come very often.

　While it affects both of my children tremendously, my son is extremely confused. He is now threatening suicide, so I admitted him into a hospital – he has been there for six days with no positive emotional changes. He still says he wants to end his life because I am mean to him. When I (and the professionals) asked him what makes me so mean, he says 'she makes me take my medicine for no reason, makes me take a bath and she's mean – that's why my dad doesn't want to live with us anymore'. My once loving child who told me often that I am the 'Best mom in the world', now hates me. Their father has visited him (as have I) every day since he has been in the hospital and encourages his hostility toward me (i.e. When our son said 'mom is aggravating' (same words as their father uses to describe me) their father replies: 'Some people aggravate other people, but she's your mom, tell her nicely that you don't want her to visit you' and when our son said 'mom's crazy', their father replies: 'that's not nice, you're going to hurt her feelings' (again, mocking his father's words). He also admits freely to telling our children that I took them and left our home – he would have never left, he loves them.

　A very long story short, our children live with me, I am not only flexible with visitation, but often stress the need to their father the need for them to see him. I thought their depression and behaviour problems were due to the lack of their father's involvement in their lives, but have learned recently that he has been bashing me to them. I came across your web site with extensive information on Parent Alienation Syndrome. Both of our children (especially our son) have all the signs and symptoms, but it states that PAS is inflicted by the custodial parent. What do you call our problem (so I can look it up) and get advice to resolve it? Please help us

S.J.

Lisa,

Thank you so much for thinking of us and us articles. We hope you will continue to do so, and we will put this up on our website. Also, wanted to forward you a recent op-ed article I did for a publication here called Jewish Journal. Awareness of Parental Alienation is increasing. We hope it is on the cusp of public knowledge. In the states, there is an article out in the widely circulated magazine, *Best Life*, entitled, 'The Lost Children', by John Sedgwick dedicated to PAS.

The national news program, Dateline, recently did a program about the Rick Lohstroh case in Houston, where a 10 year old child, enflamed by his Mother, got her handgun and murdered his Father,(you can view that piece on our website under media) and this Monday, CNN is doing a piece on PAS with Dr. Richard Warshak.

Also, in Vancouver, an important new book was just launched. It is entitled, 'A Kidnapped Mind' by Pamela Richardson. It is the true and tragic story of the torment of a child, who eventually wound up committing suicide as a result of PAS.

Don't know if you can get copies of the book yet in the UK. Here in the states, we get it through www_.Amazon.com. We must continue to bring awareness about the cruelty of PAS and the damage to the children. Hopefully, no other family will have to suffer as ours did.

There is much research that needs to be done on the effects of PAS on children, how to ameliorate that damage, and the reunification process.

Robin

I live in Brussels. My youngest daughter is 2.5 and (as it had already happened before) again, I do not see her since 30/04/2006. I download a lot on PAS, and of course I see many similarities with own situation, but I wonder if it would be good to use it in court. It seems to be many arguments of 'opponents'. What I am convinced of, is that this process really harms the child, and that is from this point of view that maybe it is better to start.

Thanks for this very useful and knowledgeable web site !

Thierry

It has been a revitalising experience to find a UK site regarding Parental Alienation, and particularly one which does not get dragged into a battle for any particular gender. Too often the sites highlighting this despicable practice are male rights oriented, while those denying its existence are pro-women.

Anyway, I digress. I notice that the majority of PA seems to be regarding younger children, and even those that accept it seem disinclined to accept teenagers can be controlled by an expert manipulator.

I will not go into my situation heavily, except to let you know that my son who is 16 and my daughter who is 15 have been very effectively programmed into aligning with my ex wife.

I can find little research where adolescents are the programmed child, yet truly belief that my children have been programmed by a person who seems to have an innate manipulative talent that meet many of the criteria that this site and others give as causing and defining the PA process

From my experience, despite strong bonds with my children, The process was rapid with my son, but my daughter was a much slower process that has ultimately succeeded in a very painful and poignant manner. I have watched two beloved children utterly reject me over a mere 18 months. It is heartbreaking, and I have no family to help with coping with the after effects of what has transpired.

I truly believe the manipulative skills of my ex wife precludes any likelihood of ever regaining my children, and feel all I have left is to do what I can to help others in raising awareness of the reality of PAS in the hope that one day it will be properly addressed in the UK.

If you are able to direct me towards research in adolescent PA I would be very appreciative.

Yours C.A.

Greetings,

I'd like to share with you the fact that I self-published a book that deals with parental alienation and the American family court system. It also happens to cover Lyme disease, a disease that I have been dealing with for 14 years, and how in my case, it affected custodial arrangements in family court as well: how my disease, though undiagnosed at the time of custody reversal, was manipulated into removing custody from me by my ex-husband and his attorney. There is a tremendous amount of information in it pertaining to parental alienation.

Additionally, false accusations of child abuse and mental illness that did not and do not exist that were proven to not exist, play a role in our situation, as does what happened to the children in this situation ---forced to lie for their father to help him remove custody from me, their mother, and how the system allowed him to do so illegally.

I think it might be of interest to people who visit your site. If you think so, please let me know and I'll be happy to send you a copy for review. Perhaps you could offer a link on your site so others can read about our situation. I believe it offers a clear picture of just how devious a man can be, and to what lengths some people will go to alienate their own children from a loving parent for their own sick purposes, without regard to the welfare of their children.

Thank you for your time and please let me know if you are interested.

By the way, I also run two support groups and web sites, for Lyme patients, www.sewill.org (Wisconsin regional group), and www.lymeleague.com, a Lyme site for patients in the US and Canada, who post stories about their Lyme disease. I work when I can, editing medical books for a small press, write articles for magazines and other publications, and author and self-publish books in other subjects.

Dear everyone

Please find attached some feedback on PA info from the US from Robin Denison co-founder of www.parental-alienation-awareness.com. Those of us who have experienced PA know the devastating and life changing impact it has on children as well as ourselves as parents, mothers and fathers, and our extended families. We should also maximise our commitment to continue to raise awareness of PA as it is not just a UK or US problem, a Christian, Jewish, Muslim or other faith problem, it is an international problem now which needs to be tackled by all Governments, family legal systems, clinicians, the media and people from all faiths and walks of life.

I have attached below the available part (without subscription) of the *Best Life* Magazine article, entitled, Lost Children: Parental Alienation which Robin mentioned below. It is an all too familiar story.

Also attached is a link to the new book published called *A Kidnapped Mind: A Mother's Heartbreaking Story of Parental Alienation Syndrome* by Pamela Anderson that Robin mentioned.

hftp:_l/www.amazon.co.uk/exec/obidosIASIN/1550026240/aid%3D1150456891/ 203-9505075-0037528

Synopsis

How do we begin to describe our love for our children? Pamela Richardson shows us with her passionate memoir of life with and without her estranged son, Dash. From age five, Dash suffered Parental Alienation Syndrome at the hands of his father. Indoctrinated to believe his mother had abandoned him, after years of monitored phone calls and impeded access, eight-year-old Dash decided he didn't want to be 'forced' to visit her at all; later, he told her he would never see her again if she took the case to court. But, he didn't count on his indefatigable mother's fierce love. For eight more years, Pamela battled Dash's father, the legal system, their psychologist, the school system, and Dash himself to try and protect her son – first from his father, then from himself. "A Kidnapped Mind" is a heartrending and mesmerising story of a Canadian mother's exile from and reunion with her child, through grief and beyond, to peace.

Lady Catherine Meyer, the wife of Sir Christopher Meyer (former UK Ambassador to the US) who is based in the UK has also published a book on the impact of PA on her life and her children from her first marriage – httpa/www.pact-online.org/html/ directorsassociates.html.

Catherine is the President and CEO of a group called Parents and Abducted Children Together (PACT) who have recently launched a very moving and powerful film on the impact of PA which adults describe from their experiences as children – http://www. act=online.org/html/documentary.html and

http_l/www_victimsofanotherwar.com/. This film has to be seen to really understand the life changing impact of PA on children.

Please help!

I am the alienated parent. During a nasty divorce my ex husband has successfully alienated our four children from me. The children have every symptom of severe alienation. Due to lack of education in PAS, in my small rural town, no one specialising in PAS is available. The children have been in court ordered therapy for over a year . . . to no avail. The therapist continues to tell me the children just don't want to see me and she doesn't want to force them. I've read your article on the 'folie à deux' and 'folie à trois'. This is ever so prevalent in my desperate situation. The current therapist has no experience in PAS. She has agreed to work with a specialist if I can find one . . . Can you help me?

I live in Rome, Georgia USA. Approximately 60 miles northwest of Atlanta. I need someone who is in the Atlanta area or someone who can come and do an intensive week intervention.

Feel free to call or e-mail with any questions. Please help me save my children from this abuse.

Thank you, M.J.R.

Web messages

PJ

Dear readers,

PAS is very real and very devastating. It not only destroys relationships, but lives. My family was ripped apart by my ex suddenly deciding he wanted custody of our two children six years post divorce and accused me of child abuse that did not exist.

The children recounted lies they told, which was part of the trial. The courts ignored everything. He won reversal of custody with no evidence and despite us proving no child abuse occurred. He even lied on the stand.

Three years, one trial and one appeal later, we are still fighting to reverse custody to original methods: now ex has accused me of mental illness that doesn't exist to continue the saga. The children have fared poorly, my daughter was suicidal/homicidal and diagnosed depressed, and removed from school. My son is falling through the cracks.

I now see my children only four days per month, and have no custody at all. My ex has used my chronic illness of Lyme Disease to try to pretend that I cannot parent. He has an endless source of funds, we do not. Yet we continue fighting.

My daughter is entering college and no longer has interest in visiting me due to the PAS going on. My son fortunately is aware of his father's garbage but is being harmed by not being part of my life (his mother).

The court system refuses to admit my ex had done anything wrong, yet blames me because my ex has made such a long paper trail of hearsay accusations that have no evidence at all. The family court system in Wisconsin USA is a joke, and is ripping families apart without a conscience whatsoever. For shame!

31 July 2006 – Wisconsin, USA

Shaun O'C

For the people's attention, on 7th July in Courtroom 71 LJ Wall admitted in open court that PAS was not investigated in Re L,v,M and H.

That report was on the issue of domestic violence and not the psychology of PAS. It was even more relevant when the Lower Court argue that I am the one responsible for the children's attitude and hostility when they had not met me for over five years.

LJ wall is going to give a reserved judgement sometime or other on the case, I await with baited breath.

Perhaps the Court now will recognise the condition that has studiously been ignored by CAFCASS and Local Authority Social Services and schools for the benefit of the medium and long-term best interests of the innocent children caught up in this.

10 July 2006 – UK

Carl

It never ceases to astonish me how dismissive welfare bodies are of PA, and their readiness to accept the post-programmed response of children as uninfluenced.

I believe this is a product of fear of getting it wrong, utterly biased PC views, and a misguided belief in their own unfailing "we know best" attitudes.

I believe awareness is there but allowed to continue: qui tacet consentit

The authorities' act of doing "what is best for the child(ren)" is often the most harmful in reality.

Thank you for speaking for we alienated parents, Dr Lowenstein

4 July 2006 – Dorset, UK

Susan

My son, Jarrod D******* was a victim of PAS. His ex-wife, ex-mother in law and ex-father in law murdered my son on July 9 2004. Although, my story ended with a tragedy, keep up the fight for your children.

30 June 2006 – United States

Steve

It has been over 6 years (2,311 days) since I have seen my daughter Jessica. We live two miles apart and she is now 15.

A forensic psychologist studied this case for the past 14 months and has diagnosed this as severe PAS and has recommended a change of custody.

Massachusetts does not reconise PAS and the child alienation and child abuse continues to this day.

28 June 2006 – USA

P mars

The article on "folie à deux" was extraordinary. Very informative. For what its worth, the family courts in the United States is just as powerless as those in other countries.

16 June 2006 – United States

Wendy

The world needs to be aware of how a perfectly normal family with two parents can suddenly be ripped and torn apart to the detriment of all involved by PAS. The alienated parent not only is in turmoil of a marriage gone sour, but loss of children, home, life, friends are alienated as well.

Now all alone in the world, left to fight through a mire of red tape, and no support system. The degradation of the alienated parent is a crime and alienators are criminals. Where is the justice?

14 June 2006 – Canada

Heather

I am broken hearted. I have two wonderful daughters in the United Kingdom who truly believe I don't love or want them anymore. I am so desperate to alert others to the damage PAS does not only to children, but also to the alienated parents.

I am at a total loss as what to do about my situation, I am trying to fight through the courts but when their father receives legal aid and I do not then there is no end to how long he can keep this going.

I will never give up trying to see my girls but in the meantime I want to feel useful and do something to bring PAS to the forefront of every judge's mind when dealing with contact issues. My prayers are with ALL alienated parents.

29 May 2006 – USA

Lorraine

Thank you for showing how both parents feel, you give a clear understanding of the situation.

The child needs both parents, and they can offer so much, whether they are together or apart.

The child needs to grow up without this hostility.

Thank you

27 April 2006 – England

Paul

Great website and resources on PAS. I have completed your survey.

See my Yahoo forum on such topics and concerning issues, all welcome – [sorry, URLs are blocked]. I have added a link to your website from my forum too.

Yes, I did my bit for World PAS awareness day here in New Zealand too. I made posters and put around the place, including in lawyer's home letterboxes.

26 April 2006 – New Zealand

Action For Justice Network

The Action For Justice network (AFJ) of the United States has celebrated April 25, 2006 by sending out emails to all separated and divorced parents making them fully aware of the consequences of Parental Alienation caused to children.

25 April 2006 – United States

Andrea

I would just like to let everyone know that April 25th is Parental Alienation and Hostile Parenting Awareness Day all over the world.

Its encouraging to know that on April 25th, all countries will be united in the fight against PAS.

More recognition is what we need to eradicate the ignorance, and stop our children being hurt.

30 March 2006 – North of England

Andrea

One question to the doubters of PAS. If it does not exist, then how can a parent in England suffer from the same alienating experiences as a parent in Australia? Have they all read a book called "How to alienate your children?"

I am a qualified counsellor who specialises in PAS, there are not many of us!!

21 March 2006 – North of England

Dr. Lowenstein's comments

Dear Andrea,

You are absolutely right; PAS exists and people all over the world share these experiences. No wonder that my website is frequently visited from all continents!

Yours,

Ludwig Lowenstein

Grandparents Apart Self Help Group Scotland
In our dealings with grandparents who are separated from their grandchildren we have encountered alienation on 80 per cent of our members. We would like to be kept informed of any ways that can help.

14 March 2006 – Scotland

Dr. Lowenstein's comments

Dear Jimmy,
Grandparents are often forgotten as victims of parental alienation, yet they suffer as much as the children and parents do. Rest assured that I will continue my work on parental alienation and I will share my work with parents, grandparents and others through my website. Our world wide survey will commence in April and I invite all of your members to participate.
Yours,
Ludwig

Lisa
Dear all alienated parents,
Just to say you are not alone and we may not be able to change what has happened but we can influence what is to come and make everyone realise that PAS is a very real phenomenon that affects dearly loved children and heartbroken decent, caring parents.
I have battled through the Courts in the UK for over 5½ years and seen both my children systematically alienated against me. The Judge and Child Psychiatrist have finally confirmed that significant emotional harm has been done to my children by my ex-husband. The problem now is finding a way to minimise any further damage and reverse this damage if at all possible.
My case has made the UK Family Public Law Records in 2005. I cannot include a weblink on this message but my case is cited on family law week dot com under C v C [2005] EWHC 2935 (Fam).
Our love for our children is unconditional and I have to believe one day my children will find their way back to me.
Keep strong and keep believing in yourself as a decent parent.
Lisa

13 March 2006 – UK

Shaun O'C
I was arguing PAS some six years ago, and for my joy got a no contact direct or indirect order.
As a suprise to the system five years after I managed to get the judge removed from the case and then transfer to the High Court.
Yet again I find the mere mention of PAS in the UK is anathema to the closed minds of the family courts.
CAFCASS refuse to recognise it, Struge and Glaser were employed to knock it on the head and yet the existence of PAS is obvious to anyone who has seriously worked with children.

The English and to a lesser extent the Welsh courts are using the wishes and feelings of the children to put the onus on the children for mother custody at all costs.

All predicted effects on my children have come to light and yet it is as if CAFCASS instead of being the eyes and ears of the court have gone blind and deaf.

Never give up on your children, Keep the spirits up and never be defeated. It's not the fault of the children but of the system and those who perpetrate the abuse.

Shaun O'C BSC PGCE

10 March 2006 – Hampshire, UK

Dr. Lowenstein's comments

Dear Shaun,

I and many others are in full agreement with your views on PAS and how it is being ignored by the Courts of Law.

Yours,

Ludwig

Ludwig Lowenstein

Dear visitor of parental-alienation.info.

If you would like to leave a message in our guestbook, please feel free to do so, however realise that due to possible spam attacks you will be asked to confirm your message in three ways: (1) by selecting a randomly given number on the first page (2) by entering four letters on the second page and (3) by confirming your message following an email sent to you. Only then will your message be added to the guestbook.

For your peace of mind, your email address will not be used in any way; it won't be added to our mailing list and it won't be forwarded to third parties. Please refrain from using abusive language, keep your messages anonymous and seek not to insult anyone.

Best regards, Dr. L.F. Lowenstein.

21 February 2006 – United Kingdom

Index

WITHDRAWN